The Public Order of Ocean Resources

The Public Order of Ocean Resources:
A Critique of the Contemporary Law of the Sea

P. Sreenivasa Rao

The MIT Press
Cambridge, Massachusetts, and London, England

This book was set in VIP Times Roman
by DEKR Corporation,
printed on Pinnacle Book Offset,
and bound in Columbia Millbank Vellum
by The Colonial Press Inc.
in the United States of America.

Library of Congress Cataloging in Publication Data

Sreenivasa Rao, Pemmaraju.
  The public order of ocean resources.

  "Adapted and enlarged from the . . . [author's thesis] presented to the Yale Law
School in 1970 under the title: Offshore natural resources exploitation and the world
public order."
  Bibliography: p.
  Includes index.
  1. Marine resources conservation—Law and legislation. 2. Maritime Law. I. Title.
Law   341.7'62   75-12741
ISBN 0-262-18072-3

To my parents

Contents

Preface

Until recently, the ocean space and its resources were regarded as inexhaustible. Based on this assumption, traditional maritime law allowed each participant on the high seas to engage in accepted activities without undue interference from others.

However, contemporary realities made the earlier assumption invalid. It is now increasingly realized that there are limits to the extent to which the resources of the sea could be exploited. Fishery stocks, with respect to certain species, have been, and could be, over-exploited. Problems of economic recoverability closely influence the availability of nonliving resources from the sea. With the growth of offshore petroleum drilling activities and increased volume of traffic at sea, risk of collision at sea is now an important concern for coastal zone management. Further, marine pollution due to oil and waste disposal can no longer be ignored if critical components of the ocean ecosystem are to be protected.

The changing realities have made it imperative to change the structure of the traditional law of the sea. However, modernization of maritime law, which is the principal theme of the Third Law of the Sea Conference at Caracas, Venezuela, does not come easily. It is fraught with a clash of divergent interests and opposing claims. In the contemporary debate on law of the sea, conflicting claims have been advanced to touch every aspect of the traditional as well as the projected uses of the oceans. These claims relate to:
a. The extent of territorial waters;
b. The extent of the continental shelf;
c. Exploitation and conservation of living resources of the sea;
d. Permissibility of military uses at sea;
e. Management of marine pollution; and
f. Preservation of freedoms of the sea.
Each of these claims gives rise to several subclaims, and they are generally interrelated.

The present study concerns the problems relating to marine mineral resource exploitation—the limits of continental shelf regime, the law of mineral resources in maritime areas beyond the limits of continental shelf, and the accommodation of mineral resource use with other competing uses of the sea.

The first chapter explores different interests that underlie the divergent claims. As these interests are closely affected by various social factors, the chapter describes the participants, their objectives, situational features attendant upon mineral resource use, availability of base values (or capabilities), strategies employed to achieve desired objectives, expected outcomes, and overriding conditional factors. In addition, the first chapter refers to the various claims arising out of the process of marine mineral resource use and the decision-making system available to resolve these claims. Before proceeding to examine trends in decision relevant to claims, the second chapter deals with a set of preferred policies. Such a clarification of policy, it is hoped, would provide a basis for appraising the trends in decision and for choosing, in the end, alternatives that would best promote common interests. The third chapter examines various claims about the extent of the continental shelf; these claims, which relate to access to deep ocean areas, are considered in the fourth chapter. The fifth chapter concerns the accommodation of mineral resource interests with several interests other than security interests. Examination of security interests is reserved for consideration in the sixth chapter. The last chapter discusses probable future trends in decision and articulates alternatives, where appropriate, to achieve common interests through the process of marine mineral resource use.

The framework of the study thus outlined follows a policy-oriented approach originally formulated by Professors Myres S. McDougal and Harold D. Lasswell of the Yale Law School in analyzing contemporary legal problems. Further, the study is adapted and enlarged from the doctoral dissertation the author presented to the Yale Law School in 1970 under the title "Offshore Natural Resources Exploitation and the World Public Order."

The preparation of this study would have been impossible without the help and encouragement I received over the last seven years from various institutions and individuals. I offer my grateful thanks to Woods Hole Oceanographic Institution, where I was Fellow of the Marine Policy and Ocean Management program from September 1972 to August 1974; to the Woodrow Wilson International Center for Scholars, where I was a member of its Ocean Study Group from January 1971 to June 1972; and to the Yale Law School, where I studied from September 1967 to July 1970. These institutions offered me not only their unique intellectual atmosphere but generous financial assistance. I would like also to mention my special gratitude to the Rockefeller Foundation and particularly to Dr. Ralph Richardson, Jr., for the grant of financial aid to enable me to stay at the Woods Hole Oceanographic Institution for two years.

I am indebted to Professor Myres S. McDougal of the Yale Law School for guidance and critical review of my work. Both as a teacher and as a friend "Mac" is invaluable. I am also grateful to Professors Harold D. Lasswell, Leon Lipson, and Michael Reisman of the Yale Law School, to Dr. David A. Ross of the Woods Hole Oceanographic Institution, and to Professor H. Gary Knight of Louisiana State University, who reviewed several chapters of my book and offered useful comments.

I also profited from my association with many colleagues at the Woodrow Wilson International Center. At the Woods Hole Oceanographic Institution I enjoyed the support and advice of Dean Robert Morse, Mr. George Cadwalader, and many other colleagues. Indeed, it was a special privilege to know and work with Mr. Benjamin H. Read, who was then Director of the Woodrow Wilson International Center for Scholars, and Dr. Paul M. Fye, President and Director of the Woods Hole Oceanographic Institution, who provided immense support as I labored on my study.

Furthermore, the help I received from Miss Kaleroy L. Hatzikon, Miss Gaenor Willson, Miss Patricia Pykosz, and Miss Helen Clayton in typing the manuscript is acknowledged with sincere thanks.

I thank all these institutions and individuals without, however, imposing any responsibility on them for the way in which the book is written or for the opinions expressed herein. I should also like to add that the book was completed before I joined the Government of India service and that it does not reflect any of the official Indian positions.

P.S.R.

The Public Order of Ocean Resources

1

Marine Mineral Resource Use, Participants, Claims, and Decisions

Participants

Generally every entity that shows interest in the process of marine mineral resource use and seeks to influence it either directly or indirectly can be regarded as a participant. In this sense the participants can be categorized as coastal states, landlocked and geographically disadvantaged states,[1] international organizations, nongovernmental bodies, and private business associations.

The interest of the coastal states in the offshore nonliving resources stems directly from the law of the sea and particularly from the Geneva Convention on the Continental Shelf of 1958. According to the Convention, they have exclusive rights over the natural resources of the adjacent submarine areas. Obviously, the interests of the coastal states transcend the continental shelf area, first, because the limits of the continental shelf area remain largely undetermined[2] and, second, because, as coastal states, they enjoy a natural advantage for controlling and profiting from any activity in the ocean environment.

If the interest of the coastal states in the process of marine mineral resource use is thus marked because of their long and open coastlines, the interests of the landlocked and geographically disadvantaged states are also evident precisely because of the lack of them. There are about 30 landlocked countries.[3] In addition, 20 so-called shelf-locked countries[4] and Zaire as a near-landlocked country consider themselves as geographically disadvantaged states.

The views expressed by this group of countries in connection with the United Nations debate on the law of the sea reveal their desire to minimize the effects of their "geographically disinherited position."[5]

The delegate from Czechoslovakia explained some of the reasons for their interest:

This area underlying the high seas, the seabed and the ocean floor beyond the limits of national jurisdiction is of interest to us firstly because we could deepen our knowledge in the respective scientific disciplines by learning about new aspects unknown to us, and so far remote to us, and secondly because, as a small landlocked country with a limited raw material basis, we see here an opportunity to participate, at least partially, in the exploitation of the rich deposits in the sea.[6]

For different reasons, the role of international organizations in the process of marine mineral resource use is important and to some extent even indispensable. Several of these agencies—for example, the Intergovernmental Maritime Consultative Organization (IMCO), the Food and Agricultural Organization (FAO), and the Intergovernmental Oceanographic Commission (IOC)—have direct responsibilities to promote orderly and productive activities at sea.[7]

Furthermore, the United Nations and a number of its specialized agencies through their expertise have been playing a crucial role in the clarification of policies and the articulation of regulations relevant to the management of marine mineral resource use.[8] In addition, they also provide necessary forums for discussion of national views on the subject.

A number of nongovernmental organizations with both national and international membership and academic and professional institutions specializing in legal, technical, scientific, and engineering aspects of the oceans are also active in shaping the institutional structures for regulation of marine resource use.[9]

The private business associations whose chief concern is wealth have a tangible stake in the process. Their concern can be directly measured by the magnitude of their investment in offshore areas around the globe.[10]

Objectives

The social process is defined as the application of institutions by individuals to resources for value maximization.[11] Different values that mankind seeks to gain may be categorized as power, wealth, enlightenment, well-being, skills, affection, respect, and rectitude. Thus the objectives of participants in the process of marine mineral resource use may be conveniently referred to in terms of various values.

The importance of managing the marine environment to the advantage of national power and security is well recognized. Customarily naval power has been employed to protect economic interests, gather intelligence, exert diplomatic pressure, enforce economic sanctions, interdict belligerent goods, blockade adversary ports, and as an additional source of military strength by transporting, supplying, and offering combat support to conventional forces in distant but limited conflicts. More recently, it has also been used to conduct atomic and scientific tests at sea and to recover astronauts on their return from space voyages. The opaque surface of the sea itself is of significant strategic value in the enhancement of offensive and defensive power of the countries.

The process of marine mineral resource use can have both positive and negative influence on the pursuit of power at sea. Positively, advances in science and technology aimed at better recovery of resources of the sea could also be used to improve the naval capabilities. For example, efforts to devise new bathyscopes that can withstand greater hydrostatic pressure and provide increased flexibility and speed of underwater movement and scientific studies relating to configuration of the ocean floor, wave, and weather conditions, and general interaction between the oceans and the space above it are all as important to the exploration of ocean resources as they are to the purposes of the navy.[12] Furthermore, the same technology that could be used to erect giant floating platforms at sea could also be employed, theoretically, to construct artificial military bases.[13]

Negatively, policies and prescriptions that a coastal state is authorized to apply to promote marine mineral resource use may be invoked at times to obstruct foreign security uses in adjacent offshore areas.[14] Also, as more of the ocean space is used for extraction of mineral resources, the same area may not be available for certain military activities such as target practice.[15]

It is also possible that countries in their bid to maximize power and security, while remaining militarily strong, will want to preserve optimum freedom to use the seas for defensive and offensive goals, whereas the militarily weak nations will attempt to achieve the same objective by seeking to curtail the freedom of the former.[16]

Of all the attractions the oceans hold out to mankind, the lure of wealth is certainly a dominant one. In addition to means of transportation and communication that it affords, the wealth it embodies is of four kinds: (1) biological, (2) chemical, (3) physical, and (4) geological resources.[17]

The present study will not be concerned with biological and physical resources as an object of wealth. It will also not deal with the chemical resources—that is, materials that are dissolved in water, which are not of immediate economic value.[18]

Marine geological resources could be categorized in three groups: (1) organic deposits, (2) detrital deposits, and (3) authigenic deposits. Of these, oil and gas, which are *organic deposits,* are highly valued.

As K. O. Emery of the Woods Hole Oceanographic Institution and a leading marine geologist of the world explained, "Oil that occurs in rocks (and thus is termed petroleum) is a product of partial decomposition of phytoplankton that grew upon the nutrient salts dissolved in water, using sunlight as an energy source for the biochemical reactions." He further noted that "While nearly all oil and its associated gas must be within or near the ancient, original, organic-rich source sediments, thick sequences of fine-grained marine sediments 20 to 200 million years old, the most common sources for oil and gas, occur . . . in certain special environments on the continental shelf." [19]

Favorable marine areas for accumulation of oil and gas deposits include (a) large deltas of very old major rivers, (b) closed basins, and (c) long, narrow troughs that parallel the coast and trap sediments from the land. However, presence of thick sediments cannot alone guarantee formation of oil and gas unless accompanied, first, by "coarse-grained, permeable reservoir beds (usually sandstones) interleaved with the source sediments" which permit the flow of oil and gas through the strata to the wells that tap them. In addition, there must also be a geological structure that serves to concentrate oil and gas from broad areas of a reservoir bed into a small area, an oil field. These structures may occur in the form of folds caused by lateral compression of a region of bedded sediments; and by local bending caused by penetration of salt pillars (salt domes) into overlying sediments, and by regional compaction of thick sediments over buried hills.

As of 1972, exploration for oil and gas was progressing in offshore areas of more than 80 countries. It involved about 400 drilling units and 134 companies. The expenditure was estimated at $4 billion. So far, about 26 countries announced commercial production, and 13 reported discoveries of commercial potential. [20]

Among areas of high offshore activity are the United Kingdom and Norwegian sections in the North Sea, Indonesia, Trinidad and Tobago, Nigeria, Tunisia, Libya, the Persian Gulf, Sable Island in Canada, the United States (the Gulf of Mexico, the Santa Barbara Channel, and the Gulf of Alaska), the USSR (the Caspian Sea, the Sea of Azov, the Black Sea, the southern part of the Barents Sea, and the Sea of Okhotsk), the South China Sea, and Northwestern Australia. [21]

In the near future several other areas may add to offshore oil and gas production. The Sunda Shelf off Indonesia, the continental margins of West Africa, the Tunisian-Sicilian platform, the Adriatic Sea, and the submerged part of the Nile Delta, the continental shelf off the mouth of the Amazon River and off southern Brazil, the Argentinan Shelf, parts of offshore areas bordering southern Chile, Peru, and Ecuador, and in the United States several new untested marine areas (for example, the outer shelf off Florida, the southern shelf off Texas, the Bering Sea, the Chukchi Sea, and the Beaufort Sea shelf, the Georges Bank, Baltimore Canyon area, and the Blake Plateau basins on the eastern seaboard) all have high offshore petroleum potential.

Furthermore, geological conditions, insofar as is known, also point to two of the world's most extensive shelf areas—the shallow sea floor beneath the Laptev and East Siberia Seas north of Siberia, and the shelf basin area off China, extending for 2,000 miles southward from the Yellow Sea through the East China Sea to Hainan off southeast China—as possible future sources of offshore oil and gas deposits.[22]

Several countries appeared to have issued licenses to explore for and exploit oil and gas deposits in marine areas deeper than 1,000 meters. However, as of 1974, no nation has reported production from offshore areas deeper than 200 meters.[23]

Detrital deposits are the result of erosion of preexisting rock, with the eroded material being carried to the oceans by rivers or some other mechanism.[24] Once in the ocean, the detrital material will be carried by waves and currents and eventually deposited on the sea floor. Sand and gravel and heavy minerals such as titanium, zircon, diamonds, tin, monazite, iron, and gold are among the detrital deposits. Exploitation of some of these deposits is thus far limited and yields modest economic returns.

Minerals belonging to *authigenic deposits* accumulate slowly on the ocean floor as chemical and biological precipitates of chemicals derived from the continents and carried in solution within the sea water. Calcium carbonite (gem corals and argonite mud) and phosphorite and manganese nodules may be mentioned as examples of authigenic deposits. The phosphorite nodules are common on the shallow banks off California and eastern Florida (U.S.A.), South Africa, Peru, and Chile. Competition from inexpensive land sources delay their exploitation.[25]

Manganese nodules, however, have greater economic potential than the phosphorite nodules.[26] They are a black to brown colored hydrous manganese dioxide concretion and contain silica, manganese, iron, nickel, cobalt, lead, and aluminum. Of these, copper, nickel, and cobalt are of interest to nations.[27] The manganese nodules occur over wide areas of the ocean floor. According to a recent study, the North Pacific has by far the most extensive deposits over large areas. The densest concentration lies between 6°N and 20°N and from 110°W to 180°W.

While there are large provinces of nodules in the Atlantic and the Indian Oceans, because of high sedimentation in those parts, they are poorly developed.[28] The nodules of the Pacific are of both geological and economic importance. Here the most valuable deposits rich in nickel and copper are available. Most nickel-rich nodules occur in siliceous deposits at depths from 4,000 to 5,600 meters, with maximum nickel values in nodules obtained from 4,900 meters.

For the sake of completeness, mention should be made of pools of hot brines as also being of possible economic value. The hot brines discovered at the bottom of the Red Sea contain abnormally high concentrations of copper, zinc, and silver. However, problems of recovery and separation of deposits presently impede their utilization as a resource base.[29]

In sum, of the different kinds of geological resources, oil and gas deposits are of greatest economic value. Among the minerals, the manganese nodules hold out real promise.

The gap between rich and poor peoples, the awesome predictions about world population growth, and the growing scarcity of raw materials seem to weigh heavily on policy-makers concerned about offshore resources.[30] To them thoughtful consideration of the use and regulation of these marine mineral resources provides an opportunity to tackle some of the world's problems effectively, thus enhancing the well-being of all countries, especially the developing countries.[31]

As part of this objective it is proposed that benefits resulting from offshore resource use should not be monopolized by a limited group, particularly by the technologically developed participants.[32] Attempts at a monopoly are regarded as a new kind of colonialism and as a potentially dangerous form of discrimination.[33]

Furthermore, well-being as an objective has also been emphasized within the context of the exploitation of ocean resources. First, concern has been expressed that adequate consideration should be given to the economic interests of some of the underdeveloped countries that are the chief primary ore producers of the same minerals that may be produced from the ocean floor.[34] Second, pollution as a hazard to biological resources and to recreational facilities is another consideration. Finally, the well-being of the people who might operate in the oceans for resource exploitation and other uses is also stressed.[35]

Though of incidental import, the pride of pioneering in new adventures to master the mysteries of nature is an ancient urge of humanity. In our age, scientific excellence and technological prowess are in themselves regarded as determinants of leadership and respect.[36]

The quest to explore the depths of the ocean, to unravel the mysteries surrounding its natural processes, and to win most of its resources has in recent years motivated several new scientific and technological breakthroughs.[37] In their bid to promote new insights into the marine environment, several nations vie with each other for leadership. That this is an objective in the context of marine resources use is well demonstrated, for example, by the U.S. Marine Resources and Engineering Development Act of 1966, which listed as one of its goals "the preservation of the role of the United States as a leader in maritime science and development."[38]

Even though the study of ocean science cannot be termed as a direct objective of the process of marine resource use, it is essential for the effective and rational exploitation of resources of the sea.

Knowledge relating to the continental drift, geological structures, configuration of the ocean floor, composition and distribution of sedimentary basins, and relationships between different depths and marine zones and the types of resources available is found increasingly useful in the study of better ocean resource management.[39] Research in marine technology and engineering concerning stationary and neutrally buoyant platforms, drilling rigs, submarine dredges, high-capacity low-cost vertical transport systems, submarine crawlers, and bottom-hovering vehicles is certain to aid the process of offshore resource exploitation.[40] Studies in the interrelationships of the atmosphere and the oceans help in the prediction of oceanic and terrestrial weather. Analysis of processes relating to tides, surface waves, tsunamis (large waves created by submarine earthquakes), and oceanic circulation patterns yields information necessary in planning proper safeguards for the people and equipment involved in the resource development at sea.[41]

Oceanography that deals with the chemical and biological reactions in sea water and their influence on the biological composition of the oceans adds insights into effects of marine pollution caused by the introduction of oil and other substances into the marine areas. It is also of direct relevance to identify different elements settled in sea water and on the ocean floor.

Situation: Geological and Temporal Features

The geological features of the ocean floor are of importance, for, as will be noted subsequently, claims have often been made to advocate or support exclusive appropriation of offshore resources on the basis of certain alleged configurations of these features.[42] While examination

of these claims is reserved for purposes of later discussion, an attempt
will be made here to sketch in necessary detail the information available about the formation and location of some of the frequently cited
features of the ocean floor.

Any appreciation of the geological features of the planet Earth gives
rise to a sense of wonder at the wide ocean stretches and the varied
structure of the continental mass. It is now known that the ocean floor
is marked by significant reliefs, steep valleys and canyons, trenches,
mountain ridges, and rises.

The transition from the continents to ocean depths can be said to
occur broadly in three phases.[43] Usually, there is a stretch of shallow
area followed by a sudden steep break in gradient of the ocean floor,
which merges gently into abyssal depths. In geological terms, the shallow area is known as continental shelf, and the steep floor is known as
continental slope.

The gradient of the continental shelf varies from ⅛° to 3°. While the
shelf terminates at different depths around the world, on an average,
according to a 1957 U.N. report prepared by marine geologists, the
edge of the shelf is located at a depth of 300 fathoms.[44] In width, the
shelf varies from 1 mile to 800 miles; the widest shelf known to exist is
in the North Polar region off Siberia.[45] Important exceptions to the
normal occurrence of the shelf should be noted in areas where the
ocean floor is continuously shallow, with less than a 200-meter depth,
as is the case of the Persian Gulf, and in areas where no shelf exists at
all, with the depth nearing almost a mile along the coast, as is the case
off Chile. Furthermore, the topography of the continental shelf is not
smooth and is often interspersed with hills, troughs, deep basins, and
banks. According to F. P. Shepard, the topography of the shelf
bears a close relationship to the coasts it borders on and is influenced
by oceanic currents. Also it has been found that the shelves off coastal
lowlands are wide and those off mountain ranges, particularly young
mountains, are narrow.

The continental slope, which connects the shallow ocean floor to the
deep ocean floor, is regarded as the greatest relief feature on the face
of the earth. It takes the form of a gentle curve. While the point where
the slope commences is relatively easy to locate in view of the dramatic break that normally occurs at the end of the shelf, the termination of
the slope is more difficult to identify as it gradually merges into the
abyssal depths.[46] Moreover, the delineation of boundaries between the
shelf and the slope, and between the slope and the abyssal depths, is

complicated by the fact that the ocean floor is characterized by a variety of other deformations.[47]

The slope itself is studded with deep canyons, chains of valleys, and other geological features.[48] The gradient of the slope ranges from 3° to 45°. Its distance may extend from 10 to 25 miles. The depth at which the slope might merge with the abyssal depths varies. The height of the slope in some cases may exceed even the highest mountain peaks known to the mainland and may be anywhere between 12,000 feet and 30,000 feet.

The abyssal depths are denoted by an ocean bottom whose slope is less than 1:1000[11].[49] Its average depth is estimated at 13,000 feet. About 60 percent of the surface of the earth lies at more than 7,000 feet below the sea level. The ocean bottom is also punctuated by rises, ridges, seamounts, flat-topped elevations that are known as guyots, deep sea fans and deep sea channels, and trenches. The Pacific Ocean, however, is noted for its chain of trenches.[50] For example, the Chile-Peru Trench extends for a distance of up to 2,500 miles. Among the more conspicuous features of the deep ocean floor are the seemingly endless mountain ridges that principally bisect all the oceans.[51]

One of the considerations for a prospective entrepreneur before starting the process of exploitation of ocean resources is the length of time he can have exclusive rights of access to an area of ocean floor. The claims in this regard are likely to vary with the type of natural resource and the economics of the exploitation involved. With respect to the exploitation of mineral resources of the deep ocean floor, whether surface or subsurface deposits, assessments of these claims still take the form of speculations.

A profitable exploitation of manganese nodules on the deep ocean floor, for example, may demand a tenure of twenty years of exclusive access to an area of maritime floor of roughly 1,000 square miles.[52] In the case of petroleum production the claims are not for definite time periods but for an identified area for as long as that area yields oil and gas. The exploitation of the natural resources on the ocean floor usually also gives rise to claims to exclusive authority and control of the superjacent waters by way of claiming protective zones.[53] These claims are not expected to be different from the claims to exclusive access to the ocean floor as far as the temporal features are concerned.

The process of exploitation of offshore resources occurs on both unorganized and organized levels, and the problems of institutionalization of controls readily present themselves.

On the unorganized level, generally speaking, exploitation of the
ocean resources, chiefly oil and gas, like the exploitation of the continental deposits, is a highly competitive enterprise. The participants
often zealously guard their skills and probable areas of profitable
exploitation. Also frequently the selfsame entrepreneur may not carry
the business operations through all the phases of exploitation, beginning with extraction all the way through to the marketing of purified or
beneficated mineral. Different phases are operated by different specialized participants, each depending on the other for success. Impersonal
and unplanned forces of the market thus govern the relationship
among the various participants.

On the organized level, however, there are areas where the participants have common interests. For example, to the oil industry,
preventing the pollution of the marine environment, influencing the
national decision-makers in formulating suitable policies regarding the
import of oil, and other policies generally beneficial to the industry as
a unit are of common concern. These interests are pursued generally
through organized institutions. For example, in the United States, the
National Petroleum Council provides a suitable forum for organized efforts of the industry. There are also several organized national groups,
like the trade unions, that devote attention to problems of particular
interest to them. Where the matters have transnational interest, the
participants utilize various governmental and nongovernmental agencies
in organizing their attitudes and in helping to adopt adequate regulatory
policies.

The pace of offshore resource use is often influenced by expectations
of crisis in the international community. For example, fears of an
"energy crisis" have greatly stimulated exploration and exploitation of
oil and gas from the oceans. Many countries, both the developed and
the developing, reacted to the rising prices of crude oil and worldwide
inflation in general with a sense of urgency to search for petroleum in
adjacent marine areas.[54] National and international breakdowns in
public order usually have adverse effects for the process of marine
resource development. The Nigerian Civil War of 1967–1968 is said
to have slowed down that country's petroleum production rate.[55]

Even in the case of manganese nodules, participants exhibit certain
anxieties. The mineral industry, especially in the United States, regards
as serious what it considers the lack of progress in international
decision-making on policies, prescriptions, and institutions relevant to
management of resource production in deep ocean areas. As an alterna-

tive, the private business associations from the United States have urged enactment of interim domestic legislation to safeguard their investments in the recovery of manganese nodules from the sea.

The international decision-makers, especially those who represent developing nations, feel that the moves of the industry are a pressure tactic and a threat to the creation of an equitable regime for the deep ocean resource use.

Base Values: Power, Wealth, and Skills

The use of resources from the ocean is heavily dependent on a number of capabilities or base values: it is not a matter of mere coincidence that only the most powerful territorial communities are also the most capable participants in the process of ocean resource development. For example, the United States and the Soviet Union, each of which possesses advanced technology relating to submarines and each of which has huge naval fleets at its disposal, are the only nations that can hope at the present time to collect extensive and valuable oceanographic data.[56]

Further projects conceived for strengthening the naval defense system of a country have a beneficial spin-off for civilian uses of the sea. In this connection the following annual report on the United States Navy activities may be noted:

. . . [The Navy collected] over 100,000 miles of seismic sub-bottom profiles and ship-towed magnetic data; 860 Nansen casts for submerged water analysis; hundreds of bottom photographs, geological cores, biological and radiological samples, and current measurements; and many thousands of measurements of propagation of acoustic energy over a wide spectrum of frequencies.

The report added,

While the above oceanographic surveys are intended for military use, others which are closely allied to them are available for civilian use. These include the mapping, charting and geodetic efforts.[57]

In addition, the expensive oceanographic vessels of the U.S. Navy lend assistance to educational institutions for research and surveying purposes.

Power as a base value is also significant in other respects. Oceans cover such a wide area of the earth that it is practically impossible to subject activities there to close national surveillance on a scale familiar to activities being conducted within the national territorial confines. To that extent there is less protection or security available to entrepreneurs operating in the marine areas. The sense of lack of security becomes particularly acute if the offshore resource exploitation is subjected only to a flag state jurisdiction. It is easily understandable that, under such circumstances, the greater the power at the disposal of each individual entity, the greater the security it can offer to entrepreneurs under its control.

Wealth as a base value is of definite importance to the process of offshore resource extraction. This is due to the fact that each phase of the process entails detailed attention from groups of highly skilled participants whose services and materials are expensive. For example, a United Nations study of 1970 estimated the average costs of exploratory drilling for oil and gas to be between $350,000 and $2 million per well and for wells currently being drilled in the North Sea to be as much as $15 million.[58] Furthermore, it is noted that these costs vary with depth, distance from the adjacent coast, and weather and wave conditions. Thus, the operating costs of exploratory drilling under prevailing weather conditions in the North Sea may be twice as much as the cost of drilling at similar depth in areas with generally favorable conditions such as in Indonesian waters. Again, in the Arctic Circle, the costs of production of offshore oil and gas may be several times higher than drilling in the North Sea.

Production and completion costs also rise sharply with water depth, and furthermore, they are subject to environmental constraints. Hence, production costs may rise from $1.5 million in shallow waters of 100 feet to $4 million in 350 feet and $12 million in 600 feet. Platforms costing between $1 million and $2 million in the Gulf of Mexico would cost between $8 million and $15 million at a similar depth in Cook Inlet, Alaska. Transportation and storage costs are also related to water depth and oceanic conditions. Thus, an underwater pipeline of only 8 inches in Alaska is 1.5 times more expensive than the average 30-inch pipeline in the Gulf of Mexico.[59]

The high cost of offshore development has an important bearing on the size of fields that can be economically exploited. Reservoirs that might be considered rich in recoverable oil or gas on land are not necessarily profitable in the oceans. Furthermore, while relatively small offshore fields may be profitably exploited from a relatively calm marine area where the production costs are low, in the Arctic only giant fields provide economic incentives. It is not surprising therefore that at present 81 percent of the world's offshore petroleum production comes from 58 giant fields, which contain 500 million or more barrels.[60]

The costs of manganese nodule production are also quite demanding. For example, Deep Sea Ventures, Inc., announced a $200 million venture. It appears that after more than one decade and $20 million spent on development work, Deep Sea Ventures, Inc., and its parent company, Tenneco, were ready for construction of a commercial-scale nodule mining system and metallurgical plant that could amount to more than $100 million. The Summa Corporation, which has a 36,000-ton prototype ocean mining ship, spent more than $60 to $70 million in efforts leading toward manganese nodule mining.[61]

Skills relating to the process of offshore petroleum use are varied and fast developing. Broadly speaking, there are five phases in the process, and each one involves different kinds of skills. John P. Albers usefully summarized the information regarding four phases:

The exploration phase of operations normally commences with seismic surveys, in which the geophones or recording devices are trailed behind the exploring vessel and record reflections of artificial earthquake waves created in the vicinity of the vessel. . . .

Following such geophysical exploration the next step is the drilling of an exploratory well. Such wells could be drilled from four types of vessels. In the first case, the vessel consists of a barge which is sunk to the seafloor, the superstructure remaining above the surface of the water. Such vessels are no longer constructed and their use is confined to Gulf of Mexico. A second type of vessel is the semisubmersible, which is towed or self-propelled to the drill location and is then partially submerged in the water. A third type of exploratory vessel is the jack-up rig, the emplacement of which requires the lowering of the legs to the seafloor which are then jacked up to maintain the drilling platform at the appropriate elevation above the water surface. The fourth exploratory drilling vessel is the drill ship which operates like other vessels but contains on its deck a drilling rig as well as other pertinences required for drilling of wells.

The second phase of offshore petroleum operations takes place after the discovery of a petroleum deposit. In this case a means is required for both the drilling of wells in the field discovered and their production. At the present time the practice is to install permanent platforms the legs of which are emplaced in the seafloor. From this platform as many as 62 different wells may be drilled directionally to produce the oil or gas reservoir. Platforms of this type are restricted to waters of 600 or 700 feet in depth. In greater water depths it will be necessary to drill the wells from either a floating vehicle of the type used for exploratory drilling or from some sort of self-contained unit on the sea floor.

At the present time several production units are being developed which can produce wells with all equipment located on the sea floor, the drilling platform being removed. . . .

A third aspect of offshore petroleum operations is related to transportation of the petroleum from the fields to shore. In some places the production is simply stored on one or more of the platforms of the field and transferred to barges which carry it ashore. In other cases, and necessarily in the case of gas fields, gathering lines are laid on the seabed between the various platforms in the fields and these gathering lines are then hooked into trunk lines for transportation of the crude oil or natural gas to a point onshore. In many places these pipelines are buried in the sediment of the sea floor but in other cases they lie on the surface. . . .

The fourth aspect of offshore petroleum operations is the storage of the petroleum. In most cases, the oil is stored on platforms and transferred to barges. . . . In some places the petroleum is stored in very large tanks which rest on the sea floor. . . . However, such sea floor tanks are necessarily restricted to special conditions of stable seabed and calm waters, such as are found in the Persian Gulf. These tanks are not used elsewhere in the world.[62]

In addition to these essential four phases, there is another phase of marketing and product delivery, which requires organizational and business skills. Almost all these skills are concentrated among a relatively few transnational business associations.[63]

Mining of manganese nodules also requires special skills.[64] As part of development of means to recover the nodules from the ocean floor, thus far two different methods have been introduced. The Deep Sea Ventures, Inc., relies on a hydraulic air-lift pump system. A continuous line bucket system is used by the Japan Resources Association. Both these methods have already undergone preliminary tests and are at an advanced stage of development.

The third system, employed by the Hughes Tool Company, is believed to involve a hydraulic pipe system with a pump located on the sea floor. In this system mining is done by lowering the apparatus to the sea floor, sweeping a given area at a time, and collecting ore in the path of a long rotating arm pivoted at a hub base. During the operation, the surface support vessel remains in a fixed position by use of dynamic positioning with respect to mining operators. Thus it avoids problems associated with moving a pipe through the water. Another feature of this system is a silt separator and ore-cleaning tank and an integral crusher as part of the bottom assembly. Transport of the material to the surface can be accomplished by hydraulic pumping.

Once the nodules are gathered from the ocean bottom, separation of different elements they contain is necessary to obtain needed materials. The metals of interest, with the exception of manganese, are present in the nodules as impurities in a siliceous matrix. This siliceous material is acid insoluble. As such, all techniques involve a leaching process of one form or another. The nodule material is extremely porous, thereby providing a very high surface area for reaction with the leaching agent.

There are at least three different kinds of leaching: (1) a hydrogen chloride method used by the Deep Sea Ventures, Inc., (2) sulfur dioxide roasting and water leaching developed by the United States Bureau of Mines, and (3) a selective leaching technique preferred by John L. Mero. All of them start with a crushing and dyeing process. This is done to increase the exposed surface area, thereby decreasing the reaction time for leaching, and to accomplish an initial transformation in the chemical state of the contained manganese.[65]

Strategies

Given the differences in capabilites, the principal instruments of strategy that participants might be expected to employ in promoting their respective objectives are both economic and diplomatic. The relevance of two other instruments, ideological and military, in this connection cannot, however, be totally ignored. The significance of the different strategies should be stressed not only with regard to the way they are utilized for promoting preferred policy choices but also with regard to the likely effects of one outcome or the other on all the four instruments of strategy.[66]

Because only a few economic and national entities have potential capabilities for exploiting the resources of the ocean bed at present, the majority of the participants are likely to show deference to the interests of the few economic and national entities, depending on the immediate advantages they perceive. Economic advantages will play a large part as trade-offs among different groups to secure desired policy choices either in the context of exploitation of offshore resources or in the general context of world social process.

Participants will also be concerned with economic strategy for two other reasons. Those countries that are now the chief producers of primary ore products would like to safeguard their economic position from being adversely affected by development of deep ocean resources. Likewise, countries that are usually dependent on imports for the several minerals that could be produced from exploitation of the deep oceans would evaluate the cost advantages of ocean resource production.[67]

Where the situation is relatively unorganized, the process itself is not yet intensively pursued, and where the policy alternatives are only in the stage of active exploration, employment of diplomatic strategy holds first importance.

The developing countries that lack the necessary skills attempt mainly to organize themselves in the chambers of international conferences and to demonstrate common policy fronts wherever possible. Private business associations that do not have direct access to forums of international policy-making, however, influence other participants through their respective national and international agencies.

The significance of ideological strategy in the context of offshore resources exploitation should be noted, as it is the shaping and sharing of wealth that is central to it, and this is a process that is familiarly enmeshed in ideological concepts. In this connection, appeals to such well-known systems as capitalism or laissez faire[68] and communism or socialism,[69] and references to such historical concepts as imperialism[70] and colonialism[71] and the birth of new ideological concepts like the common heritage of mankind[72] can be seen.

By invoking these concepts, the participants exhibit their preferences for securing or avoiding realization of particular features in the context of marine mineral resource use. Thus, at one extreme, those who believe in capitalism argue for freedom of access to natural resources of the ocean, labor, and markets. This group of participants also demands adequate incentives for deriving reasonable profits as a condition precedent to the investment of capital in the production of resources from the sea. Another group of participants who are of Marxian persuasion, at the other extreme, insists that the process of offshore resource exploitation should not be allowed to become yet another occasion for the "capitalists" to monopolize profits to the detriment of the "proletariat."

The concern of the underdeveloped countries and of peoples long the victims of colonialism and imperialism is still different. This group of participants is not so much touched by the doctrinal differences between a capitalist and a communist economy. They are very sensitive to the widespread incidence of poverty among their people and their resultant inability to participate in the process on a par with technologically developed nations if an unregulated access to these resources is allowed. By proposing new concepts like the "common heritage of mankind," they suggest that the interests of the underdeveloped countries must be given due consideration and priority in any regime that may be agreed upon by the world community to regulate the exploitation of deep ocean resources.

The process of marine mineral resource use, confined as it is relatively to shallow waters, has proceeded without the participants so far having to rely on their military strength for realization of their respective preferred choices. However, the situation may change as the operations extend to even greater depths of the oceans.

The world community expectations of authority and control with respect to the exploitation of marine mineral resources belonging to the "continental shelf" are fairly well settled. This accounts in great measure for the peaceful conditions surrounding exploitation of these resources thus far. But there are no such settled expectations as to the extent of the "continental shelf" or, if some limit to it is assumed, as to the policies and institutions that will be responsible for an orderly and peaceful exploitation of the resources in submarine areas beyond the limits of the continental shelf. While there are encouraging efforts to resolve the resultant uncertainty, there is as yet no guarantee that generally acceptable decisions with respect to the outer limits of the continental shelf and the regime beyond will be forthcoming.

In the absence of widely agreed-upon compromises and commonly held expectations and in the face of the ever-accelerating pace of the ocean science and technology, the temptation for the participants to make unilateral decisions to exploit resources belonging both to the continental shelf and to much deeper waters of the oceans will be great indeed. If such unilateral decisions were made, and participants were to attempt to appropriate exclusively resources of the submarine areas by force, chances for reliance on military strength would, of course, greatly increase for defense of individual choices.

The possibility of invoking military strategy will, however, be conditioned by the availability and persuasiveness of other strategies and the relativity of gains perceived by the participants.

Outcomes

The two major stakes as outcomes of the process of marine mineral resources are the *wealth* and *well-being* of the international community. One indication of the wealth generated from the seas is the growing strength of offshore oil and gas operations. Although petroleum has been produced from the oceans since 1890, drilling began in earnest in

1950. Fifteen years later, offshore output accounted for about 16 percent of total world production.[73] By 1971 there were about 779 production and 678 exploratory wells in waters less than 200 meters deep and 10 in waters deeper than 200 meters.[74] According to one source, by 1973 about 20 percent (of 18 billion barrels) of world production of petroleum comes from the sea, and it may reach 30 percent by 1980.[75] So even by 1971 it was estimated that 9.5 percent of world production of natural gas resulted from offshore development. In terms of monetary value, by 1974 annual offshore petroleum production was valued at $9.5 to $10 billion.[76]

Opinions vary as to the total petroleum potential of world oceans, especially as to prospects in different marine zones. However, according to one U.N. study, there may be a total of 2,272 billion barrels of oil equivalent at sea.[77] It may be noted that, as of 1974, there were 100 billion barrels of oil and 131 billion cubic feet of natural gas as proved reserves.[78] Despite these estimates, the quantity of actually recoverable oil and gas from offshore areas is determined mainly by the economic factors of extraction, competitiveness of alternative energy sources, and demand.[79]

Of the other varieties of geological resources of the sea, according to 1973 estimates, sand and gravel yielded about $200 million. These were extracted mostly from near-shore areas of quiet water where dredging for harbors was also required.[80] From the areas close to the coast approximately $10 million worth of tin and magnetite were also produced. Although so far it is uneconomical to recover gold, platinum, and diamonds from the oceans, it is expected that by 1980, $1 million worth of gold and platinum may be extracted. Furthermore, while the annual value of gem coral and argonite mud taken from offshore areas is less than $5 million, by 1980 perhaps $3 million of other minerals and $6 million of coral may be obtained. In addition, it may be noted that the value of the recoverable manganese nodules varies with each individual estimate anywhere from $6 billion to more. However, one indication of the future economic potential of the nodules is that there are about 33 international companies engaged in their exploration and they have already invested several million dollars in the process.[81]

As ocean technology improves and more energy becomes available, several uses of the sea that will enhance the well-being of mankind can be anticipated.[82] In this connection, some commentators indicate the following possibilities: The oceans can be put to use as a medium for new modes of transportation. Several new kinds of fresh foods may be produced. Scientific investigations of the ocean floor and atmosphere can be conducted better with underwater laboratories. New recreational centers and health cures can be contemplated. Furthermore, marine zones for safe disposal of waste can be identified to ease present strains of pollution on the mainland. Several new uses of the sea, for example, deep water ports, may also become a reality in the future.

The outcomes thus outlined will have a significant influence on other value demands. For example, demands on skills to translate human aspirations into the realm of reality can be easily perceived. Also, new and increasingly persuasive appeals will be made to values like affection and rectitude that may result in wider and more equitable distribution of benefits among the various groups of mankind.

Moreover, there is the possibility that the process of marine resource use may affect future considerations of power and security in the international community. Indeed, unless prompt measures are taken to reduce the existing tensions in the world and build mutual confidence and cooperation among the maritime powers, especially the two superpowers, chances are that the ocean bed may be utilized by the participants as an arena of military rivalry. Such a prospect heightens the pace of the armament race and complicates efforts to realize even partial measures of disarmament. Deterioration of peaceful conditions in the world that may result thereby will affect adversely the promises the oceans hold for the welfare of humanity.

Conditioning Factors and the Process of Claim

The preceding analysis, which focused on the different features of interaction, is largely conditioned by certain factors that particularly characterize the process of marine mineral resource use. An understanding of these factors is necessary for any rational policy formulation and for examination and appraisal of the trends that are described and discussed in subsequent chapters.

The process of exploitation of the offshore resources, just like any other resource development, is conditioned by technological, economic, and social limitations. As of today offshore exploitation has proceeded up to a depth of 200 meters.[83] However, progress is being made in this regard. The picture, in fact, is so bright, given other favorable conditions, it is expected that even the greatest depths are not beyond the reach of effective exploitation.

One of the major factors inhibiting the extension of man's capability to exploit the ocean bed on a larger scale for a wider variety of deposits at all depths is economic. Most of the deposits obtainable from the ocean bed are also available in abundance on the continents in the form of alternative sources.[84] Therefore, at any given moment a producer of offshore deposits will be concerned with their competitive quality as opposed to the alternative sources, and several factors may affect competitive quality of the offshore deposits. Greater industrialization of the world may demand a larger supply. Technological breakthroughs may make offshore exploitation just as easy and accessible as the exploitation of continental deposits. The territorial division of the land mass among contending national groups may deny some of the continental deposits to opposing factions. All these unpredictable, but no less probable, factors will significantly improve the chances of offshore exploitation on a wider scale.

There are social limits on the exploitation of the resources, whether continental or offshore. Exploitation of resources will have to be viewed in the broader context of the world social process. Only when offshore resource exploitation can be managed with the least, or what is sometimes called justifiable, interference with other uses of the sea and land does it have a chance of promotion. Several prospective and present uses of conflicts must be kept in perspective, and accommodation of the varied uses must be attempted in the common interest, if the greatest net value is to be derived from the process of offshore natural resource exploitation.[85]

It is appropriate to refer to other conspicuous differences between the developed and developing countries and among the ideological blocs that seem to override every other feature in conditioning the world social process including the process of exploitation of ocean resources. The types of organized structures of authority and control that can be created to regulate the process and the degree of their effectiveness in promoting the desired policy choices that underlie common, community interest depend chiefly on these factors.

On the whole, whatever the limits, whether technological, economic, or social, as has been pointed out, they

are themselves uncertain and shifting and very much relative to scientific perception of possibilities, technological advances, and individual and social valuations of what is important to preserve or to exploit in the natural environment.[86]

A diverse set of claims governs the process of marine resource use and the attendant conditioning factors. Claims are demands made by participants to the established decision-makers of the world constitutive process seeking prescription and application of the commonly accepted policies that have a bearing upon particular distribution of values among the members of the community.[87]

While every participant in the process of interaction could possibly be regarded as a claimant, coastal and landlocked states, developed and developing nations, and intergovernmental organizations may be referred to as the major claimants. The role of states and intergovernmental organizations, in this connection, is particularly facilitated by the formal access accorded them to present claims before established transnational decision-makers. Private business associations and individuals in their capacity as pressure groups can, however, be expected to be influential in the formulation of specific kinds of claims by states and intergovernmental organizations.

The objectives of claimants in presenting their claims to the established community decision-makers, generally stated, are to secure preferred value outcomes through peaceful and persuasive means. An identification of the preferred outcomes in the context of offshore resources exploitation may be conveniently attempted by noting different categories of claims and subclaims.

An outline of the variety of claims and subclaims follows:
1. Claims about limits for national resource jurisdiction at sea (noted in Chapter 3).
   A. Claims about the extent of the continental shelf.
      a. Claim that the legal shelf extends indefinitely toward ocean depths.
      b. Claim that the shelf is (or should be) subject to certain limits:
         i. Distance,
         ii. Depth,
         iii. Exploitability,
         iv. Geological configuration,
         v. Varying combinations of above limits.
   B. Claims about "economic zone" or "patrimonial sea."
   C. Claim that there should be an intermediate zone of mixed national and international jurisdiction over resources.
2. Claims about access to deep ocean areas (noted in Chapter 4).
   A. Claim that the deep oceans are to be subject to exclusive national jurisdiction.
   B. Claim that there is (or should be) a freedom of deep ocean mineral resource use.

C. Claims relating to an interim deep ocean regime.
D. Claims that the deep ocean mineral resource use be subject to an organized inclusive access, as, for example,

   i. To comprehensive control,
   ii. To licensing competence,
   iii. To entrepreneurial activities.

3. Claims relating to accommodation of competing uses of the sea (and several subclaims noted in Chapter 5).
4. Claims relating to security and disarmament in the sea (and its subclaims noted in Chapter 6).

A detailed exposition of the various categories of claims will be attempted below where the trends in decision are examined. Though some of the claims depend for their resolution on the viability or otherwise of most other claims mentioned, it is convenient not to assign undue priorities in listing them.

The Process of Decision

The process of decision involving the resolution of the different categories of claims, as noted above, comprises decision-makers, their objectives, arenas of decision-making, base values, and strategies or instruments of policy at the disposal of decision-makers to make their decisions effective and operational, outcomes in the prescription as well as in the application of policies, with important effects not only upon the claimants but also upon the community in general. Several features of the world constitutive process of authoritative decision that regulate the conduct of participants in the marine environment have been outlined elsewhere in sufficient detail.[88] However, a brief characterization of some of the significant elements of the process of decision relating to the exploitation of offshore mineral resources will be presented here.

The world constitutive process, decentralized as it is, leaves states, especially the coastal states, as the most prominent decision-makers with respect to claims that seek or deny access to oceans for different purposes. Under the terms of the Geneva Convention on the Continental Shelf of 1958 and pursuant to expectations originating from the uniformities in behavior among the members of the international community, the coastal states exercise exclusive competence over the exploitation of "natural resources" belonging to the "continental shelf." By issuing or refusing to issue permission to a participant to exploit mineral resources in a specific maritime zone, the coastal states could affect community expectations as to the extent of the continental shelf. The coastal states are, in addition, invested with authority and control to provide for the accommodation of different uses of the seas, conservation of marine resources, and pollution of the oceans in the continental shelf area.[89]

Several international organizations must also be referred to as decision-makers in this connection, for they are the sources for the promulgation of various international policies and procedures of consequence to the resolution of claims in the context of offshore resource exploitation. Thus the Intergovernmental Maritime Consultative Organization (IMCO) concerns itself with developing standards relating to safety of navigation and other technical maritime matters such as measurement of tonnage and prevention of pollution of the seas.[90] Together with the Intergovernmental Oceanographic Commission (IOC), the IMCO is further striving to develop uniform standards regulating the use of manned and unmanned ocean data stations, the operation of drilling rigs, production platforms, dredges, and other devices and the prevention of possible hazards to international navigation from the exploitation of offshore natural resources.[91] While the International Atomic Energy Agency (IAEA) deals with legal standards aimed at preventing pollution of the sea through the disposal of radioactive waste,[92] the Food and Agricultural Organization (FAO) is involved in regulating any marine activity that may affect the living resources, particularly fishery resources of the seas.[93]

Nongovernmental organizations, academic bodies, and pressure groups also participate, but indirectly, in the process of decision-making by issuing reports and propagating particular choices through lobbying and sometimes by special invitation.

The objective of the decision-makers in prescribing specific policies or applying them to resolve a given claim, to the extent possible, is to attempt to locate areas of common interest and provide procedures through which such widely recognized interests of the world community could be realized. States as decision-makers must act with the necessary degree of caution and concern for common interest and with a sense of reciprocity. This is rather compelling because the states that are the most significant decision-makers in the world arena are also its most noted claimants.[94]

The necessity to conform their decisions to the common interests of the world community, insofar as such common interests can be defined, is equally important in the case of international organizations in their role as decision-makers. There are no transnational organizations that are today invested with an effective coercive force other than the moral and material support extended by the members of the world community to enforce the decisions they make. In other words, it is commonly known that the international organizations more often than not must rely for successful implementation of their decisions on the voluntary compliance from a bulk of the participants whom they seek to affect through their decisions. The voluntary compliance on the part of participants will not be forthcoming if the decisions are not in the common interest.

However, to emphasize that clarification of common interests and the conforming of their decisions to such clarified interests of the world community are often demanded of decision-makers and to indicate that in practice they do make the necessary effort to realize this objective is not to suggest that in reality community decisions always correspond to the common interests. In a world as diverse and dynamic as ours, the task of clarifying the common interests and translating their purport to specific value demands is not an easy one. In certain novel situations where there is little uniformity in past behavior and where the decision function is concerned especially with the promotion of new policies and prescriptions, the complexity in conceiving the common interest is all the more obvious.

Indeed, the situation of offshore resource exploitation is very much to the point here. The development of science and technology, by rapidly extending the depths at which the marine resources can be exploited, has threatened the flexibility of the doctrine of the "continental shelf." Within less than fifteen years of the adoption of the Geneva Convention on the Law of the Sea, the world community is forced to reevaluate the decisions it made in 1958 and reformulate the common interests concerning different uses of the seas.

Fortunately, the difficulties involved in the clarification of common interests in this regard are largely remedied by the availability of several arenas of decision to the members of the world community. By interacting through these arenas, participants project their individual interests, bargain on the conflicting perspectives, and ultimately hope to accommodate and arrive at areas of common interest.

The most active arenas of decision at the international level, with respect to the exploitation of offshore resources, have been the United Nations, the committees it created, and the Eighteen-Nation Disarmament Conference (ENDC), which later became the Conference of the Committee on Disarmament (CCD). More important as an arena of decision-making are the Third Law of the Sea Conference held in Caracas, Venezuela, from June 20 to August 28, 1974, and whatever subsequent conferences may be held thereafter.

Where the decision-making utilizes the channels of international organizations, the bases of power for implementing the decision are, of course, commensurate with the cumulative powers granted them. These powers may originate from their unique structures of authority and control or from the collective bases of power of such other participants as are willing to subscribe to the implementation of their decision.

2
Clarification of Basic Community Policies: Criteria for Rational Choices

The claims that participants present to the decision-makers with regard to marine mineral resource use raise the basic problems of access, competence, and accommodation of competing interests. Resolution of these problems involves deliberate choices. While it is not assumed that only one set of choices is available, it is understood that the choices made are the product of particular policy preferences. Scholarly observers, like community decision-makers, have to become involved in the task of policy clarification not only to indicate to their audience the vantage points from which they make their critical appraisal of trends in decision but also to highlight their own preferences in a situation of conflicting choices.

As marine mineral resource use is only a part of broader and more comprehensive world public order, the task of clarification of policies will begin with the definition of basic goals of world public order and then focus on the particular features of interaction surrounding the mineral resource use.

World Public Order and Basic Goals

One of the curious paradoxes of the contemporary world is that it is subject to two diametrically opposed trends of great importance. On the one hand, the peoples of the world, as never before, have become truly interdependent because of the giant strides man has taken in the fields of science and technology. It is not an exaggeration to characterize the world community in terms of a "spaceship"[1] or a "global village."[2] On the other hand, the world community has never been more fragmented. There are more than 135 territorial groups, each claiming sovereignty and independence of action.

It is obvious that, in view of this paradox, the world public order, to be viable as an instrument to guarantee peace and prosperity of the community it regulates, must reconcile these two parallel trends of interdependence and segmentation.[3] The successful reconciliation of these opposing tendencies depends on the ability of appropriate institutions to project and protect the common interests of the world community. The common interests, in this connection, in conformity with the trends of interdependence and segmentation, may be divided into two categories: inclusive interests and exclusive interests.

Inclusive interests refer to those events that affect the entire world community or a large segment of it. The common interest requires that where certain events affect more than one territorial group, their management must be entrusted to institutions that facilitate a process of collective, international decision-making. Only when different entities are allowed to participate in the decision-making is it possible to appreciate and synthesize their divergent perspectives relating to an event that concerns them all. Exclusive interests, on the other hand, are denoted by events of relatively local significance pertaining to only one territorial group in comparison with others. Accordingly, it is in the common interest to leave the regulation of local events to the instituions authorized and controlled by the concerned territorial community.[4]

When we refer to the interests of the community, whether they are inclusive or exclusive, two major goals become particularly apparent. Both derive their prominence from the all-pervasive and dominant developments of modern science and technology. These are two distinct but closely interrelated goals. One is to preserve minimum order, and the other is to strive for promotion of an optimum order.

Maintenance of Minimum Order as an Inclusive Interest

The existence of an international community is beyond argument when the effects of total war waged with the most destructive weapons available are considered. There cannot be another world war without annihilating all of mankind, and limited wars are rightly regarded as the seedbeds for such a world war. The dimensions of the destructive capacity of modern weaponry have totally transformed the significance of coercion as a proper method of settling disputes. Uninhibited indulgence in coercion in international relations carries imminent danger to every individual on our planet. Indeed, the greatest danger to a system of world public order comes from ignoring or neglecting the grave implications of the frequency and the intensity with which the strategy of coercion is employed today.[5]

There is no region in the world that has not experienced a sense of growing expectation of crisis. The sources of world tensions cannot be ascribed to any one single factor. Several factors have often been mentioned in this context, for example: (a) opposing ideological blocs; (b)

failure of and gaps in international communication; (c) the frustration of
the demands for higher standards of living among the poor; (d) continued manufacture, purchase, and exchange of arms; (e) recruitment
and training of armed forces; (f) preservation of military pacts; and (g)
overemphasis on parochial perspectives involving nationalism, patriot-
ism, and ethnic, racial, and family divisions.[6]

Threats to world security can be traced to chronic inadequacy of
techniques intended either to deter coercion or to promote peaceful
resolution. We may mention at least four such techniques in this connection. They are as follows: building up of a nuclear arsenal (nuclear
deterrence); creation of military alignments or regional arrangements;
employment of the peace-keeping machinery of the United Nations;
and the peaceful settlement of disputes through international tribunals,
mediation, and conciliation. Most of these techniques overlap in their
use.

Ironically, some of these techniques forged for the purpose of re-
straining violence and crisis factors have, in fact, contributed to their
furtherance. Typical of this trend are nuclear deterrence[7] and military
alignments.[8] The other techniques have frequently broken down, ex-
posing their shortcomings.[9] For example, the Organization of the African Unity was not of much consequence in dealing with the disastrous
Nigerian Civil War. The U.N. peace-keeping machinery proved futile
in settling the Arab-Israeli conflict, not to speak of other less dramatic
situations. The conflict in Southeast Asia was a reminder of the limitations of all known techniques designed to enforce peace. The limitations of peaceful settlement of disputes, especially the strategy of judicial settlement, which is dependent on the willingness of disputants to
invoke it to maintain international peace, are too obvious to explain or
illustrate.[10]

The conclusion is therefore clear: threats to minimum world public
order—that is, to the security of the world community—are too varied
and explosive. And the means or strategies available to meet the challenge of saving the world from the haunting possibility of a nuclear
holocaust are too few and only partially successful. The implication of
such a conclusion for the purposes of relevant policy formulation is
that special efforts are needed to commit the community to minimizing
threats to world public order and to discourage the use of coercive
strategies in pursuing desired values. It must be realized that preservation of the minimum order is fundamental to the coexistence of the

divided world arena, as well as to its integration and to the promotion of universal goals.

Inclusive Interests and the Promotion of Optimum Order

The goal of maintenance of minimum order, though essential to prevent the world community from drifting toward cataclysm, serves only a negative function. In the ultimate analysis, the survival and well-being of humanity depend on the building of a world order that reflects and is responsive to the aspirations of all the peoples of the world. Only by striving more positively to eliminate the underlying causes of international tension, and only by promoting a more equitable world order than exists today, will we ever be able to inherit the abundance that modern science and technology offer to mankind.

An optimum world public order as we conceive of it must facilitate the realization of two important goals: first, the optimal promotion of values such as power, enlightenment, wealth, well-being, skills, affection, respect, and rectitude; second, the widest distribution of such values among the different groups of the world community.[11]

The ability of man to reach the moon dramatically signifies not only his perseverance to prevail over the nature but also the state or the power of science and technology at his command. Though the spectacular space achievement was engineered mainly by the American and the Soviet astronauts, when it is hailed as a "giant leap for mankind," it reflects a sense of realization. In essence, the important feat of putting man on the moon indicates that equally great accomplishments in other fields, such as in improving the welfare of fellow human beings, could very well be achieved if there were a broad political consensus on the measures needed.

The advanced state of science and technology that has been revolutionizing the methods of industrial production and the way of life around the world, however, has paradoxically been instrumental in furthering several serious hazards to human existence and the environment. These hazards are indicated, for example, by popular protests against pollution, exhaustion of nonreplenishable resources, and extinction of some species of animals and birds.[12]

The sobering truth of the matter is that science and technology are merely instruments. Persons who wield them must employ them wisely and in the common interest. Only when it is realized that the effects of applied science are far-ranging and often transcend the immediate scope and space of its utilization will it be possible to control its damaging effects and attain an optimum production of values. Only then will the net production of values be greater.

It must be further emphasized that optimal production of values in a given context, especially in the context of natural resource exploitation, will be achieved only by striving for the minimization of wasteful production processes—that is, by conserving resources as far as possible, by accommodating multiple uses at sea, and by controlling the market without overproduction of resources.

The interdependence of the world community needs to be stressed even more strongly when it comes to the distribution of values produced among all the members of the international community. The dangers inherent in the ever-growing gap between the developed and the developing nations and between their standards of living are more subtle and less readily appreciated than the dangers of an abused application of science and technology. Competent and perceptive observers have often pointed out the correlation between economic backwardness and the breakdown of order.[13] No fresh case has to be made in the present context to emphasize the need to help different territorial groups of the world to "achieve a minimum threshold sufficient to support a self-sustaining level of accumulation of values in modern institutional forms."[14]

Maintenance of Minimum Internal Order and Promotion of Optimal Order as an Exclusive Interest

As in the case of inclusive interests, the exclusive interests that deserve to be protected may be identified as maintenance of minimum internal public order and the promotion of optimum internal public order. Some of the comments noted while clarifying the inclusive interests are also relevant here and need not be repeated.

Threats to internal public order from such events as riots, strikes, racial or student unrest, demands for minority protection, small-scale insurgencies, and other general disorders may be treated, normally, as matters of relatively exclusive concern. Each territorial community within whose confines such threats occur is, under ordinary circumstances, the best agency to deal with them. These situations on occasion may assume such grave proportions as to be of genuine inclusive interest. However, at what point and under what circumstances matters that are originally of exclusive interest become matters of international concern could and should be decided only by a contextual examination.

Threats to the territorial integrity of a community may also arise frequently. These threats may take the form of an actual armed attack or of sustained subversive activity. Because adequate world machinery is yet to be set up to protect the territorial integrity of each community, obstacles should not be created to prevent nation-states from guarding themselves against external threats. To this extent the threats to territorial integrity of a community may be termed as a matter of exclusive interest to it.

Nation-states demand exclusive authority and control over resources and activities within their respective boundaries as a means of improving the prosperity of their peoples, and these demands are commonly honored. In their bid to promote optimum internal public order, to a limited extent they also claim authority and control over resources and activities beyond their immediate boundaries. Such claims are advanced and respected where on balance it can be shown, as far as its value maximization is concerned, that the impacts of resource exploitation or other activities have greater direct effects on the community in question, and when the territorial community is willing, on a basis of reciprocity, to defer to similar demands by other territorial communities. By way of illustration, we may mention here the claims to control fishing in contiguous zones, to control the flights of foreign aircraft over one's territory, and to prescribe customs and sanitary and other health regulations with respect to all people entering one's territory as belonging to the category of exclusive interests that bear upon the promotion of optimum internal public order.

The Context of Marine Mineral Resource Exploitation

Given the context of marine mineral resource exploitation, it is appropriate to examine more specific policies that will further the cause of the basic goals of the world public order. In discussing these policies, it may be useful to consider the following topics:

1. The characteristics of the mineral resources;
2. Participation in the marine environment;
3. The objectives of the participants;
4. The situational imperatives;
5. The base values needed;
6. The strategies employed; and
7. The outcomes expected.

The Characteristics of Mineral Resources

To determine the conditions necessary to encourage the most efficient production of the marine mineral resources and to derive maximum benefits from such production, particular attention must be paid to the characteristics of the resources under consideration.

With respect to oil and gas resources, one important characteristic is that they are exhaustible and nonrenewable. That is, they are stock resources.[15] Further, it is appropriate to regard oil and gas deposits as scarce stock resources for two reasons: (1) even though they are available over wide maritime areas, costs of production at any given time limit the number of economically attractive areas; and (2) presently, control over these areas is unevenly distributed among different countries, while the demand for more energy is constantly growing throughout the international community.

A scarce stock resource is apt to attract more than one producer. If the experience so far gained from the exploitation of oil and gas deposits of the submarine areas is any indication, the possibility of several producers bidding to exploit oil and gas deposits from the same area is extremely high. If conflicts among them are to be prevented, such a possibility calls for organized procedures of allocation of resource zones among different producers. These procedures should serve the basic goals of the world public order by specifying the size of the offshore area, the duration for which exclusive rights are granted over the area to a producer, the measures necessary for the conservation of the resource, and, most of all, the methods of choosing a producer from among several competitors.

Manganese nodules are widely scattered resources. The minerals that the exploitation of manganese nodules is anticipated to produce face competition from a variety of alternative sources. Their exploitation on a large scale may be deferred until some time in the near future. The kinds of problems associated with their exploitation are still unclear, but from the evidence so far available, one can reasonably assume that producers would like to have exclusive rights over specific marine areas for definite durations to engage in the exploitation of manganese nodules. Thus, in the exploitation of manganese nodules, procedures of orderly and peaceful allocation of exclusive rights will also be needed to promote efficient and economic production of the resources and to prevent conflicts among the various participants. The formulation and implementation of such procedures, to be in the common interest, must be subscribed to by a significant majority of the members of the world community.

Participation in the Marine Environment

Customarily, the oceans have been open to inclusive enjoyment. Different participants are involved in various uses of the seas with a minimum of interference in the interests of others.[16] The oceans also constitute wide areas of the world that are still not exclusively appropriated by any territorial group. This fact provides a unique opportunity to preserve the seas and the resources and benefits they represent as a symbol of shared use.

Because of valuable past experience regarding human interaction on the high seas and because of the future promise that the oceans hold as a common heritage of mankind, it is desirable to encourage, insofar as possible, methods of collective use and exploitation of the marine mineral resources.

Objectives

Consistent with the basic goals of the world public order are several interests that deserve consideration in the context of marine mineral resource exploitation. First, threats to the maintenance of minimum public order may arise in several different forms: (a) participants who seek strategic advantages may occupy suitable offshore areas in the name of resource exploitation and indulge in offensive activities against a coastal state; (b) in the absence of any international consensus on the ways of acquiring exclusive titles and tenures to the submarine areas, participants may clash with each other in an effort to monopolize the most attractive submarine areas; and (c) once the production of marine mineral resources becomes economically more popular, the production bases in the ocean environment may be regarded as targets of blackmail and disruption by the adversaries.

Second, from the perspective of the promotion of optimum order there is the necessity (a) to accommodate different uses of the seas, (b) to encourage equitable distribution of benefits resulting from marine mineral resource exploitation, and (c) to provide for conservation of natural resources.

Any regime intended to regulate marine mineral resource exploitation must consider all these interests and must suitably reflect the basic goals of the world public order.

Geographical Situation

The situation of the mineral resources is relevant only insofar as they affect the community interests outlined above. For example, if mineral resources of potential economic significance are confined to one location or to a few submarine areas, inequities in the acquisition of these resources might result if the resources are exploited through an unorganized access. Under these circumstances, procedures to ensure orderly and equitable access to the resources are necessary. In the case of marine mineral resources this need has already been described (see Chapter 1 and its notes).

Furthermore, the situation of mineral resources in a particular area may sometimes require that the exclusive interests of an adjacent state be given due weight in the exploitation of these resources. This may happen if the resources form a single pool that extends into the territory of the adjacent state.

Base Values

Marine mineral resource exploitation requires a variety of capabilities on the part of participants. These capabilities are usually concentrated among a few of them. If the common interests of the world community are to be promoted, the relative concentration of base values should not be allowed to result in a monopoly of the benefits derived from the exploitation. For such a monopoly might increase the gap between the developed and developing nations, a gap that has widely been regarded as inimical to the common interests of the world community.

Strategies

The obvious disparities among the participants have direct influence on the kind of strategies that participants may employ in the process of offshore resource exploitation. Measures need to be taken, in this connection, to discourage employment of strategies promoting interests that may be at variance with the promotion of optimum order involving both efficient production of resources and equitable distribution of the resulting benefits.

For example, participants who control scarce strategic mineral resources may be tempted to raise the prices at which they are offered to the consuming countries. These price rises could be so unreasonable as to disrupt the well-being of developing countries seriously and throw the world economy itself into a depression.[17] This is not an unthinkable situation, as the use of "oil weapons" by Arab nations and the resulting oil crisis have recently demonstrated.[18]

These factors indicate the need to preserve access to marine minerals through uniformly applicable and generally acceptable procedures. Such procedures would minimize the necessity for each participant to rely ultimately on use of naked force as a strategy to defend its acquisition of the resources.

Outcomes

The oceans hold both great promise and serious peril to the future of mankind. To utilize the benefits they offer and to minimize the detriments involved to the world community, the interdependence of members of the world community must be recognized as most important in the context of marine mineral resource exploitation.

Regulation of Marine Mineral Resources

Basically, three forms of regulation of marine mineral resource exploitation can be conceived: first, the resources may be divided among the coastal states, and their exploitation may be subjected to their exclusive authority and control; second, the exploitation of the resources may be regulated through an unorganized inclusive access or "flag state" jurisdiction, a jurisdiction that is presently applicable to navigation and fishing on the high seas; third, the resource exploitation may be managed by an organized inclusive access involving structures of international authority and control.[19] Each one of these forms of regulation has its merits and drawbacks from the perspective of promotion of the basic goals and the policies noted above.

Exclusive Appropriation of Marine Minerals by the Coastal State

Regulation of marine mineral exploitation exclusively under the competence of the coastal state is a method already in operation in the continental shelf area, and it will be convenient to extend the same procedure to the offshore areas beyond. Participants have developed certain expectations regarding the operation of this method: they can identify the agencies that issue leases; they can supervise the process of exploitation, the policies applicable, the remedies available in case of damage, and the norms of behavior of each of the agencies or nations involved in the process. Settled practices and uniformities in expectations will enhance efficiency of operations.

The method of exclusive appropriation of the marine minerals by the coastal state also has the apparent advantage of minimizing the risks of monopoly of the benefits by a few who have the means to recover the resources from the sea. Under this system, a developing coastal state can lease the marine mineral rights to an acceptable foreign agent, even if it could not exploit them on its own.

In addition, it is necessary to consider three other factors—(1) security of the coastal state, (2) geological continuity of marine minerals with other resources lying within the territory of the coastal state, and (3) geological appurtenance of the submarine areas—and the justification these all afford in approving the form of the coastal state's exclusive appropriation. These are factors, as will be seen in Chapter 3, often advanced by advocates of extended coastal state jurisdiction over marine minerals following the example of the Truman Proclamation on the subject.

SECURITY OF THE COASTAL STATE AND THE POSSIBILITY OF MISSILE SITES OR SUBVERSIVE ACTIVITIES

The exploitation of oil and gas deposits in shallow waters is conducted by erecting huge installations, often the size of an artificial island, involving very extensive matériel and several men working at the site of operations. The presence of such an activity off the shores of a coastal state may be seen as a threat because the coastal state demands exclusive authority and control in the interest of its internal security and public order. The precise nature of the threat is, however, not very clear. For purposes of examination, we will assume two major instances as being of potentially exclusive concern to the coastal state and will evaluate the imperative nature of the method of exclusive appropriation. The first instance relates to the possibility of an adversary power concealing missiles while claiming to engage in offshore mineral resource exploitation. The second instance refers to the possibility of a hostile state utilizing the exploitation operation site as a springboard to indulge in subversive activity against the coastal state.

With respect to the concealment of missiles, insofar as it is a real issue, the first question to be considered is whether it could be accomplished without being exposed by the adversary intelligence. For once the site of missile masking is known, the threat to the security of a state may be expected to be reduced by the adoption of countermeasures.

The two superpowers, the United States and the USSR, which are potentially capable of attempts to mask missiles, are known to possess highly sophisticated intelligence machinery to detect mutual missile strength and the places where they can be launched. In this connection, mention may be made of satellite surveillance, which can spot not only missile sites above the ground but also missile sites situated underground with grass grown over them.[20] Indeed, the availability of supersensitive cameras has made it possible to locate from high altitudes a dinner plate on the ground or even a button on a man's shirt. As far as detection of nuclear submarines is concerned, the initiation of long-range hunter killer airplanes, the Lockheed P-3C Orion has added to the strength of United States antisubmarine warfare.[21] By unilaterally improving their capacity to inspect or watch each other's missile and nuclear strength, both the superpowers have so greatly reduced the risk of surprise attack that today a few of the competent military experts can comment that on-the-spot investigation is no longer necessary to implement proposals of nuclear disarmament.[22]

In the same connection, we may also note that fixed missile sites can be more easily detected than mobile missile sites. This further reduces the risks involved in attempts to conceal missiles in fixed installation areas. Considering the fact that the high seas have been constantly patrolled by intelligence ships and planes, one may also wonder whether it would be at all possible for either the United States or the USSR to build missile sites without being observed by the other. Successful masking of missiles in submarine areas therefore appears to be a very remote possibility.

Then the following question may be raised: Suppose that such a remote possibility materialized, and one of the two superpowers successfully masked missiles in a submarine area; what difference would it make in the general context of nuclear deterrence? It is well known that nuclear deterrence is maintained principally between the superpowers through their so-called "second-strike" capabilities. Second-strike capability, in simple terms, refers to the capacity of a superpower to cause very extensive damage to an enemy after suffering the effects of a surprise nuclear attack from him. This capacity is maintained through both offensive and defensive strategies. In the foreseeable future it is hard to imagine any breakthrough in such a nuclear stalemate. One can almost assuredly conclude that missiles concealed in a submarine area add little to the quality of the surprise attack of superpowers. The position would not be vastly different as far as their second-strike capability is concerned. In other words, the threat to the coastal state's security from masking a missile is not a serious one.

It is possible, however unlikely it may be, that participants could use their installation sites as springboards for indulging in subversive activities such as smuggling and propaganda affecting the interests of the nearest coastal state. Then, the question is whether, to counter the threats involved, it is necessary to grant exclusive competence to coastal states over marine mineral resource exploitation. The answer appears to be in the negative. For the coastal state under the terms of general principles of international law is already invested with the right of self-defense against any threats to its security materializing out of unlawful activities conducted off of its shores or elsewhere.

GEOLOGICAL CONTINUITY, EFFICIENCY, AND ECONOMY

It is a fact that the boundaries of a coastal state, just as those of any other state, were not drawn with particular attention to the geological distribution of the deposits or pools of mineral resources contained therein. The boundaries of states are largely the result of political, cultural, and historical processes. But the location of natural resources is a purely geological phenomenon. It is therefore no surprise to come across a pool or a deposit of mineral resources being divided between a coastal state and the submarine areas that lie beyond the limits of its territorial waters.

An efficient and economic exploitation of a pool or deposit of natural resources normally requires an evaluation of the extent of the entire deposit. In the case of oil and gas deposits such an evaluation is especially crucial in order to determine the number of wells and the intervals at which such wells should be spread over the entire deposit. Both of these considerations in turn determine the most economic and efficient exploitation of the oil and gas deposits. In the case of marine mineral resource deposits that are geologically connected with the adjacent coastal state, there seems to be some advantage in conceding them to its exclusive competence.

However, when we examine numerous precedents where rivers, mountains, forests, and mineral deposits have belonged to more than one state, it is instructive to note that the efficient and economic use of common resources does not necessarily suffer for lack of exclusive appropriation of the entire deposits or pool of resources by one state. Common interests of participants have generally prevailed to crystallize cooperative arrangements for developing and deriving benefits from the resources. In the case of marine mineral resource exploitation itself, instances of mutual cooperation and joint efforts to develop a deposit or pool of mineral resources that lie across the territorial boundaries of two states are not rare.[23]

The conclusion, again from the perspective of desirable policy, is that the geological continuity of a marine mineral resource with the resources of the adjacent coastal state in itself does not necessarily mean that the entire deposit must be exclusively appropriated by the state.

SUBMARINE AREAS AND THE EQUITY OF EXCLUSIVE APPROPRIATION

Exclusive appropriation of the submarine mineral resources, at least up to a point, by the adjacent coastal state has widely been supported for considerations of equity. Earlier it was suggested that the mineral resources of the continental shelf essentially belonged to the adjacent coastal state because the continental shelf was geologically appurtenant to it. More recently the same consideration was invoked to justify coastal states' exclusive appropriation of offshore mineral resources, with only one difference. This time it was suggested that the submarine areas comprising continental margin, which goes further beyond the continental shelf region, are said to be geologically appurtenant to the adjacent coastal state.

For purposes of clarification of policy the question is this: What weight should be given to considerations of equity present in such a situation of geological appurtenance in assessing the merits of the method of exclusive appropriation?

The first and foremost difficulty in treating the geological features of the ocean floor as a basis for the allocation of mineral resources among the coastal states is the lack of any precise means to determine the specific point up to which it is said the submarine areas are appurtenant. The impossibility of arriving at a scientific determination as to what constitutes the boundary of a "continental shelf" was one of the reasons that forced decision-makers earlier to desist from a dogmatic reference to the features of the ocean floor in their evaluation of the merits of claims to appropriate exclusively marine mineral resources. The situation appears to be no better even when the reference is changed from an emphasis on "continental shelf" to the "continental margin." (See Chapter 1.)

Second, even if the limits of the geological extension of the coastal landmass into submarine areas could be approximated, however arbitrary such an approximation might sometimes be, the actual extent of the submarine areas that would be allotted to various coastal states' exclusive competence, on the basis of the geological configuration of the ocean floor, is bound to be different. Such differences are apt to result in claims of discrimination that, to be resolved, demand further arbitrary choices that have no relationship to the community interests at stake.

Furthermore, attempts to revise national boundaries, whatever the scope of competence for which such attempts may be made, on the basis of geological appurtenance of the landmass might lead to interminable international conflicts. For, after all, insofar as the concept of continental drift is accepted, the entire earth is one landmass, especially the submarine areas that are now divided by the deep oceans.[24] Under the circumstances, the coastal states situated opposite each other could, by invoking the fact of geological appurtenance, legitimately claim the same submarine areas, ignoring the dividing deep oceans. Taken to its logical limits, the theory of geological appurtenance of the adjacent landmass could be equally well invoked to claim revision of national boundaries of the coastal state on the landward side as they could be invoked to extend boundaries on a state's seaward side. If, however, such an argument is regarded as absurd because the interests of another state on the landward side are considered inviolable, the absurdity of coastal state's claim on the seaward side should be duly emphasized in the interest of the entire world community, and the sense of common sharing of the high seas and the resources they symbolize should be held equally sacred.

Because of the foregoing reasons, it is believed that the three factors—security of coastal states, geological continuity, and geological appurtenance—are not by themselves persuasive reasons to justify the method of exclusive appropriation of offshore mineral resources by the coastal state.[25]

Furthermore, any attempt to divide the ocean's mineral resources among the coastal states directly affects the equal opportunity that the landlocked and other geographically disadvantaged states value in the exploitation of mineral resources of the high seas and could justifiably be regarded by them as a discrimination against their interests. In this sense, division of offshore mineral resources among the coastal states is not consistent with the goal of the widest sharing of benefits resulting from their exploitation.

It must also be pointed out that exploitation of offshore mineral resources is economically far more costly and technologically far more difficult than the development of onshore natural resources. The developing countries that depend on foreign economic and technical assistance for the development of their resources naturally cannot be expected to derive benefits from mineral resources off their shores without a similar commitment from capable and willing external sources to help them in the process. Whatever the reasons, the mineral resources of the submarine areas off the coasts of several developing countries remain largely unexplored and unexploited. The truism is, as far as developing countries are concerned, the mere claiming of exclusive rights over offshore minerals does not contribute to a prompt maximization of their values. Thus, even though all the coastal states may have equal rights over the mineral resources of the sea, the benefits to be gained by the developed countries from a wide extension of coastal state jurisdiction would outweigh the advantages a developing state could claim.[26]

In addition, it is obvious that a grant of equal rights over offshore submarine areas does not assure that all the coastal states will have equal returns from the resources to be found there, since their distribution and quality would vary from area to area. It is entirely possible that some of the coastal states, although extensive maritime areas are under their control, may never receive any appreciable returns because the mineral resources found there are not economically attractive. These considerations suggest that the method of exclusive appropriation of offshore submarine areas by the coastal states may not necessarily lead to the widest distribution of returns from their exploitation even among the coastal states, let alone the landlocked and other geographically disadvantaged states.

Unorganized Inclusive Access
According to the second form of regulation of marine mineral resource exploitation, access would essentially be left free to every participant. The activities of each participant would furthermore be regulated by the state under whose protection and competence it chooses to operate on the high seas.

The "flag state" approach regulates such uses of the high seas as navigation, fishing, and scientific investigation. In each of these instances a relatively unorganized inclusive access has thus far proved to be generally in the common interest. Two important considerations, in our opinion, contribute to this outcome with respect to each one of these uses of the sea.

When the participants engage in navigation, they do not consume the ocean space as a resource. In other words, any number of participants with a minimum of ground rules can exercise their freedom of navigation without interfering with the similar freedom of others. Moreover, no participant needs wide exclusive maritime areas for a prolonged duration to operate on the high seas for purposes of navigation. As such, navigation does not substantially interfere with other uses of the seas.

Similar considerations apply to the freedom of scientific investigation on the high seas. Participants normally do not require any exclusive rights to submarine areas. Very rarely, if ever, do the scientific investigations by one participant adversely affect the interests of other participants, whether they are related to the conduct of scientific investigation or to the utilization of oceans for other purposes.

The regulation of fishing on the high seas through the "flag state" approach assumes first that fish are a renewable resource and, within certain limits of conservation, accommodates more than one participant without adversely affecting anyone's catch. Second, in this case, the "flag state" approach has proved satisfactory, because until recently the participants did not need property rights to any specific submarine area. The duration for which a fishing fleet operated in any particular part of the ocean was short enough and the technology of fishing was such that it did not adversely affect a given area for others who were fishing or using the sea for other purposes, but this situation is rapidly changing.[27]

The use of the oceans for navigation, fishing, and scientific investigation thus conceived is strikingly different when one considers marine mineral resource exploitation. Mineral resources are stock resources. Exploitation of a deposit in a particular area by a participant totally excludes the exploitation of the same deposit in the same area by other participants. This is one reason why producers always vie with one another to gain exclusive rights to a mineral resource deposit of proved economic value. Property rights involving exclusive titles and lengthy tenures are central to the process of mineral resource exploitation, whether offshore or otherwise, as discussed in Chapter 1.

Where exclusive maritime zones are created and allotted to participants for mineral resource exploitation, a certain amount of interference with other uses of the sea involving the same areas cannot be avoided, and it is even taken for granted. This is an important consideration that distinguishes marine mineral resource exploitation from the more traditional uses of the seas in which case the "flag state" approach is presently applicable.

One of the consequences of the "flag state" approach, if applied indiscriminately to the marine mineral resource exploitation, is that the resources would be claimed by the first comer, by the participant who could discover and get to them the most quickly. Where more than one participant seeks the same deposit of resources, there would be few procedures available to provide for orderly and peaceful allocation of it among them, short of negotiating from the position of strength or forcing out one of them by actually invoking military power. Furthermore, when a participant claims certain deposits of mineral resources and thereby asserts a right to exercise competence over a specific submarine area for a particular duration, there would be no commonly acceptable procedures under which its right to exploit such resources could be weighed against the interests of others to fish, navigate, conduct scientific investigation, and to engage in other possible uses in the same portion of the high seas. In other words, the size of the submarine area desired for mineral resource exploitation, the duration for which it is intended to be occupied exclusively, the amount of interference that may be caused to other interests in the use of the same areas of the ocean are all decisions that, in the case of unorganized inclusive access, each individual participant would be authorized to make, at least initially. One more obvious consequence of the "flag state" approach is that marine mineral resources are apt to be appropriated exclusively by the technologically most developed countries because of their monopoly of the means to exploit them.

These consequences would adversely affect: (1) the pursuance of inclusive interests, (2) the promotion of optimum world public order, and (3) the maintenance of minimum order.

Organized Inclusive Access

For the many reasons noted above—such as (a) the need to discourage monopoly of scarce stock resources such as oil and gas by other than the entire community; (b) the need to avoid undesirable effects on international mineral market due to ocean mineral production; (c) the importance of allocation of ocean resources among competing producers; (d) the requirements of accommodation and reconciliation of different uses with resource production in the same area; and (e) the desirability of coordinating national activities to improve the knowledge relating to oceans and the benefits derivable therefrom—there is a tendency to reject the "flag state" approach; but there is still a strong case for organizing the process of marine mineral resource use through the authority and control of international machinery.

While some flexibility must be allowed in the ultimate design of the specific structure of such an international regime, it is useful to indicate a model framework that is consistent with the identified policy preferences. For the purpose of this framework, the process of marine mineral exploitation may be divided into three phases: (1) the preexploitation or exploration phase, (2) the exploitation phase, and (3) the postexploitation phase.

THE EXPLORATION PHASE

The phase of exploration consists chiefly of field surveys, experimental drilling, and general assessment of chances of recovery of the mineral resources. As such, exploration licenses could be given mostly on a nonexclusive basis and for modest fees. Furthermore, it is best if the process of exploration is allowed to proceed with a minimum of organized regulation and interference. The only obligation on the part of explorers would be that they should share their information fully with the concerned agents of the international community. To aid in the process of exploration, the international machinery would help teams of ocean scientists to conduct research freely. Such scientific investigations, which provide basic data on the marine environment, its resource potential, and other problems concerning exploitation in the area, could be promoted either through the provision of free access to the individual ocean science institutes or through collaboration among the participants. The international agency itself, after having acquired enough royalties through the exploitation of known reserves of marine minerals, could help by undertaking provisional explorative studies of offshore areas.

THE EXPLOITATION PHASE

The phase of exploitation begins as soon as a mineral resource deposit is identified and as soon as prospective producers exhibit an interest in claiming exclusive rights of title and tenure to a given submarine area. In view of the initial expenses, the technology, and the marketing capabilities, among other things required to exploit marine mineral resources, it is believed advisable for the international agency, at least for some time, to lease out the exploitation rights rather than undertake the operation on its own.

At this stage, various participants may be encouraged to submit applications for a lease to be granted by a designated international body, which should be essentially composed of technical experts drawn from different fields related to marine mineral resource exploitation. This international body should have the competence to draw up the final lease terms.

In drawing up the terms of the lease, the international body should be concerned with preventing pollution of the marine environment, accommodating various competing uses of the seas, conserving natural resources, and fixing the royalties to be paid by the participants to the international body.

In order to pay adequate attention to the accommodation of competing uses, before the international body grants exclusive rights to participants to a given submarine area, it should consult with the concerned international specialized agencies and other interested participants on the possible protection of multiple interests in the area. In those cases where more than one use of the area is apparent, the international body together with the other participants should decide on the ways of accommodating the conflicting uses.

Where more than one participant applies for the grant of exclusive rights to a given submarine area, the international body should choose the one who agrees to pay the highest royalties to the international body.

THE POSTEXPLOITATION PHASE

The postexploitation phase is related principally to the management of funds obtained from the collection of royalties or premiums paid by the entrepreneurs. The resulting fund, of course, will have to meet the incidental expenditures of maintaining an international body to regulate marine mineral resource exploitation. However, if there are still some funds available, they could be expended for the economic development of the world community. The management of the funds for this purpose should be left to an international body that adequately represents both the developed and the developing countries. These funds could also be entrusted to an existing international agency devoted to the formation of world economic development. As an alternative, the United Nations Economic and Social Council could be given authority to allot the available funds to programs approved by it.

There might also be other variations in the proposed international machinery that would yield optimum value dividends to the world community. However, the real issue is whether the international community composed of sovereign, independent states would agree to create an autonomous, efficient, and self-supporting international agency to regulate marine mineral resource exploitation.

One of the crucial factors that affects the efficiency of the international machinery is the way its decision-making function is organized. If such a function is diffused in an unwieldy bureaucracy and if the components of the machinery are not sufficiently coordinated because the prevailing political consensus did not permit a better arrangement, there is a danger that the resultant international machinery indeed may not be conducive to promoting the preferred policies. Furthermore, to be efficient, the international machinery must be framed to suit the economic returns of the resources entrusted to its care.

If efficient international machinery is not within the realms of present political probability, one alternative for achieving the most desirable policy objectives is to rely on the method of exclusive appropriation of the marine minerals by the coastal state and to modify it in certain necessary ways.

The modification of the coastal state's exclusive authority and control over the mineral resources of the sea could take several forms. For example, in return for the exclusive competence, a coastal state might be required to pay an agreed percentage of the profits from mineral resource exploitation to an international fund.[28] The fund could be used, among other things, to promote equitable world economic development. The coastal state might also be required to give preferential treatment in providing access to the mineral resources under its jurisdiction to those who are denied such resources. In addition, the coastal state might be compelled to agree to a system of compulsory third-party settlement of disputes arising out of its management of marine mineral resource exploitation and to the accommodation of inclusive interests in the area under its exclusive control.

Moreover, it is also important that a fairly unified system of management of marine resources in the different coastal state jurisdictions should be encouraged to provide for a stable process of exploitation. This consideration, of course, must be tempered by the need to promote healthy business competition among the countries to stimulate growth opportunities within the industry of marine minerals and for the benefit of worldwide consumers.

Whatever form of regulation of marine minerals is chosen, it is necessary for the participants to adopt policies that aid the most efficient process of marine mineral exploitation and the widest sharing of benefits resulting from such a process in order that the twin basic goals of world public order—maintenance of minimum order and promotion of an optimum order—may be achieved.

3
Limits for National Resource Jurisdiction

Claims about the Extent of the Continental Shelf

Under the doctrine of the "continental shelf," which has been widely recognized by the world community both through customary practice and through the Geneva Convention on the Continental Shelf of 1958, the coastal state enjoys exclusive authority and control over the exploitation of mineral resources of the continental shelf. The Geneva Convention on the Continental Shelf, in its Article 1, defines the term "continental shelf" as

The seabed and subsoil of the submarine areas adjacent to the coast but outside the area of the territorial sea, to a depth of 200 meters or, beyond that limit, to where the depth of the superjacent waters admits of the exploitation of natural resources of the said areas.[1]

In other words, the coastal state's exclusive authority and control over mineral resources of the submarine areas are subjected to two qualifications: (1) that the areas be adjacent; and (2) that the depth of the superjacent waters be exploitable.[2]

Considering the apparent open-endedness of the area over which the coastal state's competence extends as the technology for exploiting the marine mineral resources improves its range, it can be claimed that there is no limit to the continental shelf. However, if emphasis is placed upon the wording "adjacent," which qualifies the submarine areas in the definition of the continental shelf, a counterclaim can assert that even if technology is available to exploit the deepest areas of the oceans, the coastal state cannot extend its exclusive authority and control over such submarine areas for purposes of mineral resource exploitation therein if those areas are not situated adjacent to it.

Another claim, which in a sense can also be regarded as an alternative counterclaim to the claim that the reach of the continental shelf is indefinite, is that the framers of its definition clearly intended to limit the area of the seabed and subsoil over which the coastal state is supposed to have exclusive competence. Nevertheless, it can be further claimed that they left the actual definition of limits to the authority of the future decision-makers.

The problems of policy concerning the limits of the continental shelf have already been examined in Chapter 2. We will therefore proceed to examine here the different trends in decision relating to these claims.

Trends in Decision

Pre-International Law Commission Phase

Although claims to offshore submarine areas were not unknown earlier,[3] it was President Truman who proposed a new conception in the field of international law by proclaiming, on September 25, 1945, the exclusive jurisdiction and control of the United States over "the natural resources of the subsoil and seabed of the continental shelf beneath the high seas but contiguous to the coasts of the United States."[4]

The Truman Proclamation invoked four basic considerations as the rationale for its doctrine: (1) that the "effectiveness of measures to utilize or conserve these resources would be contingent upon cooperation and protection from the shore"; (2) that the "continental shelf may be regarded as an extension of the mainland of the coastal nation and thus naturally appurtenant to it"; (3) that "these resources frequently form a seaward extension of a pool or deposit lying within the territory" of the coastal nation; and (4) that "self-protection compels a coastal nation to keep close watch over activities off its shores."[5]

Reflecting an awareness of the possible repercussions of this position on the inclusive interests of the world community, the Truman Proclamation and an official press release from the White House on the same day attempted to define the limits of the area for which the exclusive access was claimed. The assumption of control and jurisdiction over the shelf, the Proclamation pointed out, did not affect the "character as high seas of the waters above the continental shelf and the right to their free and unimpeded navigation."[6] Moreover, the Proclamation confined the continental shelf to areas "beneath the high seas but contiguous to the coasts of the United States." The press release issued from the White House went further in defining continental shelf: "Generally, submerged land which is contiguous to the continent and which is covered by no more than 100 fathoms (600 feet) of water is considered as the continental shelf."[7]

Following the Truman Proclamation, about twenty countries issued similar decrees claiming exclusive access to the continental shelf and invoking, or at least indirectly referring to, the same basic justification of coastal states' economic and security interests in the adjoining submarine areas.[8] Of the twenty countries, at least sixteen cited some criteria suggesting a specific limitation on the extent of the shelf they were claiming. Honduras, Ecuador, Australia, Portugal, and the United States referred to the depth of 200 meters or 100 fathoms as the outer limit of their shelf.[9] Chile, Costa Rica, Mexico, and Peru relied on a distance criterion of 200 nautical or marine miles as the extent of their shelf.[10] Saudi Arabia, India, and the United Kingdom stressed adjacency or contiguity in describing their shelf.[11] Argentina and Guatemala seemed to extend their claims as far as (but only as far as) the geological configuration of their shelf extended beneath the high seas.[12] Iceland and the Republic of Korea even more clearly delineated their continental shelves by referring to the various points of the sea to which the boundaries of their shelf extended.[13] Israel alone adopted the criterion of exploitability.[14]

Three states, Nicaragua, Panama, and the Philippines, did not specify any particular limits.[15] However, Nicaragua expressed a desire to limit its shelf either by law or through agreement with other states.[16] Panama and the Philippines did not commit themselves to any definite limit with respect to their shelves and used the phrase "continental shelf" only to refer to a finite geological concept generally acknowledged at the time.[17] One might assume, however, that they were merely attempting to be cautious in the absence of a thorough knowledge of the extent and geological configuration of their shelf rather than contributing to the concept of an indefinite continental shelf. Even if this assumption is not acceptable, it is clear that a significant majority of nations favored the concept of the finite extent of the continental shelf by express provisions in their national declarations.

Consideration by the International Law Commission
Once the interest of the international community in the mineral resources of the continental shelf had thus been evidenced in the numerous unilateral proclamations and in other national decrees, the International Law Commission in its Second Session in 1950 took up the task of formulating general principles to regulate exploration and exploitation in the continental shelf region. Naturally, the first question before the Commission in that session was to define precisely the area to be designated as the continental shelf, for, as we have noted, the practice of states and the opinions of geologists were inconsistent on the matter.[18]

Expressing concern for those states that did not have a continental

shelf in the geological sense of the term, J. L. Brierly suggested to the
International Law Commission that the legal characterization of the
continental shelf should ignore its geological origin and reflect the
possibilities of exploitation of the submarine areas.[19] Manley O. Hudson
seemed to endorse the suggestion when he proposed that

Control and jurisdiction over the seabed and subsoil of submarine areas
outside the marginal sea may be exercised by a littoral State for the
exploration and exploitation of the natural resources therein contained,
to the extent to which such exploitation is feasible.[20]

Such a formulation of the shelf in terms of exploitation without indicating any outer limits, although it had the merit of ignoring the vagaries
of nature, was opposed for lack of clarity. As Jean Spiropaulos put it,

With regard to Mr. Hudson's proposal, which was based on technical
possibilities, it might be dangerous to permit a State to extend its rights
to the middle of the ocean. The issue was whether the Commission
wished to limit the rights of the coastal State to a certain distance from
its coasts or whether it should be permitted to extend them to any distance whatsoever so long as exploitation was possible.[21]

Concerning the desirability of limiting a coastal state's rights to a definite point, even the members who supported the criterion of "exploitability" agreed with those who advocated a geological (or depth) criterion. The Commission itself favored a degree of precision, adopting by 6
votes to 4, with 2 abstentions, Brierly's suggestion that the area over
which the exclusive rights of the coastal states were to be recognized
needed definition, although it need not depend on the existence of a
geological shelf.[22]

Taking this recommendation of the Commission into consideration,
J. P. A. François, the Rapporteur on the Regime of the High
Seas, at the Third Session of the Commission in 1951, proposed that in
defining the shelf a maximum depth of 200 meters be accepted as the
outer limit. Explaining the choice of 200 meters as the depth, he
pointed out that

. . . the main feature of [the] definition was that it entirely disregarded
the geographical and geological concept of the continental shelf. . . .
The first advantage derived from that course was that it enabled the
inclusion of the seabed and subsoil of shallow waters.

Referring to the contemporary expectations of exploitability of the submarine areas, he added that

. . . experts maintained that it was not possible to work the resources of the sea at a depth more than 200 meters. . . . As regards the working of submarine resources, . . . the limit of 200 meters was not final, but conformed to existing technical limitations. That is why it had been adopted in a number of conventions.[23]

At the end of the 113th meeting of the Third Session, rejecting all other proposals, the Commission adopted a definition of the shelf and fixed its outer limits at a depth of 200 meters.[24] However, the matter of delimitation of the shelf was brought up again at the suggestion of some members who strongly opposed the 200-meter depth limit on the grounds that it discriminated against states without any shelf in the geological sense and that the limit ignored the future possibilities of exploitation.[25] A subcommittee was appointed at the 117th meeting to deal with these objections. It unanimously recommended at the 123rd meeting that the phrase "does not exceed 200 meters" be dropped from the earlier definition of the shelf. It proposed substituting the phrase "is such as to permit the exploitation of the natural resources of the seabed and subsoil."[26] The recommendation was adopted at that session.

When the Draft Articles on the Regime of the High Seas were circulated among the states for their comments, at least twelve states expressed their position on the delimitation of the shelf.[27] With the exception of two states (Chile, which did not have any continental shelf as that term is understood in the geological parlance, and Syria), all of them preferred a precise delimitation of the shelf to the vague formula adopted by the Commission. Five states, Belgium, Iceland, the Netherlands, the Union of South Africa, and the United Kingdom, some of which had wide shallow submarine areas off their coasts, preferred the 200-meter or 100-fathom depth limit. Yugoslavia preferred the 200-meter limit with maximum and minimum distance specifications. Egypt preferred a precise depth limit with provision for a periodical revision. France suggested a 300-meter depth limit. Two states, Brazil and Norway, both of which had considerable shallow submarine areas off their coasts, wanted a clear limit to the continental shelf, although they did not indicate any preferences as to how and where to limit it.

In view of the comments from the states and their preponderant weight in favor of a fixed limit, the Commission once again, at the 197th meeting, on the proposal of the Rapporteur, adopted by 7 votes to 4, with 2 abstentions, the depth of 200 meters as the outer limit of the shelf.[28]

The Commission did not deal with the continental shelf matter until 1956. In the meantime, twenty American states had met in Ciudad Trujillo in the Dominican Republic, during March 15–28, 1956, and had resolved, at the end of long deliberations, among other things, to submit for consideration by the American states the conclusion that

The seabed and subsoil of the continental shelf, continental and insular terrace, or other submarine areas, adjacent to the coastal state, outside the area of the territorial sea, and to a depth of 200 meters or, beyond that limit, to where the depth of the superjacent waters admits to the exploitation of the natural resources of the seabed and subsoil, appertain exclusively to that State and are subject to its jurisdiction and control.[29]

At the end of the "Resolution of Ciudad Trujillo," of which this recommendation was a part, most of the participants reserved their respective positions on the controversial issues mentioned therein. Even the preface to the Resolution, as could be noted, carefully avoided any commitment on the part of the participants to any of its conclusions.

However, when the International Law Commission came to reconsider the matter of the continental shelf in 1956, F. V. García-Amador, Chairman of the Eighth Session, proposed that the definition of the shelf be suitably modified to include the criterion of exploitability as mentioned in the "Resolution of Ciudad Trujillo."[30] The Rapporteur and a few other members disagreed, fearing it would bring vagueness into the concept.[31] The Chairman defended his proposal on the ground that there were already instances where states, like Chile, were exploiting the oceans for coal at depths nearing 1,000 meters by shore-based installations. He therefore argued that the criterion of exploitability alone could accommodate such practices as well as future possibilities for exploitation. Some members tried to distinguish exploitation of the ocean floor by shore-based installations from sea-based installations and pointed out that exploitation by sea-based installations had thus far been done at depths much less than 200 meters.

Georges Scelle touched on the heart of the issue when he attacked the amendment to include the criterion of "exploitability":

Adoption of the concept whereby the continental shelf extended as far as exploitation of the natural resources of the sea-bed was possible would tend to abolish the domain of the high seas.[32]

The Chairman lost no time in rejecting any such interpretation of his proposal. As he pointed out,

. . . the words "adjacent to the coastal State" . . . placed a very clear limitation on the submarine areas covered by the article. *The adjacent areas ended at the point where the slope down to the ocean bed began, which was not more than 25 miles* from the coast [italics added].[33]

Gerald Fitzmaurice, who supported the Chairman's proposal, also expressed the view that the criterion of "exploitability" could not be unduly stretched to reach any ocean depths. Opposing a suggestion by Sushi Hsu, another member of the Commission, Fitzmaurice said he

. . . could not agree with Mr. Hsu that recognition of the exclusive right of Coastal States to exploit the natural resources of the seabed beyond the depth of 200 meters, on condition that the areas were in adjacent waters, and that exploitation was possible, was tantamount to appropriation of a part of the high seas. Such a statement implied a complete misunderstanding of the concept of the continental shelf and of submarine areas. . . .[34]

Following these explanations, the Chairman's amendment to include the criterion of exploitability was approved by 7 votes to 5, with 3 abstentions.[35]

Finally, Draft Article 67 of the Law of the Sea (which was to become Article 1 of the Geneva Convention on the Continental Shelf) was adopted by the International Law Commission in 1956. It defined the shelf as

. . . the seabed and subsoil of the submarine areas adjacent to the coast but outside the area of the territorial sea, to a depth of 200 meters (approximately 100 fathoms) or, beyond that limit, to where the depth of the superjacent waters admits of the exploitation of the natural resources of the said areas.[36]

The Geneva Conference on the Law of the Sea of 1958
Mixed feelings were expressed by the participants at the Geneva Convention on the Law of the Sea, in 1958, for whom Draft Article 67 formed the basis in defining the continental shelf. Depending upon their reactions to the definition of the shelf, the participants could be roughly divided into four groups. All except the third group expressed a willingness to translate the intention of clearly limiting the shelf into a tangible form in terms of either depth or distance or geological configuration of the submarine areas.

One group of states felt that the continental shelf was a geological and geographical phenomenon and that the outer limits of the shelf should be fixed by taking this factor into consideration. France, for example, reflecting this position, argued against the employment of the exploitability criterion in defining the legal shelf. According to the French representative,

The Commission has studied the question of the continental shelf for the simple reason that the shelf was a recognized geographical and oceanographical institution, which had been known and defined over a quarter of a century earlier. Professor Gidel . . . had already spoken of it in 1930. The Commission had thus adopted the line of reasoning that its function was to confirm, first, that the notion was acceptable in international law, and secondly, that the State enjoyed in the area a competence limited by international law. Starting from those premises, it had sought to define that competence, both territorially and functionally.

Opposing attempts to leave the outer limits undefined, he went on to say,

That would ultimately mean that each State had a right to proceed as far as it could, not just at any one moment but forever, and that there was a "sector" of water opposite its coasts over which it would have exclusive rights as soon as it could assert them. In those circumstances, it might be safer not to depart unduly from the Commission's intentions and not to put forward a new theory according to which States would have rights over veritable "sections" of the high seas off their coasts, the acceptance of which would nullify the universally recognized principle of the high seas.[37]

The delegation from Argentina, which had a million square kilometers of continental shelf, also stressed the geological origin of the shelf.

Geology and oceanography had established that the continental shelf consisted of an extension of the continent itself under the sea, and it was that scientific conclusion which constituted the basis of President Truman's proclamation of 1945 upholding the jurisdiction of the State over the continental shelf and of subsequent proclamations of Peru, Chile, and Argentina couched in similar terms.[38]

Later in the debates Argentina pointed out that the criterion of exploitability in the Commission's definition contributed to confusion of the concept of the legal shelf,[39] and proposed, like France, to delimit the shelf by employing only the depth criterion of 200 meters.[40] Panama, through its delegate, while substantially adhering to this philosophy, suggested that the legal shelf should end where the continental shelf geographically ends.

In the light of the views expressed in recent years by a number of technical bodies such as the International Committee on the Nomenclature of Ocean Bottom Features, [the] delegation considered the term "continental base" would be more accurate than "continental shelf," for the former referred to the continental shelf and the continental slope. More than a question of terminology was involved, for if the expression "continental base" were used it might be possible to delimit the extent of the shelf.[41]

However, he did not indicate how delimiting the "continental base" could be any easier than defining the outer limits of the continental shelf.

A second group of states took the view that any definition of the continental shelf in legal terms should principally reflect the possibilities of exploitation of the submarine areas. To this group, that consideration was paramount in delimiting the shelf. Thus M. W. Mouton, the representative of the Netherlands, suggested that

There were two different methods of exploiting the natural resources of the continental shelf. The first involved the use of fixed or floating installations which might interfere with shipping and fisheries, and that type of exploitation could be limited to a depth line; however, it might be preferable to specify a depth line of 550 meters, rather than 200 meters, as being nearer to the deepest edge of the continental shelf, and more likely to result in an agreement which could remain unaltered for a long period.[42]

Although the Indian government fully supported the use of the criterion of exploitability and did not believe that Draft Article 67 was open to ambiguity, it was prepared to accept a definite outer limit to the legal shelf. India proposed a depth limit of 1,000 meters, which in its opinion would cover future expectation about exploitability of the submarine areas. Later it revised this limit in favor of the 550-meter depth in the interest of a greater consensus. The Netherlands, Sweden, and the United Kingdom supported the 550-meter depth limit suggested by India, dropping their own proposals to that effect.[43]

The third group of states opposed any attempts to amend Draft Article 67. The views of the Colombian delegate were representative of this group when he said that

The article provided a permanent solution for the problem of the definition of the continental shelf and for that of the scientifically possible exploitation; safeguarded the States without a wide shelf, while in no way causing prejudice to those States that had such a shelf because the latter would have unimpaired enjoyment of their shelf; guaranteed equality of rights to all coastal States, which would enjoy equal rights in the submarine area, since they would stem from the basic right of self-preservation and defense of States.[44]

The final group of states insisted that Draft Article 67 should be amended because of its lack of precision. To the Chinese representative it did not matter which criterion was employed as long as the definition of the shelf was made more precise.[45] To some states the depth criterion of 200 meters was preferable because it conveyed an exact notion of the outer limits of the shelf. As the representative of Tunisia pointed out,

> In its definition, the International Law Commission had made use of two criteria, the mathematical notion of the 200-meter isobath and the more subjective notion of possible exploitation, the latter of which must depend on the technical capacity of the coastal State. Those two criteria were to some extent contradictory. . . . It appeared that the best criterion for defining the continental shelf was the 200-meter isobath, which was in accordance both with the geological configuration of the continental shelf and with the availability of its resources.[46]

On the exact method of delimitation there were again different opinions. Yugoslavia and Canada suggested a combination of limits. Yugoslavia proposed that the depth criterion of 200 meters should be coupled with the specification of a maximum of 100 miles in the case of those states that had an extended continental shelf, and a minimum distance of 50 miles in the case of those states whose continental shelf was narrow, to define the extent of the legal shelf.[47] Canada recommended a combination of the criterion of geological configuration of the shelf with the depth criterion. Thus, it proposed that the legal shelf should end where the geological shelf ends, provided its edge was clear and identifiable. In the absence of an identifiable edge, Canada suggested that a specific maximum depth, perhaps 550 meters, could be fixed as the outer limit of the legal shelf.[48]

None of the proposals seeking to delimit the shelf by fixed criteria could get the majority needed for adoption.[49] The French proposal to limit the shelf at a depth of 200 meters was rejected by 48 votes to 12 with 7 abstentions. Panama's recommendation to limit the legal shelf at the edge of the continental slope was rejected by 38 votes to 4, with 26 abstentions. The Indian solution of limiting the shelf at a depth of 550 meters was rejected by 31 votes to 21 with 16 abstentions. The proposal by Yugoslavia lost by 39 votes to 2, with 21 abstentions, and that of Canada was defeated by 39 votes to 16, with 12 abstentions. In the end, Draft Article 67, as amended by the Philippines to include similar continental shelves around islands, was adopted by 51 votes to 9, with 10 abstentions.[50]

In the plenary meetings France once again attempted to delete the phrase "or, beyond that limit, to where the depth of the superjacent waters admits of the exploitation." On a separate vote taken on this phrase 48 states voted to retain it, 20 states voted against retention, and 2 states abstained. Article 67 as a whole was then adopted by 51 votes to 5, with 10 abstentions.[51]

Later, in ratifying the Convention of the Continental Shelf, France made clear its understanding of the extent of the shelf in terms of Article 1:

In the view of the Government of the French Republic, the expression "adjacent" area implies a notion of geophysical, geological, and geographical dependence which *ipso facto* rules out an unlimited extension of the continental shelf.[52]

On this interpretation of Article 1, only two parties to the convention reserved their position, and none contested it.

Post-Geneva Conference Phase
Following the adoption of the continental shelf convention, many states promulgated new regulations to govern the exploitation of "natural resources" in the "continental shelf" after their "sovereign rights" had been recognized beyond doubt.[53] Not all of them gave special attention to the area encompassed by the term "continental shelf," except for repeating the definition in Article 1. However, four states clearly mentioned the outer limits of their legal shelves: Australia and the United Kingdom described their boundaries exactly, Ecuador delimited the shelf at a depth of 200 meters, and Ghana at a depth of 100 fathoms.[54]

In 1967, Malta proposed in the United Nations that the exploitation of the resources of the seabed and the ocean floor beyond the limits of present national jurisdiction be reserved "exclusively for peaceful purposes" and "in the interests of mankind."[55] This proposal again revived the following questions: What are the outer limits of the continental shelf, and from what point does the "area beyond present national jurisdiction" begin? Shigeru Oda, a noted Japanese expert, addressing himself to these questions, observed that

. . . the concept of exploitability must be constantly reinterpreted in terms of the most advanced standards of technology and economy in the world. Hence, the exploitation of submarine resources at any point must always be reserved to the coastal state, which is empowered to claim the area when the depth of the superjacent waters admits of exploitation. It can be inferred that, under this convention, all the submarine areas of the world have been theoretically divided among the coastal states at the deepest trenches. This is the logical conclusion to be drawn from the provisions approved at the Geneva Convention.[56]

He added, however, that as a matter of *lex ferenda* he was not in favor of allowing the deep sea to be divided among the various coastal states. He therefore urged early action by the international community to separate deep sea areas from the continental shelves before claims are made "over deep sea areas in terms of exploitability as provided in the convention."[57]

Oda's interpretation of the criterion of exploitability is based on three assumptions: (1) that it should be interpreted according to the standards of technology available to the most developed nation; (2) that if technology is available to exploit one type of "natural resource" at a particular depth, the continental shelf jurisdiction will cover the exploitation of not only that resource but all other kinds of natural resources up to that depth of water; and (3) that mere technological feasibility of exploitation even without actual and physical exploitation at a particular depth of water is enough to extend the reach of coastal states' exclusive competence to that depth. The first and second assumptions are well supported by the views of other experts such as M. S. McDougal, W. T. Burke, and Richard Young and by the legislative history of Article 1 of the Geneva Convention on the Continental Shelf of 1958.[58] According to Article 2 (2) and (3), the rights of coastal states are exclusive and do not depend upon occupation or on any express proclamation. Furthermore, if the coastal state does not explore or exploit the resources of the shelf, no one else could undertake the same without its consent.

With respect to the second assumption on the resources exploited, L. F. E. Goldie offered an explanation not shared by anyone else and argued that

Since different resources call for different techniques in their exploitation the exploitability test should, in order to remain true to its meaning, only be applied as a basis for extending a coastal state's sovereign rights over the exploitation of each specific resource as that resource becomes "exploitable."[59]

Thus, according to Goldie, the Continental Shelf Convention is comprised of different extents of exclusive access for different kinds of natural resources.

Even though Goldie's explanation may have some merit in terms of rational policy, it cannot be upheld as a proper interpretation of the test of exploitability. It is obvious that at no time did the authors of the doctrine of the continental shelf refer to different kinds of natural resources or to varying techniques of their exploitation. All natural resources, which they defined in Article 2 (4) to include mineral and other nonliving resources together with the living organisms belonging to sedentary species, were considered together.

Despite the fact that Oda's first and second assumptions are correct, the third assumption, which is central to the issue of the limits, is not widely supported. It is possible to argue that mere technical feasibility is not enough and that actual exploitation must take place at a given depth of water before coastal states' exclusive competence could be extended to that depth. For example, speaking on this subject in 1970, Burke pointed out that exploitability means "production that has been demonstrated, as actually being underway and in this sense the deepest well presently in operation is 340 feet."[60]

Even if a broader interpretation than that is adopted, such as Richard Young's, it still does not follow, as Shigeru Oda feared, that the "deep sea resources have already been placed by the Convention under the control of certain specified States."[61] Young believed that

Once you demonstrate, and demonstrate bona fide, the capability to exploit, then the fact of whether you have actual exploitation or not is irrelevant. For example, in the Santa Barbara Channel a well has been drilled in just short of 400 meters of water. As I understand it, this could have been a producing well. Unfortunately, as sometimes happens, it was a dry hole. I would suggest that if that well were drilled with the intention and capability of becoming a producing well, that action demonstrates exploitability and meets the test. Hence, I would say that we are now somewhere out around the 400-meter line as a limit of exploitability.[62]

The true test of technical exploitation is met not by a few sporadic attempts to judge the suitability of available technology and know-how at a particular depth by way of exploration but by the beginning of actual exploitation. The International Law Commission and the Continental Shelf Convention consistently distinguish exploration from exploitation, and Article 1 conspicuously omits any reference to exploration.

Further, Oda, in his interpretation, did not give due weight to the criterion of adjacency, which exists in the definition of the continental shelf along with the criterion of exploitability. The members of the International Law Commission, in their final formulation of Article 1, clearly and unanimously held the view that coastal states' exclusive access was not meant to extend into deep ocean areas in disregard of the criterion of adjacency. Oda himself admitted that the authors of the definition of the continental shelf had not intended to extend coastal states' exclusive competence indefinitely into the depths of the ocean. In view of this fact, it is hard to accept the theory that the Continental Shelf Convention has already divided the natural resources of the oceans among the coastal states of the world.

Invoking the criterion of adjacency, several commentators have maintained that there is a limit to the extent to which a coastal state could extend its exclusive competence over the natural resources of the sea. Furthermore, several of these observers pointed out that insofar as the doctrine of the continental shelf is essentially a geological concept, the exploitability test read in that context meant that the exclusive jurisdiction of the coastal state was extended up to the foot of the continental slope or the edge of the continental margin, which included both the shelf and the slope.[63]

R. Y. Jennings, a well-known British scholar, pointed out that

. . . the intention in Article 1 in imposing the term "adjacency" was to base the national jurisdiction over submarine area—as in the Truman proclamation—upon that principle of appurtenance, continuity of dependence upon the land which underlies not only continental shelf claims but all claims of coastal States to maritime territory. This notion included not only proximity but also structure and formation and all of it is appropriately expressed by the term "adjacency" in its ordinary plain meaning.[64]

As a basis for this conclusion, Jennings referred to the International Law Commission's "Commentary" in 1953, that it never intended to reject the geographical test of continental shelf but only wanted to qualify it so as to "include within the definition of the regime formations which could not strictly be called shelf."[65] Proceeding further, he interpreted the effect of combining the criterion of exploitability with the criterion of "adjacency" as follows:

. . . it seems fairly obvious that the exploitability test means that national jurisdiction is extended over the "continental slope," whether or not the slope be actually "near" the coast, because the slope together with the shelf forms part of that buttress of the coastal land mass which makes it appurtenant and geographically part of it and therefore adjacent.[66]

The National Petroleum Council, an advisory body of the Department of Interior of the United States government, had also taken the position that coastal states were entitled, under Article 1 of the Convention on the Continental Shelf, to claim submarine areas encompassing the continental margin. The Council pointed out the following reasons for its conclusions:[67]

(a) That the International Law Commission "left no doubt that the 'adjacent' areas to which the Convention relates include the submarine areas having 'propinquity, contiguity, geographical continuity, appurtenance or identity' with the continental land mass";
(b) That the Ciudad Trujillo Conference of 1956 is of particular significance in construing the Convention's definition;
(c) And that the Ciudad Trujillo Conference unanimously adopted a Resolution (Document 95) which reads:
 "The sea-bed and subsoil of the continental shelf, continental and insular terrace, or other submarine areas, adjacent to the coastal state, outside the area of territorial sea, and to a depth of 200 meters or, beyond that limit, to where the depth of the superjacent waters admits of the exploitation of the natural resources of the sea-bed and subsoil, appertain exclusively to its jurisdiction and control.";
(d) That García-Amador, who was the Chairman of the International Law Commission in 1956 and who was principally responsible for the adoption of the criterion of exploitability, indicated the scope of Article 1 as essentially involving "present legal powers" up to a 100-fathom line and "potential or future powers" to be employed by coastal states on developing the necessary technology to exploit the slope and the corresponding point of the terrace;
(e) Finally, that the coastal states in practice are issuing leases either for exploration or exploitation at increasingly greater depths than 200 meters.

In its pronouncement concerning the *North Sea Continental Shelf* case between the Federal Republic of Germany, on the one hand, and the Kingdom of Denmark and the Kingdom of the Netherlands, on the other hand, the International Court of Justice seemed to endorse the view that geological appurtenance was the central basis of the doctrine of the continental shelf. The court pointed out that

. . . the institution of the continental shelf has arisen out of the recognition of a physical fact; and the link between this fact and the law, without which the institution would never have existed, remains an important element for the application of its legal regime. The continental shelf, by definition, is an area physically extending the territory of most coastal States into a species of platform which has attracted the attention first of geographers and hydrographers and then of jurists.[68]

Referring perhaps to this language of the court, the National Petroleum Council asserted that its conclusion that the legal shelf extends down to the abyssal ocean floor was justified.[69]

Some of the states participating in the discussions of the United Nations Ad Hoc Committee to Study the Peaceful Uses of the Sea-Bed and the Ocean Floor Beyond the Limits of National Jurisdiction also stressed the inherent limitations of the concept of continental shelf as a geological and geographical phenomenon. As the representative of Italy said,

Some jurists held that the flexibility of exploitability criterion of the Geneva Convention on the Continental Shelf would allow the extension of national jurisdiction over the entire seabed. His delegation did not share that view, for the concept of a continental shelf presupposed the existence of some limit. Geophysically, the earth was divided into continents and oceans, while extension of the continents beneath the seas was termed the continental shelf. That extension must not be confused with the ocean floor even if that area could be economically exploited.[70]

The Canadian delegate, relying on the factor of "geological appurtenance," declared,

In the view of the Canadian authorities, the present legal position regarding the sovereign rights of the coastal States over the resources of submarine areas extending at least to the abyssal depths is not in dispute.[71]

Argentina similarly believed that under the doctrine of the continental shelf it had exclusive jurisdiction over offshore natural resources to the "lower limit of the continental margin." [72] This mode of interpretation places heavy emphasis on the so-called "geological appurtenance" test and regards it as equivalent to the test of "adjacency." According to this, the criterion of adjacency further limits the criterion of exploitability from extending the exclusive access of the coastal states beyond the continental margin.

Although the geological appurtenance theory has been invoked many times, it is difficult to agree that by a combination of adjacency and exploitability, the outer limits of the legal shelf are set where the continental margin ends. Indeed it is ironic that the criterion of exploitability, so vigorously advocated as the only test capable of ridding the legal shelf of the vagaries of the geological shelf, should be invoked to perpetuate the very same inequities of nature that it tries to avoid. Whatever else the International Law Commission did, at least it unequivocally dissociated itself from the geological test by adopting the "exploitability" criterion. It said that

While adopting, to a certain extent, the geographical test for the "continental shelf" as the basis of the juridical definition of the term, the Commission therefore in no way holds that the existence of a continental shelf, in the geographical sense as generally understood, is essential for the exercise of the rights of coastal State as defined in these articles.[73]

Even the Truman Proclamation, which initiated the doctrine of continental shelf, did not single out the geological appurtenance of the submarine floor and the geological extension of natural resources of the mainland into the marine areas as its only rationale. It did add at least two other reasons: coastal states' security and the economy of offshore operations. However, as noted above, the Commission finally found it necessary to disregard the geological tests and honored coastal states' exclusive access on the basis of exploitability and adjacency as having close bearing on coastal states' security and the economy of exploitation operations.

It appears that the significance of the Ciudad Trujillo Conference for the interpretation of limits of continental shelf is also unduly exaggerated. First, the conference unanimously adopted the Resolution (Document 95) only for the consideration of the American states. It was not purported to set forth the final and official position of the American states.[74] Moreover, that Resolution did not equate the criterion of exploitability with the "continental or insular terrace." In fact, the criterion of exploitability was proposed as an alternative to the geological test, which according to the American states must include not merely the geological shelf but the "continental or insular shelf" as well. As it turned out, the International Law Commission at the insistance of García-Amador finally agreed to incorporate the alternative criterion of exploitation and did not give approval to any geological test involving either a geological continental shelf or an insular terrace or continental margin.[75] For these reasons, claims that the continental shelf doctrine is based essentially on the geological appurtenance or natural extension of coasts into the marine area misrepresent the true purpose of that doctrine. The position taken by the International Court of Justice was therefore incorrect.

García-Amador's interpretation that coastal states could enjoy exclusive rights of exploitation down the continental slope and part of the insular shelf if they develop technology and actually exploit these areas is basically supportable as long as they are within the bounds of "adjacency." But, as a matter of fact, to claim exclusive rights well before

actual exploitation takes place on the slope and insular shelf is not
valid according to the same interpretation. Therefore, the conclusion
of the National Petroleum Council, Jennings, and other commentators
that Article 1 has clearly extended the exclusive access of coastal
states to continental margin should be rejected as without proper legal
foundation.[76]

Thus, it is submitted that, in assessing the implications of the criteria
of adjacency and exploitability, the geological continuity or contiguity
is not of as much importance as the effects of offshore exploitation on
the exclusive interests of coastal states and the techniques of actual
exploitation. As these were essentially matters of emerging offshore
technology, definition of the exact limits of the legal shelf was not attempted by the Commission. Similarly, for lack of adequate knowledge
of the actual techniques of offshore natural resource exploitation, the
Geneva Conference failed to agree upon any one formula limiting the
legal shelf. As Burke said,

The Geneva Convention formula incorporating the outright cession of
the area within the 100 fathom line and the contingent further incorpo-
ration of the area in which exploitation becomes feasible is in practical
effect a means of postponing decision regarding the limit upon exclusive exploitation. Although delegates were aware that technology could
expand the area for feasible exploitation, it was apparently the general
belief that the 100-fathom criterion was ample for a substantial period
of time. In this light it is worthwhile to note the preparatory document
by Dr. Mouton which sought to provide the Conference with the latest
technical information concerning the possibility of exploiting the mineral resources of the subsoil.[77]

Francis T. Christy expresses a similar opinion:

This openendedness resulted from the inability of the Convention delegates to anticipate the possibilities of deep water exploitation and from
the apparent inequities of a geologically determined boundary. . . . The
Geneva Convention in avoiding the demarcation of a clear-cut limit
simply postponed the day of decision.[78]

While the exact limits of the legal shelf are thus left open, a reasonable assessment of the context in which the definition of the continental
shelf is formulated reveals that the coastal states are not authorized to
extend their monopoly to the middle of the oceans.[79] The report of the
United Nations Ad Hoc Committee on the subject significantly cor-
roborated this evaluation. The report noted the views of various member states on the outer limits of legal shelf.

It was generally agreed that there is an area of the seabed and ocean floor which is not subject to national jurisdiction and that this fact, which seemed obvious, needed emphasizing because of the broad interpretation of which Article 1 of the Continental Shelf Convention was susceptible. It was pointed out that none of the members in the Working Group had suggested that either international law or Article 1 of the Continental Shelf Convention authorizes the extension of limits for an indefinite distance into deep ocean floor.[80]

Recent Attempts to Agree upon Fixed Limits for the Continental Shelf

The almost unanimous conclusion that the coastal state cannot indefinitely extend its exclusive competence over the continental shelf into the oceans raises another as yet unsolved issue: What should be the outer limit of the continental shelf?

One group of participants preferred very narrow limits. These varied from a depth limit of 200 meters or a distance limit of 20 to 30 nautical miles to more.[81] This group appears to have been motivated by the following considerations: (a) that, except for a narrow belt of territorial waters, the oceans never exclusively belonged to the adjacent coastal states; (b) that the entire world community now depends for its welfare so much on the ocean resources and environment that it is in the common interest to manage them through inclusive authority and control, preferably under the competence of international institutions; (c) that the coastal states have a tendency to interpret liberally limited jurisdiction initially accorded to them, which will eventually assume the nature of territorial sovereignty claims; hence, any new claim to extend the area of coastal state jurisdiction should be viewed with the greatest suspicion; and (d) that the natural resources of the sea offer a unique opportunity to improve the financial reserves of the United Nations or other international institutions that are devoted to promoting rapid economic development of the developing countries.

Opposing attempts to define coastal state jurisdiction narrowly, several states and other observers advanced the following reasons: (a) that the coastal state is already invested with exclusive jurisdiction over the natural resources of the seabed and ocean floor up to the limits of the "continental margin"; and that any attempts to limit the jurisdiction to 200 miles is in violation of its well-established rights; (b) that the continental margin is naturally appurtenant to the adjacent coastal state; (c) that to vest exclusive jurisdiction over the resources of the sea in the international organizations is not practical or feasible at this state of the world political process; (d) that the international bureaucracies are as bad as or even worse than national ones; (e) that the economic and security interests of the coastal states demand that their exclusive jurisdiction over offshore natural resources be extended over a wider, not a narrower, submarine area. Accordingly, proponents of wide limits desire a depth limit of 3,000 meters or a distance limit of 200 miles, or a limit in terms of the foot of the "continental slope" or the edge of the "continental margin," whichever gives a wider maritime area to the coastal state.[82]

The Intermediate Zone
A third group of participants felt that there was no reason to polarize exclusive and inclusive interests. Proposing three resource zones that include an intermediate zone—which separates on one end coastal states' exclusive jurisdiction and on the other end a zone that should be under comprehensive control of an international agency—this group argued: (a) that by giving the coastal state the authority to decide on who could exploit the natural resources in the intermediate zone, its economic and security needs can be safeguarded; (b) that by requiring the coastal states to pay an agreed amount of royalties from the profits they receive from resource exploitation in the intermediate zone to an international agency, financial reserves could be built up to meet the costs of equitable world economic development and of pursuing other worthy causes; (c) that by prescribing standards at the global level and leaving their implementation, as far as the intermediate zone is concerned, to the discretion of the coastal state, many of the problems of international bureaucracy could be avoided; (d) that by emphasizing the role of the coastal state in the intermediate zone as an agent of the international community, the danger of diminishing the international domain of the seas could be minimized.

A United States proposal, consistent with this philosophy, was to limit the exclusive coastal state jurisdiction to a 200-meter depth and to limit the intermediate zone to the edge of the continental margin.[83] However, a seven-state draft treaty set 200 meters or 40 nautical miles as the limit for exclusive coastal state jurisdiction and another 40 nautical miles as the limit, beyond that area, for the intermediate zone.[84]

Despite some of the advantages from a common interest perspective, the proposals for the creation of an intermediate zone did not fare well at the negotiating table of the United Nations Seabed Committee.[85] The reason, as two close observers noted, was that "to varying degrees, they entailed limitations on coastal state resource management policy that many coastal states considered undesirable, potentially confusing, or unnecessary to achieve the objective of the proposals."[86]

The Economic Zone and the Patrimonial Sea

As the participants approached the opening of formal sessions of the Third Law of the Sea Conference at Caracas, Venezuela, two proposals, one for an exclusive "economic zone" and the other for an exclusive "patrimonial sea," appeared to receive substantial attention from them.[87] The first proposal, advocated by a majority of African nations, preferred a distance limit of 200 miles for the economic zone over which the coastal state could have exclusive jurisdiction for the purpose of authorizing and controlling the exploitation of living and nonliving resources.[88] The economic zone is to lie beyond the 12-mile territorial sea.

The proposal for patrimonial sea had originated from the Santo Domingo conference of a group of Caribbean countries.[89] According to this, the coastal state could have exclusive jurisdiction over the living and nonliving resources of the patrimonial sea with an outer limit of 200 miles and a similar exclusive jurisdiction over the natural resources up to the edge of the continental margin. The proponents of the "economic zone" differ from the advocates of the "patrimonial sea" in that the latter insist that the limit for natural resources should extend up to the edge of the continental margin. Both the proposals differ from previous proposals in that, while the former seeks to regulate both the living and nonliving resources under exclusive coastal state jurisdiction, the latter deals with only natural resource exploitation as conceived under the doctrine of the continental shelf.

Several proposals advanced by other states appear to be only variations of either the economic zone or the patrimonial sea concepts. Iceland suggested that the coastal state should be entitled to choose its own limits for the exclusive jurisdiction and control over the natural resources of the maritime area adjacent to its territorial sea. The outer limits of this area are to be "reasonable, keeping in view the geographical, geological, ecological, economic and other relevant local considerations, and shall not exceed 200 nautical miles." Brazil employed similar language with respect to fixing the limits but preferred to call the area "territorial sea." According to the proposal of Pakistan, in addition to a territorial sea of 12 miles, every "coastal state shall also have the right to establish its exclusive economic zone not exceeding 200 nautical miles calculated from the baseline used for the determination of the limits of the territorial sea." Japan was prepared to accept a "coastal seabed area" (the limits of this zone were left open for negotiation) over which the coastal state could exercise exclusive jurisdiction limited only for the exploitation of mineral resources.[90]

China proposed that the coastal state should have an exclusive economic zone not exceeding 200 nautical miles, measured from the baselines of the territorial sea, and that beyond its territorial sea or economic zone, it should also have exclusive jurisdiction over the continental shelf, the limits of which have to be defined "reasonably" according to the geographical conditions of the coastal state. In addition, "the maximum limits of such continental shelf may be determined among states through consultations." Ecuador, Panama, and Peru, while advocating that the sovereignty of the coastal state should extend up to a limit not exceeding 200 nautical miles, were prepared to consider provisions for cases in which the continental shelf extended beyond a distance of 200 miles.[91]

Australia and Norway agreed with others that the coastal state could have an exclusive economic zone, not exceeding 200 nautical miles, for the primary benefit of its citizens. However, with respect to the continental shelf area, differing from the rest of the formulas thus far advanced, they noted that

. . . the coastal State has the right to retain, where the natural prolongation of its land mass extends beyond the (economic zone–patrimonial sea), the sovereign rights with respect to that area of the sea-bed and subsoil thereof which it had under international law before the entry into force of this convention: such rights [do] not extend beyond the outer edge of the continental margin.[92]

In other words, according to the Australian and Norwegian plan, if, by the time the new convention on seabed resources comes into operation, the exploitation of mineral resources reached a depth of, say, 600 meters, the coastal state could have exclusive jurisdiction over the seabed area up to that depth, even if in some cases it gives it a maritime area exceeding 200 miles. However, in no case could such a depth exceed the outer edge of the continental margin that may occur at depths ranging from 2,500 meters to 3,000 meters. This formula thus has the merit of staying within the limits of a reasonable interpretation of coastal states' rights under the continental shelf doctrine and at the same time exhibits an agreeable political sensitivity by proposing a 200-mile limit for the exclusive economic zone. Insofar as it is aimed at preserving established or well-recognized rights of coastal states under the doctrine of the continental shelf, it has a sound policy objective: the promotion of stability of offshore operations currently under way.

Argentina, which has an extended continental margin, opted for by far the broadest limits for coastal state jurisdiction over the resources of the sea. First, it proposed a limit of 200 miles or 200 meters, whichever gives greater maritime area for the exclusive economic zone or patrimonial sea. Second, the coastal state could claim exclusive jurisdiction over the seabed and the ocean floor up to the "outer lower edge of the continental margin," which in no case is to be less than 200 miles.[93]

The response of the so-called geographically disadvantaged states to these proposals for exclusive coastal control over wide resource zones of the sea has been understandably one of concern. These states insist that their legitimate rights and interests must be duly accommodated before concepts of economic zone or patrimonial sea are accepted.[94] Presenting the perspective of a geographically disadvantaged state, S. Jayakumar of Singapore reacted to the proposals of economic zone or patrimonial sea by stating that "unless the interests of such geographically disadvantaged countries were accommodated," his delegation "would be unable to accept any such proposal." He suggested several alternative ways by which these interests could be accommodated:

> . . . firstly, the nationals of the regional or neighboring landlocked or shelflocked countries could be recognized as having the right to exploit the living resources in the economic zone on an equal footing with the nationals of the coastal state concerned. The nationals of those neighboring countries would, of course, observe all management and conservation regulations of the coastal state. A second possibility was to have not an exclusive economic zone but a zone in which the coastal state would exercise preferential rights to exploit the resources, while having full rights of management and conservation. A third possibility would be that of a regional economic zone; in other words, the zone adjacent to the territorial sea of coastal states in one region would be deemed to be reserved for the exclusive use of all states in that region regardless of their geographical position.[95]

Singapore, together with Afghanistan, Austria, Belgium, Bolivia, and Nepal, proposed more specifically that the geographically disadvantaged states and their subjects must have a right to participate in the exploration and exploitation of the living resources of the economic zone of neighboring coastal states "on an equal and non-discriminatory basis."[96] However, according to the same proposal, the geographically disadvantaged states were prohibited from transferring their rights in the economic zone to third parties. In addition, it was indicated that a developed coastal state with an exclusive economic zone should contribute a portion of the revenues it derives from the exploitation of living resources to an international authority to be distributed "on the basis of equitable sharing criteria."

However, all coastal states with an exclusive economic zone, the proposal of the six states noted, should make contributions to an international authority from the revenues derived from the exploitation of nonliving resources. It was pointed out that

. . . the rate of contributions shall be . . . percent of the revenues [the word "revenues" will have to be defined] from exploitation carried out within 40 miles or 200 meters isobath of . . . zone, whichever limit the coastal state may choose to adopt, and . . . percent [it is understood that different rates should apply to developed and developing countries] of the revenues from exploitation carried out beyond 40 miles or 200 meters isobath within the . . . zone.

Here again, the international authority was to distribute these contributions "on the basis of an equitable sharing criteria."[97]

The six states' proposal did not specify who would be the intended beneficiaries of the proposed revenue-sharing scheme. It was also not clear if the elimination of certain countries from the revenue-sharing was intended and what criteria were to be used in achieving equity in this regard. Perhaps the six states, being aware of the complications involved in any revenue-sharing scheme, left the matter open for further negotiation.

Uganda and Zambia, two landlocked countries from Africa, in a separate plan, advocated regional or subregional management of resources of the economic zone. The United States and Malta indicated that the coastal states should agree to share with the international community a part of the revenue they received from the mineral resource exploitation in the exclusive coastal seabed area.[98] (Malta called this area "exclusive national ocean space"). In addition, Malta proposed that the coastal state should assume an obligation to "provide adjacent landlocked countries with access to mineral and other nonliving resources of its national ocean space on conditions similar to those applicable to its own nationals."

In view of these demands for some form of accommodation of the interests of geographically disadvantaged states in the exclusive economic zones, the fourteen-state proposal (sponsored by the African coastal countries) noted that

Nationals of a developing landlocked state and other geographically disadvantaged states shall enjoy the privilege to fish in the exclusive economic zones of the adjoining neighboring coastal states. The modalities of the enjoyment of this privilege and the area to which they relate shall be settled by agreement between the coastal state and the landlocked state concerned. The right to prescribe and enforce management measures in the area shall be with the coastal state.[99]

Argentina and Brazil similarly required the coastal state to enter into negotiations with other regional geographically disadvantaged states to arrive at fair agreements in their mutual interest. However, the proposal of these states, like that of the African coastal states, limits the issue of accommodation of interests only to the sharing of fishery resources.

China, however, proposed that

A coastal State shall, in principle, grant to the landlocked and shelflocked States adjacent to its territory common enjoyment of a certain proportion of the rights of ownership in its economic zone. The coastal State and its adjacent landlocked and shelflocked States shall, through consultations on the basis of equality and mutual respect for sovereignty, conclude bilateral or regional agreements on the relevant matters.[100]

It thus implies that the coastal state should share with the geographically disadvantaged states a certain proportion not only of fishery resources but of all other natural resources including "living and nonliving resources of the whole water column, seabed and its subsoil within the economic zone."

Several of the coastal states doubted the rights of landlocked and other geographically disadvantaged states to seek accommodation of their interests in the economic zone or patrimonial sea. This belief partly explains some of the restrictive conditions under which they offered a few privileges to the others in the proposed broad exclusive resource zones. According to J. S. Warioba of Tanzania,

It was fair to say that the rights of landlocked States had been recognized only as a result of continued and arduous negotiations, and the present rules did not recognize their rights with regard to the living resources of the sea.[101]

Similarly, S. M. Thompson-Flores of Brazil argued,

I believe the road to this agreement [for accommodating of interests of
the geographically disadvantaged states] is through the discussion of
these problems within the regional groups of states because the problems of Bolivia or Paraguay will not be solved by China or the Philippines, and the problem of Afghanistan and Nepal will not be solved by
Brazil or China. . . . This is true for many reasons: one of which is
that the resources of the sea areas adjacent to the coast belong to the
coastal states concerned in the same way as the resources of the landlocked states belong to them. Some landlocked states have resources
which the coastal states do not have. For instance, Zambia has coffee.
Tanzania might say, well, we have fish, you have coffee, let's reach an
agreement.[102]

This kind of logic, however, unfortunately misses the point that the
coastal states do not have rights unilaterally to extend their seaward
boundaries from the existing limits to new and broader limits without
the approval of the international community, of which landlocked and
other geographically disadvantaged states constitute an important segment. Jayakumar made this point very clearly when he responded to
the claims of certain of the coastal states as follows:

Now, it is this kind of argument which perturbs countries like mine
which are also involved in the seabed discussions, because you are
elevating what is an accidental, geographical situation to a basis for
legal rights. . . . it would mean that all the ocean space in the world,
including all that which is now considered the high seas, could be
carved up for exclusive national appropriation by the coastal states
which are in a position to do so and who could argue on the same basis
of immediate adjacency to the ocean space.[103]

Referring to the same problem within the U.N. Seabed Committee
meetings, he also said,

One or two delegations from coastal countries had suggested that if the
landlocked and other geographically disadvantaged countries were to
have certain compensatory rights in the extended jurisdictional zone,
then there should be a reciprocal right of the coastal states to share in
the land resources of those disadvantaged States. That argument was
illogical, because there was no parallel situation with regard to land
resources; no country, coastal or otherwise, could unilaterally extend
its territory in order to acquire new wealth.[104]

In sum, at this stage of the negotiations, it appears that the limits
of the continental shelf or the exclusive resource zones depend on
three factors:

1. Accommodation of interests of geographically disadvantaged states;
2. The recognition that may be given to more inclusive interests within the exclusive resource zones; and
3. The kind of international machinery that may be regarded as acceptable to regulate the resources of the areas beyond agreed national jurisdiction.[105]

Appraisal

The expectation that the coastal state cannot indefinitely extend its exclusive control over the continental shelf is almost universally shared. The criteria of adjacency and exploitability and the very usage of the term "continental shelf" itself, even after its geographical connotation was deliberately underplayed in the legal definition, clearly signify the notion of limitation. While there is room for controversy on the exact outer limits of the continental shelf at any given time, it is persuasive to argue that the rights of coastal states are limited by actual exploitation within the ultimate criterion of adjacency.

The criterion of adjacency cannot be referred to solely in terms of depth or distance as some commentators appear to do. It can be given more meaningful content by consideration of such factors as the techniques of actual exploitation, the cooperation needed from the coastal state for the economy and efficiency of offshore operations, and the effects of these operations on the exclusive interests of coastal states such as security, protection from pollution, and utilization of marine environment for the maximization of values. These are the factors, it may be recalled, that provided the basic rationale for the acceptance of the doctrine of continental shelf by the world community.

However, if a uniform outer limit for the continental shelf were to be assumed for all coastal states, it is obvious that an arbitrary choice unrelated to the original expectation about the definition of the continental shelf has to be made. Despite the legal vacuum it apparently implies, it is fair to conclude that fixing a specific limit is a task left to future decision-making. For all the current controversy, it is well that the international bargaining is focused on the issue of limits.

In this context, one of the crucial issues confronting the decision-makers attending the Third Law of the Sea Conference is to arrive at a limit for the coastal state's resource zone that will adequately balance its exclusive interests with the inclusive interests of the international community.

Several of the limits proposed fail to give due weight to the multiplicity of interests involved. Either they seek to bring under coastal control all the potentially valuable ocean resources, or they fall short of settled expectations as to the rights of coastal states under the doctrine of the continental shelf. This is the case when the limits suggested are as wide as the 3,000-meter depth or as narrow as the 200-meter depth. Many of the more recent suggestions aim at some compromise between these two extremes.

The reasons cited for extending the limits of the shelf to the edge of the continental margin—geological appurtenance of the ocean floor, the security and economy of the coastal states—on closer observation are essentially self-serving. They are not conducive to establishing that limit which in and of itself has the legal sanction and the merit of contributing to the common interest.

In the final analysis, it is not as important to decide what limit or combination of limits could be advocated as to reach agreement on methods of resource sharing, within these limits, between the coastal states and other geographically disadvantaged states in the region. In this process, it is important to stress the primacy of coastal state interests in resource exploitation, preservation of the marine environment, and protection of its national security. It is equally important to impress upon the coastal state that, although it is allowed to enjoy exclusive control over the marine resources, it is done with the assurance that it acts as an agent of the international community.

As an agent of the international community, the coastal state should have specific duties such as promoting inclusive interests, including the right of navigation belonging to all the members of international community; sharing the benefits resulting from the ownership of ocean resources with geographically disadvantaged and underdeveloped countries; and adopting responsible resource management policies and practices.

Furthermore, it is vitally important not to set the limits so far from the coasts as to deprive a potential international agency, which may be established for the areas beyond national jurisdiction, of all the valuable resources. Indeed, it would be ironical if the developing countries, which will constitute a predominant majority at the Third Law of the Sea Conference and have fought so hard to establish a well-structured international agency to regulate maritime areas beyond national jurisdictions, should leave it no resources of real economic significance.[106]

In this sense, many developing coastal nations, principally the sponsors and supporters of the economic zone and patrimonial sea concepts, at least so far advocate what appear to be contradictory positions.[107]

According to available information, there are hardly any economically attractive nonliving resources beyond a depth of 3,000 meters, except for manganese nodules, whose value at the moment is still in doubt. So also, beyond a distance of 200 miles, the potential for fisheries is rather minimal (except for those fish that belong to the highly migratory species) compared to what it is within 200 miles.

Consequently, the concepts of economic zone or patrimonial sea, to serve common interests and become acceptable to a majority of nations, should be modified, as suggested, for example, by the United States, Malta, and China, by providing the right of access to geographically disadvantaged states for the living and nonliving resources, and by providing for a concept of reasonable revenue-sharing, in addition to an obligation to promote inclusive interests. Possibly even the geographically disadvantaged states that enjoy access to ocean resources within the economic zone or patrimonial sea may be required to pay an ocean tax either to the coastal state (which in turn may pass it on to the international community) or directly to an international agency.

The methods of accommodating the interests of geographically disadvantaged states within the economic zone or patrimonial sea may prove to be politically too complicated to be satisfactorily worked out. In that event, as an alternative, coastal states should agree to confine the extent of their exclusive maritime areas to a reasonable limit, perhaps 1,000 meters or 100 miles, in order to bring a sufficient amount of marine resources under international authority to make its regulations feasible. Moreover, the coastal state may be required to pay to an international authority a certain percentage of the value of the resources it exploits within its exclusive maritime area. The percentages may vary, however, among different coastal states, depending upon their economic status.[108]

An arrangement of this sort would provide a realistic way of promoting the interests of geographically disadvantaged states. It would be a kind of insurance against the disappointment of certain coastal states that for one reason or another are unable to gain any profit from their maritime areas. And it would encourage the work of institutions of inclusive authority and common sharing, the only bodies that can fully appreciate and cope with the intricacies of an increasingly interdependent world.

4
Access to Deep Ocean Mineral Resources

Claims and Counterclaims

The claims and counterclaims that will be discussed in this chapter deal with issues concerning the regulation of mineral resource exploitation in the deep ocean areas—that is, those maritime areas that are different from and lie beyond the limits of the continental shelf or such other exclusive coastal state resource zone as may be agreed upon by the international community.

Principally, two categories of claims and counterclaims can be identified in connection with the regulation of deep ocean mineral resource exploitation. The first category of claims invokes mainly the doctrine of freedom of the seas to conclude that there is a "freedom" of exploitation of deep ocean mineral resources just as there are other freedoms of the high seas, like fishing and navigation, and that every state is entitled to this freedom within reasonable limits of noninterference with other interests.

A counterclaim asserts that the doctrine of freedom of the seas cannot provide a basis for the regulation of an activity—exploitation of marine mineral resources in the international areas—that now exists but did not exist during the time that the doctrine was formulated and developed. Furthermore, it may be argued that the prevailing guidelines for international law applicable to activities on the high seas cannot possibly accord that degree of certainty and security of investment essential to the offshore mineral resource exploitation operations.

A second category of claims and counterclaims is centered around the particular design of international rules and machinery that may be entrusted with the regulation of marine minerals resource exploitation in the international areas. The form of these claims depends on one's perception of the inclusive interests involved. The policy implications of the claims and counterclaims have already been discussed in Chapter 2, and the analysis of this chapter will be focused on the relevant trends in decision and their appropriate appraisal.

Trends in Decision

Prevailing Views on the Freedom of Exploitation
Ever since the doctrine of freedom of the seas was established, there has been a recurrent controversy among the commentators about clas-

sifying the legal status of superjacent waters, the bed, and the ocean floor of the high seas.[1] There is general agreement that the superjacent waters of the high seas cannot be appropriated by any single participant and that they are a *res communis,* a common property of the world community open for inclusive enjoyment.[2]

However, views vary with respect to the legal status of the seabed and the ocean floor.[3] Some writers believe that the seabed cannot be distinguished from the high seas and, as such, hold it as a *res communis,* not open for exclusive appropriation.[4] Others think that the seabed as distinguished from the superjacent waters is a *res nullius,* that is, a thing belonging to none and open to exclusive appropriation and sovereignty.[5] Similarly conflicting positions have been expressed with respect to the status of the ocean floor.[6] Most of these classifications on the legal status of the high seas unfortunately have never exhibited particular sensitivity to the different uses to which the oceans are normally put.

The legal status of the seabed and the ocean floor became a matter of fresh debate when the Truman Proclamation claimed, and when other coastal nations followed it in claiming, *ipso jure,* exclusive authority and control over the mineral resources of the "adjacent submarine areas." These national decrees did not invoke the traditional concepts of *res nullius* or *res communis* as their basis. C. H. M. Waldock, who believes that the seabed and the ocean floor are a *res nullius,* challenged the validity of this novel claim to exclusive appropriation of the offshore mineral resources. According to him, no state could exclusively claim mineral resources of the submarine areas beyond the territorial waters without first establishing an effective occupation over a desired area.[7]

However, the views of Waldock did not meet with wide approval. An overwhelming majority of scholars and statesmen regarded neither the *res nullius* nor the *res communis* concepts, with which it was customary to characterize the submarine areas, as relevant to evaluating the validity of the claims to appropriate exclusively the mineral resources of the continental shelf. For example, H. Lauterpacht, who supported the new doctrine of continental shelf initiated by the Truman Proclamation, argued,

It is apparent that the views of writers on the question of the occupation and appropriation of the bed of the seas and its subsoil, insofar as they were voiced prior to the proclamations and declarations in the matter of submarine areas, must be regarded as being of distinctly limited importance for the reason that in the nature of things they are not evidence, on this subject, of the practice of states. There was no such practice save for the odd cases of the sedentary fisheries of Ceylon, Madras, Tunis, Bahrein, and probably in some parts of Western Australia. The opinions of writers were based on their deductions from and their interpretation of the principle of the freedom of the seas at a time when problems such as those which prompted the appropriation of submarine areas in the middle of the twentieth century had not arisen.[8]

The *Abu Dhabi Arbitration,* the one case where the concept of *res nullius* as a basis for approving the claims for exclusive appropriation of mineral resources of the continental shelf was directly at issue, also rejected its applicability. Lord Asquith of Bishopstone, the Arbitrator, observed, "To treat this subsoil as *res nullius*—a 'fair game' for the first occupier—entails obvious and grave dangers so far as occupation is possible at all. It invites perilous scramble."[9] Several commentators lent their weight to such an appraisal.[10] M. S. McDougal and W. T. Burke assessed and approved the reasonableness of claims, stressing the significance of promoting "both the peaceful, orderly development of such resources and their productive, rational exploitation."[11]

The International Law Commission also discarded the concepts of *res nullius* and *res communis* as inadmissible from the very beginning of its consideration of the basis for the doctrine of the continental shelf. The following brief comment refers to one of the earliest decisions of the Commission in favor of recognizing the coastal state's claims to appropriate exclusively, *ispo jure,* mineral resources of the continental shelf:

There were three possibilities for that area of control: it might be argued that it was *res nullius*. That must be counted out as being incompatible with the principle adopted on the previous day. If the shelf were *res nullius,* it could be acquired by any state, whether littoral or not; and that was inadmissible. It could be argued again that it was *res communis*; but that too was incompatible with the previous day's decision. *Res communis* was common property, and the continental shelf in that case could not be subject to the control and jurisdiction of any particular state. It would be better to say that the continental shelf belonged *ipso jure* to the littoral state.[12]

During the same period, the International Law Commission considered the status of the mineral resources of the submarine areas that lay beyond the continental shelf. One of the members suggested that exploitation of the deep ocean mineral resources should be regarded as a freedom of the high seas.[13] Such a declaration would have meant that the mineral resources could be exclusively appropriated by the first comer, as long as he did not unjustifiably interfere with the interests of others in utilizing the marine environment. However, a majority of the Commission did not think it appropriate to decide the status of the deep ocean mineral resources, because as the Rapporteur of the Commission mentioned, at that stage their exploitation "was a purely theoretical question."[14]

The reluctance of the Commission to prescribe policies regulating the exploitation of the deep ocean mineral resources and, especially, its doubts in regarding it as a freedom of the high seas were further evident from its definition of the freedom of the high seas. Freedom of the high seas, according to the Commission, comprised the traditional four freedoms "and others which are recognized by general principles of international law."[15] Explaining its definition of the freedom of the high seas, the Commission said that "The Commission has merely specified four of the main freedoms, but it is aware there are other freedoms such as freedom to undertake scientific research on the high seas."

At the same time the Commission also explained why it did not include the exploitation of deep ocean mineral resources as a freedom of the high seas. It observed that

The Commission has not made specific mention of the freedom to explore or exploit the subsoil of the high seas. It is considered that apart from the case of the exploitation or exploration of the soil or subsoil of the continental shelf . . . such exploitation has not yet assumed sufficient practical importance to justify special regulation.

The Geneva Convention on the High Seas, in 1958, adopted the definition of the freedom of the high seas as proposed by the Commission. Thus Article 2 of that Convention said that freedom of the high seas comprises, *inter alia,* both for coastal and noncoastal states:

(1) Freedom of navigation;
(2) Freedom of fishing;
(3) Freedom to lay submarine cables and pipelines;
(4) Freedom to fly over the high seas.

These freedoms, and others which are recognized by the general principles of international law, shall be exercised by all States with reasonable regard to the interests of other States in their exercise of the freedom of the high seas.[16]

Article 2 therefore left open the question of whether the exploitation of deep ocean mineral resources was a freedom of the high seas as recognized by the general principles of international law.

A few commentators, however, referring to Article 2 and the doctrine of the freedom of the high seas, suggested that there is a "freedom" to explore for and exploit the deep ocean mineral resources. Thus one commentator said,

Consistent with Article 2 [of the Geneva Convention on the High Seas, 1958], a State is free to engage in activities on the high seas which are not specifically prohibited by international law, so long as these activities do not interfere with the "interests of other States in their exercise of the freedom of the high seas." [17]

The United States National Petroleum Council was of the same opinion:

International law imposes no prohibition upon the freedom of a state or its nationals exploring for and exploiting the resources of the seabed of the high seas provided the freedom is exercised with reasonable regard to the interests of other states in their exercise of the high seas freedoms. [18]

W. T. Burke, citing the Commentary of the International Law Commission, came to the same conclusion. [19]

The commentators who relied on Article 2 did not furnish any evidence as to the expectations of the international community about whether the freedom of the high seas also included freedom to explore and exploit the deep ocean mineral resources. Thus their assertions do not take us any further than the Geneva Convention stage, at which point there was hardly any presumption in favor of such an alleged freedom.

Furthermore, the contention that the lack of a prohibition against the exploitation of the deep ocean mineral resources must be regarded as approval of the activity by the world community must be rejected. For, in this case, the lack of such a prohibition could very well be attributable to the lack of the activity itself. Burke's suggestion, that the records of the International Law Commission did endorse the exploitation of the deep ocean mineral resources as an implied freedom of the high seas, was based on an incorrect and incomplete reliance on the Commission's interpretation of the doctrine of freedom of the seas. If anything is clear from the records of the Commission, it is that it did not want to take a position on the status of the deep ocean mineral resources.

The U.N. Debate and the Emerging Law of the Deep Ocean Area

The status of deep ocean mineral resources has been one of the major issues before the United Nations Seabed Committee. Initially there were two views. One view, advocated by the technologically advanced countries, was that the existing prescriptions of international law and particularly the doctrine of freedom of the seas should be used as a basis for regulating the exploitation of deep ocean mineral resources.

According to Y. A. Malik, the representative of the USSR to the United Nations,

It was the view of [this] country that in its study the Committee should above all take into account the existing international legal principles and standards relating to the sea-bed and ocean floor. It was common knowledge that the more general principles in that field had been laid down in the international conventions on the high seas and the continental shelf, in the partial nuclear test ban treaty, as well as in some other international agreements. . . . In formulating the legal problems that required a further and thorough study one must proceed from the fact that the formulation of legal rules governing the activities of States with respect to the use of the sea-bed should be based on the existing principles of international law; it should not restrict the principle of freedom on the high seas and other rights enjoyed by states under the international rules now in force.[20]

Japan was a little more explicit in translating the purport of the existing principles of international law into the present context. It indicated that

While it was important that the sea-bed and the ocean floor should be used for the benefit of all mankind, it was also important that the Committee's discussions should not discourage States from exploring the sea-bed and the ocean floor or exploiting their resources.[21]

In the same connection, the French Government commented that

The application of the principle of *res communis* precluded appropriation and, in that connection, existing agreements on outer space could be applied to the sea-bed and ocean floors beyond the limits of present national jurisdiction. If the principle of the exclusion of appropriation could be accepted, so too, could certain concepts of the existing international regime governing the high seas in relation to activities such as fishing.[22]

Denmark was of the same opinion. As one of the major principles of a future regime it recommended that

No State may validly purport to subject any part of the sea-bed and the ocean floor, or the subsoil thereof, to its sovereignty. Exploration and use shall be free for all States, including non-coastal States, without discrimination of any kind, cf. Article 2 of the Convention on the High Seas, signed at Geneva on 29 April 1958 and the Articles I and II of the Treaty of 27 January 1967, on Principles Governing Activities of States in the Exploration and Use of Outer Space, including the Moon and Celestial Bodies.[23]

These states, which favored initially an unorganized inclusive access to the deep ocean mineral resources, did not appreciate the differences in characteristics of the process of deep ocean mineral resource exploitation from the other uses of the seas, such as navigation and fishing, and from the exploration of outer space. They also did not identify any problems that were unique to the process of deep ocean mineral resource exploitation. Furthermore, no attempt was made by this group of states to decide how they would approach such problems (widely acknowledged to be worthy of attention in the present context) as arranging the peaceful and orderly allocation of exclusive titles and tenures to submarine zones among the participants, the efficient production of mineral resources, the accommodation of competing uses of the seas, and the equitable distribution of benefits among all the members of the world community.

The indifference of those countries that argued for a free-for-all approach to these problems was opposed by a majority of the members of the U.N. Seabed Committee, most of which were developing countries. First, it was pointed out that the traditional concepts of *res nullius* and *res communis* could not be regarded as applicable to regulation of deep ocean mineral resources. According to Ambassador Arvid Pardo of Malta,

The current state of the law could not be considered satisfactory. The doctrines of *res nullius* and *res communis,* which had been rejected by the International Law Commission, were equally unacceptable.[24]

The Government of Libya said,

In connection with the legal status of the sea bed beyond the limits of national jurisdiction, we are with those who believe that neither the concept of *res nullius* nor that of *res communis* is appropriate to the area in question.[25]

The representative of Honduras to the United Nations, after examining the origin of the Roman law concepts of *res nullius* and *res communis,* questioned their relevance to justify twentieth-century claims as follows:

On the basis of these juridical concepts derived from Roman law, polemics have continued throughout history in respect of the delimitation of marine areas. But it would be inappropriate to seek in Roman law justification for the doctrines of modern international law since the development of modern law began many centuries after Rome lost its role as the great source of civil law which extended to the limits of its empire.[26]

Second, this group of states felt that an unorganized inclusive access that would allow the mineral resources of the deep ocean areas to be appropriated exclusively by the first comer, and the technologically capable, would be inimical to the common interest. As M. Vakil, the Iranian delegate to the U.N. Seabed Committee, observed,

We may agree that the sea-bed and ocean floor must serve exclusively peaceful purposes, that there must be no appropriation of them beyond the limits of national jurisdiction, that all mankind must be the beneficiaries of the riches to be won from them, that research and investigation must be free. We may even say that the developing areas of the world should be particularly favored. But these declarations will remain mere rhetoric until we face the hard question of organizing a system of obligatory deference to the common judgement concerning what uses are compatible with and serve these principles.

Such declarations of principle as we adopt must not be taken by the major Powers, which in this context means those with the greatest technological and financial capabilities, as a license to make free with what belongs to all of us. The sharing of benefits from the exploitation of this new environment is not compatible with the all too common idea that sheer capability of exploitation confers a right to proceed without close regard and respect for the legitimate interests of others.[27]

He urged, in effect, that "this self-willed approach as it concerns the utilization of the seas must be curbed from the outset." Malta opposed a "free-for-all" approach to the exploitation of the deep ocean natural resources because, if permitted, it would be, in its view, "inequitable to landlocked countries, and would likely lead to waste of natural resources, pollution of the marine environment, impairment of the living resources of the seas and conflicts between States."[28]

Edward Hambro, a well-known expert on international law, representing the Norwegian government, regarded an unorganized inclusive access to the deep ocean natural resources as "even more dangerous than the coastal state theory," which is the alternative that would have divided the ocean's mineral resources among all the coastal states. According to him, such an approach would "unreasonably favor the developed countries, especially the coastal ones, and again leads to the vicious circle of the rich getting richer and the poor, poorer."[29]

The Chairman of the United Nations Ad Hoc Committee, H. S. Amerasinghe of Sri Lanka, voiced the dilemma of the developing countries and their opposition to permitting unorganized inclusive access to the deep ocean mineral resources. He pointed out that

The wide disparity in economic standards between the developed and the developing countries will be further widened and the feeling of world-wide instability that arises from the existence of such a disparity will be intensified if the resources of the seabed and the ocean floor become the bounty of those who have the technological and financial capacity to exploit these resources and convert them to their exclusive benefit.

It is a commonplace in modern life that technological and financial capacity exist together and that he who has one has both. The developing nations have neither. They must rely on the developed nations and especially the most powerful nations for support and active cooperation if their expectations are to be realized, their apprehensions overcome and their steady economic advance assured.[30]

U.N. Declaration of Principles to Govern the Deep Ocean Areas

Despite the continued differences among members of the U.N. Seabed Committee as to the status of the deep ocean areas and as to the kind of policies and prescriptions applicable to the exploitation of resources therein, the U.N. General Assembly passed Resolution 2749 (XXV) on December 17, 1970, entitled Declaration of Principles Governing the Seabed and the Ocean Floor, and the Subsoil Thereof, beyond the Limits of National Jurisdiction.[31] The resolution was adopted by a vote of 108 in favor, none against, and 14 abstentions. The Soviet Union and other East European nations were among those states which abstained.

The U.N. Declaration, among other things, noted that

1. The deep ocean area and its resources are "the common heritage of mankind";
2. The area shall not be subject to appropriation by any means by states or persons, natural or juridical, and no state shall claim or exercise sovereignty or sovereign rights over any part thereof;
3. No one shall claim, exercise, or acquire rights with respect to the deep ocean areas or its resources incompatible with the international regime to be established and the principles of the Declaration; and
4. On the basis of the principles of the Declaration, an international regime applying to the area and its resources and including appropriate international machinery to give effect to its provisions shall be established "by an international treaty of a universal character, generally agreed upon."

To realize the goals of the Declaration, the U.N. General Assembly at the same time, by Resolution 2750 (XXV), decided to convene a comprehensive conference on the Law of the Sea to deal with the precise delimitation of the seabed area, a regime for the high seas, territorial waters, international straits, the continental shelf, fishing, contiguous zones, the preferential rights of coastal states, and the prevention of marine pollution.

The significance of the U.N. Declaration of Principles for the deep ocean areas must be appraised in the context of another important U.N. resolution known as the Moratorium Resolution 2574D (XXIV), which said that

. . . pending the establishment of an international regime:
(a) states and persons, physical or juridical, are bound to refrain from all activities of exploitation of the resources of the area of the sea-bed and ocean floor, and the sub-soil thereof, beyond the limits of national jurisdiction;
(b) no claim to any part of that area or resources shall be recognized.

C. W. Pinto, the representative of Sri Lanka, expressed the feelings of all those who voted in favor of the Moratorium Resolution when he explained its purport thus:

In our view, it was a solemn expression of the opinion held by a substantial majority of the members of the United Nations that there existed a moral obligation on all countries, developed and developing, to cooperate with one another to achieve a rational and equitable regime for the seabed, and not to take any action in the interim period which would have the effect of prejudicing that endeavor. Apart from this, my delegation felt that it could be of real practical assistance both in preventing the problems that might attend premature exploitation and in building up pressure for early agreement on an international regime.
We saw it as addressed primarily to the private sector in the developed countries who would thus be placed on notice that the rules of exploitation of the deep seabed had not yet been worked out. The private investor, being well-known to be a prudent and cautious individual, with plenty of alternative and lucrative investments on dry land as it were, might be slow thereafter to invest in ventures operating on the deep ocean floor while the law remained in a state of flux.[32]

Both of these U.N. resolutions—the Declaration of Principles and the Moratorium Resolution—were regarded by several observers as being legally without binding effect upon the members of the international community. While the first committee was considering the final draft of the Declaration of Principles, announcing that it would abstain from voting, the Soviet Union stressed that "naturally the approval by the General Assembly of this draft cannot impose legal consequences on States since such decisions are merely of a recommendatory character."[33]

The United Kingdom delegation also expressed a very cautious view.

First, like any other resolution of the General Assembly, the draft declaration has in itself no binding force. Secondly, and arising from this, the draft declaration of principles must be regarded as a whole and interpreted as a whole; and as a whole it has no dispositive effect until we have an agreement on an international regime and, as part of that agreement, we have a clear, precise and internationally accepted definition of the area to which the regime is to apply.[34]

The Australian delegate concurred in this assessment and said that the principles could be regarded as "general guidelines for the establishment of a regime for the seabed and as an earnest desire of the great majority of members to have the regime," but, he added, "we would not see them as having any binding or mandatory effect upon States in the meantime."[35]

During a Senate hearing on the Moratorium Resolution in the United States—where private industry has business interests in the development of deep ocean areas—several opinions were expressed regarding the lack of binding force of the U.N. resolutions. However, there was no agreement among the commentators about whether future exploitation operations could be undertaken in the deep ocean areas in complete disregard of the U.N. resolution. Northcutt Ely recommended

. . . that the U.S. Government . . . announce that it does not regard itself as bound by the Moratorium Resolution, but, to the contrary, will continue to encourage the exploration and exploitation by its nationals of the seabed beyond national jurisdiction, under the international law applicable to the high seas, with due regard to the similar rights of all other nations, and subject to ultimate regulation by whatever international regime may be created by a treaty to which the United States becomes a party.

John G. Laylin, a Washington, D.C., attorney and spokesman for the hard mineral mining industry, however, stated that the United Nations recommendation might be considered a measurement of growing trends in customary international law and that the resolution could not be ignored, "for it was at the very least a protest vote revealing a desire on behalf of the developing countries to be included in the economic benefits derived from the deep seabed." He thought the United States should "encourage exploitation but on a basis of equitable sharing of benefits."[36]

John R. Stevenson, Legal Adviser in the Department of State, while approving the opinion that the Resolution was not legally binding, indicated that according to the U.N. Charter the United States was required to give "good faith" consideration to it in determining its policies. Assuring the Senate that his department did not anticipate any efforts to discourage U.S. nationals from continuing with their current exploratory plans, he observed that

In the event that U.S. nationals should desire to engage in commercial exploitation prior to the establishment of an internationally agreed regime, we would seek to assure that their activities are conducted in accordance with relevant principles of international law, including the freedom of the seas and that the integrity of their investment receives due protection in any subsequent international agreement.[37]

A few commentators from other countries took a similar view that the U.N. resolutions were not binding and that the exploitation of deep ocean areas was sanctioned subject to the principle of freedom of the seas. For example, W. Goralczyk of Poland, arguing that free access to deep ocean areas and their free exploitation were consequences of the principle of freedom of the seas, noted that

. . . the Declaration, as a resolution of the United Nations General Assembly, is not legally binding on member states, the less so of course on states which are not United Nations members, because the United Nations has no legislative power.
The Declaration of Principles therefore cannot change the existing rules of international law which apply to matters rigidly in this way.[38]

E. D. Brown, referring to the U.N. Declaration of Principles and specifically to the concept of common heritage of mankind, commented that "it is not a legal principle but embodies rather agreed moral and political guidelines which the community of States has undertaken a moral commitment to follow in good faith in the elaboration of a legal regime for the area beyond the limits of national jurisdiction."[39]

Even those delegates who strongly supported the U.N. resolutions appeared to emphasize not so much their legal significance as their political and moral implications. S. M. Thompson-Flores of Brazil argued:

Even if we set aside the question of states' responsibilities with regard to United Nations decisions, the indisputable fact remains that the so-called Moratorium Resolution reflects the considered view of the vast majority of world public opinion. Abiding or not by its terms is not a purely juridical matter; it has very definitely political implications.

Alvaro de Sota of Peru expressed a similar opinion:

Now, we are talking about a future international regime and though it can be disputed that this is international law . . . I do believe it represents a moral and political commitment on the part of States which backed the Declaration, at least on the Executive branches of those states, to abstain from any sort of activity and to withhold their nationals from any sort of activity until such a regime is established.[40]

Many of the comments noted above thus take a restrictive view with respect to the effect of the U.N. resolutions, and as such they fail to appraise accurately the importance that the resolutions have in influencing an international regime for the deep ocean area. The U.N. Declaration of Principles and the Moratorium Resolution present more than moral and political commitments. They have precise legal significance insofar as they answer the question posed earlier: Is there any freedom of deep ocean mineral resource exploitation?

It was pointed out above that until 1958, at which time the Geneva Convention codified the customary law of the sea, it was clear that the decision-makers did not want to legislate on an activity that did not exist at that time.

The international community began to consider deep ocean mineral exploitation, especially manganese nodule exploitation, only in the mid-1960s. After much debate, the General Assembly in 1969 passed the Moratorium Resolution, through which a majority of states unequivocally expressed their opposition to allowing exploitation of deep ocean mineral resources through flag state control. A year later, the U.N. General Assembly with near unanimity once again reiterated its view that no freedom of deep ocean mineral exploitation should be permitted, and that the activity should be subject to regulation by an international agency. In addition, the General Assembly also outlined a few basic policies that could no longer be ignored, no matter what specific prescriptions may be fashioned hereafter.

In view of the manifest intent of the majority of states, as expressed through the adoption of U.N. General Assembly resolutions, a strong presumption in law arises against the legality of any deep ocean mineral resource exploitation that seeks protection from a flag state and whose operations are in direct violation of the policies identified by the United Nations.

Even those who are otherwise skeptical about the binding force of U.N. resolutions, given suitable contextual circumstances, concede their legislative effect in strengthening a new customary prescription.

The specificity of the subject matter at issue, the consensus expressed through the process of voting, the expectations created by the resolution in the international community, and the actions pursued after the adoption of the resolutions are among the relevant contextual circumstances that transform a U.N. resolution from a mere recommendation into a legislative force capable of creating a customary prescription binding the international community.[41]

Mindful of this potentiality of the U.N. resolutions, John G. Laylin, who strongly believed in the freedom to exploit deep ocean mineral resources, counseled against total disregard of the Moratorium Resolution.[42] Alan Beesley, though rejecting the binding force of the U.N. Declaration of principles, declared,

However, we already have an indication of the will of the international community, and in fairly specific and, I would say, legal terms. It is worth looking at that Resolution not as just another U.N. resolution. (I do not hold with the school of thought that any resolution of the U.N. should be looked at as "just another resolution.") I accept that it does not have legal binding force, but it certainly has a good deal of legal content, and I think we could capitalize on it if we wished to.[43]

Proposals for Interim Deep Ocean Regime
While the United Nations continued its deliberations on developing acceptable international machinery for regulating the deep ocean mineral resource exploitation, private industry in the United States concerned with such activity expressed great frustration at the lack of prompt agreement on the matter. Claiming adequate knowledge about the resources, possession of needed technology, and availability of financial investments, the mineral industry in the United States felt that the only impediment in the way of deep ocean mining operations was the absence of an international regime that could guarantee proper safeguards for investments.[44] As a solution to the dilemma, leaders of the U.S. mineral industry suggested that the United States government offer protection of its flag and enact an interim deep ocean regime for the mining of minerals in the area, pending the outcome of international negotiations. To this end, the American Mining Congress submitted draft legislation for the approval of the United States Congress and Senate.[45] Explaining the central features of the proposed interim legislation, Laylin pointed out that it

1. (a) restrains persons subject to the jurisdiction of the United States from mining the resources of the deep seabed except under licenses issued by the United States or any other state with comparable legisla-

tion (a "reciprocating state") and in accordance with the regulations laid down to promote orderly and nondiscriminatory development; (b) permits foreign individuals and corporations acting through companies incorporated in the United States to mine under a United States license.

2. contemplates that landlocked states will enact comparable legislation and issue licenses in any section of the Area not previously licensed by a reciprocating state.

3. contemplates that non-industrialized states may enact comparable legislation under which licenses could be issued to companies with advanced technology and know-how wherever owned so long as these companies accept for the licensed activities the jurisdiction of the licensing state.

4. attempts to encourage those delegations in the UN Seabed Committee that have thus far delayed progress or advanced proposals they know are not acceptable to states whose adherence to a multinational convention is essential, to get down to work on a sensible set of heads of agreement for a 1973 convention and treaty or set of treaties on the Law of the Sea.[46]

The proposed interim legislation also envisaged the establishment of an "escrow fund" to become available eventually for assistance to developing reciprocating states. In addition, the licenses issued under the interim legislation may be made subject to

any international regime for development of the deep seabed hereafter agreed to by the United States, provided that such regime fully recognizes and protects the exclusive rights of each licensee to develop the licensed block for the term of the license and provided further that the United States fully reimburses the licensee for any loss of investment or increased costs of the licensee incurred within forty years after issuance of the license due to requirements or limitations imposed by the regime more burdensome than those of this Act.[47]

Appraisal

The interim legislation, presented by Senator Lee Metcalf to the United States Senate, has several positive elements:

a. It is designed only as an interim measure and not as an alternative to an international regime that may be adopted as a result of contemporary law of the sea negotiations.

b. It seeks to protect the investments of the American mineral industry in the absence of an agreed international regime for the deep ocean area.

c. It provides insurance for the industry against unacceptable risks that may arise out of an agreed international regime.

However, many of the provisions of the interim legislation and a few of the assumptions underlying it are not conducive to the promotion of common interests:

a. The size of the contemplated "escrow fund" meant for the assistance of the developing countries will be determined exclusively by the developed states, and the United States is not permitted to contribute to this fund more than the amount other developed states are willing to pay.

This provision, by ignoring the wishes of the developing countries in determining the size of the fund, is in direct violation of the concept of the common heritage of mankind, which has been identified as the cornerstone of the international regime presently being negotiated. The interim legislation, by restricting assistance from the fund only to the reciprocating developing countries, is in further violation of that concept.

b. While the interim legislation allows other states, including developing and/or landlocked states, to issue licenses to applicants as well, it is obvious that it is the developed countries and their industries that will be its primary beneficiaries. All conditions being equal, mining applicants are apt to seek licenses from the country where they are citizens. For the near future there are no business interests in the developing countries capable of venturing into the deep oceans.

Alternatively, the developing countries will have to offer extra incentives or concessions to foreign companies to persuade them to operate under their authority. While these concessions, if they involve less exacting environmental and work standards and tax restrictions, might be beneficial to the profit-oriented industry, they might prove to be detrimental to the other community interests.

c. The sponsors of the U.S. interim legislation made it clear that they intend it as an instrument to force the U.N. negotiations to conform to the preferences of the industry and to do so quickly. Senator Lee Metcalf, for example, while introducing the legislation, had this to say:

One reason for concluding that legislation merits consideration at this time is the increasing evidence that some of the more militant nations represented in the U.N. Seabed Committee would deny U.S. industry effective access to the minerals of the deep seabed.[48]

That this is not an accurate appraisal of the mood of the negotiations of the U.N. Seabed Committee needs no proof for anyone familiar with the discussions in that forum. It is beyond doubt that the international community is attempting to establish policies and guidelines for the deep seabed where there is at present no clear law applicable to marine mineral exploitation. The industry itself recognizes this and indeed urges the international community to agree on these policies as quickly as possible. Once this is done, a clarified international regime would actually enhance chances for protection of investments made by the industry. It is therefore hard to agree with Senator Metcalf that a group of "militant" nations are attempting to deny the mineral industry access to the deep oceans. The effect of such dramatic statements on the international negotiations can only be adverse. Under the circumstances it is clear that some of them regard the interim legislation as an attempt to thrust a fait accompli upon the international community.[49]

d. Furthermore, as one observer rightly noted, the interim legislation does not help even the industry that it seeks to protect:

Now, what is bad about this interim measure is basically, in our opinion, that it promotes conflict over claims to ocean resources between developing nations and developed nations. It could even lead to serious conflict between developed nations. It does not share equitably the resources of the deep seabed.

It seems to me there would be very little to go to anyone except the developing companies, after depletion allowance had been taken under United States domestic law, with a permanent license fee of only $5,000. We don't think that this interim measure provides stability for those investing in ocean enterprises, as is necessary. And we don't think that it really gives any voice to the international community in this common resource of the international community.

There is no effective international authority and no basis for settling conflicts, no tribunal, and there really is no protection for anyone. So we think that this is not even a good interim arrangement, if one should eventually be necessary. We do not think that it is in the interest of the United States or other countries to take this particular route. We are open-minded as to "when"; but certainly as to "how," this is not the way we think makes sense.[50]

It is unfortunate that the interim legislation has been submitted to the U.S. Senate at a time when the international community is actively engaged in fashioning an international regime. The legislation merits examination by a responsible country like the United States only if the international negotiations should fail irrevocably. Even then many of its provisions would have to be modified to propose more equitable sharing of resources among the members of the international community and more orderly procedures of allocation of deep ocean resources among prospective producers. It is certainly legitimate for the industry to expect prompt agreement on principles of law relating to the security of their investments. But that concern cannot be divested from the equally reasonable interests of other parts of the community.[51]

For all its defects and the poor timing of its introduction, the interim legislation has one positive side: it reminds the international legislators that the legal decision-making process cannot be indefinitely delayed and allowed to lag behind technological and economic needs of the society. And any unreasonable stalling of an international agreement on deep ocean areas would only give the special interests an opportunity to gain at the expense of common interests.

If agreement on setting up international machinery to govern the deep oceans is long delayed, while there may be a need for appropriate interim legislation, such legislation must not be proposed with complete indifference to the U.N. Declaration of Principles, which approved the following concepts with sufficient clarity:[52]

a. That the area and its resources are a common heritage of mankind;
b. That they should be developed for the benefit of all peoples, particularly upholding the interests of developing countries that lack the means for gaining, on their own, an equitable share from their exploitation;
c. That the international community has agreed to subject the process of deep ocean mineral exploitation to an international regime to be concluded eventually in terms of a universal international treaty.

Thus the U.N. Declaration of Principles categorically rejected the flag-state control of deep ocean resources and invalidated claims for the exclusive appropriation of resources without the state paying a reasonable share to other members of the community. Furthermore, according to the Declaration, such resources could be exploited only under policies that are consistent with an efficient and safe use of the marine environment.[53]

The Question of Organized Inclusive Access

Nongovernmental Proposals for International Machinery
Both before and after the initiation of current law of the sea negotiations, there were several nongovernmental proposals for the creation of international machinery to regulate exploitation of mineral resources of the deep ocean areas. The reasons that motivated such proposals, of course, were varied.[54]

The fact that marine mineral resources outside the boundaries of national jurisdiction did not come under the exclusive competence of any one particular group of the international community prompted a member of the International Law Commission, as early as 1950, to suggest that the responsibility for organizing their exploitation be entrusted to an institution representative of the entire international community.[55] The International Law Commission did not, however, favorably respond to his suggestion because, in its view, such a scheme was fraught with "insurmountable difficulties."[56]

Georges Scelle, another member of the International Law Commission, who did not conceal his contempt for the continental shelf doctrine, expressed his concern for the preservation of the marine environment as a legacy to all mankind. The recognition of exclusive rights over submarine areas, whatever the scope and purpose of the activities for which such rights are claimed by participants, according to him, would inevitably downgrade the high seas as a symbol of inclusive enjoyment.[57] As an alternative to the approval of apportionment of marine mineral resources among different territorial groups, Scelle proposed that their exploitation be authorized and controlled by an international agency belonging to the family of the United Nations.[58]

The United Nations authority and control over the exploitation of marine mineral resources was, in a few instances, recommended as part of a "grand design" to strengthen and support it as an instrument for regulating relations among the nations of the world. Thus in 1955 the World Association of Parliamentarians for World Government, for example, requested the government of the United Kingdom to advocate the authority and control of the United Nations over the exploitation of mineral resources of the high seas.[59]

For similar reasons, the Commission to Study the Organization of Peace, in its tenth Annual Report, recommended that "the floor under the high seas be recognized as 'res communis' and its ownership and control be conceded to the United Nations."[60] Grenville Clark and Louis Sohn endorsed the idea in their model revision of the Charter of the United Nations and suggested that the United Nations could exercise trusteeship over the high seas.[61]

The White House Conference on International Cooperation convened by President Lyndon Johnson in Washington, D.C., from November 29 to December 1, 1965, considered, among other things, appropriate arrangements for the regulation of "certain natural resources" that "are unique in that no one has exclusive rights to their use or exploitation." In this connection, the conference of American scholars gave some attention to the deep ocean mineral resources and observed that

Because these resources are clearly outside national jurisdictions, the possibility of their exploitation raises two problems: the efficient and orderly exploitation of the nodules, and the distribution or sharing of mining rights to areas that are sufficiently large to permit them to operate economically and without fear of congestion or interference. And if rights are to be granted for resources that are the common property of the world community, their decisions on the allocation of these rights or on the methods of acquisition must be made within the framework of international law. A specialized Agency of the United Nations would be the most appropriate body for administering the distribution of exclusive mining rights.[62]

The World Peace Through Law Conference held in July 1967, which was attended by nearly 2,000 lawyers and judges from all over the world, joined the ranks of those who advocated the United Nations' authority and control over the deep ocean mineral resource exploitation. Its main motivation and hope was that through such international control the benefits resulting from such exploitation could be directed toward improving conditions for more than half of mankind, which "finds itself underprivileged, underfed, and underdeveloped."[63] More recently, after Ambassador Arvid Pardo introduced his proposal in the United Nations, many institutions and individuals have expressed their support for an organized inclusive access for the deep ocean mineral resources.

In the United States, the Commission to Study the Organization of Peace,[64] the American Assembly,[65] the New England Assembly,[66] the Center for the Study of Democratic Institutions,[67] and Senator Claiborne Pell[68] were among those who preferred international control over the process of deep ocean mineral resource exploitation.

The idea had also found supporters elsewhere in the world. The Deep-Sea Mining Committee on the Exploration and Exploitation of Minerals on the Ocean Bed and in Its Subsoil of the International Law Association in its draft report opted for an international agency, "for instance, a new or an existing specialized Agency or an organ of the United Nations."[69] The Brown Report accepted in principle the establishment of an intergovernmental organization.[70] The United Nations Committee of the World Peace Through Law Center followed up its own earlier recommendations and reiterated its support for the idea of setting up an international body to regulate access to marine minerals and to help the world community to share its benefits.[71] Two scientists, one American and the other Soviet, had put forward a joint plea for regarding the mineral resources of the oceans as the common property of all peoples of the world and for instituting suitable arrangements to divert the profits derived from their exploitation to aid in the economic growth of the developing countries.[72]

Most of the private models suggested for the regulation of deep ocean mineral resource exploitation suffer from one of two principal disadvantages: either they are too sketchy and inadequate to comprehend and coordinate all the different interests involved in the process, or they are too unrealistic and ambitious to gain the necessary political acceptance and to promote efficient and economic supervision of the resource exploitation.

Thus, the treaty proposed by U.S. Senator Pell did not contain any procedures for implementing some of its wise policy recommendations to encourage the growth of developing countries, to protect the interests of coastal states from threats to their security and environment, and to manage rationally multiple uses in the same maritime area.

In contrast, the Center for the Study of Democratic Institutions under the leadership of E. M. Borgese had produced a very comprehensive framework for the regulation of all ocean uses, of which marine mineral resource exploitation was only a part. As the original draft statute of the Center pointed out, it viewed the occasion ''not so much, or not only, for a systematic approach to the scientific, technological, and economic development of ocean resources but for the creation of a model for the development of new principles of international law, organization, and cooperation.''[73] Much as one would like to encourage the visionary exhortations of the Center for the Study of Democratic Institutions with respect to organizing the world community into a mold of ''participational democracy,'' the difficulties in accepting its approach to transnational problems are obvious.

Nation-states, whether rich or poor, are particularly sensitive to any system of centralized decision-making over which they do not have undisputed control. Even when they are forced by the facts of life to accept new international machinery, as they have done before, its authority and control cannot often rise above the limits of voluntary compliance. Under these circumstances, it is useless to propose utopian models of world government.

While the Center for the Study of Democratic Institutions is right in criticizing the failings of existing international institutions, it somehow misses the reality that their weaknesses are nothing but a reflection of the disagreement and fragmentation that characterize the contemporary world community. In the absence of any dramatic improvement in the attitudes of the nations of the world, the Center's impatience to create a new era of international organization can only remain overambitious and illusory.

Proposals before the United Nations and an International Regime
The Declaration of Principles passed by the United Nations General Assembly in 1970 provided impetus to many countries to propose concrete models for the regulation of deep ocean resource exploitation through an international regime. Even those states, such as the USSR and Poland, which had earlier opposed international control of ocean resources, submitted their own models in this regard. By 1971, the U.N. Seabed Committee had about twelve separate designs before it dealing with an international regime.[74]

While there were several common elements among the various proposals, there were also significant differences in the basic philosophy that guided them and in the details of the machinery advocated. One set of proposals, put forward by the United States, the United Kingdom, and Japan, favored confining the authority of international machinery essentially to the regulation of mineral resources. Another set of proposals, exemplified by the Latin American, Maltese, and the Tanzanian drafts, conceived very broad powers for the international agency, which included control not only over the international area itself but also over all activities undertaken there. Furthermore, the sponsors of some proposals, including the United States, the United Kingdom, France, and Japan, felt that the authority of international machinery should be restricted to the issuing of offshore licenses. Another group of states, including the Latin American countries, believed that the international agency itself should be entrusted with the exclusive power to undertake exploitation of ocean resources. Ambassador Andres Aguilar of Venezuela explained the philosophy behind the Latin American proposal thus:

A very important issue is at stake here. To developing nations the concept of common heritage implies not only sharing in the benefits to be obtained from the exploitation of the resources of the area but also, and above all, an effective and total participation in all aspects of the management of this common heritage. To be more precise, the developing nations seek to participate in all the activities to be carried out in this area: in scientific research, in exploration and exploitation, and in management and distribution of the benefits to be derived.[75]

In addition, the Latin American and the Tanzanian drafts emphasized the need for the international agency to control the fluctuation of prices of minerals, especially when such instability would seriously affect the economics of developing countries that are the principal producers of raw minerals.[76]

However, representing those opposing such extensive powers, especially the authority of the international agency to exploit the resources, Leigh Ratiner of the United States pointed out that his delegation felt

. . . it would be unconscionable from the standpoint of common law for the authority both to regulate deep sea mining activities and to engage in them itself. That would place States engaged in similiar activities at a disadvantage and raise doubts as to whether due process of law was being observed.[77]

Finally, some proposals favored a minimum of international bureaucracy to manage deep ocean areas. France, which reflected this approach in its working paper, noted that

The essential purpose of the working paper presented by France is to ensure the equitable and effective operation of the international regime. . . . The word "effective" implies a regime that has no complex structure producing expenditure and delays but manages its resources rationally through the administration's impartiality and competence.[78]

In contrast, there were proposals that advocated a broad system of agencies and subsidiary agencies with a view to covering every conceivable administrative contingency and to providing a system of checks and balances during the operation of the proposed international regime. The draft proposal by the United States, which, like Malta, envisaged the most elaborate machinery, had the following policy as its basis: "The regime and machinery should be structured in a manner that realistically reflects the principal interests of different groups of States."[79]

Given the differences in their perspectives, the proposals varied in the emphasis they placed on specific agencies of the international machinery and on their functions and powers. Basically, most of them contemplated an Assembly (a plenary organ), a Council (an executive and representative organ), a Secretariat (an administrative organ), and a Tribunal for dispute settlement. The proposal by the United Kingdom also had a distribution agency (to disburse the net profit among member nations) whose board of directors had to be elected by the Assembly. The French plan suggested establishment of only two bodies—a Permanent Board and a Conference of Plenipotentiaries—to provide meeting places for the exchange of views, negotiation, and arbitration among participants of the deep ocean regime. Poland envisaged the development of the international machinery in two stages: for the transitional period, it indicated the establishment of an Assembly, Council, and Secretariat, and after the transition period, the machinery could be enlarged to include a Technical Board, Economic Board, Registration and Licensing Board, and an Arbitration Tribunal. However, the USSR and Japan limited their machinery to only an Assembly, Council, and Secretariat. A group of Latin American countries proposed the creation of an International Seabed Resources Enterprise in addition to an Assembly and Council. In contrast, some of the landlocked and shelf-locked countries proposed that such an agency should be created later by the Assembly at the recommendation of the Council. Malta outlined comprehensive international machinery that, in addition to an Assembly, Council, Secretariat, and Tribunal, included major subsidiary organs—an Ocean Management and Development Commission, a Scientific and Technological Commission, and a Legal Commission. The United States draft also had specified three subsidiary commissions: a Rules and Recommended Practice Commission, an Operations Commission, and an International Seabed Boundary Review Commission.[80]

Functions and Powers of the Organs of International Machinery

The Assembly A few of the general functions envisaged for the Assembly included the election of Members of the Council; examination of reports from the Council; approval of the budget of the machinery; creation of the necessary subsidiary agencies; consideration of plans for distributing the net income of the international agency among members of the international community; and proposal of amendments to regulations affecting the international machinery. Most of the proposals also authorized the Assembly to consider any matter concerning the operation of the international machinery and to take action on matters over which other organs within this machinery would not have specific control.

Besides the generally supervisory functions, it was also suggested that the Assembly be given certain additional powers. Thus the proposal by a group of the Latin American countries would give the Assembly authority to approve regulations framed by the Council with respect to conclusion of service contracts and joint ventures between the international agency and judicial persons duly sponsored by states. In addition, the same proposal would require that the Assembly decide what offshore area would be available for exploration and exploitation of resources therein. Furthermore, the United Kingdom and the USSR in their models gave the Assembly the authority to appoint the Secretary-General for the Secretariat of the machinery. The USSR's model also gave it the power to expel members on the recommendation of the Council. In addition, the same proposal required the Assembly to draft standards concerning marine pollution. Malta proposed that the Assembly approve any rules with regard to the exercise of borrowing powers by the international machinery and have the authority to allocate expenses not covered by the income among the member states. Finally, the Latin American and the United Republic of Tanzanian proposals regarded the Assembly as the "supreme organ" of the international machinery. On decision-making within the Assembly, different formulas were presented. Japan, some of the Latin American countries, Poland, and the United States proposed a simple majority vote.[81] Malta indicated a weighted voting formula.[82] Canada preferred decision by a two-thirds majority vote. The USSR favored a two-thirds majority vote for substantive decisions and a simple majority vote for procedural decisions.

The Council All the proposals before the U.N. Seabed Committee considered the Council to be a central organ of the international machinery. According to the United States proposal, the Council would prepare the budget and submit it to the Assembly for approval, prepare annual reports on the work of the machinery, determine rules of procedure, create and supervise the functioning of subsidiary organs, and appoint the Secretary-General of the Secretariat. In addition, the Council was also authorized, under the U.S. scheme, to issue emergency orders, maintain emergency funds, coordinate the procedures of the international machinery with those of the United Nations, and organize assistance to developing countries to develop their maritime capabilities.

While some of the above provisions were endorsed by other models, they also included a few functions for the Council which the United States model did not touch upon. For example, the United Kingdom's proposal provided for a periodic review of licensing and other technical procedures by the Council. The United Republic of Tanzania, the USSR, some of the Latin American countries, and Malta, in their plans, required the Council to take action to avoid marine pollution due to offshore exploitation operations and to provide for conservation of seabed resources. Japan, the United Republic of Tanzania, and Malta wanted the Council to issue licenses for exploration and exploitation of ocean resources in the international area. According to the United Kingdom's plan, while the Council should have the authority to license, it wanted that power to be delegated to the Secretary-General.

The proposals by the USSR, several of the Latin American countries, and Japan envisaged for the Council supervisory and regulatory authority over the activities of licensees and sublicensees. While the United Republic of Tanzania's scheme would have the Council fix liability for damage arising out of offshore exploitation operations, the USSR proposed that it set arbitration procedures in case of disputes. It is also interesting to note that the Latin American proposal required permission from the Council for all scientific research in the international area. On the other hand, Malta wanted it to exercise such regulatory functions with respect to military uses as may be conferred upon it by a unanimous vote. In contrast to a few schemes that appeared to give the Assembly residual powers, the USSR proposed that the Council have these powers.

The composition of the Council and the voting within this body provoked great diversity in the various proposals. For example, some of the Latin American countries and the United Republic of Tanzania advocated election of all the members. Other countries, including the United States, the United Kingdom, Canada, and Japan, wanted the Council to have both designated and elected members.[83] Still others, Malta[84] and the USSR[85] among them, divided the membership of the Council into categories and prescribed special election procedures.

The United States and Japanese schemes called for a 24-member Council, of which 6 would be designated and 18 elected. Furthermore, they proposed that the Council have at least 12 developing countries and 2 or 3 landlocked or shelf-locked countries among its members. Canada and the USSR specified 30, the Latin Americans 35, and the United Republic of Tanzania 18 members for the Council. While most countries favored a three-year term for each member, the USSR suggested a four-year term.[86]

In addition to a careful blending of geographical regions, technological capabilities, and economic status in the composition of the Council, the United States[87] and Malta[88] proposed a special system of voting. Canada, Japan, the United Republic of Tanzania, and the Latin American countries advocated a two-thirds majority for decision on substantive matters. The USSR, on the other hand, preferred consensus or unanimity for decisions on substantive matters and simple majority for procedural matters.[89]

International Seabed Enterprise Differing from other models, the proposal by certain of the Latin American countries called for the creation of an International Seabed Enterprise as a principal organ of the international machinery. Its chief function would be to authorize and control all technical, industrial, and commercial activities. The Enterprise under this scheme would be invested with a separate legal personality and all implied powers enabling it to operate as a business and administrative organ.[90]

The Tribunal At least five proposals dealt with a dispute settlement tribunal as part of the machinery they advocated. The U.S. plan would establish a permanent tribunal with five, seven, or nine independent judges (no two members may be of the same nationality). The tribunal would be authorized to decide all disputes and to advise on all questions relating to the interpretation and application of the convention that would create the international machinery. It would have authority not only to give advisory opinions to the agency but also to seek advisory opinions from the International Court of Justice. Judges of the tribunal would be elected by the Council from a list of nominations submitted to it by the Contracting Parties. Each of the judges would serve for a term of nine years, with a provision for reelection. The U.S. scheme also elaborated on the procedure for submission of disputes to the tribunal. In addition, the U.S. proposal referred to sanctions applicable to parties who failed to carry out obligations imposed on them by the judgments of the tribunal. Initially, the Council would decide on measures necessary to give effect to the decision. As part of these sanctions, the Council could decide to suspend temporarily, in whole or in part, the rights of the delinquent Party under the Convention. However, any such suspension of rights of the Contracting Parties must not impair the rights of licensees who have not contributed to the failure to perform obligations arising out of judgment of the tribunal.

Malta also envisaged the creation of a permanent International Maritime Court but left the provisions governing it as the subject of a separate statute. Canada favored a small body of legal and perhaps technical experts, elected either by the Council or by the Assembly, to settle disputes concerning the operation of the international machinery. It suggested that provision be made for appeals to the International Court of Justice on decisions from the tribunal.

The United Kingdom's plan called for a tribunal to settle disputes by a process of conciliation as well as adjudication. It proposed that the existing international dispute settlement mechanisms, including the International Court of Justice, play a part in resolving disputes concerning offshore resource exploitation activities. Japan also contemplated a simple tribunal to be constituted on an ad hoc basis, with three members, each party to the dispute being entitled to nominate one member and the Chairman to be chosen by the designated members. In the event that the International Seabed Authority was a party to the dispute, the Japanese proposal indicated that the Secretary-General should have the authority to appoint a member to the tribunal. It further stated that, upon agreement among the parties to the dispute, there could be an appeal to the International Court of Justice on decisions rendered by the tribunal. In the absence of such special stipulation, the decisions of the tribunal would be final.

The Secretariat As a principal organ of the machinery, the Secretariat was intended in most proposals to gather data relevant to offshore activities, to keep records, and to prepare reports for submission to the Assembly and the Council. However, the United Republic of Tanzania and some of the Latin American countries in their models envisaged other important functions as well. The Tanzanian proposal gave the Secretariat the function of inspection over maritime activities. On the other hand, the Latin American scheme required the Secretariat to perform an advisory role to the Enterprise and to arrange for distribution of information gained from scientific research.[91] Malta wanted to prohibit the Secretary-General or members of his staff from having any financial interest in any of the offshore operations over which the Secretariat is invested with supervisory roles.[92] The United Kingdom and Japan proposed that the Secretariat be authorized to carry out such other functions as may be delegated to it.[93]

Lease Terms One of the essential functions of the international machinery according to all the proposals would be to authorize and control the process of marine mineral resource exploitation. For this purpose most of the models except the one authored by a group of Latin American states presented a system for granting leases to prospective producers. An overview of the lease terms is as follows:[94]

Leases could be granted only to states, or Contracting Parties.[95] States could organize exploration and exploitation on their own or could form joint ventures with other states or business associations or could sublease the areas to others.[96] Each state would be entitled to only a limited maritime area for lease. The area available to each state for exploiting the resources therein would be fixed according to an agreed formula.[97] States would normally be expected to supervise offshore operations in the areas under their exclusive competence. However, the international agency could inspect these activities on its own initiative or at the request of one of the Contracting Parties.[98] Generally the leases would be nonexclusive for prospecting or exploration purposes and exclusive for production or exploitation of resources.[99] All the leases would require a license fee, and at the production stage the operations would be subject to royalties also. Expropriations or unjustifiable interferences with offshore operations would be prohibited.[100] Specified work requirements must be observed. Violations of lease agreements would have to be reported to the Tribunal if the Contracting Parties did not agree to correct them. A sanction for violation of the lease terms would be revocation of the lease itself.[101]

Equitable Sharing of Benefits All the proposals appear to agree that revenues derived from the leasing of marine resources should be defrayed to achieve three principal purposes: (1) to meet administrative expenses of the agency; (2) to improve the knowledge relating to ocean resources and techniques of their exploitation; and (3) to provide financial dividends to all the Contracting Parties with special consideration for the underdeveloped countries.

In order to accomplish these objectives, the following different methods were suggested:

The U.S. draft sought to utilize the existing international agencies as far as possible. The U.N. special fund or the creation of a distribution agency was suggested in the U.K. plan.[102] The French scheme, which emphasized reliance on individual states for the regulation of deep ocean mineral resources, proposed that the states themselves choose ways best suited to their tastes in promoting the three objectives.[103]

According to the Tanzanian draft, the Assembly should determine the formula for sharing. It further suggested that a distribution agency be created with three to five persons "to assess all the income available to the Authority from the sale of raw materials, from license fees, royalties, and any other charges or payments." On the basis of such assessments, the Tanzanian draft recommended that the net income be shared among members of the international agency "according to the inverse ratio of their respective contributions to the annual budget of the United Nations." In the case of states that were not members of the U.N., it noted that "their share of income shall be determined by the agency according to their stage of development."

The Latin American draft emphasized that special consideration should be given to the interests and needs of developing countries, whether coastal or landlocked, in the equitable distribution of income among all states. Malta provided for a certain scale of distribution if the net income of the international agency was less than $50 million, and another scale if the income was more than $50 million. Under its scheme, in either case, "not less than 85 percent of this revenue shall be allocated to States whose gross national product does not exceed $800 per capita." Japan left the net income to be used in promoting the growth of developing countries in accordance with rules to be established by the international agency.[104]

Appraisal

With respect to the international machinery proposed to govern the process of marine mineral resource exploitation, considerable consensus on several aspects appears to have emerged among different groups of the international community. Subject to some differences of opinion as to which organ of the machinery must discharge what functions, there is agreement that the international authority must attempt to (a) promote knowledge relating to the oceans, their resources, and exploitation techniques; (b) organize a leasing system to provide for an orderly and phased allocation of marine areas among states for development of their resources; (c) discourage the monopoly of ocean areas and their resources; (d) supervise offshore resource exploitation operations with a view to avoiding marine pollution, undue interference with other uses of the sea, and wasteful exploitation and depletion of resources; and (e) provide for pacific settlement of disputes arising out of offshore operations.

However, a number of issues remain unresolved. These are related to (a) the comprehensiveness of powers to be accorded to the international machinery; (b) its structure and the functions of specific organs; (c) representation and voting in the principal organs; and (d) sharing of benefits resulting from ocean use among the members of the international community.

Most of the unresolved issues are in some way interrelated. The issue of the functions of specific organs is directly connected with the issue of representation and voting therein. While the developing countries would like the Assembly (where together they would constitute a predominant majority) to be the "supreme organ," the technologically advanced countries would prefer the Council (where they advocate weighted voting or veto power) to assume responsibility for the main business of the international machinery.

Problems relating to voting are not peculiar or novel to the process of the law of the sea negotiations. They are inherent in the very art of decision-making in the international arena.[105] They reflect a basic dilemma of the international community: Should decision-making be based on the one-state-one-vote principle, or should it defer to the inequalities that exist with regard to power, wealth, respect, and rectitude among the participants?

The developed countries advocate weighted voting or even veto power on the ground that they would be the principal investors of capital, technology, and skills necessary to gain the needed benefits from the oceans. Accordingly, they argue that they should have a significant say in the way in which the offshore operations are conducted. Any other system of decision-making that would deny them such a major role, the developed countries claim, would be an unacceptable form of taxation without proper representation.

On the other hand, the developing countries oppose weighted voting or the veto as a violation of the principles of universal representation and sovereign equality. It is also feared that a system of weighted voting or veto power would perpetuate the economic and technological backwardness of the developing countries, hence their dependence upon the developed countries.

One solution to the problems of decision-making appears to be to depoliticize the process of offshore resource exploitation as far as possible. Many of the functions that most nations agree the international machinery must undertake in the interest of optimal utilization of benefits from the sea could be usefully entrusted to an organ manned by experts in their capacity as international civil servants.

The proposals advocated by the United States, the United Republic of Tanzania, the Latin American countries, and Malta ignore this aspect of the problem and make the process of marine mineral resource exploitation subject to the approval of such political organs as the Assembly, the Council, or the Enterprise. The United Kingdom plan comes close to advocating the policy of depoliticization by proposing the delegation of resource management functions to the Secretariat. However, even this scheme is not fully satisfactory as it requires the

Secretariat to be responsible to the Council, which is of course a central political organ.

In their concern to neutralize different political groups, several of these proposals suggest a vast network of principal organs. However, these attempts do not face up to an important policy consideration, that is, to tailor the bureaucracy of the machinery to the essential functions and the income and other means expected to be available to it.

It is certainly possible to conceive broad powers for the international machinery, including the power to undertake the exploitation of marine resources on its own, without literally forcing it to do so when it is economically and technologically beyond its means. The Latin American proposal to make the Enterprise the sole producer of deep ocean resources, at least in the initial stages of its operation, may well prove to be a costly and risky undertaking for the international community.

If a wide exclusive resource zone is given to the coastal state, as several influential proposals before the Caracas Law of the Sea Confer ence argue, much of the deep ocean area may cease to be economically attractive in the immediate future. For this reason, it may be prudent, as Poland suggested, to start with rather modest machinery and to enlarge it as functions and income demand later.[106]

With respect to the sharing of benefits, some countries, for example, the United Republic of Tanzania and Brazil, have suggested that the net income of the international agency be distributed among states, giving special consideration to the poor nations. From a common interest perspective, this is an unacceptable mode of utilizing benefits derived from the seas. This is so, first of all, because the net income of the agency may be so small, at least for some years, that, when divided among 150 states, the share of individual countries will have a negligible impact upon their domestic economies;[107] the overall effect upon the international economic scene, as a result of such a scheme, would be even less noticeable. Second, even when the apportionable sums are respectable, cash payments to individual countries would encourage disparate and uncoordinated economic investments, often with no net gains for an organized and balanced world economic development. Suggestions for creating special Distribution Agencies to manage the net income of the International Agency are also to be rejected, as they tend to multiply bureaucracy and hence prove to be uneconomical.

There are several international agencies specializing in promotion of global economic growth and in transfer of capital and technical assistance from developed to developing countries. An important problem

of these agencies is not the lack of well-thought-out development programs for the developing countries but more often the lack of necessary funds to implement those schemes. Rather than create one more
bureaucracy, it appears reasonable therefore to channel the net income
of the International Agency through the existing transnational development agencies. Such a policy not only would reduce the initial establishment expenses for the International Agency but would give it the
benefit of the experience that these international agencies have already
accumulated in their operation. In addition, the integration of the new
machinery governing the oceans with the existing specialized agencies
of the United Nations would lend them much-needed morale and a
boost in status.

5

Competing Uses of the Sea

Multiple Uses and Conflicts

As the exploitation of offshore nonliving resources has become more widespread, it is necessary to examine its place among the many other uses of the sea. This chapter will assess the processes of conflict and accommodation resulting from the introduction of nonliving resource exploitation into the context of various competing uses of the sea.

For the purpose of this analysis, the nature and intensity of each of these uses of the sea will first be identified; then an assessment of the conflict—actual or potential—between each of these uses and nonliving resource exploitation will be made.

Fisheries

For centuries man has turned to the sea for the exploitation of its fishery resources. In recent years, because of world population growth and consequent demands on available food resources, coupled with enhanced technological efficiency, the number of fishing vessels and the amount of fish caught have greatly increased.

At present, nearly 15,000 fishing vessels larger than 100 gross tons and involving nearly 101 countries engage in fishing around the world.[1] According to one account, by 1972 the fish catch stood at 62 million tons, with a value of U.S. $8 billion. In the near future, the catch may even reach 100 million tons and may earn as much as U.S. $20 billion.[2]

The growth in fish catches and the introduction of modern techniques for locating and exploiting the fishery stocks of the seas have caused fears of overexploitation. According to some fishery experts, the problem is so serious that even under perfect conditions of regulation and control, the optimum harvest from the sea will provide less food than is required by present, let alone future, populations. As one solution to the problem, many marine biologists are considering aquaculture, defined as "the techniques of raising useful aquatic species under some control of the organism and its environment."[3]

Aquaculture is not a new phenomenon. China, Japan, and Egypt for over 4,000 years, Java and India for over 3,000 years, and parts of Europe for over 2,500 years have been engaged in some form of aquaculture. However, most of the present activity in this field has been carried on without scientific aid. So far the major culture industries involve shellfish, principally oysters and mussels, with substantial milkfish and mullet production in some Asian countries, shrimp in the Far East, yellowtail (a large fish) in Japan; other estuarine animals such as lobsters, clams, abalone, scallops, pompano, and plaice are raised in certain areas. For most of these species, commercial production is insignificant, with most of the culture being still in the laboratory or early pilot stage.

Only a limited part of the sea, the shallow region near shore, appears suitable for aquaculture. In most cases, the activity may be confined to depths of less than 30 meters. Nonetheless, there are still enormous areas available for the conduct of aquaculture. According to the available data, in some Asian countries—excluding China, Japan, and India, which are the leaders in aquaculture—about 400,000 hectares of coastal waters are under cultivation, and a total of 1,500,000 hectares are believed to be suitable. In Africa, a single country, Nigeria, has at least a million hectares of mangrove area that could be converted into sea farms. At least half of this area could conceivably be more profitably used for aquaculture than for other activities. There are additional millions of hectares along the shores of Africa, South America, and many other regions of the world that are suitable for aquatic farms.

Aquaculture as a maritime activity requires large exclusive areas. These areas have to be selected, among other things, on the basis of temperature, water quality, immunity from predators, and availability of sources of food and oxygen. Other uses of the sea, such as commercial fishing, recreation involving fishing and boating, waste disposal, and offshore nonliving resource exploitation, cannot coexist with aquaculture as these activities will interfere with water transportation, water quality, and the conditions necessary for its pursuit.[4]

Most forms of aquaculture involve the complicated preparation of enclosures and their protection. These in turn require exclusive use of varying amounts of the water area. For example, plots that are 3 feet wide and 30 feet long are used for oyster culture in the Philippines.[5]

In the case of fisheries, conflict with nonliving resource exploitation can arise if waters are polluted with oil, and for other reasons as well.

OFFSHORE OIL POLLUTION

The problem of oil pollution of the sea has gained wide attention in the past few years. Several sources of oil pollution have been identified. These include tanker and other ship operations, offshore oil production, refinery operations, oil wastes, and accidental spills. According to one source, in 1969 nearly 2,180,000 tons of petroleum hydrocarbons were lost into the marine environment for one reason or another. The projections of similar losses for 1975 vary between 2,246,000 and 3,405,000 tons, and for 1980 between 3,325,000 and 4,752,000 tons.[6]

Offshore oil production appears to rank low among the sources of oil pollution. For example, it was responsible for only 100,000 tons of the total amount in 1969, which incidentally was the year when Santa Barbara blowout occurred. The projections are that by 1975 oil pollution, because of offshore production, may range between a minimum of 160,000 tons and a maximum of 320,000 tons, and by 1980 it may be between 230,000 and 460,000 tons.

The experience of offshore production, to date, indicates that oil pollution from this source, however dramatic it may be, is not serious. As one U.S. petroleum expert noted, "of the 16,000 wells drilled in the U.S. waters only 25 have resulted in blowouts and of these only three were serious enough to cause severe pollution and consequent interference with commercial and pleasure uses of the seas."[7]

According to an oil industry spokesman, the safety of offshore oil and gas production can be maintained through the use of well-designed surface and subsurface safety valves in the production process; the monitoring and collection of oil leaks; sophisticated fire-fighting equipment, consisting of high-volume seawater pumping facilities supplemented by portable chemical extinguishers, and, in some cases, by automatic sprinkler deluge systems; and the maintenance of contaminant booms and oil-recovery devices. While the technology for safety surface systems is well established, various industrial groups as well as individual firms are attempting to

—Improve surface equipment standards and manufacturing quality control;
—Further reduce the incidence of critical human procedural errors through continued and perhaps accelerating training and safety programs;
—Extend the application of sand erosion monitoring and control equipment.[8]

There is considerable discussion about the effect of discharged oil, both crude and refined, on the marine environment and living organisms.[9] In the case of the Santa Barbara oil spill of 1969, it is reported that while it did not adversely affect the fish population in the area, it caused real harm to birds, benthic plants, and animals in the intertidal zone and contaminated beach and shore facilities.[10] Later, studying the effect of a relatively small spill of refined petroleum, which occurred in West Falmouth, near Woods Hole, a group of scientists of the Woods Hole Oceanographic Institution pointed out that "oil is much more persistent and destructive to marine organisms and to man's marine food resources than scientists had thought." Furthermore, in the opinion of these scientists,

. . . crude oil and oil products are persistent poisons, resembling in their longevity DDT, PCB's and other synthetic materials . . . [and] like other long-lasting poisons that, in some properties, resemble the natural fats of the organisms, hydrocarbons from oil spills enter the marine food chain and are concentrated in the fatty parts of the organisms. They can then be passed from prey to predator where they may become a hazard to marine life and even to man himself.[11]

Future research will undoubtedly throw more light on the effects of oil on the sea. Much appears to depend upon the kind and quantities of oil discharged and upon the nature of the place and the organisms involved. Meanwhile, whenever there is an oil spill in the ocean, claims are bound to arise for compensation of real or apparent damages sustained because of "oil pollution."

In the case of the West Falmouth oil spill, the damage to the local shellfish resources, almost a year and a half after the incident, was estimated to be $118,000. The owner of the oil paid compensation of $100,000 to the town of Falmouth and $200,000 to the Commonwealth of Massachusetts for the losses they suffered in marine fishery re-resources.[12]

However, it is not often easy to assess the precise dollar figure in each case of damage due to oil spill. Sea fish, for example, may be rendered unsalable because they are unhealthy or tainted, or they may not be caught at all because they are driven away from normal fishing grounds.

OIL AND GAS OPERATIONS AS A CAUSE OF CONFLICT

As part of the process of offshore petroleum production in some cases and necessarily in the case of gas fields, gathering lines are laid on the seabed between the various platforms in the fields; these gathering lines are then hooked into trunk lines for transporting the crude oil or natural gas to a point on shore. Such pipelines either are buried in the sediment of the sea floor or lie on the surface. In the latter case, the pipelines may interfere with dragger operations and may foul up large fishing nets. In rare instances they may also break and result in the pollution of the marine environment.

Conflicts may also arise as a result of abandoned wells, the casing of which has not been cut off at a sufficient distance below the sea floor, or as a result of junk material lost during the development of a field. Here again, the problem need not be a very serious one if proper governmental legislation and supervision takes place.[13]

THE EFFECT OF MARINE MINING ON THE OCEAN ENVIRONMENT

Marine mining activity, excluding the extraction of petroleum from the ocean floor, can also result in conflicts, especially in the "sublittoral zone" of the continental shelf—the area between the intertidal zone and the edge of the continental shelf—where they are most likely to take place. One authority on marine mineral technology assessed the nature of the problems that can be anticipated in this regard:

This [the marine mining activity in the sublittoral zone of the continental shelf] is of concern to scientists and engineers alike because this area comprises the bulk of the zone of light penetration—the zone teeming, where conditions are favorable, with marine life.

At the moment, science cannot anticipate what effect marine mining will have on the environment. It is certain, nevertheless, that there is a tremendous potential effect due simply to the magnitude of the operation. . . .

Marine mining may effect a series of changes in the physical environment. The locally deeper sea floor may cause alterations in wave refraction that can erode beaches. Fine particles from the mine, if they do not muddy the swimming water, may settle into new beaches in unwanted places or into silt beds hazardous to navigation.

Possible effects on marine life are far more complex. Excavation will destroy bottom-dwelling organisms and soil stabilizing vegetation. Excavation explosions will damage air bladders and vascular systems, particularly in very small fish and larvae. Some nutrients and chemicals could have a beneficial effect depending on the chemistry of the water mass, but heavy metals, released [and] not completely recovered by the mining system, could be concentrated in certain fish in lethal amounts.

Turbidity will retard photosynthesis and thereby reduce the basic productivity of the area. Fish, whose gills become clogged with the suspended particles, may die. A change in heat radiation can be expected, also changing the ecological character of the area. During settling, the suspended particles can scavenge organic waste and, upon deposition, drastically reduce the the oxygen available to sea-floor organisms, smothering fish food, shell fish, and spawning grounds.

After a sea-floor mine has been worked out, the environment will reach equilibrium. But the deposition of fine-grained material over a large area down current can constitute an unstable mass with the resultant problem of frequent resuspension, and can frequently eliminate biologic succession.[14]

It must be pointed out, however, that so far the marine mining activities that are conducted in relatively near-shore areas have not caused serious problems. The possible complications noted above must be assessed, and appropriate legislation may have to be adopted to regulate all future mining activities that are expected to be extended into the outer continental shelf area.

Navigation

The principal purposes of navigation at sea are security, scientific research, and commerce. Conflicts between security and nonliving resource interests will be discussed in a separate section.

SCIENTIFIC INVESTIGATION AT SEA

Scientific investigation of the sea or the study of oceanography dates back at least to 1872, when the celebrated British Challenger Expedition set off to collect samples of animals of the sea and the sea floor around the world.[15] Since then oceanography as a science has become increasingly important.

In the United States, one of the leaders in this field, there are more than 1,500 oceanographers studying the chemistry, physics, geology, geophysics, and engineering of the oceans. About 500 or so research vessels are at the service of these scientists. The federal government spends about half a billion dollars on the pursuit of oceanography. Many millions of dollars also come from nongovernmental sources— industry, foundations, and individual philanthropy.[16]

Many other countries, including the USSR, Japan, the United Kingdom, Canada, France, West Germany, South Africa, Denmark, other European nations, and some Latin American, African, and Asian countries, also have growing oceanographic programs.[17]

In the past few years, the international community's interest in oceanography has acquired such prominence, in terms of people, resources, and the finances involved, as to be recognized as "big ocean business."[18] The importance of oceanography for the well-being of mankind cannot be overstated. Covering nearly 70 percent of the earth, the oceans contain abundant natural resources. Furthermore, most of the natural phenomena that profoundly affect human continental life seem to be closely connected with oceanic processes.

Oceanography is directed, among other things, toward learning patterns of distribution of ocean resources and improving methods for locating them, comprehending the limits of their renewability and the effects of their exploitation on global ecology, providing better access to the maritime areas for nonresource uses such as navigation in general and recreation, examining the interaction between the earth and the atmosphere, controlling and modifying the weather, and more effectively anticipating natural disasters such as hurricanes and earthquakes.[19]

Much progress has been made in identifying the resource potential of the continental shelves and some of the problems of pollution that may arise in the course of their exploitation. Recent studies have also led to revolutionary new concepts of the history of the earth. Theories so far propounded about ocean circulation may soon result in better comprehension of climatic fluctuations.

Yet in many respects our present knowledge about the oceans may be only a beginning. A group of distinguished oceanographers pointed out that we need to move rapidly ahead with several important research projects to lay the groundwork for the exploration and exploitation of nonliving resources of the sea, for the improvement of techniques of conservation and harvesting of marine living resources, and for the establishment of a worldwide system of pollutant monitoring at sea. To carry out these and other vital oceanographic research projects, large capital investments and the pooling of research vessels, technicians, and scientists will be necessary.

Indicating the magnitude of certain needs of this research, Roger Revelle, a distinguished oceanographer, pointed out:

These include: some twenty-five survey ships to make the echo-sounding surveys required for detailed bathymetric charts of the world ocean; perhaps forty major research ships, half of which should be equipped for fishery research; about twenty fishing vessels for systematic resource evaluation; thirty-seven weather ships for weather stations in the Atlantic and the Pacific; a small aircraft carrier and escorts for magnetic surveys; three deep-sea drilling vessels; about two hundred "ships of opportunity" (merchant ships, naval vessels, and fishing boats), equipped for both meteorological and oceanographic observations; a nuclear powered submarine for studies in the Antarctic; two small, self-propelled manned submersibles with depth capabilities up to several thousand meters; several hundred deep-sea anchored buoys, instrumented for meteorological and sub-surface measurements; and an equal number of instrumented drifting buoys. A world-wide precision navigational system, using combined satellite and long-wave radio navigation, should be established to enable survey and research ships to fix their position within a few hundred meters, and a radio communication system for telemetering oceanographic data from ships and buoys should be developed. Earth-viewing satellites should be equipped for sensing temperatures and other surface and near surface ocean properties. Fixed monitoring stations should be established near river mouths and elsewhere near shore. These seagoing facilities must be backed up by research laboratories, biological sorting centers, analysis centers for pollutant monitoring programs, standardization and test facilities, data centers, and facilities for production and distribution of charts and other publications. Greatly increased arrangements for training and education of specialists in a wide range of scientific disciplines and engineering skills will be required, particularly for the developing countries.[20]

More fundamentally, international cooperation is required for the success of future scientific research at sea not only because the magnitude of the task and the size of the investment (in terms of wealth, knowledge, skills, and planning) involved are too enormous to be mobilized by a single institution or country but also because the areas of investigation fall under different countries' jurisdiction, however precisely and conservatively they may be defined.

Except for rare instances, scientific investigation at sea does not require the exclusive use of a maritime area for extended periods of time. Thus it can be assumed to be a compatible use with the nonliving resource exploitation and involves no particular spatial conflict problems.

However, problems involving conflicting jurisdictional claims can easily arise in the case of research at sea. Questions such as who should regulate what kind of a research in what areas are increasingly being asked. Indeed, as we will see below, the issue of the extent to which a coastal state is entitled to control research conducted in the continental shelf area has become one of the most critical problems of accommodation of multiple uses at sea.

INTERNATIONAL COMMERCE

International commerce has a capacity of 57,000 ships, representing a total of 268 million gross tons. It yields an annual revenue of about $40 billion. In less than a decade, the merchant fleet has changed in design and has grown in size about ten or more times. Consequently, nearly 228 oil tankers, known as giant ships, with 100,000 gross tonnage or more and a draft of 70 feet or more, are now in operation, transporting crude and refined oil from producing to consuming countries.[21] The daily movement of oil in 1972 totaled about 29 million barrels.[22]

The movements of the world merchant fleet are dominated by the flow of crude petroleum and refined products from their points of origin in the Middle East, the South China Sea area, and the north coast of South America to such destinations as Western Europe and North Africa, Japan, the United States, Canada, and other Western Hemisphere countries. For the purpose of international trade, nearly 62 straits are used, of which the Straits of Bosporus-Dardanelles, Dover, Florida, Gilbraltar, Hormuz, Lombok, Luzon, Malacca-Singapore, Mozambique, Skagerrak, and, should the Suez Canal be opened, Bab el Mandeb are considered to be the most important.[23]

The shipping lanes, situated above the continental rises, slopes, and shelves of the oceans, become congested with traffic as they approach major ports. Some of these ports are located in areas where offshore oil and gas drilling activities are also very extensive.

According to recent data, in the Gulf of Mexico area alone there are some 1,800 platforms.[24] An offshore platform can be used to drill as many as 62 different wells. It was estimated that by 1973 the United States had about 16,000 wells drilled in its offshore areas. The offshore installation can and did pose serious navigational hazards, whether due to human error or weather conditions or poor light and sound signals. A recent study of the collisions between commercial vessels and offshore installations in the Gulf of Mexico, undertaken for the purpose of determining the impact of offshore nuclear plants in areas of vessel traffic, reported eight collisions during a ten-year period (fiscal year 1963 to 1972) involving vessels of over 1,000 gross tons. During the same period, there were also twenty-two other collisions; fifteen of them involved vessels of less than 100 gross tons, and the remaining seven involved vessels between 100 and 650 gross tons.[25] The study added that in all these collisions, there was no loss of life involved, and damage to the rig was insignificant. Of the twenty-two small vessels, two fishing vessels were a total loss.

Offshore Islands

The construction of artificial islands at sea is being actively considered in order to solve problems posed by heavy industrial traffic and other environment-burdening activities in densely populated coastal areas. Such islands may be used as sites for deep-draft ports, industrial plants, disposal and treatment of wastes, power generators, small cities, and recreational facilities.

DEEP-DRAFT HARBORS

The growth in the size of the mechant ships, especially the oil tankers, has in recent years posed problems of access to several major ports. The depth of the existing channels leading toward these ports is not sufficient to accommodate the giant ships. In several cases, deepening the channel facilities may not be an acceptable alternative. Detailing the problems involved, one recent study noted that

Providing sufficient depth of channels to existing ports for supertankers would involve major extensions in the length of the offshore positions of the channel, especially in areas such as the Gulf of Mexico, where the slope of the continental shelf is relatively small. Movement of bed material by offshore currents could result in a high shoaling rate in the channel.

There are other constraints on accommodating these ships in existing harbors, for example, the existence of highway and railway tunnels under harbors or entrance channels and the need to move or build docks and other directly adjacent landside loading and terminal facilities. The cost of channeling through bedrock or moving tunnels or other structures almost certainly far exceeds the benefits to be gained by giving supertankers access to conventional harbors.

The same study concluded that therefore "one possible solution to this problem is to build offshore terminals.[26]

Efforts are already being made in the United States and other parts of the world to assess the desirability of establishing a few deep-draft ports in the offshore areas.[27]

OFFSHORE POWER GENERATORS

In assessing the energy demands of the United States, one source noted that "if present trends continue for the next fifteen years, we will need approximately 67 percent more oil, 33 percent more coal, and 100 percent more natural gas than we have consumed to date." In the same context, it was pointed out that

We must add as much new generating capacity as has been constructed since the invention of the lightbulb. If the increase continues at the present rate, the same amount of capacity—as much as has been constructed through 1969—would then have to be added in the following five years.[28]

In other words, it was estimated that the power needs of the United States would require over one billion kilowatts of installed electric generating capacity by the year 1990.

The power needs of Western Europe are also high. It was suggested, for example, that by 1975 it would require 1,600,000 kwh of electricity, though currently constructed plants can provide only one-half of that amount.[29]

It is against this background of critical energy needs of the international community that the feasibility of two different techniques of generating power at sea must be considered.

1. *Atomic Power Plants* Several designs are suggested for offshore atomic power plants. Basically, these involve either floating platforms or fixed structures. A fair economic analysis favors floating platforms over fixed structures.[30] According to one observer, offshore floating atomic reactors could become a familiar sight along the coasts of the United States and elsewhere by the middle of 1980.

As an indicator of the future prospects within the United States, a new business organization, Offshore Power Systems, was recently incorporated to set up an offshore power plant on a floating platform off Jacksonville, Florida. There are also plans to install a pair of floating nuclear reactors at a cost of $1,000 million in 45 feet of water on a site within the three-mile limit off New Jersey. The plants are expected to be mounted aboard 400-foot-square barges, honeycombed with water-tight bulkheads. Together, the plants and barges will stand 200 feet above the waterline.

The atomic power plants will be protected from storms at sea by semicircular breakwaters made from sand, gravel, rock, and concrete. Each breakwater, with a 50-foot breadth at the top and a 300-foot breadth on the ocean floor, will be designed to withstand gusts of 300 mph and to turn back waves as high as 50 feet. These plants are expected to come into operation by 1980.[31]

2. *Tidal Power Plants* Tidal power plants may also be considered as a supplement to conventional sources of electricity. This kind of power plant has several advantages: it avoids thermal pollution problems; it results in no radiation effects; it utilizes the almost inexhaustible supply of renewable resources; and it has several additional uses, such as for a railroad or improved navigation for estuarine ports. Nearly 100 sites have been suggested as favorable for the establishment of tidal power plants.[32]

Despite these advantages and the existence of appropriate sites, it appears that construction costs for tidal power plants far exceed the returns. So far, France is the only country with a tidal power plant in operation; built on the Rance River, it produces 544,000 kwh of electricity. The USSR, however, has completed an experimental plant.[33]

The construction of tidal power plants is most favored in bays, inlets, estuaries, and gulfs where there are narrow openings to the sea which allow for a large tidal exchange.

INDUSTRIAL DEVELOPMENT AND WASTE DISPOSAL

Off the westernmost part of Rotterdam Harbor, Holland has an artificial island constructed for industrial development. Another offshore island under the authority of the Amsterdam municipality is used for a similar purpose. Recently, a study considered the feasibility of establishing an artificial "sea island" on the Netherlands' continental shelf for several purposes including industrial development. The study examined the desirability and suitability of three different sizes of islands, their costs, the required engineering planning, and the various objectives that can be accomplished through the construction of an offshore "sea island."[34]

This study also noted the attractiveness of utilizing "sea islands" for waste disposal and treatment and for tackling problems of industrial pollution. With regard to the problems of pollution, the authors of the study pointed out that

In our opinion, the solution is not to be sought or found in curtailing industrial development, but rather in a direction where in the first instance residential and working areas must be clearly separated from one another. Moreover, uniform standards must be determined regarding the influence exerted on the environment; and if such plants by which pollution is caused are situated in a somewhat isolated location, such as an island, it would be possible to carry out regulations more efficiently.

In densely populated industrial areas, which often border shallow seas, the building of artificial islands may, against the background of this philosophy, provide a solution for many of these problems.[35]

SEA CITIES AND AIRPORTS

Several countries also have plans for the construction of offshore artificial islands. The United Kingdom is considering the building of a large international airport and a deep sea harbor at Maplin Sands, near Foulness to the northeast of London.[36] In at least three countries, Belgium, the United Kingdom, and the United States, off Hawaii, designers are examining the prospects for establishing an offshore "Sea City."[37] In almost every instance, an artificial island would require an exclusive maritime area including protective zones. In addition, many precautions would have to be taken, because of the specific objective of the island, to avoid interference from others using the area. Clearly, in the vicinity of a power plant, exploration for and exploitation of mineral resources and oil and gas resources would be risky.

Where waste disposal and industrial plants and sea cities are located, exploitation of offshore nonliving resources may raise problems of pollution and spatial conflict. Construction of oil rigs in the proximity of deep-draft ports and airports will certainly restrict the flow of traffic and create navigational hazards. Therefore, numerous problems of conflict have to be considered before allowing offshore mineral resource exploitation to coexist with other uses of the sea that also require exclusive maritime areas for their operation.

Recreational Activities

Recreational activities constitute one of the important uses of the sea. The islands of Hawaii, the Bahamas, Puerto Rico, Malta, and coastlines everywhere are popular as recreational centers. In the United States, for which relevant information is available, nearly 44 percent of the population favor water-related recreation over other forms.[38] Furthermore, according to one source, in 1968 nearly 112 million people participated in ocean-oriented activities and spent about $14 billion on them.[39]

The coastal zone—which is defined as including backland, the area in the vicinity of shore land, the beach, and the continental shelf—supports at least 27 kinds of activities relating to recreation, tourism, and aesthetic amenities.[40] Some of the popular recreational uses of the coastal zone are swimming, surfing, skin and scuba diving, pleasure boating, fishing, and water skiing.

Offshore mineral resource exploitation can pose problems for recreational use of the area in several ways. The drilling rigs and installations may exhibit themselves as unsightly structures, spoiling the scenic landscape. When erected in numbers, they may severely restrict the area available for boating, surfing, swimming, and other activities. Finally, and most important, in the case of a "blowout" the resultant oil pollution can deal a severe blow to the recreational opportunities of the area.[41]

Underwater Archaeology
Underwater archaeology is one of the growing uses of the sea. Over centuries significant historical and economic treasures have been lost at sea. In recent years, tools, techniques, and modern knowledge of marine sciences are brought to bear on locating and excavating the underwater archaeological treasures. For example, the government of Jamaica is engaged in excavating the relics of Port Royal, a city lost to the sea as the result of an earthquake that occurred about 300 years ago. There have been other interesting cases in different parts of the world involving either location or retrieval of significant archaeological finds. An ever-increasing number of scientists are now probing the waters of the Caribbean and Mediterranean. The Baltic Sea is also expected to have a high potential for the pursuit of underwater archaeology.[42]

In view of the value of underwater archaeology for the study of the past and for the lure of adventure and wealth it holds, it is important to accommodate these interests with that of offshore nonliving resource exploitation. The problems of conflict, if they arise at all, would involve the use of space, when the same maritime area is sought for both these uses. Underwater archaeology and offshore exploitation of mineral resources may thus be regarded as incompatible uses in the sense that they cannot coexist in the same place at the same time.

Artificial Reefs

In some remote cases conflicts may also arise between artificial reefs and mineral resource exploitation at sea. Artificial reefs made out of sunken ships, junked cars, and other waste materials can serve as useful habitats for fisheries. These reefs are often instrumental in increasing the fishermen's catch.

The case of the *San Diego,* a sunken ship, illustrates the type of conflicts that can result between interests involving artificial reefs and other marine uses. The *San Diego,* which provided a useful habitat for fish, was purchased by a metal company with a view to recovering the metals of its hull. The fishermen of the area opposed the company's move as it would deprive them of their livelihood.[43]

A similar situation of conflict could arise if mineral resource production were to be planned from the area in disregard of the artificial reefs that act as fish habitats.

Categories of Claims

The claims relating to the accommodation of multiple uses that arise out of the process of conflicts described above will generally invoke, on the one hand, the doctrine of the freedom of the seas and the rights of different users. On the other hand, the exclusive resource enjoyment rights granted to the coastal states may be invoked to support the counterclaims.

It should be pointed out that the coastal state, even under the new regimes of the ocean that have been proposed, will continue to have exclusive jurisdiction over resources of an area that may be described as the continental shelf or the "exclusive resource" zone. It is equally certain that beyond the limits of such exclusive coastal state's resource zone, the resources of the sea will be regulated through an international regime. In the latter area, which may be termed the "international area," problems relating to accommodation of multiple uses will also arise that are of equal importance.

For purposes of examining the trends in decision, the claims relating to multiple uses at sea may be identified as follows:

1. Claims relating to the accommodation of multiple uses in the continental shelf or "exclusive resource" zones;
   A. Claims relating to liability for pollution arising from marine mineral exploitation;

B. Claims relating to conflicts involving navigational and mineral interests;

C. Claims relating to the conduct of scientific research in the continental shelf or "exclusive resource" zones;

D. Claims relating to the accommodation of uses that require exclusive ocean space in the continental shelf or the "exclusive resource" zone;

2. Claims relating to the accommodation of conflicting uses in the "International Area."

Once again, subclaims similar to the categories described in the preceding section of this chapter will have to be considered.

Policies Relevant to the Accommodation of Multiple Uses at Sea

Shared use of the oceans will inevitably result in conflicts since multiple uses operate "in a physical world of finite space and resources" and they are conducted "at the direction of purposeful humans."[44] In each interaction the conflicts among multiple uses of the sea vary in intensity and occur in different combinations. For this reason, it is necessary not to postulate absolute and inflexible guidelines and priorities aimed at accommodation of competing and conflicting uses of the sea.[45]

Generally the context in which conflicts appear provides the criteria and indices necessary for resolving problems relating to accommodation of multiple uses. Several factors involved in the context may be noted in this connection. These include the nature of uses and users; objectives purported to be served; economic interests they represent; geographical space and time duration required by each use; community preferences expressed in favor of one or another use through organized or unorganized institutions; opportunities for technological innovation; immediate outcomes, long-term effects, and expectations of crisis attendant upon approval or denial of access to each use.

Furthermore, for the purpose of establishing priorities among different uses, which are sometimes mutually exclusive, a distinction can be usefully made between those uses that serve the basic needs of community and those that only enhance desirable options for participants. For example, if the conflict is between access for pleasure boating and fishing for commercial purposes, or between establishing an artificial island for housing gambling casinos and exploitation of oil and gas resources in the same area, the choice in favor of the latter kinds of activities to the exclusion of the former can be justified on the ground that they will help to meet the basic needs of the community.

In more general terms, the conflict between competing uses and particularly those between the exclusive interests of the coastal state and the inclusive interests of the general community could be resolved by considering the contextual factors. These may include, among other things, (a) the interests to be protected; (b) the significance of those interests to the coastal state; (c) the scope of authority asserted; and (d) the relationship between the claimed authority and the interests at stake.[46]

Within the broad framework of these considerations, the conflicts between offshore nonliving resource exploitation and other uses of the sea can be resolved and accommodated. More specifically, advance notification of the request for permission or lease to exploit nonliving resources in a given area must be made to other users of the area.[47] Any objections in this regard must be considered by the appropriate forums.

In addition, certain requirements may also help to minimize the possibilities of conflict between offshore nonliving resource exploitation and other uses and to lessen the impact of conflict where it cannot be avoided. These requirements include (a) prior permission for utilizing explosives in geological prospecting of maritime areas; (b) implementation of stringent safety measures to prevent accidents; (c) adequate preparedness to meet accidents; (d) proof that producers of nonliving resources have the financial ability to meet the costs of damage caused to other uses and users of the sea as a result of accidents; (e) proper identification of offshore structures to avoid undue interference with other uses; (f) removal of junk and proper sealing of wells after the exploitation of oil and gas resources so that other users can safely return to the area.

Trends in Decision

Evolution of the Law Relating to Multiple Uses in the Continental Shelf or the "Exclusive Resource" Zones
FREEDOM OF THE SEAS VERSUS THE DOCTRINE OF THE CONTINENTAL SHELF

For many centuries, the principle of freedom of the seas was regarded as an important function of international law. The principle of freedom of the seas meant, as G. Gidel noted in 1932, "that in time of peace every state and its inhabitants may make use of the high seas for navigation, fishing, the collection of its fauna and flora, the laying of submarine cables, and flying above it."[48] With few exceptions, the principle of freedom of the seas signified free and inclusive access to oceans, noninterference in others' activities, and the honoring of flag state jurisdiction over the activities of individual participants. Within the fold of these broad principles, the international community, until very recently, was able to accommodate multiple uses with a minimum of conflicts between users.

One major exception to the principle of freedom of the seas was the comprehensive and continuing authority and control granted to coastal states over their territorial sea. The international community also recognized the occasional exercise of limited exclusive authority and control by a coastal state for specified purposes, such as security, customs, and health, in maritime areas contiguous to the territorial sea.

However, by the end of the nineteenth century, the width of the territorial sea claimed around the world varied only between a minimum of three and a maximum of twelve miles. With the exception of the Soviet Union, which favored twelve miles, the rest of the coastal countries preferred either three or four or six miles of territorial sea.[49] The modest limits claimed for territorial sea was yet another indication of the special weight given to the principle of freedom of the seas.

At the time it claimed exclusive jurisdiction over the resources of the continental shelf, the United States, which had championed the doctrine of the freedom of the seas, took special care to state that the Truman Proclamation of 1945 was not meant to affect the "character as high seas of the waters above the continental shelf."[50] A large majority of coastal states that followed the example of the United States in claiming exclusive jurisdiction over the continental shelf adjacent to their shores exhibited similar respect for freedom of the seas. However, a minority of Latin American countries, which included Argentina, Chile, Costa Rica, and Peru, claimed sovereignty not only over the seabed and subsoil of the continental shelf but also over the superjacent waters and the air space above the continental shelf. Furthermore, some of the Latin American states, like Chile and Peru, claimed 200 miles as the outer limits of their continental shelves.[51] A majority of states regarded the attitude of the Latin American countries as a threat to the freedom of the seas. The United States, the United Kingdom, and other countries sent protest notes to these Latin American countries.[52]

The initial reaction of scholars to the unilateral proclamation on the continental shelf was mixed. One group of writers was of the opinion that claims relating to continental shelf, despite their express assurances, were incompatible with the principle of the freedom of seas. On this ground, these writers argued for the rejection of the doctrine of the continental shelf. Noting that the exploration for and exploitation of the continental shelf resources would involve fixed permanent installations, protective zones, and coastal state policing around them, George Schwargenberger warned that

Of necessity, therefore, any such claim amounts to the pretension of exercising exclusive control over a portion of the surface of the high seas. Thus *prima facie,* it constitutes a challenge to one of the basic rules underlying the principle of the freedom of the seas. . . . In fact, any claim to the right of exclusive appropriation of the resources of the continental shelf is the thin end of a dangerous wedge.[53]

Another group of commentators took a different view. Sir Hersch Lauterpacht argued that the doctrine of the freedom of the seas was not immutable, that the original assumptions on which it was founded were no longer applicable without important qualification, and that it was capable of adaptation to new circumstances. Admitting that the offshore installations "must constitute some obstacle in the way of unimpaired navigation both by their actual presence and by the necessity of protecting them from negligence or malicious design of passing or approaching vessels," the distinguished scholar added that

Unless abused, they may offend against the theory but not true object of the freedom of the seas. . . . The possibility of interference with the high seas is disturbing and provides a cause for apprehension only when viewed against the background of a rigid conception of the freedom of the seas impervious to reasonable requirements of economic life and scientific progress.[54]

Lauterpacht was conscious of the conflicts that might arise between the particular interest of the coastal state to enjoy exclusively the resources of its continental shelf and the more general interests of the community in protecting the inclusive access to the oceans for a variety of purposes. However, he believed that the situation did not pose any special problems and that "evaluation of conflicting interests and the effective recognition of those which, on balance, are entitled to protection is a constant feature of judicial activity as, indeed, of law in general."[55]

M. W. Mouton, a Dutch scholar, was of similar opinion. Referring to the sovereignty of states, he asked

. . . how could any State claim absolute sovereignty where in a community of States the rights and powers of one State are necessarily limited for the single reason that the State is not the only one and other States have rights and powers which form ipso facto a limitation on the rights and powers of the first State[?]

Extending the same logic to freedom of navigation, the author observed that "In pure theory and 'ad absurdum' we could say that pure freedom of navigation would only exist if but one ship sailed the oceans." Then Mouton discussed a few examples of possible conflicts between navigational interests and offshore oil and gas interests and pointed out that resolution of such conflicts "largely depends on the location, and of course the distance between them." He added,

If located somewhere in a bay or gulf, not frequented by shipping we can safely say that no practical obstacle exists. . . . It is, however, quite clear that if oil companies were left free in putting their constructions wherever they wanted, irrespective of other interests, a serious obstruction to shipping may arise, for instance, in narrow passages, straits frequented by shipping or approaches to harbors, in short, in shipping routes.

He concluded that

We maintain that building construction in the high seas is using the freedom of the seas just as much as navigating on these seas, or fishing in these seas or laying telegraph cables on the bottom of these seas. If Grotius had known about telegraph cables and oil derricks, he would have included them in the kind of use one can make of the high seas. . . .

The only thing we can reasonably ask is to avoid building these installations just there where congestion of shipping exists. In order to achieve a reasonable application of different ways of using the high seas, it would be recommendable to create an international body, judging plans submitted to it and giving binding decisions.[56]

CLARIFICATION BY THE INTERNATIONAL LAW COMMISSION

The International Law Commission, which in 1950 started its deliberation on progressive development and codification of international law, had quickly endorsed the view that the doctrine of continental shelf was essentially compatible with the principle of freedom of the seas. Following that premise, its members concentrated their efforts on the articulation of appropriate limits for coastal states' exclusive jurisdiction over the continental shelf.

After debating different formulations for over six years, the International Law Commission in its final drafts provided for limits of coastal states' exclusive authority and control over the continental shelf in the following terms:

First, it declared that the coastal state was granted only "sovereign rights" over the continental shelf. This implied rejection of coastal states' sovereignty and

. . . laying down the regime of the continental shelf only as subject to and within the orbit of the paramount principle of the freedom of the seas and of the air space above them. No modification of or exceptions from that principle are admissible unless expressly provided for in the various articles.[57]

Second, it stated that the exploration for and exploitation of the continental shelf resources "must not result in any unjustifiable interference" with navigation, fishing, or conservation of living resources of the sea. While admitting that the term "unjustifiable interference" sometimes involved subjective evaluation, the Commission defended the choice of the term on the ground that it allowed for the application of tests of equivalence and relative importance of the interests involved in reconciliation of inclusive and exclusive interests.[58] García-Amador explained the intention of the International Law Commission as follows:

The Commission was not unaware of the fact that the progressive development of international law which takes place against the background of established rules must often result in the modification of those rules by reference to new interests and needs. The extent of the modification must be determined by the relative importance of the needs and interests involved. To lay down, therefore, that the exploration and exploitation of the continental shelf must not result in any interference whatsoever with navigation and fishing might result, in many cases, in rendering somewhat nominal both the sovereign rights of exploration and exploitation and the very purpose of the articles as adopted. The case is clearly one of assessment of the relative importance of the interests involved. Interference, even if substantial, with navigation and fishing might, in some cases, be justified. On the other hand, interference, even on an insignificant scale, would be unjustified if unrelated to reasonably conceived requirements of exploration and exploitation of the continental shelf.[59]

In other words, it rejected any attempt to fix inflexible priorities among different uses of the sea. More specifically, it avoided giving undue prominence to the continental shelf interests over other interests.

Third, applying its general concepts to particular situations, the International Law Commission pointed out that installations established for the purpose of exploitation of continental shelf resources could be used by the coastal states neither to claim a belt of territorial sea around them nor to advance the base points for determining the extension of the territorial sea. In addition, the coastal states must give others due notice of any such installations constructed and must maintain permanent means for warning others of their presence. Furthermore, it was provided that installations could not be constructed in areas where "interference may be caused in recognized sea lanes essential to international navigation" even if they were necessary for exploration or exploitation of the continental shelf. Moreover, the coastal state must permit the laying of cables and pipelines in its continental shelf area; however, it could prescribe "conditions" for giving such permission. And, according to the Commission, the coastal state had no jurisdiction over the scientific research conducted in the superjacent waters. However, such consent was required only "for research relating to the exploration or exploitation of the seabed or subsoil." Even in this regard, the Commission expressed the belief that "the coastal State will only refuse its consent exceptionally, and in cases in which it fears an impediment to its exclusive rights to explore and exploit the seabed and subsoil."[60]

RESPONSES FROM THE GENEVA CONFERENCES ON THE LAW OF THE SEA, 1958

The Geneva Conference on the Law of the Sea held in 1958 approved these recommendations of the International Commission with minor differences. Accordingly, Article 2(1) of the Convention on the Continental Shelf states that the coastal state exercises sovereign rights over the continental shelf for the purpose of exploring it and exploiting its natural resources; Article 3 notes that the rights of coastal states do not affect the legal status of the superjacent waters as high seas, or that of the air space above those waters. Article 4 contains a prohibition against obstructions to the laying and maintaining of submarine cables and pipelines on the continental shelf; Article 5(1) proscribes "any unjustifiable interference with navigation, fishing or the conservation of the living resources of the sea" and provides for the protection of "fundamental oceanographic or other scientific research carried out with the intention of open publication"; Article 5(2), 5(3), 5(4), and 5(6) lay down qualifications for the establishment of permanent installations in the continental shelf area.

However, in a few provisions differing from the Commission, the Convention on the Continental Shelf provides for a slightly different emphasis on a coastal state's rights. Under Article 5(7), a provision adopted at the suggestion of Yugoslavia, it indicates that the "coastal State is obliged to undertake, in the safety zones [around the installations], all appropriate measures for the protection of the living resources of the sea from harmful agents."[61] Thus, the Convention afforded a much sharper focus on the obligations of the coastal state with respect to pollution arising out of the exploitation of the continental shelf. The International Law Commission earlier was satisfied with merely suggesting in its commentary that "everything possible should be done to prevent damage by exploitation of the subsoil, seismic exploration in connection with oil prospecting and leaks from pipelines." [62]

While the provisions of the Geneva Convention with respect to protection of living organisms may be considered an improvement over the Commission's version, its article on scientific research can be said to have only added to the equivocation of the Commission in this regard. In Article 5(8), the Continental Shelf Convention stipulated that "the consent of the coastal state shall be obtained in respect of any research concerning the continental shelf and undertaken there," and added that

Nevertheless, the coastal State shall not normally withhold its consent if the request is submitted by a qualified institution with a view to purely scientific research into the physical or biological characteristics of the continental shelf, subject to the proviso that the coastal State shall have the right, if it so desires, to participate or to be represented in the research, and that in any event the results shall be published.

This formulation entertained more qualifications with respect to the freedom of scientific research than were originally recommended by the International Law Commission. In addition, one is struck by its ambiguities. Shigeru Oda's observations may be recalled here to illustrate the point. He said,

Paragraph 1, based on the Danish proposal as adopted 25:20:10, appears strange even at first glance, since oceanographic or other scientific research may be inevitably affected by the very existence of the installations or equipment used for the exploitation of the continental shelf. If the provision means that the coastal State is prevented from interfering with scientific research in the superjacent waters, it merely states a truism. The coastal State entitled to the rights granted under Article 2 is obliged to see to it that injunctions of paragraphs 5 and 6 of Article 5 are observed by any enterprise connected with the exploitation of the continental shelf. There remains the question of how the research provided for in paragraph 8 differs from the research noted in paragraph 1; whether such research may not be the same as the exploration of the continental shelf reserved exclusively to the coastal State. [63]

Despite the ambiguities and equivocation in the language, it must be pointed out that the Convention, like the Commission, prohibited the coastal state from restricting the conduct of scientific research in the shelf area as long as such research did not physically interfere with the activities authorized by it.[64]

By way of summary of the law relating to accommodation of multiple uses of the sea, as it developed up to 1958, the following points may be emphasized: (1) all present and prospective uses of the high seas must be equally accommodated; (2) continental shelf exploitation must not result in any unjustifiable interference with other uses of the high seas; (3) in cases of conflict, resolution must be achieved in accordance with the tests of equivalence and relativity of interests involved; (4) under no circumstances must absolute and inflexible priorities among different uses of the sea be assumed.

NATIONAL LEGISLATION

Both prior to and after the adoption of the Geneva Convention on the Continental Shelf, several states indicated through their national legislation that the exclusive authority and control assumed over the continental shelf area was not meant to interfere with other legitimate uses of the high seas. These included navigation, fishing, scientific research, and the laying of communication cables and pipelines. Some of them had special provisions to prevent marine pollution arising from exploitation of natural resources in the continental shelf area. A few countries adopted rather detailed regulations incorporating policies regarding accommodation of different uses in the continental shelf area.

As an example, Norway ruled that offshore mining operations should not cause "unreasonable impediment or nuisance to shipping, fishing or aviation" and that they should avoid "damage or risk of damage to marine life or to underwater cables or other underwater installations" and "risk of pollution to the seabed and its subsoil, the sea and the air."[65]

In addition to the general prescriptions, the Norwegian decree of April 9, 1965, provided the following regulations to safeguard other interests in the continental shelf area:

a. The placement of drilling platforms and the erection of provisional or permanent installations in the continental shelf area require the approval of the Ministry of Industry.

b. The licensee should give adequate notice to others about the type and position of the installations being used, as well as the light and sound signals about them.

c. Survey vessels and aircraft engaged in continental shelf operations should keep safe distances from fishing vessels.

d. Detonation would be prohibited in the vicinity of vessels engaged in fishing or in the vicinity of floating or stationary gear or where schools of fish are discovered. Furthermore, detonation should not cause damage to underwater cables and pipelines.

e. Drilling would be prohibited within one nautical mile from cables and pipelines or installations and within two nautical miles from telephone or telegraph amplifiers.

The Norwegian decree also had regulations on the abandonment of wells, on the use of radioactive equipment, and on safe practices in exploring for and exploitation of petroleum resources in the continental shelf. In undertaking these activities, the licensee was required to adopt good oil field practices. With respect to the prevention of marine pollution, it said that

In case of explosions from blowouts, etc., in the well, all necessary steps shall immediately be taken in accordance with good oilfield practices to re-establish safe working conditions and bring the well under control. In addition, all necessary measures must immediately be taken to repair, as far as possible, all damage sustained.

On liability for violations, the Norwegian decree provided that "willful or gross negligent violations of this decree or of the provisions contained in regulations issued pursuant to this decree are punishable according to the applicable law in force."

By a separate decree of January 31, 1969, Norway promulgated regulations regarding scientific research on the natural resources of the seabed or its subsoil in Norwegian internal waters, territorial waters, and "in the part of the continental shelf which is under Norwegian sovereignty, but not in areas subject to private property rights." It was provided that a license for such research be granted without fee and for one particular investigation, unless otherwise decided in an individual case. Such a license would entitle the licensee to carry out the following operations:

a) Magnetic surveys
b) Gravimetric surveys
c) Seismic surveys
d) Thermal conductivity measurements
e) Radiometric measurements
f) Collection of samples from the seabed or its subsoil, provided that drilling is not involved.

Where other techniques of exploration were involved, the Norwegian Ministry of Industry and Handicrafts could grant permission on application.

As some of the conditions for issuing a license, the Ministry could demand Norwegian participation in the scientific research and could require that the expedition submit reports to the Ministry, that the findings be published and copies of publications or reports be submitted to the Ministry, and that any other information and material relevant to the proposed research be submitted to the Ministry on request. Finally, the scientific research must be conducted in a safe manner and must not unreasonably interfere with other activities and interests in the area.

However, as an exception to the general trend among states to honor inclusive interests in the continental shelf area, a few coastal states, for example, Brazil, the People's Democratic Republic of Yemen, and the USSR, prohibited foreign scientific research in their continental shelf area without their consent.[66] In addition, there were several countries that did not have specific continental shelf legislation concerning the management of multiple uses. Among them were Costa Rica, Cyprus, Greece, Guatemala, Iceland, Nicaragua, Oman, Peru, Turkey, and Western Samoa.

Against the background of the general principles of international law with respect to the accommodation of multiple uses, let us examine some of the claims that arise in the process of managing continental shelf operations.

Specific Claims in the Continental Shelf and "Exclusive Resource" Zones

Pollution from Mineral Exploitation
The record of the offshore mining industry is admittedly impressive in maintaining safety and preventing pollution. In most cases, careful planning and testing of the machinery associated with the conduct of operations should be credited for the good record. However, the possibility of breakdowns in the offshore operations and the resultant threat of marine pollution always looms large and cannot be ignored. Indeed, the experience of the United States in the case of the Santa Barbara oil blowout serves as a sobering reminder of the kind of accidents that can happen and of the kinds of claims which they give rise to.[67]

THE SANTA BARBARA CASE OF 1969
Santa Barbara, California, is a famous resort city in the United States. About 60 percent of the city's revenue comes from visitors, and an additional 20 percent is derived from so-called "clean industries" such as research, educational, and developmental institutions.[68]

In order to preserve its special idyllic setting, the California legislature passed the Cunningham-Shelf Act of 1955. The Act prohibited offshore drilling for petroleum in an area sixteen miles long and extending three miles out from the coast. In additon, the city and the county of Santa Barbara enacted zoning controls that outlawed shore-based oil extraction along the length of the sixteen-mile border.[69]

It must be noted that beyond the three-mile limit, the federal government exercises authority and control over offshore areas adjacent to California. Early in 1966 the federal government expressed an intention to lease the Santa Barbara channel area for petroleum recovery. The proposed lease area was about thirty miles from the city's beaches. Despite protests from the citizens and officials of Santa Barbara, the federal government, in February 1968, advertised 110 blocks of seabed area consisting of 5,700 acres each and received bids totaling $603 million for 75 of them.[70]

On January 28, 1969, one of the wells owned by the Union Oil Company suffered a blowout, resulting in the "Oil Disaster of 1969." For the next eleven days, the well lost reddish-brown crude oil in the Pacific Ocean at the rate of nearly 1,000 gallons per hour.[71]

The incident gave rise to three lawsuits:

1. On February 18, 1969, the state of California, the city and the county of Santa Barbara, and the city of Carpenteria claimed from the U.S. Secretary of the Interior $500 million for damage done to their interests because of oil pollution. The claim rested on three grounds: deprivation of claimants' property rights "without due process of law and for unlawful purposes"; negligence on the part of the Department of the Interior in arranging for the drilling in the Santa Barbara Channel; the conduct of an ultrahazardous activity by the federal government.

2. The state of California and other claimants at the same time brought a class action in the Calfornia Superior Court on behalf of themselves and others similarly situated against the Union Oil Company, operator of the federal lease on which the oil blowout occurred, its partners in the channel oil-drilling venture, Mobil Oil Corporation, Gulf Oil Company, and Texas, Inc., the drilling contractor, Peter Barden Drilling, Inc., and 500 unnamed persons.

The plaintiffs alleged five grounds for the class action: the defendants engaged in ultrahazardous activity, resulting in damage of not less than $500 million for the plaintiffs; they were negligent in the conduct of drilling operations, causing damage of not less than $500 million; the defendants permitted oil to escape from their well and thereby damaged, polluted, and contaminated plaintiffs' lands, waters, fish, wildlife, and personal property in the amount of not less than $500 million; the defendants negligently caused the destruction of various birds, fish, mammals, mollusks, and crustaceans protected by the laws of California; contrary to the laws of California, the defendants negligently permitted oil to be deposited into the waters of the state and thereby put plaintiffs to great expense of not less than $10 million in cleaning up the oil so deposited.

3. In February 1969, the Seacoast Marine Corporation, representing pleasure boating suppliers, sellers, and users; Dorothy Ferre, representing the users of the public beaches; three property owners; and Harrison Hall, representing the local fishermen, filed the third suit in the central District Court of California against the Union Oil Company and its partners. The claim, based on negligence and the conduct of ultrahazardous activity, was for damages of not less than $1.3 billion.

The defendants, the Union Oil Company and others and the federal government, adopted *damnum absque injuria* (injury without damage) and sovereign immunity, respectively, as defenses. However, the substantive issues presented by these legal actions have so far not been definitively decided and have been obscured by procedural and jurisdictional squabbles.

Meanwhile, the Union Oil Company agreed, though without admitting liability, to pay for the cleanup costs on public and private beaches, to pay compensation to a majority of the boat and property owners, and to have the federal district court send claim forms to 17,000 persons likely to have suffered damage from the oil slick.[72]

One of the issues raised by the Santa Barbara incident was whether offshore oil exploitation could or should be regarded as an ultrahazardous activity. Closely related to this issue was the question whether, in case of oil pollution, the person responsible could or should be held absolutely liable.

Under common law, in cases of damage resulting from ultrahazardous activity, defendants are held absolutely liable without proof of negligence or fault on their part. The principle of absolute liability was enunciated in the *Fletcher* v. *Rylands* case, where the water in a reservoir broke through into the unused shaft of a coalmine and flooded the adjoining mine of the plaintiff. In this connection, the court held that

. . . the person who for his own purposes brings on his lands and collects and keeps there anything likely to do mischief if it escapes, must keep it in at his peril, and, if he does not do so, is prima facie answerable for all the damage which is the natural consequence of its escape.[73]

This principle was found applicable in the *Green v. General Petroleum Corporation* case, where the defendant driller was held liable for damage from a "blowout" despite an express finding of "due care" in the conduct of his operations. The California court that decided on the case said,

Where one, in the conduct and maintenance of an enterprise, lawful and proper in itself, deliberately does an act under known conditions, and with knowledge that injury may result to another, proceeds, and injury is done to the other as the direct and proximate consequence of the act, however carefully done, the one who does the act and causes the injury should, in all fairness, be required to compensate the other for the damage done. The instant case offers a most excellent example of an actual invasion of the property of one person through the act of another. The fact that the act resulting in the "blow-out" was lawful and not negligently done does not, in our opinion, make the covering of respondent's property with oil, sand, mud, and rocks any less an actual invasion of and a trespass upon the premises.[74]

California is one of the many states that declared that "the drilling of an oil well is an ultrahazardous activity because it necessarily involves the risk of serious harm to lands, waters, fish, wildlife and personal property of others." The federal government, after the Santa Barbara incident, as noted above, imposed strict liability on the operators for removal of pollutants in case of accidents.[75] However, under the Outer Continental Shelf Lands Act of 1953, operators' liability toward third parties is governed by applicable law. In other words, depending on the state in which the claim arises, the availability of the grounds for absolute liability will be determined.[76]

Despite variations in state laws on the subject, Milton Katz of Harvard Law School believes generally that in activities such as offshore oil development there has evolved a doctrine of enterprise liability whether based on a theory of "strict products liability, on responsibility for abnormally dangerous activities, on the doctrine of *Fletcher v. Rylands*, or on nuisance."[77]

Indeed, beachfront owners, farmers of the seabed, pier owners, resort owners, and small boat owners, who are frequently damaged by oil pollution, have recovered compensation on grounds of nuisance or trespass. In *Arizona Copper Co.* v. *Gillespie,* the United States Supreme Court recognized that there is a remedy for injury from pollution regardless of the importance of the operation to either the public or the operator.[78]

While the United States, Canada, and a few other countries like India appear to hold offshore mining operators absolutely liable at least for certain purposes, several other countries have made operators' liability in all instances conditional upon the proof of negligence. In such cases, to establish negligence or the lack of it on the part of offshore mining operators, the test of "good oilfield practice," "reasonable care," and "accepted standards of petroleum technology" have to be applied.

According to these tests, whatever a majority of operators has decided to put into practice to ensure the safety of operations will constitute the standard on the basis of which negligence will be determined. Under these circumstances, there is real danger that offshore mining operators will give profits priority and will neglect the research and development of the technology necessary to improve the safety of offshore operations. Many states, in prescribing negligence as a ground for recovery of damage, may have been motivated to encourage offshore mining development without undue deterrents for the operators.

However, in the case of damage to other states and their nationals as a result of offshore operations conducted under the supervision of a state, the injured person would have no difficulty under international law in seeking reparation. Clyde Eagleton, in his influential work on international responsibility, pointed out the relevant well-established prescription thus:

If, by international law, a state enjoys exclusive jurisdiction within its boundaries, it does so upon the understanding that the state will endeavor to prevent or repair injuries to other states or their nationals within its jurisdiction.

Furthermore,

The obligation put upon the state by international law is an absolute one, and it is unnecessary to show that the state has been careless in the choice of its agents. The state is left free to create or authorize such agents as may be able to meet its international obligations. If these obligations are not satisfied by it, no question can be raised as to fault in the selection of its agent; the state cannot plead that it was not at fault and therefore not responsible. It is for the state to find a more effective system. It is in complete control of these agents, which cannot be reached by other states. It alone has given them their power to injure, and it must accept responsibility for any injuries occasioned through the exercise of this grant of power.[79]

In view of the responsibility to pay compensation to foreign states and their nationals as a result of damage caused to them by offshore operations conducted under its exclusive control, the coastal state, especially the developing coastal state, would be well advised to impose strict liability on the conduct of the offshore mining operators.

The imposition of strict or absolute liability in case of offshore petroleum operations is justified by the fact that most experts regard it as an ultrahazardous activity. V. E. McKelvey, Director of the U.S. Geological Survey, characterized them as "high-risk operations."[80] C. W. Jenks, a well-known international law expert and the Director of the International Labor Organization, regarded these operations as ultrahazardous and said,

It does not imply that the activity is ultrahazardous in the sense that there is a high degree of probability that the hazard will materialize, but rather that the consequences in the exceptional and perhaps quite improbable event of the hazard materializing may be so far-reaching that special rules concerning the liability for such consequences are necessary if serious injustice and hardship are to be avoided. Liability is shifted from fault (including negligence) to risk with a view to spreading more fairly the possible consequences of improbable but potentially dangerous misadventure, making the burden of insurance or the provision of other security for compensation in the event of misadventure a cost of the adventure, and eliminating a burden of proof which, in view of the nature of the risk, the victim cannot reasonably be expected to discharge and, in many cases, could never discharge; he can prove legal causation, in the sense of showing a required relationship between the fact of certain activities having been undertaken and the fact of damage, but he cannot prove what actually had happened or hope to prove fault or negligence.[81]

L. F. E. Goldie, in a persuasive presentation, similarly argued that

A plaintiff enterprise might be completely unable affirmatively to prove negligence, or even to establish any equivalent to res ipsa loquitur, not through any lack of validity to its claim, but due to the limited utility of those concepts in such situations. Hence, it is most strongly urged that the draftsmen of the relevant conventions and legislation should ensure, for reasons of policy and fairness, that negligence should be presumed, not as a permissible inference of fact, a res ipsa loquitur extrapolation from circumstantial evidence, but by virtue of a rule imposing the burden of disproof on the enterprise to which, under rules of absolute liability, the harm would be channelled.[82]

As for the deterrent that adoption of the absolute liability principle might pose for offshore developers of petroleum, one might recommend, as Milton Katz did, that the oil companies and other offshore mineral developers be permitted "to pool their resources to establish an insurance fund, whether as self-insurance or with the participation of insurance companies."[83]

The deterrent effect upon the offshore mining developers resulting from the imposition of absolute or strict liability can be further mitigated by the establishment of an upper financial limit for liability. Goldie pointed out that

A refusal of this security to the industry might destroy the object of imposing absolute liability—the protection of individuals who are helpless in their exposure to the risk created. To create a liability which might restrain the enterprise's liquidity, and perhaps even bankrupt insurance carriers, would achieve little more than the creation of an illusion of protection. Indeed, such a burden might threaten the international credit or economic stability of the country whose operations occasioned the disaster.[84]

Navigational and Mineral Interests
The trends in decision relating to the conflicts involving navigational and mineral interests may be either preventive or remedial and may be either restorative or redemptive. The development of traffic separation schemes aimed at channeling vessels along a fixed route may be mentioned among the trends in decision that attempt to prevent collisions between vessels and between vessels and mineral installations. Once collisions occur, a second category of decisions comes into play, and these are aimed at allocating liability among the parties involved on the basis of which damages are redeemed.

THE CONCEPT OF SHIPPING FAIRWAYS
The Gulf of Mexico is one of the areas that has witnessed growing competition among different uses for maritime space. Conflicts involving navigational and petroleum interests became evident in 1948, when one of the oil companies applied to the U.S. Corps of Engineers for permission to set up drilling platforms in the Gulf of Mexico near the entrance channel to the Galveston harbor. In response to an advertisement of the oil company's request by the Corps of Engineers, the American Merchant Marine Institute filed objections to the proposed action on the ground that fixed installations in the area would pose serious navigational hazards.

The result of the confrontation and the negotiations between the oil company people and the American Merchant Marine Institute, with the Corps of Engineers acting as a moderator, was the establishment of a shipping fairway five nautical miles wide leading up to the entrance to the Galveston harbor. Within the fairway, all structures were prohibited. As a result, the oil company's application was rejected since part of the area in question fell within the established fairway. Following the successful establishment of the first fairway, a more organized procedure was instituted to locate and modify fairways in the Gulf of Mexico. One observer summarized the current procedure thus:

New fairways, or modifications of existing fairways, may be proposed by the Corps, by mineral or navigational interests, or by other interested persons or agencies. Upon initiation of such a request, and in accordance with its established procedure, the Corps publishes a notice of the proposed promulgation or change (the substance of which will have been previously negotiated among the oil and navigational interests, the Corps, and other interested parties) calling for objections to the proposal. If there are none, the addition or modification is adopted upon the expiration of the time for filing of objections (usually thirty days). If objections are filed, a public hearing, of which due notice has been given, is held, but in some instances it is possible to handle the objections on an informal basis. In effect, the Corps acts as a mediator, and its practice is not to make any official promulgation without agreement of all interested parties. The latter commonly include fishing interests, the Department of Defense, the Department of the Interior and affected state agencies and local port authorities.

Following the resolution, at private meetings or public hearings, of any differences of opinion concerning the location of fairways, the Corps issues a notice of the action taken and adjusts its official maps accordingly. Since 1968 fairway designations have also been published in the Federal Register and printed on United States Coast Guard and Geodetic Survey charts.[85]

THE TRAFFIC SEPARATION SCHEMES

In addition to the development of shipping fairways in the Gulf of Mexico, the United States has also adopted voluntary traffic separation schemes for approaches to New York, San Francisco, Seattle, Boston, the Cape Cod Canal, Portland, Maine, Providence, Rhode Island, Los Angeles, Chesapeake Bay, Delaware Bay, and the Santa Barbara Channel. In accordance with the schemes, the vessels traveling to and from these United States ports are advised to use designated routes to avoid collisions and ease traffic tie-ups.[86]

The traffic separation schemes are not unique to the United States. Several countries of Europe have adopted similar schemes to regulate traffic flow. The Intergovernmental Maritime Consultative Organization through its Maritime Safety Committee has long advocated the desirability of establishing such schemes. Under its auspices, the international community has recently adopted a new convention revising the International Regulations for preventing collisions at sea. The revised Regulations, which take into account current technical developments, regulate the navigation of ships through separation schemes and are a significant improvement over the existing rules.[87]

The designation of shipping fairways and traffic separation schemes in most cases are only recommendatory in nature, and compliance with them is not compulsory for the navigating vessels. Two factors appear to be operating in this situation: First, the discretion of the ships' captains has long been regarded as the ultimate guarantor of the safety of vessels during voyages. For this reason, the creation of compulsory routes would limit the discretion of the ships' captains and might expose the vessel to real dangers in bad weather and other emergencies. Second, compulsory routes might on occasion entail unacceptable costs to vessels by denying them access to the shortest and most economic routes from port to port. Under such circumstances the question arises whether imposition of obligatory routes upon the shipping industry is an unreasonable interference with its legitimate rights under the doctrine of the freedom of the sea.

It cannot be denied that the coastal state has proper authority under the doctrine of the continental shelf to regulate reasonably other uses including navigation in the shelf area in the interest of the safety and efficiency of mineral resource exploitation. Designation of mandatory routes to and from its ports is reasonable, provided the coastal state has given navigational interests the opportunity to represent their case and has allowed them full participation in the process that led to their adoption. Any reasonable accommodation of the navigational and mineral interests resulting in the establishment of recommended or required paths of navigation would give additional weight to the net costs and benefits offered to the community by the available choices.[88]

THE LAW OF COLLISIONS AND LIABILITY

The United States admiralty law has fairly well-developed policies and prescriptions for dealing with claims of liability in case collision occurs between a navigating vessel and an offshore installation. Generally, in collision cases, liability is based upon fault. That is, in a collision between vessels A and B, four possible outcomes can be envisaged: Where vessel A or B alone is entirely at fault, it will be required to pay full compensation for the innocent vessel. Where neither of the vessels is at fault, each will be asked to absorb its own loss. Finally, where both vessels are at fault, without regard to the degree of their fault, the total loss will be divided equally between the two vessels. Thus, according to the principle of divided damages, if vessel A had a damage of $350,000 and vessel B had a damage of $250,000, the total damage of $600,000 would be divided equally, and vessel B would be required to pay $50,000 to vessel A in addition to absorbing its own loss all by itself. The principle of divided damages is strictly honored by higher United States courts despite persistent criticism and attempts by lower courts to apportion damages according to a system of proportionality for the liability involved. In addition, it must be noted that where a collision occurs between a moving vessel and an anchored vessel, the moving vessel is presumed to be at fault. It has been customary for the courts to equate offshore installations with an anchored vessel.[89]

For the assessment of liability, U.S. courts refer to the Rules of the Road that govern all maritime traffic when in the U.S. waters and to the International Rules of the Road, which are applicable to U.S. nationals only when on the high seas. All maritime nations have, by common consent, adopted virtually identical provisions with respect to the conduct of their own vessels on the high seas. These rules, which set standards of prudent seamanship in clear language, deal with the basic obligations of vessels in regard to navigation lights, sound signals, steering and sailing rules in both restricted and unrestricted visibility. As for the offshore installations, fault is measured by their conformity with the Coast Guard's applicable Rules and Regulations for Artificial Islands and Fixed Structures on the Outer Continental Shelf and the permit for its construction issued by the Corps of Engineers or a similar body.

Furthermore, it is a fact that most collisions between offshore fixed structures and navigating vessels occur when visibility is limited either by darkness or by inclement weather. Therefore, courts insist that the offshore installations comply assiduously with the required light and sound signals, in order to be free from liability. If a vessel can prove that the lights or sound signals of an installation were weaker than required, the operator of the structure has the tremendous burden of proving that such a violation could not possibly have contributed to the casualty.[90]

Thus far courts have not found occasion to determine the degree of fault attached to a vessel that has collided with an offshore structure after departing from a required or recommended path. In such cases, it is appropriate for the courts to presume fault on the part of the vessel, provided the departure from the recommended or required path is not justified on grounds of emergency, poor visibility, lack of information regarding a route that should have been available through due channels and charts, or any other reasonable cause.

The United States Admiralty law dealing with collisions, insofar as it reflects the general body of common law and equity on the subject, has very persuasive force with respect to similar cases elsewhere in the world.

Scientific Research in the Continental Shelf Area

In recent years, following the adoption of the Geneva Conventions on the Law of the Sea, it has been claimed that coastal states are increasingly asserting control over research conducted in the continental shelf area. The U.S. Department of State pointed out that, during the period from 1963 to 1971, on at least 36 occasions American scientists were refused permission to work in foreign offshore areas. In addition, another source noted about 22 instances in which scientists abandoned requests for clearance because of long delays and discouraging statements or action encountered during the clearance process. It was further suggested that in many unreported cases scientists did not even apply for access to certain countries because of past negative responses. Data are not readily available as to how scientists from other nations have fared in pursuing research at sea. Furthermore, the available data do not identify the countries that are responsible for these refusals, the nature of projects refused, and the areas involved in such refusals.[91]

From a survey of national legislation, which is often couched in general terms, it is readily apparent that coastal states do not necessarily perceive their obligations to protect scientific research in the shelf area in a similar way. While a few states expressly exclude the regulation of research from the exercise of the continental shelf authority, others merely imply it. Still another group of states is silent on the conduct of scientific research in the shelf area, even though they have specifically undertaken to safeguard freedoms relating to navigation and fisheries. Furthermore, a very small group of states claims that all research conducted in the shelf area should be subject to their prior authorization. In addition, there are a growing number of states (which are still in the minority) that claim more than twelve miles of territorial sea and insist that all research undertaken in the claimed area is subject to their consent. The attitude of the last group is not relevant in the present context in assessing the nature of coastal state's obligations in protecting scientific research in the shelf area.

Despite the variations noted above, several coastal states have adopted one simple criterion in judging whether research is subject to their prior consent. In many cases, the coastal state concerned requires its consent for any research project that involves physical contact with the shelf area. For example, it was noted that, according to this criterion, "measurements of magnetic fields of gravity, or the taking of acoustic sub-bottom reflection measurements, or water samples would not be considered to be shelf research." On the other hand, research involving the dredging and coring of the ocean floor, the laying of nets in the seabed area, and any action on the shelf itself is considered to be within the exclusive competence of the coastal state. Even though these guidelines exist, there is no guarantee that in the future the coastal states will not put more liberal interpretations on their authority to control any kind of research conducted in the shelf area.[92]

Indeed, in the United Nations Seabed Committee, several states advocated that scientific research be subject to the prior authorization and regulation of the coastal state when it had to be conducted in maritime zones under their sovereignty or exclusive jurisdiction. In other words, according to these countries, scientific research in internal waters, territorial seas, continental shelf and the subsoil thereof, and zones of special economic jurisdiction could be carried out only with the consent and under the control of the coastal states. The African states, members of the Organization of African Unity, the Latin American states, parties to the Santo Domingo Declaration of June 9, 1972, China, Pakistan, the Philippines, Iran, Tunisia, Romania, and Yugoslavia are some of the countries that support such a position. In addition, these countries insisted that, whenever an application was made requesting the consent of a coastal state for the pursuit of a project, the research in question could not be conducted without the express authorization of the coastal state. Thus they opposed a proposal by Italy that silence on the part of the coastal state for a specified number of days in regard to an application for consent could be treated as approval of the project.[93]

The developing countries, which advocate controls, fear that research at sea could be used by foreign countries as a cover for the pursuit of military and industrial intelligence. Incidents such as that involving the *Pueblo,* which undertook intelligence activity in the name of ocean science research, lend some credibility to such fears. It is also possible that marine industries might use the scientific data available from oceanographic expeditions to their advantage when engaged in lease negotiations with the less informed developing nations.[94]

It was also suggested that, in addition to the consent requirement, the coastal state should be entitled to take part on an equal footing in the scientific research carried out by other countries within its jurisdiction, and that it should receive data and samples as soon as they are available. It was further held that publicatiion of the results of the research at sea should in no way be prejudicial to the interests of the coastal state and should be subject to its prior consent. Even with respect to research in areas beyond the limits of a coastal state's jurisdiction, it was pointed out that the nearest coastal state should be given advance notification of the proposed scientific research and the opportunity to participate in it.[95]

Although they recognize the fears of the developing countries, several participants from the developed countries, especially those from the leading oceanographic institutions, are anxious to avoid unduly burdensome coastal state controls over scientific research at sea. While indicating the need for relative freedom of access for marine scientists, as well as the ill effects of the requirement of the coastal state's prior consent, this group has listed several obligations to be imposed upon the oceanographic community to meet the legitimate concerns of the coastal states and of the developing countries. Reflecting these suggestions, Article 7 of the United States' draft on the subject lists the following set of obligations:[96]

1. Advance notification to the coastal state;
2. Meaningful participation by the coastal state in the research directly or through an international organization of its choosing;
3. Sharing of all data and samples with the coastal state;
4. Assistance directly or through an international organization to the coastal state in interpreting the data and samples;
5. Flag-state certification that the research is being conducted by a qualified scientific research institution;
6. Publication of significant research results in an open and readily available scientific journal;
7. Required compliance with all applicable international environmental standards; and
8. Prior consent of the coastal state for the conduct of scientific research in its territorial seas.[97]

In addition to these obligations, it was also indicated that the oceanographically advanced countries should be prepared to offer the transfer of technology suitable to the needs of the developing countries and third-party settlement of disputes that might arise in the course of the execution of any research project.[98]

These offers appear to have no significant effect on the attitude of the advocates of control. No matter what the outcome of the Third Law of the Sea Conference may be, it is likely that more coastal states will demand prior consent for any research conducted in maritime areas under their exclusive jurisdiction. Such controls might very well provide a sense of accomplishment for some of the developing countries.

However, the costs of enforcing rigid coastal state controls over scientific research in wide maritime areas must not be underestimated. If coastal state controls are accepted in an area of 200 miles or up to the edge of the continental margin, which reaches a depth of about 3,000 meters, nearly 40 percent of the marine area in which about 80 percent of the interesting marine science research is done will be subject to the control of the adjacent coastal state. Such coastal state controls may on occasion result in refusal of proposed research projects for reasons not connected with their scientific merit. They may also cause inexorable bureaucratic delays. Political accessibility of an area will become crucial for undertaking any oceanographic research. Such extraneous considerations will thus undercut the overall value of the research done. They may also result in unnecessary duplication of work due to the unfortunate reordering of research priorities and, in some cases, commitment of the limited number of scientists and the scarce, valuable equipment.

There are costs even for the developing countries. Under a system of rigid controls the offshore areas under their jurisdiction will not yield any scientific information. Without such information they may remain economically underdeveloped, as marine industries would rather risk their capital in better-known areas. Even if a few industries venture to lease out such areas from the developing countries, the latter will not be in an independent position to assess the value of the area in question. In this sense, the developing country will be exposed to the same industrial blackmail that it seeks to avoid by self-regulation of ocean science research. Furthermore, if the developing country wishes to have an independent evaluation of the resource potential of the area under its control, it may even have to pay an oceanographic institution for such a service. Indeed, it would be unfortunate if the developing countries had to pay for something they could have obtained free of cost under different conditions. Finally, in a world of continuing political rivalry and unequal capabilities, the developing countries may not succeed in preventing threats to national security and economic independence by rigidly controlling marine science research, for this kind of regulation gives them very little real protection. By adopting such controls, they will, however, succeed in crippling the pace and utility of future ocean science research not only to their own detriment but to the detriment of the entire world community.[99]

It is hoped, therefore, that no matter who controls science research in any maritime area, the policy will facilitate the building of a broader base of knowledge about oceans that can be used to benefit all countries, especially the developing nations.

Accommodation of Uses That Require Exclusive Ocean Space in the Continental Shelf Area

So far, we have been concerned essentially with conflicts that arise between those uses that do not require any exclusive ocean space for extended duration and the continental shelf activities that need such an arrangement. Now we will turn to the conflicts that arise between such uses as the establishment of deep-water ports, industrial and other waste disposal plants, sea cities, the laying of cables and other communication lines, and the continental shelf activities where both the types of uses demand exclusive ocean space.

One of the questions to be considered here is whether a deep-water port or industrial plant and the like can be established in the continental shelf area of a coastal state without its permission. It may be argued that insofar as an entrepreneur does not indulge in natural resource exploration and exploitation, he can establish an artificial island or installation in the shelf area without violating the exclusive rights of the coastal state. However, it can be pointed out that the enterprise by occupying a certain area of the shelf for an indefinite period denies the coastal state an opportunity to explore and exploit the resources therein. In view of this possibility of infringement of its exclusive rights, the coastal state could claim the right to prohibit occupation of the continental shelf by foreign entities.

In the case of the *United States* v. *Ray*, the issue arose whether Acme General Contractors, Inc., could construct an artificial island in an area called Triumph Reef (which is located approximately fifteen miles southeast of Dade County, Florida) without the permission of the United States government. According to Mr. Ray of Acme General Contractors, Inc., it was proposed that the island be constructed for the purpose of building and operating a ship's servicing store. The site included a coral reef and was attractive to commercial as well as sports fishermen and to marine research biologists.

The U.S. government brought a suit against Acme General Contractors, Inc., for trespassing. While the court thought the allegation was inaccurately framed, it decreed that Acme's occupation of the area would be an infringement of those rights that appertain to the United States and that are under "national and international law subject not only to its jurisdiction but its control as well." [100]

Another incident, which may be referred to as the "Abalonia incident," which did not result in judicial determination of the claims involved, is also worth mentioning in the present context. A group of entrepreneurs decided to establish a new nation called "Abalonia" in the Pacific Ocean, on Cortes Bank, a submerged geological structure located approximately 110 miles west of San Diego, California. This area apparently was rich in abalone and lobster and to a large extent remained unexploited. The purported plan of Abalonia's creators was to build a "tax-free sovereign" processing plant on the bank and to use divers to harvest the abalone and lobster. In order to create an artificial island on which to operate, the entrepreneurs obtained a 366-foot World War II troop ship and towed it out to Cortes Bank with the intention of sinking it in an area two fathoms deep. However, before they could sink the ship, unanticipated rough seas snapped one of the mooring lines, and the ship was dragged to deeper water; there the project ended.

About the same time, the U.S. Interior Department, regarding the Cortes Bank area as within its exclusive jurisdiction, offered to lease the area by publishing a notice in the *Federal Register* on December 20, 1966. Such a publication, according to Interior Department administrative practice, constituted official assumption of jurisdiction over an ocean bottom area under the authority of the Outer Continental Shelf Lands Act of 1953.[101]

If the fateful event had not occurred and the entrepreneurs had persisted in building Abalonia, the U.S. government, by invoking the precedent of the *United States* v. *Ray,* would have succeeded in preventing their proposed action. However, in both the instances noted, the areas in dispute contained resources—coral reefs in one case, and lobster and abalone in the other—which fall in the category of natural resources that would have been denied to the coastal state if the proposed occupation had been allowed.

If, on the other hand, the building of an artificial island or structure were proposed in an area in which there could not be an apparent conflict with the exclusive "natural resource" interest of the coastal state, could the state prohibit such an action merely on the ground that it took place in its continental shelf area without its prior permission? Such a situation could theoretically arise if the area selected for occupation proved to be of no interest from the perspective of "natural resources," as defined by the Convention on the Continental Shelf. In such a remote and hypothetical case, the answer appears to be clear that the coastal state cannot prohibit proposed occupation by invoking its continental shelf authority and control.

To a certain extent, the limitations on the exclusive jurisdiction of the coastal state under the doctrine of the continental shelf were exposed in the unusual case of pirate broadcasting in the European waters. In at least one of the incidents, the Reclame Exploitatie Maatschappij N.V. (R.E.M.) began transmitting radio broadcasts on July 29, 1964, and television broadcasts on August 15, 1964, from a platform supported by legs resting on the seabed and situated in international waters off Noordwijk on the part of the continental shelf that is under the Dutch jurisdiction.

This radio and television transmission was in direct violation of Dutch regulations in the Wireless Telegraphy Law of 1904, which, however, could not be extended to regulate transmission from outside Dutch territorial boundaries. Since the transmission station was outside the three-mile Dutch territorial sea, the law could not be readily applied. Also, the Dutch authorities did not feel that they could prohibit the activity in question under their continental shelf authority. Instead, they passed a separate statute extending Dutch criminal law and the jurisdiction of Dutch authority to "installations constructed on the bed of that part of the North Sea which falls outside the territorial waters and within the boundaries of that part of the continental shelf appertaining to the Netherlands." The Dutch Wireless Telegraphy Law of 1904 was accordingly applied to R.E.M. installations, and on December 17, 1964, the Dutch police sealed off the station and shut off the transmission.[102]

The Dutch authorities could have used their exclusive continental shelf competence to vacate the radio and television station in question not only because the transmission was illegal according to the Telegraphy Law 1904 but also because the station was situated in an area of actual or potential natural resource value. This approach, however, raises the issue of the burden of proof: Who should establish that the disputed area is or is not of value from the point of view of the natural resources? Should it be the coastal state, which seeks to authorize and control the fixed installations, or the entrepreneur, who wishes to establish them? In some cases, tangible proof may be very difficult to produce.

Given the fact that the coastal state is accorded exclusive rights over the resources of the shelf and also the fact that knowledge about the kinds of resources in the area and the technology available to exploit them are continuously evolving, it is fair to assume that, unless proved to the contrary, the area is of value to the coastal state. If this assumption is allowed, two conclusions will arise: (1) that the burden of proof rests on the entrepreneurs seeking to establish a fixed structure on the shelf to show that the area does not have "natural resource" value for the coastal state; and (2) that in the absence of such proof, fixed installations cannot be established in the continental shelf without the consent of the coastal state.

From the above discussion it follows further that where a fixed installation can be established in the shelf area without violating the coastal state's rights, its existence is subject to the principles of the doctrine of freedom of the seas. That is, among other things, it cannot be treated as an island in order to appropriate permanently a portion of the high seas and to claim a territorial sea around it. It should also be constructed with reasonable regard for the interests of other participants. Applying some of these principles to the establishment of fixed buoys or data stations in the high seas, the joint UNESCO-IMCO report on the legal problems associated with Ocean Data Acquisition Systems (ODAS) arrived at the following conclusions:
1. Freedom of the high seas includes the "freedom of research in the high seas";
2. No state may exercise exclusive sovereign rights of the high seas for the conduct of research by means of ODAS;
3. No state may restrict the reasonable conduct of such research by other governments or by individuals over whom it has no personal jurisdiction;
4. States are under an obligation to ensure that such research undertaken by them or by their nationals is conducted with reasonable re-

gard to the interests of other states in their exercise of the freedom
of the high seas;

5. A state is permitted by international law to place additional restrictions on the conduct of research on the high seas for its own nationals and vessels but not for persons over whom the state has no
   jurisdiction.[103]

In judging the legitimacy of fixed installations in the high seas, a crucial requirement is evidence of reasonable regard for the inclusive
community interests. To measure compliance with this requirement,
decision-makers examine several contextual factors. Among them are
the objectives sought, the location and extent of the area required, the
duration of the intended occupation, the scope and nature of the rights
claimed, and the degree to which others are affected.[104]

In the context of the U.N. seabed negotiations, a few delegations referred to the status of artificial islands and installations in the continental shelf area. Belgium, in a special letter to the U.N. Secretary-
General, requested that the question of "jurisdiction over artificial
islands or artificial installations" be included in the list of subjects to
be discussed by the Third Law of the Sea Conference. According to
Belgium,

In the event that structures of this kind were to be built, they could not
be included within any jurisdiction under existing international law.
Thus, there appears to be something of a judicial and juridical vacuum,
at variance with international public order.[105]

Interpreting the provisions of the Geneva Convention on the Continental Shelf too restrictively, as Holland did in a different situation,[106]
Belgium claimed that it had no competence to decide on the application
of a private source to establish an artificial port in its continental shelf
area. The proposed port that was meant for the unloading of heavy
tankers was to occupy permanently an area of 170 hectares and was to
be situated at about 27 kilometers from the Belgian coast.[107]

In view of the foregoing analysis on the subject, Belgium's hesitancy
in considering the legality of the proposed construction was unjustified.
It could at least have decided whether there were "natural resources"
involved in the proposed site.

In response to the Belgian request, several delegations agreed to
consider the status of artificial islands and installations as a separate
agenda item for the Third Law of the Sea Conference. In this connection, several Latin American countries advocated a much broader

definition of rights of the coastal states with respect to the continental shelf and "patrimonial sea" areas. Referring to the shelf rights, the Argentinian representative, for example, noted that

Although the extraction of minerals or oil was currently the most important utilization of the continental shelf, it was already possible to conceive of other uses which went far beyond the concept of exploration and exploitation of the natural resources of the shelf. [The Argentine] delegation therefore considered that Article 2 of the 1958 Convention of the Continental Shelf was too restrictive, since it only recognized exclusive sovereign rights for coastal states for the purpose of exploration and exploitation. It considered that the article should be amended to make the sovereignty of the coastal state not only exclusive but complete without in any way affecting the legal status of the superjacent waters, either in the area under national jurisdiction or in the high seas. The coastal state's sovereignty should extend over the whole of its submerged territory.

Uruguay, Peru, and Brazil also endorsed this view. Furthermore, with respect to the proposed patrimonial sea, Article 7 of the draft articles submitted by Colombia, Mexico, and Venezuela provided that

The coastal state shall authorize and regulate the emplacement and use of artificial islands and any kinds of facilities on the surface of the sea, in the water column and on the seabed and subsoil of the patrimonial sea.[108]

Arvid Pardo's draft of the Ocean Space Treaty approached the status of artificial islands and other installations from a slightly different perspective. It authorized the coastal state to construct, maintain, and operate "on or under the seabed of national ocean space habitats, installations, equipment, and devices for peaceful purposes." Within the same area, which extends up to 200 miles, it also allowed the coastal state to establish artificial islands, floating harbors or other installations, or unanchored floating devices for "peaceful purposes.[109]

Pardo's draft does not, however, mention whether the coastal state's rights with respect to artificial islands and installations are exclusive. Perhaps the omission is unintentional. Nevertheless, insofar as it restricts the coastal state's right to "peaceful purposes," the Pardo formulation is distinct from the Latin American position. The restriction thus suggested may not be acceptable to several delegations that regard the phrase "peaceful purposes" as ambiguous and open to subjective and conflicting interpretations.

The concept "economic zone," advocated by Kenya, several of the African countries, and others, is limited to the management of living and nonliving resources and does not deal directly with the status of artificial islands and installations in the area. But it is fair to assume that the proponents of the exclusive economic zone, following the lead of the advocates of the patrimonial sea concept, would have no objection to extending the scope of the coastal state's jurisdiction in the area to cover all activities except the freedoms specifically excluded.

While it may still be too early to predict the exact outer limits of the "economic zone" or "patrimonial sea" that will be put exclusively under the jurisdiction of the coastal state, it is almost certain that its authority in this area will be extended to include the regulation of artificial installations and islands. Considering the exclusivity and comprehensiveness of the resource interest of the coastal state, as pointed out above, it is in the common interest to extend its authority and control in this way over all activities in the area which require occupation of the seabed and ocean floor for indefinite periods. Such a step would even eliminate the problems of the burden of proof.

The legal position regarding the laying of submarine cables and communication pipelines in the shelf and in the proposed exclusive resource zones differs from that involving artificial islands and installations, which incidentally include the pipelines for oil and gas and other resources.

National legislation on the nature of the shelf rights claimed by the coastal states was mostly in conformity with the doctrine of the continental shelf as enunciated by the Geneva Conventions and as evolved through the customary process. Under its terms, the freedom to lay submarine cables and pipelines remained unaffected, subject only to the reasonable regard of a coastal state's rights over the shelf. M. S. McDougal and W. T. Burke explained the law thus:

> This was understood to mean, as the [International Law Commission] Commentary explicitly stated, that the "coastal State is required to permit the laying of cables on the seabed of its continental shelf, but . . . it may impose conditions concerning the route to be followed." This latter reference to "conditions" seems to have been intended to convey the idea that the coastal state was not liable for the additional expense required for laying more cable than would otherwise have been needed. On the other hand, it was declared during Commission discussion and stated by Professor François in his 1953 Report that the coastal state (or, more probably, the operating oil company) would be required to pay for the cost of moving cables if this were necessary before exploitation could be undertaken.[110]

While introducing and advocating the exclusive "economic zone" and "patrimonial sea" concepts, their sponsors explicitly stated that the freedom to lay submarine cables and pipelines would not be affected.

Article X of the draft articles on the "economic zone" proposed by Kenya, the Santo Domingo Declaration of June 1972, the Yaoundé Conclusions of the African states' regional seminar on law of the sea of June 1972, the draft articles submitted by Colombia, Mexico, and Venezuela, all have specific provisions to that effect. Explaining the similarities between the "economic zone" and the "patrimonial sea" concepts in this respect, Jorge Castañeda of Mexico noted that "the establishment of such (an exclusive resource) zone would in no way affect freedom of navigation or other customary freedoms, such as freedom of overflight and freedom to lay submarine cables and pipelines."[111]

On the laying of submarine cables and pipelines, the Maltese (Pardo's) draft of the Ocean Space Treaty in Article 27(5) provided that

Subject to its rights to take reasonable measures *for the regulation of navigation, for the prevention of pollution* and for the exploration and exploitation of the natural resources of *national ocean space,* the coastal state may not impede the maintenance of submarine cables and pipelines. [Italics in original][112]

The two additional rights of the coastal state—regulation of navigation and of pollution—mentioned in the Maltese formulation are not really separate from the totality of rights assumed by the coastal state under the doctrine of the continental shelf; nor are they different from the kinds of rights intended for the exclusive enjoyment of the coastal state under the economic zone or patrimonial sea concepts. Except for the elaboration of the nature of coastal states' rights contained in the Maltese draft, it sought to regulate the freedom to lay submarine cables and pipelines in the national ocean space in the same manner as the concepts of economic zone or patrimonial sea are expected to do.

Accommodation of Conflicting Uses in the "International Area"

Freedom of the Seas and the Conflicting Uses
In the "international area," which is beyond the limits of the continental shelf or other exclusive resource zones that may be accepted, conflicts among different uses will have to be resolved on the basis of the doctrine of the freedom of the seas. The doctrine of the freedom of the seas as it has evolved through the customary process is captured in Article 2 of the Geneva Convention on the High Seas. It says that

The high seas being open to all nations, no state may validly purport to subject any part of them to its sovereignty. Freedom of the high seas is exercised under the conditions laid down by these articles and

by other rules of international law. It comprises *inter alia* both for coastal and non-coastal states:
1) Freedom of navigation;
2) Freedom of fishing;
3) Freedom to lay submarine cables and pipelines;
4) Freedom to fly over the high seas.
These freedoms and others which are recognized by the general principles of international law shall be exercised by all states with reasonable regard to the interests of other states in their exercise of the freedom of the high seas.

M. S. McDougal and W. T. Burke pointed out the implication of this provision thus:

At the 1958 Conference, states succeeded in making it clearer than had the Commission that the principle of free access to the sea is a flexible one, permitting expansions of types of use as long as an accommodation may be made in accord with the standard of reasonableness. Article 2 of the Convention on the High Seas retains the Commission's enumeration of the classical freedoms and also uses the phrase *"inter alia."* In addition, moreover, Article 2 emphasizes the open-endedness by referring to "These freedoms, and others which are recognized by the general principles of international law. . . ." In supplement to these positive steps, the Conference, or the relevant committee, in rejecting certain proposals restrictive of the purposes of access to the sea, furnished further indication of the general consensus on promotion of free access for all purposes.[113]

Major components of this doctrine of the freedom of the seas relevant to management of conflicting uses of the high seas, cited on previous occasions, may be usefully recalled here:[114]

1. *Flag-state jurisdiction:* Each user of the area is subject to the authority and control of the state whose flag he flies and cannot be interferred with by others except under generally agreed conditions.
2. *Nonappropriation of the area:* Under no circumstances is a participant allowed to claim ownership or sovereignty over an area on the basis of the activity undertaken there.
3. *No unreasonable interference with other users:* In pursuing his activities, each participant must show regard to other users and should not unreasonably interfere with them.

In the case of novel activities, before they can be justified in terms of the doctrine of the freedom of the seas, the question remains whether such activities can be allowed under the "freedom" doctrine recognized by the general principles of international law. If a different regime is accepted by the world community for a novel activity, other than the freedom of the seas doctrine, a further question arises as to its compatibility with other uses. It is also possible that the Third Law of the Sea Conference may replace the doctrine of the freedom of the seas with a new international regime for regulating different kinds of present and possible uses in the international area.[115]

With respect to the seabed and subsoil of the international area and the exploration and exploitation of the mineral resources therein, the consensus is that they should be subject to the regime of the "common heritage of mankind" and to regulation by the international machinery established for this purpose.

"Principles" Relating to Activities in the International Area and Competing Uses

The U.N. General Assembly in its Resolution 2749 (XXV) of December 17, 1970, declared, among other things, that

1. The sea-bed and ocean floor, and the subsoil thereof, beyond the limits of national jurisdiction (hereinafter referred to as the area), as well as the resources of the area, are the common heritage of mankind.

2. The area shall not be subject to appropriation by any means by States or persons, natural or juridical, and no State shall claim or exercise sovereignty or sovereign rights over any part thereof. . . .

4. All activities regarding the exploration and exploitation of the resources of the area and other related activities shall be governed by the international regime to be established. . . .

9. On the basis of the principles of this Declaration, an international regime applying to the area and its resources and including appropriate international machinery to give effect to its provisions shall be established by an international treaty of a universal character, generally agreed upon. The régime shall, *inter alia*, provide for the orderly and safe development and rational management of the area and its resources and for expanding opportunities in the use thereof, and ensure the equitable sharing by States in the benefits derived therefrom, taking into particular consideration the interests and needs of the developing countries, whether land-locked or coastal. . . .

13. Nothing herein shall affect:
   (a) the legal status of the waters superjacent to the area or that of the airspace above those waters; . . .

14. Every state shall have the responsibility to ensure that activities in the area, including those relating to its resources, whether undertaken by governmental agencies, or non-governmental entities or persons under its jurisdiction, or acting on its behalf, shall be carried out in conformity with the international régime to be established. The same responsibility applies to international organizations and their members for activities undertaken by such organizations or on their behalf. Damage caused by such activities shall entail liability.[116]

The U.N. resolution may be interpreted to mean that all activities that require physical occupation of the seabed and the ocean floor of the international area and the exploration and exploitation of the living and nonliving resources therein should be subject to the regulation of an international regime and its machinery. However, navigation in and flying over the international area will be left to be governed by the doctrine of the freedom of the seas. The resolution was not clear as to the status of scientific research in the area.

Thus, in effect, the same system of accommodation of conflicting uses obtaining in the continental shelf area is proposed in terms of the "principles" resolution in the international area, with just one exception: the international machinery, instead of the coastal state, will assume the role of regulation of competing uses. With respect to navigation, where necessary, traffic separation schemes and fairways will be adopted even in the deep-ocean international area to avoid collisions between different vessels and between vessels and fixed installations. The international machinery, under the terms of the U.N. resolution, will also have to decide under what circumstances fixed installations not meant for mineral exploitation can be allowed in an area. No matter what the precise shape of the future international regime is, the practice that has been developing for the shelf area will prove useful in adopting suitable policies and regulations to accommodate different uses in the international area.[117]

Following the adoption of the U.N. Declaration on Principles Governing the Seabed and the Ocean Floor, and the Subsoil Thereof, beyond the Limits of National Jurisdiction, the issue of accommodation of conflicting uses received more specific attention from various delegations to the U.N. Seabed Committee.

Draft Proposals on the International Regime and Management of Multiple Uses

Several draft articles characterized the international area as a "common heritage of mankind." Canada explained the implication of the proposals in this regard as follows:

It should be noted that difficulties could arise from the affirmation that the international sea-bed area itself and not only its resources is the common heritage of mankind. This could be taken to imply that all cases of and activities on the sea-bed beyond national jurisdiction, and not only those activities directly related to resources exploration and exploitation, should necessarily be regulated by the international regime and machinery to be established.

The Latin American, the Tanzanian, and the Maltese drafts did not regard this as a "difficulty," and advocated affirmatively that all activities in the international area be regulated by the international machinery. The United States draft, however, proposed that each "Contracting Party" to the international regime be left free to exploit the living resources of the area, subject only to conservation measures. The United Kingdom draft, on the other hand, favored strict definition of the resources proposed to be put under the authority of the international machinery. It suggested that the regime should embrace "mineral resources of the sea-bed beyond national jurisdiction at present known, including hydrocarbons, manganese nodules, phosphate deposits and mineralized muds, but not minerals recovered from the actual water of the seas." It added further that "it would seem more natural to regard such minerals pertaining to the high seas. Sedentary living resources capable of commercial development would also be subject to the regime although we do not at present know of any such existing at substantial depths."[118]

Canada also doubted the existence of commercial quantities of fish beyond depths of approximately 1,800 meters. Keeping its options open on the status of living resources in the area, Canada argued that "it would be unrealistic to attempt to have the future regime govern all uses of and activities on the sea-bed beyond national jurisdiction." However, the Canadian proposal found it "necessary for the regime to have certain connected regulatory powers which would ensure that other activities would not unduly interfere with the development of sea-bed resources, and which would guard against pollution of the sea arising from sea-bed activities." It noted that "In principle, there should be no ban to giving the regime certain powers with regard to the laying of pipelines, for instance, since this is an activity directly related to the exploitation of sea-bed resources." Canada claimed that the international machinery should have authority and control over conflict management as part of the mandate proposed by the U.N. resolution on the principles.[119]

Several draft proposals agreed that the exploration and exploitation activities should not unreasonably interfere with other uses in the area. Toward this goal the Soviet Union's draft provided articles regulating the emplacement of "stationary and mobile installations" in the international area. Among other things,

1. The installations were prohibited from being placed in "straits and at points where they may obstruct passage on sea-lanes of vital

importance for international shipping or at points of intense fishing activities;"

2. Subject to the requirement of noninterference with the rights of navigation, the installations were entitled to safety zones of 500 meters around them and had to be maintained with appropriate navigational markings;

3. The construction or removal of the installations must be included in the Notices to Mariners or other generally recognized forms of public announcements;

4. The installations would not have the status of islands.[120]

The United Kingdom's draft pointed out that the requirement of regard for other uses included the duty to prevent and control pollution of the marine environment resulting from research into and exploration of the area, or exploitation of its natural resources, and the prevention of unjustifiable interference with navigation, overflight, and fishing. The Maltese draft endorsed similar provisions and indicated that exploration and exploitation of natural resources should not be permitted "in areas where interference may be caused to the use of recognized sea lanes essential to international navigation or where scientific findings indicate the probability that exploitation may result in extensive pollution of the marine environment. The Soviet draft gave the "Conference" of the "Agency," which would be composed of state members of the Agency, the power to draft "general principles and recommendations to states concerning the prevention of pollution and contamination of the marine environment as a result of the exploration and exploitation of sea-bed resources." The "Conference" was also given the "residual powers."[121]

The Maltese draft recommended broad powers for the "Assembly," which

. . . shall approve such rules of a general and non-discriminatory character relating to overflight of ocean space; navigation; maritime safety; communications; marine and ocean bed installations; conservation, management and development of natural resources, the conduct of scientific research, the maintenance of the quality of the marine environment and harmonization of conflicting uses of International Ocean Space as may be recommended by the Council.

The United States, the United Kingdom, the United Republic of Tanzania, and Malta in their draft proposals entrusted to the "Council" or the "executive board," as the central organ of the international machinery, primary authority and control over the accommodation of multiple uses in the international seabed area. The powers of the "Council" or "executive board" specified in different drafts included

1. Enactment of regulations pertaining to all activities undertaken in the area (Latin American nations);
2. Prevention and minimization of conflicts among different uses (United Republic of Tanzania);
3. Recommendation to the "Assembly" of rules and principles with respect to avoidance of conflicts among the uses of the area, prevention of pollution, maintenance of law and order, avoidance of threats to the integrity of the International Ocean Space (Malta);
4. The right to give emergency orders to prevent serious harm to the marine environment (U.S.A., U.K., United Republic of Tanzania);
5. Inspection of offshore activities (United Republic of Tanzania, Malta);
6. Prevention of marine pollution and conservation of resources (U.K., United Republic of Tanzania, Malta, USSR, Japan, and the Latin American group);
7. Establishment of liability in cases of damage resulting from the activities undertaken in the international area (United Republic of Tanzania).

The United States' and the Maltese drafts, in addition, provided for several subsidiary organs to help the "Council" or the "executive board" in carrying out its responsibilities for the rational and orderly management of the international area. The U.S. draft proposed the establishment of a "Rules and Recommended Practices Commission" to assure that the activities in the area would be conducted under strict safeguards for the protection of human life and safety and of the environment; to protect living organisms from damage; to prevent or reduce to acceptable limits interference arising from exploration and exploitation activities with other uses and users of the marine environment; to promote safe design and construction of fixed operations.[122]

The Maltese draft referred to the establishment of an "Ocean Management and Development Commission" to supervise compliance with the provisions of all licenses and to report periodically about it to the Council.[123]

Almost all draft proposals agreed that each "contracting party" should be made liable for any damage caused by activities carried out by it or under its sponsorship. The "contracting party" could be a state or states or an international organization, depending upon whether a draft had approved exploitation of seabed resources directly or by an international organization. In the case of a group of states acting together, it was provided that they should be made jointly and severally responsible. The provisions on liability, of course, did not specify whether the liability intended was strict or absolute or one based on fault. Japan's draft did not reject the idea of liability but suggested further study of the subject.[124]

Deliberations within the U.N. Seabed Committee
Subcommittee I of the U.N. Seabed Committee was the forum in which the details of the international regime and machinery were discussed. Subcommittee I appointed a working group to give particular attention to the powers and functions that might be assigned to the international machinery. There was considerable variation in the views expressed in the working group about the nature and scope of the functions of different organs proposed—particularly the "Assembly" (intended to be invested primarily with deliberative functions, composed of representatives of all the contracting parties) and the "Council" (a smaller organ concerned primarily with executive functions and with responsibility for day-to-day activities)—and the relationship among them. Under relevant topic headings, the views expressed may be summarized as follows:[125]
PROMULGATION OF GENERAL INTERNATIONAL STANDARDS RELATING TO A VARIETY OF TECHNICAL AND OPERATIONAL SUBJECTS
These standards relate primarily to the exploration and exploitation of the resources and to the noninterference with the other uses of the high seas in the international area.

While one group wanted the Assembly to adopt general principles, another group wished the Council to authorize them. A third group suggested that the general principles be mentioned in the international convention with an appropriate procedure for their implementation. The procedural regulations were to be prepared, according to this view, by the Council or a subsidiary organ and would come into force after being submitted directly to the contracting parties and approved by them. A fourth group, which was in substantial agreement with the third group, preferred to have the Assembly examine the procedural rules on the recommendation of the Council and submit them to the states for approval.
MARINE POLLUTION
According to one view, the Assembly should be empowered to adopt general principles and recommendations concerning the prevention of

pollution and contamination of the marine environment resulting from exploration and exploitation of the international area. A second view would, in addition, give the Assembly authority to take measures to prevent, mitigate, or eliminate pollution or threats of pollution or other hazardous events resulting from any activity in the area and to establish an emergency relief fund.

Others opposed giving such powers to the Assembly; instead, they regarded the Council or perhaps a special subsidiary organ as the proper agency to adopt general principles on marine pollution. It was further proposed that the Council be empowered to deal with emergency or hazardous events resulting from any activity connected with the exploration and exploitation of the resources of the area. Another proposal was to authorize the Assembly to approve, upon the recommendation of the Council, "nondiscriminatory informative principles" dealing with matters concerning the uses of the marine environment. Several representatives preferred to omit such provisions on the ground that they went beyond the jurisdiction of the international machinery under discussion.

SCIENTIFIC RESEARCH

While one view was to leave the freedom of research in the international area essentially unrestricted, another opinion favored the conduct of research under regulations passed by the Assembly. A few delegations even wanted the international "Authority" to carry out scientific research in the area. Another view was to leave the conduct of scientific research to a subsidiary organ that would be established for the purpose.

It was also proposed that an appropriate organ (Assembly or Council) of the international authority be empowered to promote international cooperation with regard to scientific research on the resources of the area; encourage the exchange and training of scientists and experts in the exploration and exploitation of the resources of the area; organize the development and practical application of scientific techniques suitable to the optimal utilization of the area; and help in the acquisition of facilities, plant, and equipment useful in carrying out the functions approved by the "Authority." Representatives supported one or more of those measures, but no one group of measures was able to command general support. In particular, opinions differed on the steps to be taken to accomplish those purposes.

ORDERLY UTILIZATION OF THE INTERNATIONAL AREA

According to one view, the Assembly should have the power to decide from time to time which parts of the international area should be open to exploration and exploitation of resources. It was also suggested that the Assembly should be able to provide, where necessary, for the orderly development of the area, for the preservation of the marine environment, and for keeping parts of the area free from exploration and exploitation activities. Those who opposed these views thought that such powers should either be omitted or be assigned to the Council, which, according to them, should have a major role in the regulation of activities in the international area. These activities related to the establishment of scientific stations, nature parks, and archaeological or other marine preserves in the area as well as other services for international community purposes.

Appraisal

In summary, the following points should be emphasized with respect to the prescriptions on the accommodation of multiple uses in the continental shelf area:
1. The coastal state's exclusive jurisdiction over the continental shelf area is confined to the regulation of the exploration and the exploitation of the natural resources therein.
2. The exclusive authority and control of the coastal state in this area must be exercised with reasonable regard for the freedom of the high seas and the rights of other users.
3. Reasonableness of a coastal state's interference with the uses of the superjacent waters and other uses not connected with the continental shelf activities will have to be judged on the basis of tests of equivalence and relativity. In applying these tests, decision-makers could usefully examine several relevant contextual factors.

Generally, in actual practice, such inclusive interests as navigation, fisheries, the laying of cables and pipelines, and overflight in the continental shelf area have been accommodated with relative ease and with little damage to the common interest.

However, with regard to the pursuit of scientific investigation in the area, accommodation of interests has not been very satisfactory. Despite the clear intention of the authors of the Geneva Convention, a few coastal states claim that their prior consent is necessary for any research to be conducted in the continental shelf area. While past practice and present prescriptions reject such claims, at least in the case of those research projects that do not require actual physical contact with the ocean floor of the continental shelf area, future practice and prescriptions may indeed support them. The possible change in status of the right of scientific investigation in the continental shelf area can be explained, not in terms of the so-called "creeping jurisdiction," for which we find little justification in the practice of the majc.ity of states, but as a consequence of a growing consensus among a majority of states that such a change is in the common interest. Most of these states, in our opinion, erroneously believe that exclusive control over scientific research is vital to their national security and economic well-being.[126]

In view of the fact that exclusive authority and control over the resources of the shelf have been granted to the coastal state and also because of the possibility of approval of a similar competence over the proposed economic zone, the discovery of resources through scientific research would only help, not harm, the economic interests of the coastal states. Furthermore, the obligations proposed for the future conduct of scientific research in the exclusive resource zones, such as prior notification, opportunity for the coastal state to participate, and open publication of the results, if accepted, in addition to other attendant contextual factors, would, in our opinion, enable states to distinguish genuine scientific research from military intelligence activities.

With respect to the future prospects of managing multiple uses in the continental shelf area or the exclusive resource zones, the problem appears to lie in the definition of the jurisdiction of the coastal state over such areas and the geographical boundaries within which it could be exercised. A significant group of states, including both developed and developing countries, advocates at least a 200-mile economic zone in which the coastal state would be given exclusive ownership of all the living and nonliving resources and control over scientific research. The USSR and Japan are among a group of states that opposes comprehensive coastal state authority and control over a wide maritime area.

In the international area a similar disagreement exists among two different groups of states as to the powers and functions of the proposed international machinery. One group of states, dominated largely by developing nations, argues that the international machinery must have exclusive control over all activities except navigation, overflight, and the laying of cables and pipelines. The powers of the international agency would, according to this view, include resolution of any conflicts that might arise among the various uses of the area.

Another group of states, consisting mainly of the developed countries, believes that the functions and powers of the international machinery should be confined to the exploration and exploitation of the deep-ocean nonliving and sedentary fishery resources. However, even this group of states is not opposed to the idea of allowing the international machinery to manage the accommodation of multiple uses of the area.

While there may be disagreements as to which organ of the international machinery should be given specific functions, it appears certain that policies and prescriptions of proved value in the case of the continental shelf area will become equally important in the rational accommodation of multiple uses in the international area.

6

Security and Disarmament in the Sea

The Nature of Security Uses of the Sea

Modern science and technology have changed the perspectives of maritime military strategists. These new perspectives may have altered the significance of a few of the traditional components of seapower that A. T. Mahan stressed.[1] However, the consequent changes in naval strategy have not in the least affected states' reliance on seapower to secure their differing objectives. The obvious fact is that modern navies have become more sophisticated and diversified. The age of battleships has been replaced by the age of nuclear submarines, aircraft carriers, destroyers, ocean escorts, frigates, and antisubmarine warfare carriers.

The United States, one of the leading maritime powers, has 145 submarines, of which 41 are of the Polaris type. It has 300 destroyers, 24 aircraft carriers, and perhaps 5,000 vessels of all kinds.[2] Its chief political and ideological adversary, the Union of Soviet Socialist Republics, is not far behind. As one source pointed out,

> In important categories of sea power, the Soviet Union already surpasses the United States. In others, the Soviets are catching up. The Soviet Union presently has many more conventionally powered submarines, unparalleled systems on surface ships and on submarines, and a sizable missile equipped fleet of patrol boats. They are catching up in POLARIS-type ballistic missile submarines and helicopter carriers.
> Compared to the U.S. Navy, the Soviet Navy lags in logistic support for sustained combat conditions. It is inferior in anti-submarine warfare capabilities on the high seas, in the capacity for long-range amphibious operations, and, above all, in ship-based naval air power. Major efforts are underway to overcome these weaknesses.[3]

The maritime military capabilities of the other coastal states vary widely and lag considerably behind the strength of the United States and the Soviet Union.[4]

The various components of seapower are constantly undergoing scientific and technological changes.[5] These changes involve efforts to diminish the noise of the submarine, to improve its speed and range, and to allow it to remain submerged almost indefinitely. Antisubmarine warfare capabilities are also fast improving. In the future, we may witness further progress in the deployment deep-submergence vehicles that can operate at depths of 20,000 feet. With this capacity submarines will have access to 98 percent of the volume of the world's oceans. At present, access is limited to a mere 10 percent of the ocean floor.

In due course, bottom or subbottom stations are also anticipated. Such stations will be useful as centers to command and control submerged weapon systems and for manned bottom surveillance. In addition, they can be used for servicing submarines. Furthermore, in the management of unmanned bottom detection and surveillance systems, the development of advanced instrumentation and power sources independent of surface or land support via cable can be visualized.

With regard to other security uses of the ocean floor, mention should be made of the emplacement of isotope-fueled navigation devices, undersea test ranges, bottom engineering test units, seismic detection of underground explosives, and the disposal of military waste products. In addition, states use the seas for regular target practice and for testing atomic weapons. The latter activity, although lately diminished in frequency, has by no means disappeared from the seas.

Effects of Seapower on National Aspirations

States use seapower to maximize different values:

First, security and power: War as the final arbiter in settling disputes among nations has not been eliminated as a part of international life. Accordingly, each nation must always be well equipped both to persuade others to honor its claims and at the same time to dissuade them from imposing their demands on it. States have always relied on seapower in their bid to improve national power and security.[6]

Even in the modern context, seapower is regarded as crucial to a state's sense of security.[7] The two superpowers have built their maritime supremacy as an essential ingredient of mutual deterrence. While there may be some doubt as to the deterrent value of the Strategic Air Command (B-52 intercontinental bombers) and the intercontinental ballistic missiles (ICBMs), the Polaris missile-firing submarines (SLBMs) with their capacity to elude antisubmarine warfare forces[8] offer maximum deterrence capacity to the United States and the Union of Soviet Socialist Republics against each other.[9]

Second, wealth and well-being: European powers relied on their seapower to reach and defend overseas colonies, which they controlled both as sources of raw materials and as markets for their commercial products.

Even with the virtual end of the colonial period, the importance of seapower for promoting the wealth and well-being of nations has not diminished. New economic interests in the oceans have arisen. The overcrowded planet will increasingly turn to the sea for food and nourishment, energy, and raw materials as the continental resources become depleted at an increasing rate.[10] Already science and technology have brought some of the resources of the sea within the grasp of mankind. Reliance on seapower under such circumstances can be expected to increase in direct proportion to the growth of economic investments in and returns from the seas.[11]

Third, respect and rectitude: Maintenance of seapower is also regarded as essential to preserve the image of a nation as a great power and to gain the respect of others. This was one of the reasons why Britain negotiated the terms of Washington Naval Treaty of 1921.[12] The same consideration may also partly explain the United States' effort to maintain its naval supremacy.[13]

The need to preserve law and order on the seas and to make participants behave responsibly is yet another factor that lends importance to seapower. Seapower may also be credited with the elimination of piracy and overseas trading in slaves.

In the future, as more international standards are defined and accepted for regulating the use and enjoyment of the oceans, it will become increasingly important to police them to make sure that participants responsibly adhere to such standards.

Fourth, enlightenment: While it is true that navies of the world are not created primarily to conduct oceanography, they have been among the major supporters of marine science. As is the case with outer space, much of the knowledge about the sea's potentialities for the benefit of mankind has come from attempts by defense planners to utilize the oceans primarily for power and security of states.[14] In other words, money appropriated for defense has greatly aided oceanographic research.

Conflicts between Security Interests and Mineral Resource Interests

In some cases, the use of a maritime area for security purposes may exclude other users from the same area. This would be the case when states indulge in target practice, conduct naval maneuvers, and set up fixed military installations. In these situations, it becomes necessary to evaluate whether the exclusion of other users is within the limits of reasonableness. The resulting conflict will come into even sharper focus if the areas in question also contain valuable mineral resources that can be exploited.

Even in the case of other types of security uses, such as navigation by military vessels, conflicting claims relating to the regulation of their passage rights could easily arise in the maritime zones over which the coastal state has different degrees of exclusive authority and control.

In addition, there have also been efforts to prohibit particular kinds of security uses either from the entire ocean areas or from specified regions of the sea. In general, these efforts are motivated by the hope that, if successful, such moves would contribute toward the demilitarization of the oceans and hence toward the promotion of peace among nations and permit greater utilization of the seas for nonsecurity uses.

Thus, the claims relating to the security uses and demilitarization of the oceans could be categorized as follows: (A) claims relating to access to maritime areas for security uses: (1) to the high seas; (2) to the continental shelf areas or exclusive resource zones; (3) to the contiguous zones; (4) to the territorial sea; (B) claims relating to the demilitarization of the oceans: (1) Washington and London naval conferences; (2) reservation of the oceans exclusively for "peaceful purposes" and (a) the Seabed Arms Control Treaty and (b) proposals for peace zones.

Basic World Community Policies

There are two basic world community policies or goals[15] that emerge from the United Nations Charter prescriptions[16] and from the contemporary realities of the global situation,[17] that is, (a) threats against the security of states and against the survival of mankind on earth must be minimized to the extent possible and as a matter of priority; and (b) the optimum promotion of values comprising the whole range of conditions that men everywhere seek and their widest distribution among the members of the international community must be encouraged.[18]

What are the implications of promoting these two rather broad goals in the context of security uses of the seas? On a general level two points should be made: First, those security uses of the sea that contribute to stability of the world must be preserved. Second, in prohibiting or permitting certain security uses of the sea, a primary consideration should be to minimize conflict between such uses and nonsecurity uses of the same environment.

An analysis of the above-mentioned security uses of the sea reveals that most of them, except those involving fixed installations, use the ocean as a "spatial extension resource." [19] In other words, these uses of the sea by participants do not exhaust the oceans as a resource, and there is little occasion for participants to interfere with others who are involved in the same use or other uses.

However, this does not mean that security uses of the sea which derive benefit from the oceans as a "spatial extension" resource do not sometimes require special regulation. This special regulation may in some cases be needed to minimize interference with other uses of the sea. For example, military exercises and target practice must be conducted in identified maritime zones, and they naturally require temporary suspension of other uses of the sea in the same area. Furthermore, submarines and men-of-war along with other ships require that certain sea routes be kept free from congestion or permanent occupation by other users. [20]

These kinds of interference with nonsecurity uses of the sea need not be detrimental to the common interest if the losses sustained by the latter could be compensated by the availability of equally attractive alternative maritime areas or if the duration of the interference is relatively short.

Fortunately, up to now, security uses of the seas involving navigation of submarines and men-of-war have not seriously conflicted with nonsecurity uses. Except in those maritime areas that are relatively close to the shores and that are mainly under the exclusive jurisdiction of the coastal states, it can be safely assumed that there will be very few cases of incompatibility between such security and nonsecurity uses of the seas. On the basis of this assumption, it can be argued that continued permission of these security operations in the seas is not inimical to the common interest.

However, although the operation of submarines and men-of-war at sea may be permissible from the perspective of common interests, it must also be justified in terms of the maintenance of minimum world public order. Nuclear submarines clearly stand out as being essential to the stability of deterrence between the two superpowers, the United States and the Soviet Union. At a time when the Soviet Union can match the strength of the United States in the area of Strategic Air Command (B-52 intercontinental bombers) and intercontinental ballistic missiles (ICBMs), the value of the Polaris missile-firing submarines (SLBMs), the only other component of strategic force, to the United States has been considered to be very high. As long as one of the superpowers relies on nuclear submarines for its own security and survival, an attempt to prohibit them would be not only politically and strategically impractical but dangerous to the sense of security of that state. The simple logic is that the survival of the world depends on its ability to avoid a nuclear showdown between the two superpowers. The sensitivities of other nuclear powers are also important, but to a large extent these are controlled by the sensitivities of the superpowers.[21]

Men-of-war are also a necessary component of the strategy to maintain peace and security among nations.[22] The value of warships is that in all the cases of minor conflict in the world, they provide an alternative, flexible response.[23] Without them, the great powers would perhaps be forced to use their nuclear weapons.

Once the need for nuclear submarines and warships is justified because of the lack of better alternatives for the security of states, it must be conceded further that military exercises, target practice, and the scientific investigation of the sea by military personnel and equipment are equally supportable. These activities are essential for the proper maintenance and operation of submarines and warships. Scientific investigations of the sea, by virtue of the benefits they yield for civilian purposes, thereby gain further support as a permissible activity.[24]

The case of fixed military installations is, however, different. They could be permanent and could be expected to occupy maritime areas, sometimes large enough to cause unacceptable interference with other users of the sea. In these cases, in areas under special authority and control of a coastal state, the emplacement of fixed military installations should be subject to the consent and the regulation of the coastal state.

In areas beyond national jurisdiction, the establishment of fixed military installations, which are otherwise not prohibited by common consent, must be approved along with other known uses of the high seas such as navigation, fishing, and the laying of submarine cables. Conflicts between fixed military installations and other uses must be resolved on the basis of the criterion of reasonableness and tests of equivalence and relativity.

Trends in Decision

Access to Marine Areas for Security Uses
CUSTOMARY EXPECTATIONS AND THE PURSUIT OF SECURITY ON THE HIGH SEAS
Ever since navies were developed as part of the military establishment, oceans have been used for the maximization of both the defensive and

the offensive power of nations. From the Second Punic War, B.C. 218–201, to the twentieth century A.D., innumerable instances of the influence of seapower on the world social process have been recorded by maritime historians.[25] The community of nations has always organized the institutions of authority and control which regulated their relations on the seas in such a way as to facilitate the growth and display of their individual maritime might. The efforts of Grotius in his advocacy of an open sea symbolize the recurrent desire of nations to use the oceans on a basis of equality for different purposes. The concept of "freedom of the seas," which emerged from these efforts and which controls the activities of members of the world community on the seas, provides for the freedom of navigation, among other things.

Freedom of navigation implies the freedom for states to send their military vessels, men-of-war and submarines, across the oceans. This right naturally includes free passage for military ships through straits that are not within the territorial waters of a coastal state. Wherever they are on the oceans, with few exceptions, military vessels are under the exclusive jurisdiction of the state whose flag they fly. The same prescription applies with equal force to the operation of merchant ships on the oceans.

Regard for the equal rights of all states necessarily gives rise to a restriction on the otherwise broad and extensive authority granted to states to use the oceans for any purpose whatsoever. That is, each user of the ocean must accommodate other users in such a way as not to cause unjustifiable interference with the latter's interests. The justifiability of a case of interference is determined in the particular context by an inclusive community decision.

The other well-known components of the freedom of the seas—the freedom to conduct scientific investigations in the oceans and the freedom to fly over them—contribute no less frequently to the enhancement of a state's security interests.

In addition, the right of states to conduct military maneuvers and target practice at sea has also been well established through centuries of practice. In view of the potential threat to other users of the seas from such military activities, notification of the areas earmarked for the activity and the length of time it is expected to last is generally given to them. As a normal practice, other users of the sea cooperate with the party or parties conducting the target practice and military maneuvers.[26]

Even in the context of negotiations at the Third Law of the Sea Conference, these customary expectations as to security uses on the high seas have not been seriously challenged. A majority of states believes that the proposed international machinery to regulate certain activities in the international area should not control the traditional security interests—such as navigation by military vessels, naval maneuvers, and target practice. However, a significant group of states, consisting of Asian, African, and Latin American states, argues that the proposed international machinery must be given exclusive authority over the sea-bed and ocean floor of the international area and all activities connected with them. The only exception to the comprehensive authority and control of the international machinery according to this group of states should be in the case of navigation in the superjacent waters, overflight, and the laying of cables and pipelines. (See Chapter 5.)

If the contentions of the group advocating comprehensive powers for the international agency are accepted, security uses involving fixed military installation in the international area will come under the regulation of such an agency. Even the nuclear weapon tests, which have a tendency to affect adversely the resources of the area, will come under the jurisdiction of the proposed international machinery.

THE CONTINENTAL SHELF AREA

The question as to what extent the exclusive authority of the coastal state over the continental shelf area could be invoked to prohibit foreign security uses there has often been raised. It is generally agreed that the coastal state has no authority to regulate the security uses that do not involve fixed installations. Thus, for example, navigation by military vessels, naval maneuvers, and target practice in the continental shelf area are to be regarded as part of the freedom of the high seas. Interference with such activities because of the exercise of a coastal state's continental shelf authority should be within the limits of reasonableness. However, in the case of security uses requiring fixed installations in the continental shelf area, there is no clear consensus as to the authority of the coastal state to control them exclusively.

The Geneva Convention on the Continental Shelf is silent on the latter point. However, it is of some interest to note that the Geneva Conference rejected an Indian resolution that sought to prohibit all fixed military installations whether they belonged to the coastal state or to a foreign government from the continental shelf area.[27] It was thought that the issue of demilitarization of a part of an ocean area was not a proper subject to be decided in the context of the doctrine of the continental shelf.

However, in connection with the recent law of the sea negotiations a growing number of states believe that the continental shelf authority of the coastal state and its proposed exclusive authority and control over the economic zone or patrimonial sea should be clearly extended to include control over all fixed installations, even those connected with security interests. Mexico, for example, proposed that new attempts to achieve broader ocean disarmament measures

. . . should first and foremost be directed at achieving the express prohibition of the emplacement of conventional weapons . . . on those regions of the continental shelf of any state that lie beyond the twelve-mile limit by any state other than the coastal state to which the continental shelf belongs.[28]

In addition, Mexico along with Canada and India has expressly stated that it will not allow any foreign military installations in its continental shelf area.[29]

To some extent, the view that foreign military installations cannot be established in the continental shelf area of a coastal state is supported by the doctrine of the continental shelf insofar as such installations adversely affect the chances of the coastal state to fully explore and exploit the natural resources therein. Furthermore, often such installations would also give rise to issues of self-defense of the coastal state. For these two principal reasons, M. S. McDougal and W. T. Burke stated that it was "imperative to recognize exclusive coastal control over any use of the continental shelf which requires emplacing relatively fixed installations." They argued that

It would be most inadvisable, for example, to permit an uncontrolled competence in non-coastal states to erect structures on the continental shelf, while at the same time authorizing the coastal state to exploit the natural resources of the continental shelf. The possibilities of conflict are too obvious.[30]

THE CONTIGUOUS ZONE

According to Article 24 of the Geneva Convention on the Territorial Sea and the Contiguous Zone, the contiguous zone "may not extend beyond twelve miles from the baselines from which the breadth of the territorial sea is measured." Within the zone, the coastal state is given exclusive authority necessary to "prevent infringement of its customs, fiscal, immigration or sanitary regulations within its territory or territorial seas" and punish such infringements.[31]

Except for these specified purposes, the contiguous zone, beyond the limits of the territorial sea, is to be regarded as the high seas. Thus, all states have the freedom of navigation through the zone and may use it for all other lawful security purposes, subject, of course, to the same restrictions as are applicable in the continental shelf area or exclusive resource zone.

THE TERRITORIAL SEA

Within the territorial sea area, coastal states have broad powers. These powers, for all practical purposes, can be equated with the sovereignty that they have over their internal waters and the land areas under their control. However, in times of peace coastal states cannot use their powers to interfere arbitrarily with the flow of navigation through the territorial seas. The same prescription applies with equal force to the navigation by foreign military vessels as long as their passage is "innocent." The right of innocent passage is also valid in the case of those straits that lie within the territorial sea of a coastal state but connect two parts of the high seas. The right of innocent passage received strong support from the International Court of Justice in the *Corfu Channel* case[32] and was reiterated by the Geneva Convention on the Territorial Sea and the Contiguous Zone.

According to Article 14 (4) of the Geneva Convention on the Territorial Sea and the Contiguous Zone, subject to its provisions, "ships of all States, whether coastal or not, shall enjoy the right of innocent passage." "Passage" is defined in Article 14 (2) and (3) as "navigation through the territorial sea for the purpose either of traversing that sea without entering internal waters or of proceeding to internal waters, or of making for the high seas from internal waters" and includes "stopping and anchoring, but only so far as the same are incidental to ordinary navigation or are rendered necessary by *force majeure* or by distress." Furthermore, Article 14 (6) requires submarines to navigate on the surface and to show their flag. Article 15 puts the coastal state under an obligation not to hamper innocent passage through territorial waters and requires it to "give appropriate publicity to any dangers to navigation, of which it has knowledge, within its territorial sea."

Article 16 (3) of the Geneva Convention on the Territorial Sea and the Contiguous Zone gives the coastal state the right to suspend innocent passage, temporarily, in specified areas of its territorial sea, "if such suspension is essential for the protection of its security," subject, however, to Article 16 (4), according to which

There shall be no suspension of the innocent passage of foreign ships through straits which are used for international navigation between one part of the high seas and another part of the high seas or the territorial sea of a foreign state.

Disagreeing with the Geneva Convention's clear endorsement of the right of foreign ships to exercise innocent passage through the territorial sea and the straits of a coastal state without its prior authorization, the Soviet Union, several East European countries, and Colombia made reservations at the time of signing the Convention to the effect that they had a right to require prior authorization for passage of warships. Since then, Indonesia, Turkey, and Pakistan have also required such advance permission.[33]

Despite these reservations and the practice of a minority of states, the growth of customary international law and the strong approval of it by the majority of states that participated in the Geneva Conferences seem only to emphasize the right of innocent passage for all ships through the territorial sea and the straits of a coastal state without its prior authorization. However, a more difficult issue relating to the concept of innocent passage is not to determine whether it is an established right but to identify what factors affect innocence and who makes the final decision on the innocent character of a passage.

Factors Affecting Innocent Passage The Hague Codification Conference of 1930, after considerable debate, in Article 3 of Final Act 16 defined noninnocent passage as the one "when a vessel makes use of the territorial sea of a coastal State for the purpose of doing any act prejudicial to the security, to the public policy or to the fiscal interests of that State."[34] This definition represents one of the earliest attempts to clarify the meaning of innocent passage. However, it is not clear whether a mere intention to commit acts prejudicial to the referred interests of the coastal state, without actually "doing any act," would make the passage noninnocent. It is particularly confusing if the Hague definition is examined in the context of the *Corfu Channel* case. In that case, purpose rather than the manner of voyage seemed crucial for the determination of the innocent character of passage.[35] Moreover, terms such as "security," "public policy," and "fiscal interests" are sufficiently general and tend to leave much to the claimants' discretion to justify any interpretation favorable to them.

To a certain extent, however, the ambiguities involved in the general definition of innocent passage appear to have been narrowed down by a specification of different interests in whose protection the coastal state could promulgate regulations that were considered binding on foreign ships navigating in its waters. The Hague Codification Conference listed illustratively rather than exhaustively these interests: (a) safety of traffic and protection of channels and buoys, (b) prevention of pollution, (c) protection of the products of the territorial sea, and (d) the rights of fishing, shooting, and analogous rights belonging to the coastal state.[36]

Later, the International Law Commission showed a similar inclination to specify the interests of the coastal state in an effort to clarify the scope of innocent passage. The Commission not only endorsed the list of interests originally cited by the Hague Conference but even added to the list coastal authority to prescribe regulations concerning hydrographical surveys.[37] However, regarding the general definition of innocent passage the Commission could not achieve any more clarity than did the Hague Conference. With an intent to restrict a coastal state's authority to exclude foreign ships from navigating in its territorial waters, the Commission defined innocent passage in terms of "acts prejudicial to security, or contrary to the present rules or other rules of international law."[38] Such a definition was confusing even to the members of the Commission itself, because, as McDougal and Burke point out, they could not agree whether or not passage for the purpose of smuggling or of evading export-import controls could be considered innocent.[39]

The Geneva Convention on the Territorial Sea and the Contiguous Zone differed from the International Law Commission and defined in Article 14 (6), passage "prejudicial to the peace, good order, or security of the coastal state" as noninnocent. Further, in Article 17 it required ships exercising the right of innocent passage to "comply with the laws and regulations enacted by the coastal states in conformity with these articles and other rules of international law and in particular with such laws and regulations relating to transport and navigation."

Both the formulations contained in Article 14 (4) and those of Article 17, consisting of such vague phrases as "security," "good order," "peace," and "other rules of international law," signify a marked deterioration in the efforts to clarify the meaning of innocent passage. Taken at their face value, they raise the further question as to whether a coastal state can exclude foreign ships from exercising the right of passage if they do not comply with its regulations, which are intended to protect its legitimate interests, short of "peace, good order, or security"—if such a distinction can be made at all.

A number of delegations, in approving the Geneva formulations, appear to have been moved to consider restricting the coastal state from exercising too wide a discretion in limiting the right of innocent passage. Thus, Max Sørensen, head of the Danish delegation, noted that under the Geneva Convention,

The coastal state is authorized to *enforce* its laws and regulations on foreign ships passing through its territorial sea, but is not allowed to prevent a ship from passing through merely on the ground of a violation of such laws or regulations.[40]

According to J. H. W. Verzil, a member of the Dutch delegation, the formulations are an attempt to distinguish between acts of passing ships that are directed against "peace, good order, or security" and acts of "simple nonobservance" of shipping regulations, with the sanction of exclusion applied only in the former case.[41]

However, despite these intentions, it can be argued that the coastal state is entitled under the Geneva Convention to prohibit passage of ships for violating regulations that it has promulated to protect its resources from unauthorized exploitation and pollution, as well as its immigration rules and trade regulations. These are all interests that directly or indirectly affect its "peace, good order, or security." The Convention itself indicates that such an interpretation is justifiable when it provides in Article 14 (5) that fishing vessels must adhere to coastal states' regulations as a condition of innocent passage.

In sum, despite the Geneva Convention's vague definition of "innocent passage," it appears that a number of considerations and specific interests of states provide guidance in determining its interpretation in a specific context.

Thus, the position of the guns, the strength and formation of the naval force, the purpose of intended passage, the cargo carried, and the destination in a third state are all factors that affect innocent passage. Furthermore, other factors and interests—such as protection of resources from nonnational exploitation, prevention of pollution, safe and orderly navigation, prevention of smuggling, and protection of domestic laws concerning health and trade—can provide a basis for determining innocent passage.

Moreover, it is fair to conclude that it is the coastal state that makes the initial determination with respect to the innocent character of passage. In this determination it enjoys wide, though not unlimited, discretion. If a dispute arises between a coastal state and a foreign government over the former's decision not to allow passage, it has to be resolved through the traditional procedures of pacific settlement of disputes. Where these procedures fail, it is to be expected that the controversy will be settled through the invocation of sanctions involving either reciprocity or retaliation.

The Recent Law of the Sea Debate and the Right of Innocent Passage
The fact that the law of innocent passage is weighted slightly in favor of

the interests of the coastal state obviously provides less than optimum satisfaction to those participants who desire absolute freedom of navigation on the high seas. In recent years, proponents of the freedom of navigation have been caused further anxiety by the growing trend among the coastal states toward the acceptance of a twelve-mile territorial sea limit. According to one source, out of 138 states whose national claims were noted as of early 1972, only 30 states will uphold the three-mile limit. Of these 30 states, only 7 can be regarded as important industrial states. In all, more than 90 states in Eastern Europe, Africa, and South America have claimed a twelve-mile, or broader, territorial sea.[42]

It is said that if the territorial sea limit is raised from three to twelve miles for all coastal states, at least 121 straits will cease to be international waters. At least sixteen of these straits are of high strategic value, especially for the United States and the Soviet Union. These straits are[43]

Bering Strait (West)

Western Chosen Strait (South Korea)

Malacca Strait (Malaysia)

Sunda Strait, Selat, Lombok, and Ombrai Straits (all Indonesia)

Old Bahamas Channel

Dominica, Martinique, Saint Lucia Channel, and Saint Vincent Passage (all Lesser Antilles)

Strait of Hormuz (Persian Gulf)

Bab el Mandeb (Red Sea)

Strait of Gibraltar

Strait of Dover

The list of the strategic straits may vary depending upon who is making the selection and for what purpose.

On the issue of safeguarding the freedom of navigation, in an age of expanding territorial sea claims, at least three different views can be identified from the United Nations discussions.

According to the first view, argued principally by the United States and the Soviet Union, an international corridor must be created within a national strait that is used for international navigation. Through the international corridor, vessels of all nations must be allowed freedom of passage on a basis of equality, as if it were a strip of the high seas. This means that foreign submarines will have the right of submerged travel through the strait and military aircraft will enjoy freedom of flight over the strait. Furthermore, the coastal state will be given the option to designate the international corridor, subject to the expectation that, as far as ships are concerned, it will include channels customarily employed by ships in transit. However, the concept of international corridor is not meant to affect "historical rights," conventions, or other international agreements already in force specifically relating to particular straits.[44]

Another group of states, known as "strait states," represented by Indonesia and Malaysia, is opposed to the concept of international corridors as diminishing the coastal state's sovereignty over its territorial waters. These states argue that ships of all nations can enjoy innocent passage through the straits within the territorial waters, subject only to prior authorization from the coastal state. It is further pointed out that such a method not only protects the legitimate interests of international navigation but also provides an opportunity for the coastal state to safeguard its vital interests.[45]

A third group of states believes that claims for establishing corridors of high seas in the midst of territorial waters of coastal states are as undesirable as claims requiring prior authorization from the coastal state for exercising the right of innocent passage through a strait within its territorial waters. These states, which regard the existing law as satisfactory, prefer a reaffirmation of the right of innocent passage with a clearer definition of the rights and duties of all states, including the coastal states.[46]

The second and third group of states, which constitute a significant majority, appear to agree on most points except for the issue of prior authorization. There is consensus among them that the claimed freedom to fly over the territorial straits is alien to the concept of innocent passage and that it should not be accepted.

Appraisal The case for establishing corridors of high seas through the territorial waters of a coastal state, which until recently included straits regarded as international straits, rests on grounds of customary practice. However, a majority of states believe that the regime of innocent passage should be applied to all straits within the territorial waters of a coastal state, whether or not they were customarily regarded as international straits. The latter view has the merit of advocating uniform standards for all straits.

The Soviet Union, insofar as it supports the concept of corridors, appears to hold two contradictory and untenable positions. Insisting on the exception of the so-called "historical rights" to such a concept, it attempts to provide legitimacy to its practice of requiring prior consent for all foreign military ships to go through the straits that lie within its twelve-mile territorial sea. At the same time, it favors free passage through those straits which may soon be included in the territorial sea of coastal states because of the adoption of a uniform twelve-mile limit for the territorial sea of all coastal states.

It is believed that reliance on the right of innocent passage serves the common interest better than the other two alternatives—the corridors concept and prior consent. The right of innocent passage as customarily developed and as reiterated by the Geneva Convention has several merits. As noted above, it represents a good blend of the coastal states' interests with the international community's interest in the right of transit. Even though it allows foreign ships to pass through territorial waters and straits within them without prior authorization, it obligates them to comply with the coastal state's regulations designed to safeguard a variety of its interests, including its security, the prevention of pollution in its waters, and protection against hazards created by international navigation involving nuclear vessels, among others, as noted earlier in this chapter.[47]

Under the existing system, there is no guarantee that a dispute involving the right of passage will always be settled through peaceful means. In the final analysis, states have to depend on their individual and collective power of persuasion or coercion to defend the right against any abuse. It would therefore be desirable for participants to provide an international mechanism that can be used not only to solve disputes involving the right of innocent passage but also to invoke international sanctions against those who abuse the right.

Alternatively, if an international mechanism cannot be immediately agreed upon, at least prompt action must be taken to prescribe precise international standards to prevent pollution and nuclear hazards at sea and to provide greater safety of navigation at a time when most coastal areas are increasingly being used for exploitation of oil, gas, and mineral resources and for other peaceful purposes. Once such standards are established, it is much easier for the coastal state, as well as others, to judge whether the regulations issued by the former are in the common interest.

Fortunately, the common interest in providing freedom of navigation for ships of all nations has worked so far without resulting in any significant abuses of the right of innocent passage. The same spirit of mutual respect for the interests of others can provide a satisfactory basis for regulating the future exercise of the right of innocent passage.

Possibilities for Demilitarization of the Oceans

The Washington and London Naval Conferences

The Washington and the London Naval Conferences of 1921 and 1930, respectively, represent early attempts at demilitarization or arms control as a reaction to the accelerating world armament race. Through these conferences the maritime powers did not, however, aim at total demilitarization of the oceans. They sought only to restrict the number of naval vessels of different categories that each of them could possess without sacrificing their national security and economic well-being and without unduly threatening others.[48]

The Reservation of the Oceans Exclusively for Peaceful Purposes
After World War II, with the introduction of nuclear weapons into the armament race, more dramatic demilitarization proposals were made. These involved total demilitarization and the utilization of nuclear power "exclusively for peaceful purposes." To a certain extent, the world community succeeded in committing world powers to use outer space and Antarctica "exclusively for peaceful purposes."[49] Encouraged by these precedents, and believing that the greater the ocean area disarmed, the greater the maritime area available for nonsecurity uses, Ambassador Arvid Pardo proposed that the seabed and the ocean floor be used exclusively for "peaceful purposes." He pointed out that

. . . the advantages of proceeding to utilize the deep seas and the ocean floor for military purposes might at first sight appear compelling to the country or countries possessing the requisite technology. Yet there are disadvantages to such a course of action.

Since more than one country is able to utilize the deep seas and the ocean floor for military purposes, we can expect an immediate and rapid escalation of the arms race in the seas. . . . There would certainly be a race to occupy accessible strategic areas on the ocean floor without much regard to the claims that other nations, not having the capability to occupy these areas, might put forward. Military installations on or near the ocean floor require protection against spying or harassment, this would almost inevitably lead to unilaterally proclaimed jurisdiction over large areas of the surrounding and superjacent sea; and the consequent curtailment of lawful traditional activities on the high seas would be bitterly resented by many countries. . . . It is certain that effective counter-measures are possible: thus the effectiveness of acoustic detection and surveillance devices installed in the ocean could be destroyed by insonifying parts of the ocean themselves. This would be effective militarily but it would also render near bottom navigation, for all purposes, including scientific purposes, extremely hazardous and would render fishing sonar virtually unusable.

In his opinion, therefore,

Legitimate defense needs and the balance of terror, as well as the interests of all countries, can far better be safeguarded by developing within an international framework credible assurances that the seabed and the ocean floor will be used exclusively for peaceful purposes.[50]

It may be recalled that it was in response to Pardo's initiative the United Nations decided to undertake agenda item 92, of October 6, 1967, entitled "Examination of the question of reservation exclusively for peaceful purposes of the sea-bed and the ocean floor, and the subsoil thereof, underlying the high seas beyond the limits of present national jurisdiction and the use of their resources in the interest of mankind.

During the discussion of the implications of agenda item 92, it became quickly apparent, as in the case of the two previous agreements on outer space and Antarctica, that there was no consensus on the limits and the true meaning of the proposed reservation of the oceans exclusively for "peaceful purposes." Almost all members of the United Nations showed a willingness to support such a reservation of the oceans but readily offered their own interpretations about its implications.

According to some states, a primary difficulty in approving the proposed policy was to define peaceful as opposed to nonpeaceful uses of the sea. The United States, the United Kingdom, and their supporters pointed out that acceptance of the policy of reservation of the oceans exclusively for peaceful purposes did not automatically abolish or prohibit the present or the contemplated security uses of the sea that were in conformity with the requirements of self-defense and the United Nations Charter prescriptions. Any new set of prescriptions that might prohibit certain security uses of the seas, this group indicated, would have to be negotiated through the Eighteen Nation Disarmament Conference (ENDC).[51] The United States further proposed that, as a matter of negotiation, the possibility of prohibiting the emplacement of nuclear weapons and other weapons of mass destruction might be taken up.

The Soviet Union basically agreed with the viewpoint that all new ocean arms limitation measures must be negotiated and that they could not be automatically presumed from the approval of the general policy to reserve the ocean exclusively for peaceful purposes. However, differing from the American position, the Soviet Union suggested that a more complete demilitarization of the oceans involving the displacement of all objects of a military nature would be in accordance with the spirit of the general policy.[52]

Several small nonnuclear powers also did not seem to object to the proposed method of approving the policy of reservation of oceans exclusively for peaceful purposes subject to the condition of negotiating specific ocean disarmament measures. However, these countries pointed out that almost all security uses of the sea were inconsistent with such a policy and that all of them must be prohibited, even if this was done gradually.[53]

These differing interpretations remained unreconciled, and the General Assembly of the United Nations recommended through its resolutions in 1967 and 1968 that the member nations should further negotiate on the question of reservation of the oceans exclusively for peaceful purposes.[54] The resolutions provided an impetus to the negotiations that followed their adoption in the United Nations and in the Conference on the Committee for Disarmament (CCD) on the issue.

In approaching the claim that the oceans be reserved exclusively for peaceful purposes, it can be stated, however, that the members of the United Nations have so far shown considerable pragmatism. They were able to see the differences in human interaction when such a claim was related, on the one hand, to outer space and Antarctica and, on the other, to the ocean area. In the former case, there were few, if any, established security uses. Several well-known and lawful security uses, however, could be identified in the case of the ocean area, which most of the states claimed were crucial to their self-defense. The approval of a policy of reserving the oceans exclusively for peaceful purposes, in the final analysis, would mean that states would agree to conduct fresh negotiations to identify mutually acceptable seabed arms limitation measures.

The result of negotiations in the U.N. and the CCD was the adoption of the Treaty on the Prohibition of Emplacement of Nuclear Weapons and Other Weapons of Mass Destruction on the Seabed and the Ocean Floor and in the Subsoil Thereof on December 7, 1970. For convenience, it is referred to as the Seabed Arms Control Treaty (SACT).

The Seabed Arms Control Treaty, 1971
The implications of the SACT for ocean disarmament can be analyzed in terms of responses to three types of claims: (1) claims relating to the scope of prohibitions; (2) claims relating to the geographical area; and (3) claims relating to verification. The analysis below will begin with an examination of the Soviet draft treaty on measures to stop the arms race and on disarmament that were submitted to the ENDC, which was later enlarged to become the CCD.[55]

THE SCOPE OF THE PROHIBITIONS
The Soviet draft, Article I, stated that

The use for military purposes of the sea-bed and the ocean floor and the subsoil thereof beyond the twelve-mile maritime zone of a coastal State is prohibited.

The second paragraph of the same article, however, added that

It is prohibited to place on the sea-bed and the ocean floor and the subsoil thereof objects with nuclear weapons or any other types of weapons of mass destruction and to set up military bases, structures, installations, fortifications and other objects of a military nature.

Without the second paragraph, Article I would have meant a drastic demilitarization of the oceans. It would, of course, have raised the difficult question of defining the term "military purpose." Clearly it would have implied prohibition of nuclear submarines, warships, and other traditional military uses of the sea.

By adding the second paragraph and using such words as "place" and "set up," and by clearly indicating the prohibition of certain kinds of military uses, the Soviet Union apparently intended to exclude from its draft treaty prohibitions all the military uses of the sea that benefit from the ocean as a "spatial extension" resource. Furthermore, in explaining exceptions to the proposed prohibitions, the Soviet Union asserted that the establishment or use of "means of communication, beacons and other installations have no direct military purpose" and that the use of military personnel or equipment for peaceful scientific research was consistent with its concept of reserving the oceans exclusively for peaceful purposes.[56]

Many countries welcomed the Soviet proposal. However, the United States, the United Kingdom, and Canada raised objections to it. Canada considered the Soviet draft treaty unacceptable because it did not make any provision for defensive installations, which Canada thought were important to the security of coastal states as long as nuclear submarines were permitted to traverse the depths of the ocean.[57] The United States rejected Article I of the Soviet draft treaty as "unworkable and even harmful" on grounds that it was vaguely worded and that the scope of its prohibitions was too sweeping to provide either for the security of coastal states or for an adequate verification mechanism.[58]

Canada proposed, as part of an analytical approach, that all weapons and their installations, except defensive installations, that could be used against the territory or territorial sea or air space of another state should be prohibited.[59] The Soviet Union anticipated and opposed the

Canadian approach, which it claimed would provoke endless controversy over the definition of "defensive installations." [60]

The United States, arguing that a similar problem existed with respect to the Soviet draft when one considered the phrase "objects of a military nature," proposed in a draft treaty of its own that for the present only the emplacement of nuclear weapons and other weapons of mass destruction on the seabed and ocean floor beyond a three-mile limit from the coast should be prohibited. The phrase "other weapons of mass destruction," it was explained, would cover chemical and bacteriological weapons. Such a limited prohibition, it argued, would be easy to verify and safe to accept without greatly affecting international security. [61]

The initial reaction of the majority to the American suggestions was negative. It was feared that, by excluding the installations that might serve the emplacement of conventional weapons in the seabed and on the ocean floor, the American draft treaty would legitimize and provide the incentive for the spread of the conventional armament race into the oceans. [62] The United States discounted such fears and pointed out that emplacement of nuclear installations was the only real and immediate problem. [63]

However, the United States agreed with Poland that certain installations could be set up to serve the dual purpose of emplacing conventional and nuclear weapons. Thus it readily included such installations under the scope of the prohibitions it proposed. [64]

Although the Soviet Union was supported by a majority in its approach, it was thought that without a compromise with the American position and its supporters there could be no satisfactory seabed arms limitation measure. In the interest of achieving some results on this measure, the Soviet Union agreed to cosponsor the United States proposal. The joint draft treaty that the two nations presented to the ENDC incorporated the American position totally as far as the scope of prohibitions was concerned.

The representative of the United States explained the implications of the joint draft treaty prohibitions. He excluded the following uses of the sea from its scope: the operation of nuclear submarines and warships, the conduct of military maneuvers, target practice, and peaceful nuclear explosions, the application of nuclear energy, nuclear reactors, scientific research consistent with other treaty obligations, facilities for research or for commercial exploitation not specifically designed for using nuclear weapons and other weapons of mass destruction, the deployment of submarine tracking stations, and the use of military personnel and equipment for scientific research.[65]

Responding to a query from the representative of the United Kingdom, the American delegate explained that the intended prohibitions would cover the operation of the so-called "creepy-crawlies," that is, those weapon systems that cannot move without some permanent contact with the seabed.[66]

The reaction of other states to the American-Soviet joint draft was generally favorable. However, several amendments were proposed. These amendments were directed at including in the draft treaty (a) an operative paragraph committing the parties to the treaty to undertake further negotiations to achieve in good faith additional measures of seabed disarmament,[67] (b) a clear indication of the prohibitions intended under the phrase "other weapons of mass destruction" and elimination of the phrase itself lest it give rise to contentious interpretations,[68] and (c) provision for the convening of a conference after five years to review the treaty.[69]

The joint draft treaty, which underwent three revisions, gradually incorporated all of these suggestions except for eliminating the phrase "other weapons of mass destruction." In its final form the SACT contained in Article V a commitment on the part of the parties to continue negotiations and in Article VII a provision for a review conference after five years. It also provided under Article VI that "any State Party may propose amendments to this Treaty."[70]

Appraisal These provisions of the treaty reflect the awareness on the part of negotiators of the limited character and scope of prohibitions and their desire to strive, in a manner consistent with world conditions, for further measures to prevent an arms race on the seabed.

The scope of the prohibitions thus agreed upon indeed excludes all the important contemporary military uses of the seas. Most of these activities are conducted for purposes of promoting national security and of scientific research, both of which are objectives well honored by the international community.

While the retention of the phrase "other weapons of mass destruction" serves no purpose at present except the inclusion of chemical and other bacteriological weapons under the treaty prohibition, the international community may in the future decide to include other weapons in that category.

Despite the character of the obligation stated in Article V to continue negotiations, the parties to the treaty are free to choose the place, the time, and the nature of issues to be considered in the negotiations.

The only controversy that arose during the resolution of claims regarding the scope of the prohibitions was whether they should also have included installations designed to deploy conventional weapons such as mines and torpedos. Despite the enthusiasm in some quarters for this kind of a provision, it was quickly apparent that a few major states, without whose approval no viable ocean disarmament measure would be possible, would not endorse any such move. Thus, the desire to achieve a wide consensus prevailed over the attempt to articulate a very comprehensive prohibition against military uses of the seabed. Furthermore, because the elimination of installations involving conventional weapons, though desirable, was not crucial either for the security of states or for the encouragement of peaceful exploitation of ocean resources there was no reason to insist upon their inclusion in the scope of prohibitions finally agreed upon.

In some measure, the final outcome with respect to the claims on the scope of prohibitions was determined partly by the results of a resolution of claims about the geographical area and the procedures of verification. These claims will be considered next.

THE GEOGRAPHICAL AREA

The claims relating to the geographical area within which the proposed prohibitions would or would not be permitted were motivated primarily by two factors: First, there was a concern to avoid definitions of the geographical area that might directly or indirectly affect claims regarding the extent of territorial waters. Second, in any formulation of the definition of the area, there was a need to safeguard the other rights of coastal states, especially those involving their defense and security interests.

The Extent of the Territorial Seas The Soviet Union, which presented a draft treaty on March 18, 1969, suggested under Article III that the proposed prohibition should be made applicable to a maritime area that lies beyond a limit of twelve miles measured "from the same base lines which are used in defining the limits of territorial waters of coastal States." In this connection it indicated that such a limit proposed for the sole purpose of the draft treaty was in no way intended to prejudice the positions of different coastal states on the extent of territorial seas they claimed.[71]

Despite the disclaimer, it was obvious that the Soviet Union, in choosing a twelve-mile outer limit for the maritime zone that would be exempted from the treaty prohibitions, was influenced by its own position of claiming twelve-mile territorial waters. That the two limits should coincide in the case of the Soviet Union was not accidental. As is well known, coastal states enjoy sovereignty over their territorial seas and thereby possess full freedom to use them for all kinds of security purposes. The Soviet Union wanted to save this freedom and thereby to avoid any restrictions on its territorial sovereignty.

The Soviet Union's proposal was regarded as unsatisfactory by the states that claimed territorial seas of lesser or greater breadth. The coastal states that claimed less than twelve-mile territorial seas, for example, three or six miles, felt that under the Soviet proposal an unregulated stretch of high seas of nine to six miles, as the case might be, would result. It was feared that this stretch of high seas would invite foreign military activities inimical to the security of coastal states, even though the Soviet Union denied that this was the purpose of the proposed treaty and claimed that the coastal states would have exclusive control, for these purposes, of the area within twelve miles whether or not they claimed the same extent of territorial seas. Canada, for example, argued that the Soviet proposal needed an appropriate amendment to mitigate dangers to coastal states' security.[72]

The United States, which claims three-mile territorial seas, suggested that the outer limits of the maritime zone to be exempted from the treaty prohibitions be set at three miles. Such a solution, it proposed, besides being suitable to all coastal states that claim less than twelve miles of territorial seas would also enlarge the maritime area in which the prohibition of the proposed treaty would apply.[73]

A majority of the members of the ENDC, however, preferred a twelve-mile limit, with the specific understanding that such a limit had no relationship to the outer limits of territorial seas a coastal state could claim. This preference can be partly explained by the fact that a majority of coastal states do claim more than three miles of territorial seas.[74]

The American-Soviet joint draft treaty that was presented to the ENDC later tried to eliminate any reference to the territorial sea in defining the exempted maritime zone. Instead, the treaty stated that the proposed treaty prohibitions would not be applicable to a maritime zone whose outer limit would be coterminous with the contiguous zone, a zone that was defined under the terms of the Convention on the Territorial Sea and the Contiguous Zone of 1958 and extends up to twelve miles.

The indirect reference to a twelve-mile limit and its definition in terms of the contiguous zone was opposed because of its infelicitous wording in the draft treaty. Mexico claimed, quite validly, that good drafting demanded a simpler and more straightforward definition of the maritime area than the one contained in the joint draft treaty.[75] Several countries objected to the reference made to the Geneva Convention on the Territorial Sea and the Contiguous Zone.[76] A few of them pointed out that such a reference served no other purpose than to prejudge, in a surreptitious manner, coastal states' claims to the extent of territorial sea jurisdictions.[77] The best solution, it was indicated, was to simply refer to a twelve-mile outer limit as was initially done in the Soviet and the American draft.[78]

However, those states that supported the joint draft treaty's reference to the Geneva Convention thought such a reference was the only convenient way to refer to an elaborate method of measuring the twelve-mile outer limit from the coast.[79]

Further objections were raised to the joint draft treaty because it did not solve the problem of the gap that might exist between a twelve-mile outer limit of the proposed geographical area and the outer limit of a coastal state's territorial sea, which extends up to either three or six miles. The United Kingdom, in referring to the problem, recommended appropriate rewording of the joint draft treaty to bridge such a gap.[80]

Argentina took the initiative and submitted a working paper on the definition of the geographical area that was aimed at satisfying the concerns of the states that claim less than twelve miles of territorial seas and of the Latin American countries that claim more than twelve miles of territorial sea and of those states that do not accept the Geneva Conventions on the Law of the Sea as authoritative.[81]

Implications of the Argentinian Proposals The Argentinian working paper referred to a "seabed zone" instead of a "maritime zone." In an attempt to attract the widest support, it also defined the outer limit of the seabed zone in terms of the twelve-mile outer limit of the contiguous zone referred to in Section II of the Geneva Convention on the Territorial Sea and the Contiguous Zone. It noted further that the proposed treaty prohibition would not be applicable to the coastal state within the seabed zone "or within the seabed beneath its territorial waters." The Argentinian suggestions were accepted by the cosponsors and were incorporated in a second revision of the joint draft treaty.[82]

Mexico protested against the inclusion of the phrase "or the seabed beneath its territorial waters" in paragraph 2 of Article I of the second revised version of the joint draft treaty. It warned that the phrase had the implication that any state, by unilaterally claiming territorial waters of more than twelve miles, could extend the limits of the seabed zone within which the treaty prohibition would not be applicable. Such an implication, it pointed out, would accelerate the arms race in the seabed, an objective that was contrary to the spirit of the proposed treaty.[83]

The Mexican objections were well taken and would be more widely appreciated if one considered the status of the treaty on nonemplacement of nuclear weapons in Latin America. (This is also referred to as the Tlatelolco Treaty.) Argentina and Chile signed but did not ratify the Tlatelolco Treaty.[84] As matters stand, Argentina and Chile could theoretically emplace nuclear weapons and other weapons of mass destruction in the seabed beneath their territorial waters. Such an act, if ever undertaken, might provoke the other Latin American countries that subscribe to the Tlatelolco Treaty and force them to revise their commitments thereunder. The situation could then lead to a scramble to acquire nuclear weapons, with all the serious consequences of such an armament race.

Mexico submitted two amendments to the joint draft treaty to counter the effect of the acceptance of the Argentinian working paper. First, it suggested that a separate article be included in the proposed treaty so its provisions would not in any way affect the obligations assumed by state parties under international instruments establishing zones free from nuclear weapons.[85] Through the second amendment Mexico wanted the parties to the proposed treaty to agree not to contribute in any way to the violation of the obligations in the zone referred to in Article I.[86]

The first of the two suggestions that Mexico made was accepted, and its sense was reflected in Article VIII as part of the second revision of the joint draft treaty. The cosponsors of the joint draft treaty, however, did not think that the second suggestion was necessary, because in their view the same result was already achieved through the so-called disclaimer clause they had included in the joint draft treaty.

The representatives of both the United States and the Soviet Union made it clear that the definition of the seabed zone within which the proposed treaty prohibition would not be applicable was deliberately designed not "to support or prejudice the position of any State with respect to rights or claims related to waters off its coasts including among other things, territorial seas."[87]

The Concept of the Maritime Defensive Zone To complete the examination of claims relating to the geographical area, mention should be made of a Canadian proposal for a two-hundred-mile maritime defensive zone. The Canadian proposal was intended to give the coastal state exclusive authority to use the defensive zone for security purposes not prohibited by the treaty under consideration. In other words, such a proposal would have excluded all foreign security activities whether defensive or offensive off the shores of a coastal state up to a limit of two hundred miles.[88]

Canada proposed this concept of a defensive maritime zone for two reasons. First, the proposal was intended as a condition to accepting the prohibitions of a limited nature that were advocated by the United States. Second, it was an attempt to establish unequivocally the right of a coastal state to exclude foreign security installations from its continental shelf area, a right Canada contended was not clearly articulated by the provisions of the Geneva Convention on the Continental Shelf.[89]

The Canadian proposal found some support from countries that were not strong maritime powers.[90] However, the two superpowers did not seriously consider the proposal, nor did the majority show much enthusiasm about it. Finally, Canada dropped the proposal and endorsed the joint draft treaty position even though it was not completely satisfactory and did not address the second aspect of the Canadian concern: to clearly empower the coastal state to exclude all foreign security installations even when they were defensive in character from its continental shelf area.

PROCEDURES OF VERIFICATION

Any agreement on an arms limitation measure has always been dependent on the availability of suitable verification procedures to ensure the parties to it that all possible violations would be promptly detected. Even in the context of negotiation of the SACT, this cardinal principle of effective verification played a central role. One of the reasons why the United States insisted on limiting the scope of the prohibitions in the present context was to ensure that the agreed measures on seabed disarmament could be easily and effectively verified.

While there was consensus on the principle of disarmament under effective verification, there were several differing opinions about what constituted effective verification in relation to the proposed seabed arms control measures. The Soviet Union, under Article II of its draft treaty, suggested that all seabed installations belonging to parties to the treaty be open, on a basis of reciprocity, for free access. The principle of free access, it pointed out, had important precedents in agreements on outer space and Antarctica, which, like the oceans, were areas with no national boundaries.[91]

Many countries with little or no technological capability for inspecting underwater facilities and other seabed installations saw in the condition of reciprocity a discriminatory procedure.[92] According to these countries, the condition of reciprocity emphasized a bilateral relationship between the parties participating in the verification procedures. Such a bilateral relationship, they pointed out, appeared to deny to an underdeveloped coastal state its right to seek third-party assistance if its own means were not adequate to ensure effective verification. Consequently, a developed coastal state with appropriate facilities was better situated than an underdeveloped coastal state to benefit fully from the proposed verification procedure. To mitigate the feared discrimination, it was proposed that the verification procedure in this case should assure the rights of the coastal state to seek third-party assistance.[93] A few of the countries regarded the creation of an international verification mechanism as even more desirable.[94]

The United States opposed all the above alternatives. Proposing that emplacement in the seabed and on the ocean floor of nuclear weapons and other weapons of mass destruction alone be prohibited at this time, it argued that the simple technique of observation and consultation among the parties to the treaty would constitute an effective verification procedure. It pointed out that the placement of nuclear weapons and other weapons of mass destruction in the seabed and on the ocean floor involves extensive activity and unique technological features that could very easily be verified through external observation. Such an observation could be made, it added, in the course of regular navigation of the seas. In case of doubt as to violations of the treaty, this procedure provided that the parties should resort to mutual consultation.[95]

The majority of the members of ENDC, who accepted the proposal for a treaty of limited prohibition as advocated by the United States, were still not convinced that the technique of observation and consultation could lead to effective verification. It was pointed out that the American proposal did not provide any alternatives in case the consultation among the parties failed to resolve doubts regarding treaty violations. They also felt that at some stage, where needed, direct access to the installation was necessary to ascertain compliance with the treaty prohibitions.[96]

The technique of observation, undertaken in pursuance of the freedom to navigate the seas, was also opposed by some states on the grounds that it did not pay adequate attention to the coastal states' exclusive rights over the installations embedded in their territorial waters and the continental shelf.[97]

To remedy these defects, Canada and Brazil submitted separate proposals, the main components of which may be summarized in the form of the following rights:[98]

a. The right of the parties to seek third-party assistance, including the right to appeal to the Secretary-General of the United Nations to help organize such assistance for verification.

b. The right of access to the installations, which, however, can be exercised only after notifying the coastal state of the intention to inspect the facilities over which it has exclusive jurisdiction. Brazil pointed out that the coastal state could not refuse permission to inspect installations when requested and that the provision was designed only to give the coastal state a chance to join in the verification procedures.[99]

c. The right of recourse to the Security Council of the United Nations, where consultation among the parties or the verification procedures fail to produce a satisfactory resolution of doubts regarding compliance with the treaty prohibitions.

The United States objected to the proposed right of third-party assistance. Any such right, it argued, would put onerous obligations on a few technologically developed states. The idea of organizing international assistance for verification of the seabed installations, it warned, was premature and would involve unjustifiable expenses for the international community.[100]

In response to the objections of the United States, India, for example, clarified the issue, saying that the right to seek third-party assistance did not oblige the developed countries to assist in the verification and that it was meant only to enable the coastal state to utilize third-party assistance where voluntarily provided.[101]

As for the international machinery, Canada argued that no expensive new international agency was needed. It recommended that the costs of investigation be met by the party requesting assistance if no violation was proved. Where some violation was established, it added, the expenses could be shared by all the parties or settled through other agreed procedures.[102]

In view of the strong support that the Canadian and Brazilian proposals got from the majority of states, the final version of the joint draft treaty, cosponsored by the United States and the Soviet Union, adopted these proposals with minor modifications.

Verification under the SACT The parties to the treaty have the right to observe all seabed installations in the normal exercise of the freedom of navigation. If any of the parties doubts the purpose of an installation, it must consult with those giving rise to such doubts. Where no responsible party can be identified, the doubting party must notify and consult with all the parties in the region. Other interested parties outside the region may join in such consultation and cooperation. As part of this process, the parties may agree upon appropriate procedures of verification, including the on-site inspection of installations.

Before undertaking the on-site inspection of an installation where necessary, the party or parties must notify the coastal state or others interested in order to give them an opportunity to become involved in the investigation. The results of the investigation must be circulated among the parties. If these procedures of consultation and cooperation fail to produce satisfactory resolution of doubts, the party can refer the matter to the Security Council of the United Nations for appropriate action. In undertaking the procedures of verification under the SACT, the parties can request full or partial assistance from others. Similar assistance can also be channeled "through appropriate international procedures within the framework of the United Nations and in accordance with its Charter." Finally, the procedures of verification must be implemented with due regard for the freedoms of the high seas and the rights of coastal states with respect to the exploration and exploitation of their continental shelves.

Such careful elaboration of the procedures of verification resulted from the need to balance the time-honored freedoms of the seas against the special rights granted to coastal states. This is a situation that distinguishes human behavior with respect to oceans from that involving outer space and Antarctica. In the latter environments, much simpler procedures of verification were found to be satisfactory because of the relatively small number of users and the less significant uses they were put to.

In sum, the procedure of verification under the SACT seemed to emphasize the technique of observation and consultation, and the rest of the provisions were added only as special safeguards. On careful examination the right to seek third-party assistance does not add anything new to the already existing rights of states to request and receive bilateral and multilateral aid, whether it is military or nonmilitary. The Secretary-General and various organs of the United Nations can lend only their good offices and do not have the necessary resources to provide assistance to parties for undertaking effective verification of the seabed installations. While the right of recourse to the Security Council is welcome, here again no new procedures or rights are granted to parties other than those already existing under the United Nations Charter.

It is interesting to speculate, for example, whether or not a state that is party to the SACT, but not a member of the United Nations, would have direct recourse to the Security Council. The answer appears to be in the affirmative, because the Charter of the United Nations under Article 35, paragraph 3, provides that

A State which is not a Member of the United Nations may bring to the attention of the Security Council or of the General Assembly any dispute to which it is a party if it accepts in advance, for the purpose of the dispute, the obligations of pacific settlement provided in the Charter.

Alternatively, a party to the SACT but a nonmember of the United Nations can also inform the Secretary-General of the dispute. The Secretary-General, if he thinks that the situation "may threaten the maintenance of international peace and security," is empowered under Article 99 of the Charter to bring the matter to the attention of the Security Council. Then the Security Council, pursuant to Article 34 of the Charter, can take appropriate action.

However, if one of the parties to the SACT that is responsible for noncooperation leading to the referral of the matter to the Security Council of the United Nations is also a member of the United Nations with veto power, what the Security Council can do and what other lawful strategies can be employed to resolve the dispute are another matter. Contextual factors and the attendant perception of common interests alone determine the shape of such strategies.

It may be added, in the last analysis, that not many states have nuclear weapons and other weapons of mass destruction. Even those states that have them seem convinced that to emplace them in the seabed is economically costly and has no commensurate strategic value. These factors, more than the elaborate mechanism of verification provided under the SACT, would assure compliance with its prohibitions. *Appraisal* The value of the negotiations that led to the SACT lies essentially in the clarification of the status of several security uses of the seas. At a time when the entire body of the contemporary law of the sea has been undergoing reexamination, the negotiations surrounding the seabed arms control measures considered various claims regarding the permissibility of certain kinds of security uses of the sea. A healthy attempt was made in the process of resolving these claims to give priority to the security of states involving the exercise of freedoms of the high seas and the exclusive rights granted to the coastal states over the continental shelves.

It is quite obvious that the provisions of the SACT do not represent a felicitous drafting exercise. However, what the treaty lost in felicity it gained in wider subscription. If one realizes that the treaty was negotiated at a time when both the security and the nonsecurity uses of the sea were being intensively reevaluated, perhaps one could be less critical about its scope or structure.[103]

The admission of People's Republic of China to the United Nations and the new diplomatic moves between that country and the United States, the Strategic Arms Limitation Talks between the United States and the Soviet Union, and the dialogue between the Federal Republic of Germany, on the one hand, and the Soviet Union and some of the East European countries, on the other hand, have already led to modest hopes for the reduction of crises, and this optimism in turn may contribute to further measures of disarmament or arms control.[104]

The Third Law of the Sea Conference is another major event that, if planned well and approached systematically, could resolve several outstanding problems such as those relating to the limits of the territorial seas, the special fishing rights, the limits of the continental shelf, and the nature of the exclusive resources zones. Once these problems are solved, and a more propitious international atmosphere exists for further measures of arms control, a better version of the SACT would automatically be made possible. On balance, the SACT could be cited as an example of how common interests, representing a compromise among several competing interests, could be achieved.[105]

Proposals for Peace Zones

To complete the discussion on reserving the oceans exclusively for "peaceful purposes," it is necessary to point out the attempts to declare certain marine areas to be peace zones wherein certain or all security uses would not be allowed. As two examples, the Tlatelolco Treaty and the "U.N. Declaration of Indian Ocean as a Zone of Peace" may be mentioned. Since the Tlatelolco Treaty was mentioned above, the status of the Indian Ocean as a peace zone will be examined here.[106]

Principally through the efforts of the coastal states of the Indian Ocean, the United Nations General Assembly adopted a "Declaration of the Indian Ocean as a Zone of Peace" on December 16, 1971 [G.A. Resolution 2832 (XXVI)]. The sponsors of the U.N. Declaration wished not merely to keep the Indian Ocean free of nuclear weapons, as the Tlatelolco Treaty was intended to do for the Latin American region, but to exclude from the area "great Power rivalries and competition as well as bases conceived in the context of such rivalries and competition." The resolution urged all members of the U.N. to take steps to implement the spirit of the Declaration.[107]

Subsequent to the adoption of the U.N. General Assembly Resolution 2832 (XXVI), the U.N. Secretary-General conducted a survey of the steps being taken by countries to implement it. Only four countries, Bahrain, Madagascar, the Philippines, and Yemen, responded to the call, though they did not give any concrete information other than a simple reaffirmation of the goal itself.[108]

In order to clarify the goals of the U.N. Declaration and to help achieve some specific measures leading to the promotion of the Indian Ocean as a zone of peace, the sponsors in 1972 made a further attempt to have a fifteen-member committee appointed.

The first committee approved the draft resolution submitted to it in this regard on December 5, 1972, by 72 votes to none, with 35 abstentions.[109]

All the major maritime powers including the United States, the USSR, the United Kingdom, and France were among the countries abstaining. One important reason for the abstention of these countries was the belief that the U.N. Declaration, despite its legitimate concern for security and peace for the coastal states of the region, was, as the Representative of the Soviet Union indicated, not consistent with the principles of "freedom of navigation for all vessels, including naval craft, and the carrying out of scientific research by means of such vessels."

According to Sweden, the Declaration was merely a call for consultation, and unless the states of the region in cooperation with other interested countries agreed on specific disarmament measures, it was too early for the General Assembly to endorse it positively. France noted that "only international *détente* and true disarmament can bring to the coastal States of the Indian Ocean, as to all the peoples of the other regions of the world, the security to which they aspire."

In response to these comments, and to explain the intentions of the sponsors of the Declaration and the latter proposal for the appointment of a committee, Ambassador H. S. Amerasinghe of Sri Lanka pointed out that

It was because the Declaration in all its details last year presented problems to Members of the United Nations that this year we felt that it was necessary to ask for the appointment of a committee which would study the implications of the proposal. . . .

This proposal does not in the least interfere with what was described as the basic principle of law of the sea, namely the freedom of the seas. . . .

Another argument that was adduced was that there should be no regional treatment of the problem of peace. We are not trying to dissect peace, but there is no such thing as regional or global treatment of peace. If you wait for the global treatment of peace, you will never get it. So let us therefore try to approach it regionally, step by step. . . . Why should we be denied the privilege that they [the major powers] seek? They ask us to state as a first step that all foreign military bases and installations should be removed from the Indian Ocean. But that, according to them, is the last measure that they themselves are contemplating. . . .

. . . If this Organization does not show a willingness and a readiness to study a proposal, how can we expect anything of it, how can we expect any progress in the direction of peace? . . . Our proposal is: let us start peace somewhere; start positive measures for the creation of a climate of peace somewhere. Perhaps, as I have said, the infection will spread, and I hope that nobody will get himself inoculated against it.[110]

In view of this explanation, the Declaration should be considered more as a statement of the goal to be attained than as a specific disarmament measure affecting the area.

Final Appraisal

It is generally agreed that states are entitled, on the basis of equality and mutual respect, to access to the high seas, including the continental shelf area and the contiguous zones, for security uses. Even in the territorial sea, over which the coastal state has sovereign rights, it cannot arbitrarily prohibit the innocent passage of foreign ships in times of peace.

However, the coastal state could bar foreign fixed security installations from its continental shelf area on the ground that such a use is not only inimical to its security but also contrary to the exclusive rights granted to it over the "natural resources" of the seabed and the ocean floor. In addition, in the case of passage through the territorial sea, the coastal state could maintain that the foreign ships have an obligation to respect its domestic laws concerning protection of resources and prevention of pollution, among other things.

Attempts at demilitarization of the oceans, to be successful, must be conceived in the context of global disarmament and arms control measures. Despite the rhetoric employed and a certain consistency exhibited in proposing that the oceans be used exclusively for "peaceful purposes," most participants are realistic about the limitations of such a proposal. Furthermore, they realize that several of the security uses of the sea, even though they cause occasional irritation to particular states, generally contribute to the stability of world relations.

Even as the majority of states approve security uses, they also recognize that it is in the common interest for them to be subject to the same policies and prescriptions of accommodation of competing interests at sea as are applicable to the other uses of the sea.

7
Caracas and Beyond

As the international community approaches the final phases of the Third Law of the Sea Conference, the first formal session of which was held in Caracas, Venezuela, from June 20 to August 28, 1974, it is appropriate to inquire about the shape of the future public order of ocean resources. In the preceding chapters this study has pointed out and critically appraised some of the likely results of the Conference. To recapitulate the principal results briefly, most states appear to endorse the exclusive authority of the coastal state over all the resources of the sea within a limit of 200 miles from the coast. Beyond that limit, there appears to be a growing international consensus for approval of coastal state ownership of nonliving resources up to the edge of the continental margin. This ownership, of course, may be subject to some form of revenue-sharing between the coastal state and the international community involving the proceeds gained from exploitation of nonliving resources.

In addition, a significant majority of nations support the creation of strong and comprehensive international machinery not only to regulate access to deep-ocean areas for various uses but to exploit their resources on its own. Furthermore, there is increasing agreement among nations that in the exclusive resource zones of the coastal states, scientific research and preservation of marine environment can be accomplished only with the consent and under the supervision of the coastal state. However, in the same area, except within a twelve-mile limit from its shore, the coastal state may be obliged to permit unimpeded international navigation for all kinds of vessels. Even within the twelve miles, it is likely that the coastal state would still be obliged to honor the innocent passage of foreign vessels.

Except for the law relating to navigation, the outcomes thus indicated by present trends, if enacted in an international treaty, will represent a radical break from the traditional law of the sea. The doctrine of freedom of the seas, which for centuries governed access to the sea, will soon become anachronistic.

However, a successful conclusion of the Third Law of the Sea Conference and the formal enactment of a treaty incorporating some of the trends noted would depend upon resolution of several other issues that are also under serious consideration. These are related to the accommodation of the interests of geographically disadvantaged states in the exclusive resource zones of the coastal states, compromise achievable between distant-water fishing nations and the coastal states with respect to exploitation of fishery resources, and the structure and powers of the proposed international machinery for the deep-ocean areas. On all these and other questions, such as the archipelago problem, the status of offshore islands, and the problem of drawing baselines, considerable bargaining lies ahead. Whether the participants will be able to resolve the outstanding issues amicably and in the common interest at the Geneva session in the spring of 1975 or shortly thereafter is still an open question.

Even as the process of negotiation on the historic revision of the maritime law draws to a close after seven intensive years, the threat of unilateral and much divisive action relating to the use of the seas still looms large. Several coastal states may resort to unilateral proclamations if, in their opinion, the Law of the Sea Conference does not endorse options they consider essential. Such unilateral action may also come about if the negotiation process drags on interminably and if some states believe that their national interests are going to be irretrievably compromised by the resultant legal uncertainty. Thus the international decision-makers are under great pressure to achieve acceptable compromises and achieve them soon, before events preempt negotiated settlement of the issues. For one reason or the other, if states resort to unilateral action, the future of the ocean resource law will remain unsettled. Under such circumstances, there will be no guarantee that the conflicting claims will be resolved through a peaceful process, and the goal of maintenance of minimum world public order will be seriously jeopardized. For this reason alone, even if some specific outcomes are not satisfactory from the perspective of promoting an optimum world public order, the Law of the Sea Conference and the path of negotiated settlement of issues must be pursued with the commitment and seriousness that they deserve.

One major feature of the contemporary revision of the law of the sea has been the growing individualism or nationalism among states. Every nation approaches the issues involved with one policy objective: how it can maximize the offshore areas and the resources and other values they symbolize for itself to the exclusion of others. This policy reflects a sense of isolationism, a sense of exclusivism that is indicative of a subtle distrust among nations of the utility or value of international solutions to the world's pressing problems. The unilateral approach may be gaining currency because of an action-reaction phenomenon, as one group of states resorts to this policy with respect to one set of problems and others reciprocate and adopt it for other problems as well. Emphasis on exclusivism may also be due to the desperate situation in which many nations have found themselves in facing up to growing inflation and the rapid deterioration in the quality of life for many of their people.

But it will soon become clear that contemporary problems are not amenable to individual solutions. This is so, first of all, because their sources and implications are transnational. Second, the magnitude of many of these problems, especially problems of population, food, and poverty, is so great that national resources, however impressive they may be, are not adequate to meet their challenge. Thus, whether because of crushing energy prices, unabated world inflation, depressed standards of living, or deteriorating global environment, solutions to these current crises are to be found not in the individual realm but only through unprecedented international cooperation and a conscious sense of sacrifice and compromise among all nations. These are issues from which the process of offshore resource development cannot be divested.

In deference to world realities and also in recognition of the facts surrounding the framework of the Third Law of the Sea Conference, the following recommendations are offered to organize the process of ocean resource exploitation:

1. If the conference cannot achieve final solutions to all the issues before it, the participants must attempt to separate those questions on which broad consensus has already been achieved and to incorporate them in appropriate treaty form. In this way the conference need not lose ground with respect to some issues while seeking to gain on others.

2. The limits of coastal state jurisdiction should be set in a clear and easily accountable way, for example, in terms of 200 miles or 2,500-meter depth, rather than in terms of geological concepts such as the edge of the continental margin. Such a course would set problems of boundary demarcation at rest with greater ease.

3. The coastal states must agree to pay a percentage of the value of offshore resources given to their exclusive use and enjoyment to meet international needs and interests. The proposition that applies revenue-sharing only to the area between 200 miles from the shore and the edge of the continental margin is very conservative and unsatisfactory.

4. While the creation of international machinery to control access to deep-ocean areas may be acceptable, the development of its bureaucracy and specific functions must be tailored to the actual needs of international use of deep-ocean areas. Otherwise, ambitious programs will be nothing but costly ego trips that the international community cannot sustain.

5. The coastal states, in mutual consultation, should set up uniform policies and prescriptions and, if possible, institutions to regulate the resources in the exclusive zones. Thus they will be able to contribute to the stability of expectations and efficiency of offshore operations.

6. Now that it is increasingly certain that coastal states will have control over scientific research at sea, they are under a special obligation to promote and facilitate it. Toward this end, the nations must adopt simple regulations and easily identifiable domestic institutions to which requests for access may be readily addressed. In addition, national institutions, wherever possible, must provide advance notification of the conditions under which they are prepared to agree to requests for research in maritime areas under their jurisdiction.

7. Finally, the future international treaty governing the uses of the sea should contain specific commitments by the parties to submit disputes to judicial settlement, allowing the proper role to be played by existing agencies, including the International Court of Justice.

Notes

Abbreviations

A.J.I.L.	American Journal of International Law
B.Y.B.I.L.	British Yearbook of International Law
G.A.O.R.	General Assembly Office Records
I.C.J.	International Court of Justice
I.C.L.Q.	International and Comparative Law Quarterly
I.J.I.L.	Indian Journal of International Law
I.L.C.	International Law Commission
Y.B.I.L.C.	Yearbook of the International Law Commission

Notes to Chapter 1, pp. 1–25

[1] In connection with the law of the sea, "geographically disadvantaged states" is a recent expression. It refers to those coastal states with offshore areas of less than a 200-meter depth. The expression is also used to include Zaire, a so-called near-landlocked state because it has a narrow coastline of 22 miles. Generally, coastal states that do not have long and open coastlines, which do not seem to be able to benefit from wide limits advocated for coastal states' exclusive resource jurisdiction, consider themselves to be geographically disadvantaged states. In this study the expression is sometimes used to refer to landlocked, near-landlocked, and shelf-locked states. See Chapter 3.

[2] See Chapter 3.

[3] Landlocked states are Afghanistan, Andorra, Austria, Bhutan, Botswana, Burundi, Bolivia, Central African Republic, Chad, Czechoslovakia, Hungary, Laos, Lesotho, Liechtenstein, Luxembourg, Malawi, Mali, Mongolia, Nepal, Nigeria, Paraguay, Rhodesia, Rwanda, Swaziland, San Marino, Switzerland, Uganda, Upper Volta, Vatican City, and Zambia.

[4] Shelf-locked states are Bahrain, Belgium, Cambodia, Denmark, Finland, Germany (East), Germany (West), Iran, Jordan, Kuwait, Monaco, Netherlands, Poland, Qatar, Singapore, Sweden, Togo, United Arab Emirates, Vietnam (North), and Yugoslavia.

[5] The statement of the representative of Afghanistan to the United Nations on the subject of deep ocean resources is very pertinent in reference to the anxiety of the landlocked countries. Proposing that the equal interests of landlocked countries should be recognized in ocean resource exploitation, he said,

> The underprivileged situation of the land-locked countries in matters of trade, development and access to the sea has long been recognized by the international community and reflected in relevant international documents. . . . It is highly desirable that their underprivileged situation should in all fairness be singled out in this draft as in all other instruments related to the access to the sea and the exploitation of its resources. Furthermore, our formula would have the merit of drawing attention not only to the special situation of the developing land-locked countries but to the situation of the developed land-locked countries as well. It should be understood that whatever the degree of the development of the developed land-locked countries and the extent and scope of the arrangements that these countries might have entered with the coastal States, they will remain handicapped by their geographically disinherited position.

U.N. doc. A/C.1/PV. 1595, pp. 45–46.

A similar view was expressed by the representative of Austria in the same connection:

> For my government the starting point in examining this problem was understandably the fact that Austria is a landlocked State. Thus my country is among those which would be primarily affected if technological progress, outpacing legal developments, worked only to the benefit of those countries which have free access to the sea.

U.N. doc. A/C.1/PV. 1591, pp. 24–25.

[6] U.N. doc. A/C.1/PV. 1598, p. 12. See also Chapter 3, footnotes 94 and 95.

[7] For a list of the international and intergovernmental organizations that deal with one or the other aspects of ocean environment, see the Second Report of the President to the Congress on Marine Resources and Engineering Development: *Marine Science Affairs: A Year of Plans and Progress* (Washington, D.C.: U.S. Government Printing Office, 1968), p. 191.

[8] Of the various valuable reports these intergovernmental organizations submitted for member-states' guidance in the consideration of exploitation of the deep-ocean resources, we may mention, for example, the following documents:

1. U.N. doc. A/AC. 135/4 (an outline on scientific aspects relating to the marine environment prepared by IOC);
2. U.N. doc. A/AC. 135/14 (economic implications of the exploitation of deep ocean resources prepared by the U.N. Secretariat);
3. U.N. doc. A/AC. 135/15 (effects of the exploitation of the mineral resources on the superjacent waters and on other uses of the marine environment prepared by the U.N. Secretariat);
4. U.N. doc. A/AC. 135/17 (scientific aspects of the peaceful uses of the ocean floor, prepared by the IOC);
5. U.N. doc. A/AC. 135/10 and Rev. 1 and A/AC. 135/11 (survey of various international agreements concerning the seabed and the ocean floor and the subsoil thereof underlying the high seas beyond the limits of present national jurisdiction);
6. U.N. doc. E/4487 (*Marine Science and Technology: Survey and Proposals,* a report by the U.N. Secretary-General); and
7. U.N. doc. A/AC. 135/23 (regulatory aspects of exploration and exploitation including rules respecting ocean data stations, drilling rigs, production platforms, and other devices prepared by IMCO).

For a more exhaustive list of U.N. documents, see *Ocean Affairs Bibliography,* 1971 (Ocean Series 302, Woodrow Wilson International Center for Scholars), pp. 161–187.

[9] For a list of nongovernmental organizations active in this field, see The Second Report of the President, *supra* note 7.

By way of some obvious examples we might also mention the following academic bodies: the International Law Association and its several national branches; the national societies of international law; the World Peace Through World Law Center; the Centre for Democratic Study; the American Assembly; and International Institute for Peace and Conflict Research.

[10] See *infra* note 20 for an idea of the industry's involvement in offshore mining activities.

[11] For this kind of formulation of the social process, see M. S. McDougal, "Land Policy and Control," in M. S. McDougal and David Haber, *Property, Wealth and Land: Allocation, Planning and Development* (Charlottesville, Va.: Michie Casebook Corporation, 1948), pp. 41–44, at p. 41.

[12] For a thorough account of some of the implications of current research in ocean science and technology for the purposes of power and security see John P. Craven, "Sea Power and the Sea Bed," Vol. 92, *U.S. Naval Institute Proceedings,* pp. 36–51 (April 1966). Also see, Odale D. Waters, Jr., "The Navy's Role in Oceanography" in *Proceedings of the Marine Frontiers Conference* (University of Rhode Island, July 27–28, 1967), at p. 523; and Rear Admiral Wilfred A. Hearn, USN, "The Role of the United States Navy in the Formulation of Federal Policy Regarding the Sea," Vol. 1, *Natural Resources Lawyer,* pp. 23–31 (June 1968).

[13] See Gordon J. F. MacDonald, "An American Strategy for the Oceans," in Edmund A. Gullion (ed.), *Uses of the Seas* (Englewood Cliffs, N.J.: Prentice-Hall, 1968), pp. 163–194, at p. 176.

[14] Some observers have feared not only temporary obstructions but even permanent restrictions on security uses due to special jurisdictions granted to regulate resource uses. This fear, expressed in terms of the so-called concept of "creeping jurisdiction," was mentioned by Professor Louis Henkin at a U.S. Senate Committee hearing. He said,

> I am persuaded, wherever the coastal state has sovereign rights for purposes of exploiting natural resources, it acquires in the long run, and in the less-than-long run, too, exclusive rights for other and probably all purposes. Wide continental shelves, then, will mean wide areas under the increasing control of other coastal states from which various uses by the United States could be effectively barred.

See *Hearings before the Special Sub-Committee on Outer Continental Shelf of the United States Senate Committee on Interior and Insular Affairs*, 91st Congress, First and Second Sessions (Washington, D.C., 1970), at pp. 204–205.

[15] On accommodation of competing uses of the sea, see Chapter 5, and on conflicts involving security uses, see Chapter 6.

[16] See the statement of the representative of Iceland to the United Nations:

> The Icelandic Government, furthermore, favours the principle of exclusive reservation for peaceful purposes of the sea bed and the ocean floor. As the Government of a country without any armed forces, it does not favour the exploitation of the ocean floor for military purposes.

U.N. doc. A/AC. 135/1/Add. 8, p. 2.

See also, for the views of other member states on this matter, U.N. doc. A/AC. 135/12, pp. 29–33.

[17] This categorization of ocean resources is taken from David A. Ross, *Introduction to Oceanography* (New York: Appleton-Century-Crofts, 1970), Chapter 9.

[18] The sea water contains such known minerals as salt, magnesium, bromine, and fresh water. In some parts of the world's coastal areas these minerals are presently being extracted. The sea, covering an area of about 140 million square miles, at a mean depth of 2.5 miles, holds 300 million cubic miles of water.

See John L. Mero, "Review of Mineral Values on and Under the Ocean Floor" in Marine Technology Society, *Exploiting the Ocean* (Washington, D.C.: Marine Technology Society, 1966), pp. 61–78 at p. 65. For a detailed analysis of the different minerals composed in a cubic mile of sea water, see J. W. Chanslor, "Treasures From the Sea," in U.S. Naval Oceanographic Office, *Science and the Sea* (Washington, D.C.: U.S. Government Printing Office, 1967), pp. 9–16, at p. 9.

Estimating the economic value of the minerals dissolved in the sea water, one source pointed out that "[e]very cubic kilometer of sea water contains about 40 million tons of dissolved solids having a value of more than $1 billion if extracted."

See Paul M. Fye, Arthur E. Maxwell, K. O. Emery, and Bostwick Ketchum, "Ocean Sciences and Marine Resources," in E. A. Guillion (ed.), *supra* note 13, pp. 17–69, at p. 50.

[19] See K. O. Emery, "Oil on the Shelf," Vol. 27, *Oceanus*, pp. 11–17 (Woods Hole: Woods Hole Oceanographic Institution, Spring 1973).

[20] See John P. Albers, "Offshore Petroleum: Its Geography and Technology," in John K. Gamble, Jr., and Giulio Pontecorvo (eds.), *Law of the Sea: The Emerging Regime of the Oceans* (Proceedings of the Eighth Annual Conference of the Law of the Sea Institute, June 18–21, 1973) (Cambridge, Mass.: Ballinger Publishing Co., 1974), pp. 293–304, at p. 294. See also Report of the Secretary-General, *Economic Significance, in Terms of Sea-Bed Mineral Resources, of the Various Limits Proposed for National Jurisdiction*, U.N. doc. A/AC. 138/87, at pp. 9–10.

[21] John P. Albers, idem, pp. 299–302. It is also noted that of the countries having significant production of oil, Saudi Arabia shows 33 percent from offshore; the United

States, 18 percent; Trinidad and Tobago, 33 percent; Australia, 66 percent; and Gabon, 23 percent. Other countries with large but undetermined amounts of offshore oil production include Mexico and Nigeria.

With respect to offshore natural gas production, only 10 countries reported such production at all. Among them, the United States identified a large amount of offshore production in terms of quantities (17 percent).

See John P. Albers and Richard F. Meyer, "New Information on Worldwide Seabed Resources," Vol. 2, *Ocean Management,* pp. 61–74 (1974), at pp. 66–67.

[22] John P. Albers, idem. The South China Sea and Yellow Sea geophysical features have been studied by Emery and other scientists. See also K. O. Emery and Zvi Ben-Avraham, "Structure and Stratigraphy of the China Basin," Vol. 6, *United Nations ECAFE, CCOP Technical Bulletin* (July 1972); K. O. Emery, Elazar Uchupi, John Sunderland, H. L. Uktolseja, and E. M. Young, "Geological Structure and Some Water Characteristics of the Java Sea and Adjacent Continental Shelf," Vol. 6, *United Nations ECAFE, CCOP Technical Bulletin* (July 1972). See also K. O. Emery and Hiroshi Niino, "Stratigraphy and Petroleum Prospects of Korea Strait and the East China Sea," Vol. 1, *Report of Geophysical Exploration,* pp. 1–19 (1967); John M. Wageman, Thomas W. C. Hilde, and K. O. Emery, "Structural Framework of East China Sea and Yellow Sea," Vol. 54, *The American Association of Petroleum Geologists Bulletin,* pp. 1611–1643 (September 1970).

In addition to these China Sea areas, there may be other marine areas (for example, West Africa) with petroleum potential; see K. O. Emery, *Eastern Atlantic Continental Margin Program of the International Decade of Ocean Exploration* (GX-28193): *Some Results of 1972 Cruise of R/V ATLANTIS II* (July 1972). Also see K. O. Emery, "Pagoda Structures in Marine Sediments" (in press).

[23] See the map, *Licenses and Leases Awarded in Water Deeper than 200 Meters* (dated March 1973), compiled by Shell International Petroleum, obtainable through the U.N. Secretariat. According to one source, 39 countries bordering internationally known water bodies have issued licenses or concessions that extend wholly or in part beyond the 200-meter isobath.

See John P. Albers and Richard F. Meyer, *supra* note 21, pp. 65–66.

[24] David A. Ross, *supra* note 17, pp. 337–338. Also see the U.N. Secretary-General's Report, *Resources of the Sea,* U.N. doc. E/4449/Add. 1, pp. 6–12.

[25] K. O. Emery, Paul M. Fye, and George Cadwalader, "The Seabed," in *Public Policy Towards Environment 1973: A Review and Appraisal,* Vol. 216 of the *Annals of the New York Academy of Sciences* (May 18, 1973), pp. 51–55, at p. 53, also p. 54.

[26] John L. Mero is among those who are optimistic about the economic value of the manganese nodules. See John L. Mero, *The Mineral Resources of the Sea* (Amsterdam: Elsevier, 1965), pp. 242–280; Mero, *The Mining and Processing of Deep-Sea Manganese Nodules* (Berkeley: Institute of Marine Resources, 1959); Mero, "Minerals on the Ocean Floor," Vol. 203, *Scientific American,* pp. 64–72 (December 1960).

For other views, H. D. Hess, "The Ocean: Mining's Newest Frontier," Vol. 166, *Engineering and Mining Journal,* pp. 79–96 (August 1965); John E. Crawford and John W. Padan, "The Bureau of Mines' Expanding Role in Undersea Mining," Vol. 17, *Mining Engineering,* pp. 67–70 (March 1965); Meyer G. Lurie, "Ocean Miners Prepare for the Big Plunge," Vol. 96, *Chemical Week,* pp. 131–144 (April 17, 1965); and Thomas A. Wilson, "Undersea Mining: Where Do We Stand Today?" Vol. 166, *Engineering and Mining Journal,* pp. 81–88 (May 1965).

[27] Manganese, the chief component of the nodules, is abundantly available in land deposits. These are adequate for several hundreds of years at their present rate of use, mainly as a toughener for steel. See David B. Brooks, *Low-Grade and Nonconventional Sources of Manganese* (Baltimore: Johns Hopkins Press, 1966), p. 94.

[28] D. R. Horn, B. M. Horn, and M. N. Delach, *Ocean Manganese Nodules Metal Values and Mining Sites* (Technical Report No. 4, NSF GX-33616, International Decade of Ocean Exploration, National Science Foundation, Washington, D.C., 1973).

[29] On the Red Sea deposits, see Egon T. Degens and David A. Ross, *Hot Brines and Recent Heavy Metal Deposits in Red Sea: A Geochemical and Geophysical Account* (New York: Springer-Verlag, 1969).

[30] Reflecting anxiety over these factors in the contemporary world social process, Lord C. P. Snow, a noted British novelist, said,

We can't avoid any longer the fundamental trouble we are moving into: the trouble which, in truth, we are already in. This has certainly contributed to our state of siege. Never mind our mental states, though. The trouble is elemental.
It is the contrast between the rich countries of the world and the poor. The fact that half our fellow human beings are living at or below subsistence level. The fact that in the unlucky countries the population is growing faster than the food to keep it alive. The fact that we may be moving—perhaps in 10 years—into large-scale famine.
The most dreadful of all . . . is that many millions of people in the poor countries are going to starve to death before our eyes—or, to complete the domestic picture, we shall see them doing so upon our television sets.
How soon? How many deaths? Can they be prevented? Can they be minimized?
These are the most important questions in our world today.

See, for a fuller account of his evaluation of the world social process, *The New York Times,* November 13, 1968, p. 28.
Since Lord Snow made his comments, the world has witnessed a growing intensification of these concerns, which culminated in a U.N. General Assembly special session discussion on the study of the problems of raw materials and development. For the fears expressed by almost every major country in the world on the subject, see U.N. doc. A/PV. 2207 to 2227 (of meetings held from April 9 to 26, 1974).

[31] For example, about 2,000 lawyers and judges from over a hundred nations attending the World Peace Through World Law Conference, passed Resolution 15 on July 23, 1967, which stated:

Whereas new technology and oceanography have revealed the possibility of exploitation of untold resources of the high seas and of the bed thereof beyond the continental shelf and more than half of mankind finds itself underprivileged, underfed, and underdeveloped and the high seas are the common heritage of all mankind.
Resolved that the World Peace Through Law Centre: (1) Recommend to the General Assembly of the United Nations the issuance of a proclamation declaring that the nonfishery resources of the high seas, outside the territorial waters of any state and the bed of the sea beyond the continental shelf, appertain to the United Nations and are subject to its jurisdiction and control.

Ambassador Arvid Pardo of Malta, commending this resolution to the U.N., elaborated on some of the objectives that should guide the regulation of the seabed resources as follows: ". . . the seabed and the ocean floor, beyond the limits of national jurisdiction shall be reserved 'exclusively for peaceful purposes' and shall be exploited primarily in the interest of mankind, with particular regard to the needs of poor countries." See A/C.1/PV. 1515.
On the relationship of the world social process to the process of ocean resource exploitation, see the statement of Jamil Baroody, the representative of Saudi Arabia to the United Nations, A/C.1/PV. 1592, pp. 32–55. In the same connection, pointing out that the ocean resource exploitation can either breed competition and violence or promote collaboration and welfare in the international community, E. Hambro, a distinguished scholar and statesman warned that "the deep seas can be either the graveyard of disappointed hopes or the active workshop for common endeavour." A/C.1/PV. 1593, p. 21.

[32] See the statement of the representative of Sri Lanka, H. S. Amerasinghe:

It is a commonplace in modern life that technological and financial capacity exist together and that he who has one has both. The developing nations have neither. They must rely on the developed nations, and especially the most powerful nations, for support and active cooperation if their expectations are to be realized, their apprehensions overcome and their steady economic advance assured. It is not self-abnegation and altruism that is asked of the economically and technologically advanced nations, but a rational policy that will spare the world another experience of competitive colonial expansion which though not directed at the political subjugation of peoples and territories might well result in their economic subjugation.

A/C.1/PV. 1588, p. 63.

[33] The views of the Minister for External Relations of Brazil were stated by Brazil's representative at the opening of the third session of the U.N. Ad Hoc Committee to Study the Peaceful Uses of the Sea-Bed and Ocean Floor Beyond the Limits of National Jurisdiction as follows:

Discrimination in any form is not to be accepted, but we should bear in mind that the most serious and potentially most dangerous form of discrimination is one which, as a consequence of an unqualified freedom of exploitation, would benefit exclusively the technologically and economically most advanced nations.

Quoted by the representative of Brazil to the United Nations; A/C.1/PV. 1591, p. 11.

The views of other countries that are economically and technically underdeveloped reflect the same sentiments. See, for example, Uruguay, A/C.1/PV. 1593, p. 41; Yugoslavia, idem, p. 51; Argentina, A/C.1/PV. 1594, p. 22; Pakistan, A/C.1/PV. 1601, p. 17; Tunisia, A/C.1/PV. 1601, p. 33; Trinidad and Tobago, A/C.1/PV. 1601, p. 73; Chile, A/C.1/PV. 1601, p. 86; and India, A/C.1/PV. 1591, p. 17. Representing the views of all the underdeveloped countries in this matter was the working paper on the draft Declaration of General Principles proposed by Argentina, Brazil, Ceylon, Chile, Ecuador, El Salvador, India, Kenya, Liberia, Libya, Pakistan, Peru, Thailand, United Arab Republic, and United Republic of Tanzania on the subject of the "Examination of the question of the reservation exclusively for peaceful purposes of the sea-bed and the ocean floor, and the sub-soil thereof, underlying the high seas beyond the limits of present national jurisdiction, and the use of their resources in the interest of mankind." See the Report of the U.N. Ad Hoc Committee, U.N. doc. A/7230 (New York: United Nations, 1968), pp. 62–64. Also see U.N. doc. A/AC. 135.12, pp. 34–41.

[34] For a summary of the views expressed in the United Nations in this regard see the Report of the Ad Hoc Committee, A/7230, pp. 30–32. Also see the U.N. doc. A/AC. 135/12, p. 40; and A/AC. 135.14.

[35] Report of the Panel on Oceanography, President's Science Advisory Committee, *Effective Use of the Sea* (Washington, D.C.: U.S. Government Printing Office, June 1968), pp. 27–28. See also the keynote address of Edward Wenk, Jr. (Executive Secretary, National Council on Marine Resources and Engineering Development), at the First Scientific Meeting of the Undersea Medical Society in Conjunction with the Aerospace Medical Association (Miami, Florida, May 9, 1968), p. 13.

[36] See the Report of the Organization for Economic Cooperation and Development, which mentions that

. . . since the strength, progress, and prestige of countries are today measured in part by their achievements in science and technology, scientific excellence is more and more becoming an important national goal. National resources are therefore increasingly devoted to research and development.

"Science and Policies of the Government," in Norman Kaplan (ed.), *Science and Society* (Chicago: Rand McNally Co., 1965), p. 374.

[37] Explaining his involvement for many years in marine research, William L. Chapman said,

The great dream of conquering the sea and bending it to our use, and the great expectations of the benefits that would certainly flow to all mankind, and particularly to the
United States, from this has been a sufficient goal for me to drive for these many years,
and so it has been with most of my scientific colleagues.

William L. Chapman, *Statement before the Subcommittee on Oceanography of the
Committee on Merchant Marine and Fisheries, House of Representatives,* Eighty-Ninth
Congress, First Session, *National Oceanographic Program Legislation* (Washington,
D.C.: U.S. Government Printing Office, 1965), pp. 427–428.

[38] See the First Report of the President to the Congress on Marine Resources and Engineering Development: *Marine Science Affairs: A Year of Transition* (Washington,
D.C.: U.S. Government Printing Office, February 1967), p. 14.

[39] See the report by the U.S. National Council on Marine Resources and Engineering
Development, Executive Office of the President, *International Decade of Ocean Exploration* (Washington, D.C.: U.S. Government Printing Office, 1968), p. 2.

[40] See the Report of the Commission on Marine Science, *Our Nation and the Sea: A
Plan for National Action* (Washington, D.C.: U.S. Government Printing Office, January
1969), pp. 133–134.

[41] David A. Ross, *supra* note 17, pp. 204 and 106.

[42] Keeping some of these claims in view, the study by John P. Albers and Richard F.
Meyer, *supra* note 21 (pp. 63–64), made calculations about the area of the ocean floor
that some of the countries would gain depending upon acceptance of one or another of
the limits frequently proposed: a 200-meter depth, 3,000-meter depth, or a 200-nautical-
mile distance, as follows:

By way of summary, 36 countries have coastlines more than 1,000 nautical miles long but
there are only 13 countries whose offshore areas to a water depth of 200 meters are as
large as 100,000 square nautical miles. If the seaward jurisdiction were established at a
water depth of 3,000 meters, 25 countries would have offshore areas of as much as
100,000 square nautical miles; whereas if the seaward limit were placed at 200 nautical
miles, 41 countries would have offshore areas greater than 100,000 square nautical miles.
It is interesting to note the differences in included offshore areas of the various countries
when the limits are set according to the three criteria established above. Consideration of
the 13 countries alone whose coastlines are approximately 3,000 miles long or longer
demonstrates the variations that occur in relative amounts of offshore area depending
upon which of the three jurisdictional limits are chosen [Table 1.1, p. 212]. As an example, the Soviet Union possesses the longest coastline of any nation in the world. Yet, its
seaward area to a water depth of 200 meters is exceeded by four nations, to a water
depth of 3,000 meters, by four nations, and to a distance of 200 miles by five nations. As
another example, both Chile and India have coastlines approximately 3,000 miles long.
On the basis of jurisdictional limits seaward to a water depth of 200 meters, India has an
offshore area nearly 16 times that of Chile and to a water depth of 3,000 meters, about
double that of Chile. However, on the basis of a jurisdictional limit of 200 miles from
shore, Chile incorporates nearly 100,000 square nautical miles more than India.

[43] H. Sverdrup, M. W. Johnson, and R. H. Fleming, *The Oceans* (Englewood Cliffs,
N.J.: Prentice-Hall, 1942), p. 21.

[44] David A. Ross, *supra* note 17, p. 261. According to Dr. Ross, in reality the depth at
which the greatest change of slope occurs is 72 fathoms.

[45] H. Sverdrup, M. W. Johnson, and R. H. Fleming, *supra* note 43, p. 21. For an extensive description of the shelves along the coasts of the world, see F. P. Shepard, *Submarine Geology,* 3rd Ed. (New York: Harper and Row, 1973), pp. 196–275. According to
Kuenen, the most extensive shelf on earth is that connecting Java, Sumatra, Malacca,
and Borneo. It has an area of 2,000 km^2. Other wide shelves are found, he says, south of
the Bering Strait, north of Siberia, between Australia and New Guinea, to the east of
Argentina, off Korea, and in the North Sea, all about 1 million km^2. P. H. Kuenen,
Marine Geology (New York: John Wiley and Sons, 1950), p. 105.

Table 1.1   Coastal Lengths and Offshore Areas [see note 42]

	Length of Coastline (1,000 Nautical Miles)	Offshore Area (1,000 Square Nautical Miles)		
		to 200 meters	to 3000 meters	to 200 miles
USSR	23	364	736	1,310
Indonesia	20	810	1,230	1,577
Australia	15	662	1,445	2,043
U.S.A.	12	545	863	2,222
Canada	11	847	1,240	1,370
Philippines	7	52	65	551
Mexico	5	129	343	832
Japan	5	140	441	1,126
Brazil	4	224	436	924
China, People's Republic of	3	230	281	281
New Zealand	3	71	571	1,410
India	3	132	340	588
United Kingdom	3	144	282	275
Chile	3	8	168	667

Source: John P. Albers and Richard F. Meyer, "New Information on Worldwide Seabed Resources," Vol. 2, *Ocean Management,* pp. 63–64 (1974).

[46] See F. P. Shepard, *Submarine Geology,* 1st Ed. (New York: Harper and Brothers, 1948). Shepard says, after extensively describing the shelves around the world, that "it should not have been necessary to complete the preceding tour de monde to have learned that the old concept of nicely graded shelves extending out to a so-called wave base belongs in a museum for antiques." Idem, pp. 143, 144, 175.

[47] Mentioning that there are many patterns of transition from the continents to ocean bottoms, one source divided them into three classes. In the first, the sequence of form is shelf, slope, trench, ridge, and basin (westward from Peru). The second pattern differs in having a marginal sea and island area between slope and trench (north from Venezuela). The third is represented by the sequence of shelf, slope, rise, and basin (east from New Jersey). See Maurice Ewing and Mark Landisman, "Shape and Structure of Ocean Basins," in Mary Sears (ed.), *Oceanography* (Washington, D.C.: Publication No. 67 of the American Association for the Advancement of Science, 1961), pp. 3–37, at pp. 5–6.

[48] For a description of the continental slope off the coasts around the world see F. P. Shepard, *supra* note 45.

[49] C. A. M. King, *An Introduction to Oceanography* (New York: McGraw-Hill, 1963), pp. 26, 18.

[50] For a definition of these various features, see F. P. Shepard, *supra* note 45.

[51] See C. A. M. King, *supra* note 49, pp. 43–49.

[52] Francis T. Christy, "Alternative Regimes for Marine Resources Underlying the High Seas," Vol. 1, *Natural Resources Lawyer,* pp. 63–77 (1968), at pp. 65–66.

Christy argues that even though the manganese nodules are widely distributed, producers of hard minerals, when the time arrives, still like to choose a specific submarine area and bargain for exclusive rights over such identified maritime zones. In selecting the offshore areas for the exploitation of manganese nodules, he indicates that such factors as the size of the nodules, the density of their distribution, the distance from the shore, and the wave and weather conditions would be important.

Even so, assurance of exclusive property rights is essential to encourage investors to exploit offshore natural resources, whether they are oil and gas deposits or manganese

nodules. David Brooks, a noted economist, and chief of the Division of Economic
Analysis, Bureau of Mines, U.S. Department of the Interior, says,

> The principle of exclusive rights is so fundamental to efficient mining that the industry
> often neglects to elaborate upon it. Apart from exclusive rights there is no way to insure
> that the returns from exploration accrue to the discoverer, hence no way to attract capi-
> tal to the exploration efforts nor any way to prevent the common property dilemma that
> bedevils fishing. If exclusive rights were not available one company could wait until
> another had done the needed exploration and then, having avoided these costs, move in
> on the deposit and operate on the same locale. Ignoring the obvious problem of conflict,
> it is easy to visualize problems of congestion with equipment forced to operate at less
> than optimum levels of productivity or safety. Moreover, the tendency to mine as fast as
> possible or to "high grade" would be aggravated by the need to reap the benefits of min-
> ing before another firm obtained them. But for materials like manganese deposits that are
> fixed in position and cannot move across arbitrary property lines, these problems cannot
> arise once exclusive rights are made available.

See David Brooks, "Deep Sea Manganese Nodules: From Scientific Phenomenon to
World Resource" in Lewis M. Alexander (ed.), *The Law of the Sea: The Future of the
Sea's Resources* (Proceedings of Second Annual Conference of the Law of the Sea Institute, University of Rhode Island, Kingston, R.I., 1968), pp. 32–42, at p. 37. See also for
similar views, Northcutt Ely, "The Laws Governing Exploitation of the Minerals Beneath the Sea" in *Exploiting the Ocean, supra* note 18, pp. 372–378, at p. 377.

[53] John P. Craven, "The Challenge of Ocean Technology to the Law of the Sea," Vol.
22, *Judge Advocate General Journal*, pp. 31–38 (1967), at pp. 35–37.

[54] On inflation around the world in 1974 see "Inflation Goes Around the World," *The
New York Times,* July 7, 1974, Section 4, p. 1.

[55] John P. Albers and Richard F. Meyer, *supra* note 21.

[56] The enormous task of collecting the oceanographic data is indicated by the Soviet representative to the United Nations in the following terms: "It would, for example, take a
hundred vessels about 200–250 years to produce a geological survey of the ocean floor of
the Pacific alone." See U.N. doc. A/AC. 135/WG12SRg, pp. 8–11.

If this were so, one can imagine the disadvantage of most of the nations that do not
have any significant naval fleet at their disposal in collecting oceanographic data.

[57] The Second Report of the President, *supra* note 7, p. 91.

[58] See *Mineral Resources of the Sea Including Annexes* (1970), U.N. doc. ST/ECA/125,
p. 31; and *Ocean Industry* (September 1973). The average cost of the 1,191 offshore
wells drilled off the United States in 1969 was $559,309. See U.N., ECOSOC doc.
E/4973, p. 52. Also see Herman T. Franssen, "Oil and Gas in the Oceans," Vol. 26,
Naval War College Review, pp. 50–64 (May–June 1974), at pp. 54–55.

[59] See Herman T. Franssen, idem.

[60] See John P. Albers, *supra* note 20, p. 296.

[61] Progress Report by the Secretary-General, *Sea-Bed Mineral Resources: Recent Developments,* U.N. doc. A/AC. 138/90, pp. 11–12.

[62] John P. Albers, *supra* note 20, pp. 302–304.

[63] Robert Engler, *The Politics of Oil: A Study of Private Power and Democratic Directions* (Chicago: University of Chicago Press, 1967), p. 94, for a mention of the ten corporations that control most needed skills for petroleum production and distribution.

However, of late, as more of the countries that own the oil and gas deposits become
assertive of their role in the production rate and price setting for petroleum, the long-
enjoyed dominant role of the oil industry is beginning to decrease. Nevertheless, the skills
that the industry has at its disposal make it an indispensable partner in all future arrangements concerning oil and gas production and distribution. For an excellent analysis
of changing role of the oil industry, see "The Oil Industry—Caught in a Tug-of-War,"
The New York Times, July 7, 1974, Section 3, pp. 1 and 3.

[64] For a description of manganese nodule technology, see the Progress Report of the Secretary-General, *supra* note 61, pp. 10–14, and A. J. Rothstein and R. Kaufman, "The Approaching Maturity of Deep Ocean Mining—The Pace Quickens," Vol. 1, *Offshore Technology Conference Preprints* (1973), pp. 323–344.

[65] See Wayne J. Smith, "An Assessment of Deep Ocean Manganese Nodule Exploration Technology" (an unpublished draft, Woods Hole Oceanographic Institution, 1972).

[66] For emphasis on the latter aspect, see William T. Burke, "A Negative View of a Proposal for United Nations ownership of Ocean Mineral Resources," Vol. 1, *Natural Resources Lawyer*, pp. 42–62 (June 1968), at pp. 57–59.

[67] For a mention of this aspect, see David Brooks, *supra* note 27, pp. 114–115, 120–122.

[68] See Claude Girad, "Military Uses of the Continental Shelf and the Sea-bed Beyond," in William T. Burke, *Towards a Better Use of the Oceans: A Study and Prognosis,* a SIPRI Monograph (New York: Humanities Press, 1969), pp. 175–482, at pp. 268–289.

[69] I. Kuzminov, "Superiorities of Socialism," Vol. 12 *International Affairs,* pp. 32–36 (Moscow, December 1967), at p. 38.

[70] See the views of Soviet Union and other East European countries in U.N. doc. A/C. 1/PV. 1592, pp. 16–17; A/C.1/PV. 1598, p. 57; A/C.1/PV. 1597, p. 37; A/C.1/PV. 1596, pp. 66–67; A/C.1/PV. 1702, p. 48.

[71] See the views of the Representative of Ceylon in U.N. doc. A/C.1/PV. 1588, p. 63.

[72] See the views of the representatives from the developing countries in this connection. For example, see A/C.1/PV. 1595, A/C.1/PV. 1596, and A/C.1/PV. 1597. For an exhaustive and critical analysis of the ideological instrument, see B. S. Murty, *Propaganda: Legal Regulation of Ideological Instrument of Coercion* (New Haven: Yale University Press, 1968).

[73] K. O. Emery, *supra* note 19, p. 14.

[74] John P. Albers and Richard F. Meyer, *supra* note 21, p. 65. For a detailed country by country breakdown on production and explanation activity, see John P. Albers, M. Devereux Carter, Allen L. Clark, Anny B. Coury, and Stanley P. Schweinfurth, *Summary Petroleum and Selected Mineral Statistics for 120 Countries, Including Offshore Areas,* Geological Survey Professional Paper 817 (Washington, D.C.: U.S. Government Printing Office, 1973).

[75] K. O. Emery, *supra* note 19, p. 14.

[76] See the U.N. Secretary-General's Report, *supra* note 20, pp. 9–10.

[77] Lewis Weeks, a geologist, is rather pessimistic about the hydrocarbon potential of the lower slope and rise. However, K. O. Emery, M. Ewing, J. Ewing, and E. Uchupi are very optimistic about availability of rich petroleum deposits from deep ocean areas. For Lewis Weeks's estimates, see Report of the Secretary-General, *supra* note 20. On the view of the other scientists, see *supra* note 22.

The U.S. National Petroleum Council was also optimistic about availability of oil and gas in areas deeper than 200 meters. According to one of its reports:

> Review of geological information available on oceanic areas suggests that petroleum accumulations, comparable to those which are currently commercial on land and in shallow coastal waters [less than 200 meters depth], may exist also under the deeper water parts of the ocean. Such additional areas of petroleum accumulation may occur not only under waters deeper than 200 meters on the continental shelf and continental borderland, but also under the even deeper waters covering the continental slope, the continental rise, and possibly certain parts of the deep ocean basins. The actual productive potential of such petroleum deposits as may exist under these deep waters is of course entirely conjectural.

An Interim Report of the National Petroleum Council (to the Secretary of the Interior of the United States Government), *Petroleum Resources Under the Ocean Floor* (Washington, D.C., July 9, 1968), p. 3.

Explaining the results of the Deep-Sea Drilling Project, David A. Ross also concluded that the deep-ocean areas may have significant potential for oil accumulation. Ross noted that

One of the major discoveries of the Deep-Sea Drilling Project came in the second hole drilled. This hole was located in the Gulf of Mexico on what is now called the Challenger Knoll [a knoll is a small hill on the sea floor]. The drilling ship, the *Glomar Challenger,* started drilling on the hill situated 11,753 ft. below the ship. Samples of drilled material were obtained at various depths. A sample obtained from 450 ft. below the surface was very surprising—it showed a definite indication of gas and oil. The knoll actually is a sea-floor expression of a buried geological structure known as a salt dome and salt domes are often associated with oil deposits. The surprise was finding a salt dome with associated oil deposits at such great depths. Usually these are found at considerably shallower depths, on or near the continental shelf. The results of this site suggest that oil-forming processes may act in the deep sea, an area previously thought to have an insignificant potential for oil accumulation.

David A. Ross, *supra* note 17, p. 340.
[78] Herman T. Franssen, *supra* note, 58, p. 52. Countries with large offshore reserves of crude oil include Egypt (UAR), Nigeria, Norway, the United Kingdom, Malaysia, Qatar, Saudi Arabia, the USSR, the United Arab Emirates, Australia, and the United States. At present about 76 percent of world offshore reserves are associated with the continent of Asia, if the European part of the Soviet Union is included as part of Asia.

Countries having known but large unreported gas reserves include Canada, Mexico, Indonesia, Qatar, and the USSR; countries that have reported large offshore reserves include the United States, Nigeria, Norway, the United Kingdom, Saudi Arabia, Australia, and New Zealand. The reserves of the North Sea are approximately equal to those of the United Sates, that is, 1,200 billion cubic meters. See John P. Albers and Richard F. Meyer, *supra* note 21, p. 67.
[79] *Supra* note 58.
[80] The figures given here are provided by K. O. Emery et al., *supra* note 25, p. 53.
[81] See the Progress Report by the Secretary-General, *supra* note 61, pp. 10–14. Among the major companies that are interested in manganese nodule mining the following may be noted: Summa Corporation (U.S.A.), Kennecott Copper Corporation (U.S.A.), Deep Sea Ventures Inc. (U.S.A.), Sumito Group (Japan), Deep Ocean Minerals Association (Japan), Arbeitsgemein-Schaft Meerestechnischgewinnbare Rohstoffe (AMR, West Germany), CNEXO (France), and International Nickel (Canada).

See also Wayne J. Smith, ''International Control of Deep Sea Mineral Resources,'' Vol. 24, *Naval War College Review,* pp. 82–90 (June 1972), at p. 83.
[82] For an excellent survey of the present and possible uses of the seas see Douglas M. Johnston, ''Law, Technology and the Sea,'' Vol. 55, *California Law Review,* pp. 449–472 (May, 1967). Also see the remarks of Professor M. S. McDougal on the emerging uses of the seas in ''Revision of the Geneva Conventions on the Law of the Sea—The Views of a Commentator,'' Vol. 1 *Natural Resources Lawyer,* pp. 19–28 (July, 1968), at p. 82; W. T. Burke, *Ocean Sciences, Technology and the Future of International Law of the Sea* (Columbus, Ohio: Ohio State University Press, 1966); *Our Nation and the Sea, supra* note 40, and ''Perspectives for Oceanography,'' *The New York Times* (editorial), January 18, 1969.
[83] See *supra* note 23.
[84] See Herman T. Franssen, *supra* note 58, and David Brooks, *supra* note 27.
[85] As examples of the conflicts in competing uses of the sea we might mention the following instances:
1. North Atlantic fishermen temporarily had to give up a large area of their fishing grounds while exploiters were testing for oil. Finally the fishermen forced the government to stop this interference with their fishing. See John P. Craven, *supra* note 53, pp. 35–37.

2. The Santa Barbara oil slick is the most recent example where the exploitation of natural resources came in sharp conflict with other uses of the marine environment. This also gave rise to demands for weighing the resource exploitation as a value with other values like protection of birds, beaches, and marine life. See, for an extensive coverage of oil slick incident and these demands, *The New York Times,* February 2, 1969, p. 1, col. 3, and p. 54, col. 2; February 4, 1969, p. 1, col. 2 and p. 78, col. 4, and the editorial on February 4, 1969.

3. On the other hand, as an instance of other uses of the sea interfering with natural resource exploitation, the following illustration bears out the point: Recently off California there was an attempt to remove phosphate nodules. But the project was given up as there were large numbers of live artillery shells among the nodules. See "Ocean Raw Materials," Vol. 14, *Kirk-Othmer Encyclopedia of Chemical Technology* (Second Ed., 1967), p. 163.

[86] Joseph L. Fisher, "Limits on the Exploitation of Natural Resources," Vol. 70, *Technology Review* (MIT), pp. 49–54 (May 1968).

[87] M. S. McDougal, H. D. Lasswell, and I. A. Vlasic, *Law and Public Order in Outer Space* (New Haven: Yale University Press, 1963), p. 88.

[88] See M. S. McDougal and W. T. Burke, *The Public Order of the Oceans* (New Haven: Yale University Press, 1962), pp. 36–51; M. S. McDougal, H. D. Lasswell, and I. A. Vlasic, idem, pp. 94–137; M. S. McDougal, H. D. Lasswell, and M. Reisman, "The World Constitutive Process of Authoritative Decision-Making," Vol. 19, *Journal of Legal Education,* pp. 253–300 and 403–437 (1966); and Michael Reisman, *Nullity and Revision: The Review and Enforcement of International Judgments and Awards* (New Haven: Yale University Press, 1971).

[89] See Article 5 of the Convention on the Continental Shelf of 1958, Vol. 49, *United Nations Treaty Series,* pp. 312–320 (1964).

[90] See Max Sørensen, "Institutionalized International Cooperation in Economic, Social and Cultural Fields," in Max Sørensen (ed.), *Manual of Public International Law* (New York: St. Martin's Press, 1968), pp. 605–672.

[91] See *supra* note 8.

[92] See D. W. Bowett, *The Law of the Sea* (Dobbs Ferry, N.Y.: Oceana Publications, 1967), p. 47.

[93] Report of the Secretary-General, *Marine Science and Technology: Survey and Proposals,* U.N. doc. E/4487 of 24 April 1968, Annex XI: *Activities of the Organizations of the United Nations System,* pp. 17–18.

[94] Professor Clive Parry refers to this aspect of the process of decision in these terms:

But the individual state, by definition, is but one among many. By the same right that it claims to be free of all external yoke, it must concede to other peoples a like freedom. Despite its local power, and all the local resources and loyalties which it has come so freely to command, even the greatest state is inferior to the collective strength of all the rest. A long view of its interests must call therefore for some accommodation with others. . . . A true view of the interests of any state, which are but the interests of its citizens, demands that it shall often listen as much to the claims, and respect as much the interests of others as those which appear to be its own.

See Clive Parry, "The Function of Law in the International Community," in Max Sørensen (ed.), *supra* note 90, pp. 1–54, at pp. 6–7.

Notes to Chapter 2, pp. 26–46

[1] See Barbara Ward, *Spaceship Earth* (New York: Columbia University Press, 1966), p. 45.

[2] See Peter F. Drucker, *The Age of Discontinuity: Guidelines to Our Changing Society* (New York: Harper and Row, Publishers, 1969), pp. 79–80. Describing the contemporary world situation, Drucker says:

Today the whole world, whatever its actual economic condition—and whatever the political system in force in a given area—has one common demand schedule, one common set of economic values and preferences. The whole world, in other words, has become one economy in its expectations, in its responses, and in its behavior. This is new in human history.

Underlying this common economic behavior is a community of information. The whole world today knows how everybody lives. . . . In fact, everybody will have become everybody else's next-door neighbor. The whole world, in Marshall McLuhan's words, will have become one "global village."

For some parallel assumptions see also Kenneth E. Boulding, "The Concept of World Interest," in Richard A. Falk and Saul H. Mendlovitz, *The Strategy of World Public Order: Disarmament and Economic Development,* Vol. 4 (New York: World Law Fund, 1966), pp. 494–515.

[3] Jenks makes this point very eloquently. He says,

The parallel progress of interdependence and independence has tended to paralyze rather than to promote the political genius and vitality necessary to reconcile the dilemma. The potentially tragic complication of this paradox is the ever-present danger that by failing to reconcile in a responsible manner the greater concentration of political authority required by the progress of interdependence with the wider diffusion of political freedom implied in the progress of independence we may fail to achieve either of our fundamental objectives and forfeit both peace and freedom.

See C. Wilfred Jenks, *The World Beyond the Charter* (London: George Allen and Unwin, 1969), p. 127.

[4] For this kind of characterization of common interest in terms of exclusive and inclusive interests, see the several contributions by Myres S. McDougal and Harold D. Lasswell, and their associates. In particular, here, reference may be given to M. S. McDougal, H. D. Lasswell, and Ivan A. Vlasic, *Law and Public Order in Space* (New Haven: Yale University Press, 1963), pp. 150–151. The authors define inclusive public order interests as the "Demands for values plus supporting expectations about conditions of achievement, the expectations involving high degrees of collective impact upon the relationships referred to by the goals of the world community." The exclusive public order interests, according to the same authors, are "Demands for values plus supporting expectations, the expectations involving high degrees of particular impact, compatible with the goal values of the world community, and unaccompanied by high levels of collective impact." Furthermore, it is mentioned that whereas the management of inclusive public order interests involves "Community-wide participation in decision, or a less degree of participation by more than one component community of the world arena," regulation of exclusive public order interests is achieved through "decisions by each participant acting alone."

One important caveat, issued by the authors also needs to be noted in this connection: According to the authors, the separation between inclusive and exclusive interests, "though dichotomous in form," is "intended to refer to a factual continuum," and to imply that the spectrum of reality is "more or less" rather than "either-or."

[5] For a survey of trends in coercion and the resulting expectations of crisis, see Murray Thompson, *Militarism 1969: A Survey of World Trends,* Vol. II, *Peace Research Reviews,* No. 5 (Clarkson, Ontario, Canada: Canadian Peace Research Institute, October 1968).

[6] A representative analysis of the factors contributing to world tensions was made during a conference at the University of Chicago in 1960. See the University of Chicago and World Brotherhood, *Conference on World Tensions* (May 11–13, 1960). Of particular interest are the following excerpts from the proceedings of the Conference:

a. The Conference Outline mentions that

There is general agreement that the political tensions that presently exist between the two major powers and the blocs associated with them—the Soviet Union and the United States—are the principal danger to world peace.

b. The Report of the Committee on Communications refers to the gaps in and failures of international communication as a source of world tensions. According to this Committee,

Communications, as we have come to use the word, involves all contact between peoples—whether personal, or through the flow of information and ideas.
The inhibition of such contacts in itself constitutes a major threat to peace.

c. The Seminar on Economic Relations emerged with a consensus that declared that

Out of the massive yearnings of hundreds of millions of people for a better life can come a better world, or if their yearnings are ignored a world of mounting and explosive tensions.

Murray Thomson mentions in his survey, *supra* note 5, the other factors noted in the text. He observed (at p. 85):

Militarism is a function of several interdependent social policies and processes. It is these processes which strengthen and maintain militarism, rather than a single root condition or cause.

Of related interest is the contribution made by David E. Apter, "Political Development and Tensions in New Nations," a background paper submitted to the *Conference on World Tensions* (held at the University of Chicago). Apter (at p. 5 of his contribution) notes the following factors as commonly responsible for the tensions in the new nations with their consequent implications for the breakdown of minimum world public order: (a) family division; (b) religious division; (c) antitraditionalism; (d) urban migration; (e) ethnic competitiveness; (f) racial compartmentalization; (g) economic discrimination; (h) emphasis on political solutions. Even today, the relevance of most of these factors for world tensions remains unchanged.

[7] The inherent fallacy of nuclear deterrence and the potential dangers involved in relying on that technique for the maintenance of minimum order is that the two superpowers, by constantly increasing their capacity to destroy each other, keep each other in a state of continual anxiety over their safety and survival. The escalation of mutual fear that is built into the development of the nuclear arsenal ironically contributes, in fact, to further-ing the expectation of crisis, while it is supposed to guarantee security. Albert Einstein referred to this dilemma when he said: "The unleashed power of the atom has changed everything save our modes of thinking, and there we drift towards unparalleled catastrophe." Quoted by Edward M. Kennedy in his Introduction to Abram Chayes and Jerome B. Wiesner, *ABM: An Evaluation of the Decision to Deploy an Antiballistic Missile System* (New York: Harper and Row, 1969), at p. xiv.

Furthermore, the proliferation of nuclear weapons, as more and more nations attempt to defend themselves by building up their own nuclear weapons system, is widely re-garded as a threat to the maintenance of minimum order. This belief brought about the conclusion of the Non-Proliferation Treaty and the vigorous lobbying that was required to obtain wide ratification for it.

[8] Referring to various military alignments that originated under the concept of collective self-defense, Goodrich says,

. . . all the agreements that have been entered into in the exercise of the inherent right of collective self-defense have been the product in part, at least, of the "cold war." While these agreements have been widely viewed as filling a gap in the United Nations system, it does not necessarily follow that they have strengthened the United Nations. To the extent that they have created a greater sense of peace and security and have helped to establish an equilibrium in power relations which discourages any resort to armed force, they have perhaps strengthened the United Nations by creating conditions favourable to the achievement of its other purposes. To the extent that they instill fear and distrust and harden relations at the "cold war" level they may in fact weaken the United Nations by creating conditions which make the performance of its tasks more difficult.

Leland M. Goodrich, *The United Nations* (London: Stevens and Sons, 1959), at pp. 175–176.

[9] For a discussion of the shortcomings of the technique of mutual deterrence, see Robert S. McNamara, *The Essence of Security: Reflections in Office* (New York: Harper and Row, 1968). On page 59 he says,

While thermonuclear power is almost inconceivably awesome and represents virtually unlimited potential destructiveness, it has proven to be a limited diplomatic instrument. Its uniqueness lies in the fact that it is at the same time an all-powerful weapon and a very inadequate weapon.

And, on page 67, he concludes,

History has placed our particular lives in an era when the consequences of human folly are waxing more and more catastrophic in the matters of war and peace. In the end, the root of man's security does not lie in his weaponry, it lies in his mind. What the world requires in its third decade of the Atomic Age is not a new race toward armaments, but a new race toward reasonableness.
We had all better run that race.

Ernst B. Haas gives an account of the limitations and inadequacies of regional alliances and multibloc systems, and the resulting disuse of them. See his *Tangle of Hopes: American Commitments and World Order* (Englewood Cliffs, N.J.: Prentice-Hall, 1969), Chapter Five, pp. 93–117.

Charles W. Yost, the U.S. Ambassador to the United Nations, deals with the crisis resolution by the concurrent action of the United States and the USSR and notes some of the difficulties in employing that technique as well as others. He also makes several useful suggestions for maintaining minimum order through this and other means. See Charles W. Yost, "World Order and American Responsibility," *Foreign Affairs,* Vol. 47 (1968), pp. 1–14.

[10] One recent commentator notes the limitations of international adjudication in terms of the jurisdiction granted to international tribunals, the reluctance of states to surrender their sovereignty to a supranational institution, the restrictions regarding the participants who can invoke these tribunals, and several other considerations like the fear of losing the case and distrust of the "impartiality of the judges." See Forest L. Grieves, *Supranationalism and International Adjudication* (Urbana, Ill.: University of Illinois Press, 1969), particularly pp. 170–179.

[11] M. S. McDougal, H. D. Lasswell and I. A. Vlasic provide a succinct definition of the optimum order:

By optimum order we mean a public order which, beyond authoritative orientation toward the minimum of coercion and the maximum of persuasion in the interaction of participants, is further designed to promote the greatest production and the widest possible sharing of human dignity values among all peoples.

See *supra* note 4, at p. 160.

[12] The attempt of the United States government to involve its NATO partners in a major effort to save man's environment from the dangers of the indiscriminate use of modern technology is a typical example of the response provoked by the ever-growing need to employ science for common community purposes.

See "U.S. Asks NATO to Help Save Man's Environment," *The New York Times,* October 22, 1969, cols. 1–4, page 12. Also see Nigel Calder, *Technopolis* (New York: Simon and Schuster, 1970), where the author probes the relationship between the contemporary scientific developments and the potential technological dangers of our time.
[13] Oscar Schachter observed that

At a time when large masses of mankind have reached a status of national dignity and political equality, we have witnessed the growing inequality between those who have inherited the fruits of science and technology and those who remain on the outside looking in. To be aware of the emerging technology in the midst of famine, squalor and disease adds a dimension of bitterness and cruelty for those increasingly conscious of the ideals of equal rights and opportunities. Thus science ironically widens the great fissure that now splits the globe and threatens our precious international order.

See his "Scientific Advances and International Law Making," Vol. 55, *California Law Review,* pp. 423–430 (May 1967).

On the same subject, see the statement of Elliot Richardson, then the Under-Secretary of the State Department of the United States before the Foreign Affairs Committee of the House of Representatives, *The New York Times,* June 10, 1969, page 7, col. 1.

A number of studies in the field of social sciences have focused on the relationship between economic backwardness and the breakdown of order. See, for example, Ted Gurr, "A Causal Model of Civil Strife: A Comparative Analysis Using New Indices," Vol. 62, *American Political Science Review,* pp. 1104–1124 (1968).

When we refer to the general breakdown of order in a community, we must remember that it is not always due to widespread poverty in that community. There are often many other motivating factors that can contribute to the outbreak of violence. This point can be illustrated by addressing ourselves to the disorder that occurs in the developed countries where the per capita income is high. For example, the United States experienced a series of crises because of racial prejudice and discrimination, which were often unrelated to wealth as a value distribution. Also the so-called "campus disorders" where students revolted against the establishment had more to do with the young people's disenchantment with the U.S. involvement in Vietnam War than with any economic backwardness.

However, we stress the importance of reducing the gap between the rich and the poor nations in this connection only because it is a major dimension of the crises at the international level and also because it is the most widely accepted goal.
[14] Lasswell, referring to the widespread process of international economic assistance that is motivated mainly by the need to help the underdeveloped countries to attain satisfactory levels of economic development and the resulting claims, asks the following questions:

When we review the declarations of international conferences, and the formulations that obtain increasing support in international bodies of many kinds, do we not find it necessary to take note of an unmistakable trend in the rhetoric employed? Is not the language becoming more saturated with words and phrases of obligation, approximating the conventional discourse of statute and treaty? Do we not find demonstrations of impatience to press beyond ambiguities of obligation to operational specifics, and to introduce such criteria as percent of gross national product?

These questions suggest that not only has such a necessity been recognized in the contemporary world but the capable participants are increasingly led to believe that the idea of sharing values with the less capable is becoming an obligation. See Harold D. Lasswell, "The Relevance of International Law to the Development Process," *Proceedings of the American Society of International Law* (April 28–30, 1966), pp. 1–8, at p. 5.
[15] A stock resource is defined by Ciriacy-Wantrup as one in which the "total physical quantity does not increase significantly with time." S. Ciriacy-Wantrup, *Resource Con-*

servation: Economics and Policies (Berkeley, Calif.: University of California Press, 1952), at p. 35. Also see M. S. McDougal, H. D. Lasswell, and I. A. Vlasic, *supra* note 4, p. 778.

[16] For an exposition of the contemporary uses of the seas and the process of inclusive enjoyment of the oceans, see M. S. McDougal and W. T. Burke, *The Public Order of the Oceans* (New Haven: Yale University Press, 1962); also see *supra* Chapter 1.

[17] Regarding the effects of the rise in oil prices on the less developed countries (LDCs), it is said that

With the rise in oil prices, many LDCs must draw down their precious foreign-exchange reserves to pay for the oil. Their total petroleum imports in 1974 are expected to cost $8 billion to $10 billion more than last year. This exceeds the total amount of foreign aid they receive from all sources.

With their reserves down, these countries will have less money, if any, to buy chemical fertilizers, which are made from oil or gas and also have shot up in price. Hence they will be less able to raise production of rice and other grains.

As the demand for fertilizer and food increases, many LDCs will look to the industrialized West to make up the deficits. But shortages have developed in the rich nations as well and it is far from certain they will meet their trade and aid commitments in the face of domestic pressures.

See Charlotte Saikowski, "U.S. Wary of Oil-Crisis Impact on 'Third World'," *The Christian Science Monitor,* January 24, 1974, p. 3.

[18] On worldwide depression resulting from the oil crisis, see Harry Anderson, "Oil Crisis Has Made Global Trade Wars Real Threat," *The Boston Globe,* February 12, 1974, p. 29, where it is pointed out that

The oil-exporting nations, principally the Arab states, are expected to receive between $85 billion and $105 billion this year for petroleum. That is an astounding contrast to the approximately $22 billion they got last year.

If the situation continues, it is estimated that oil-consuming nations, including the United States, will run balance of payment deficiencies in the neighborhood of $50 billion a year. And, the experts say, any voluntary price reductions by the Arabs or diminished demand for oil in the consuming countries would not change the situation greatly.

Just how will the oil-consuming nations pay the gigantic price demanded by the Arabs without ruining their own economies?

One ominous solution would be for panic-stricken, oil-starved countries to resort to cutthroat export wars, destructive trade agreements, import barriers and competitive devaluations of their currency to raise the capital they will need to pay the Arabs.

Such activity in the 1930's worsened the depression and aggravated the old national rivalries that eventually led to World War II.

Also a *New York Times* editorial warned that

The price gouging in oil has created grave economic and political strains among the United States, Western Europe, Japan and other nations including the 'Third World' countries. . . .

The oil producers could suffer the same fate—for their extortionate demands have created the danger of world-wide depression, with nations facing unpayable oil bills, struggling to restrict their other imports or devaluing their currencies to push their exports.

The New York Times, February 10, 1974, page 14, Section E.

On the "oil crisis" and its impact on world order, see also Jordan J. Paust and Albert Blaustein, "The Arab Oil Weapon—A Threat to International Peace," Vol. 68, *A.J.I.L.,* pp. 410–439 (1974); C. Fred Bergsten, "The Threat from the Third World," No. 11, *Foreign Policy,* pp. 102–124 (Summer 1973); Zuhyr Mikdashi, "Collision Could Work," No. 14, *Foreign Policy,* pp. 57–68 (Spring 1974); Stephen D. Krasner, "Oil Is the Exception," idem, pp. 68–74; and C. Fred Bergsten, "The Threat Is Real," idem, pp. 84–90.

[19] The forms of regulation are discussed here solely from the perspective of the exploitation of oil and gas and manganese nodules. For other offshore resources, the kinds of regulation applicable should be decided according to the context surrounding their exploitation.

[20] See Jeremy J. Stone, "Can the Communists Deceive Us," in Abram Chayes and Jerome B. Wiesner (eds.), *supra* note 7, pp. 193–198, at p. 195.

[21] William Becher, "New Submarine-Hunter Plane Is Shown on the Coast," *The New York Times,* October 13, 1968.

[22] John W. Finney, "Why Inspection May No Longer Be Critical for Arms Control," *The New York Times,* April 13, 1969, Week in Review Section.

[23] See Albert E. Utton, "Institutional Arrangements for Developing North Sea Oil and Gas," Vol. 9, *Virginia Journal of International Law,* pp. 66–81 (1968), at pp. 69–71. See also James E. Horigan, "Unitization of Petroleum Reservoirs Extending across Subsea Boundary Lines Bordering Seas in the North Sea," Vol. 7, *Natural Resources Lawyer,* pp. 67–76 (1974).

[24] On the theory of continental drift, see David A. Ross, *Introduction to Oceanography* (New York: Appleton-Century-Crofts, 1970), pp. 311–320.

[25] With respect to security of states as a consideration for extending coastal states' exclusive competence over maritime areas, Burke rightly pointed out that "Those who would, for security reasons, establish a wide limit for coastal control should bear the burden of establishing this need by reference to facts and not to surmises." William T. Burke, *Towards a Better Use of the Ocean: Contemporary Legal Problems in Ocean Development: Comments and Recommendations by an International Symposium* (New York: Humanities Press, a SIPRI Monograph, 1969), p. 26. For a similar view, see Ian Brownlie, ibid., p. 148.

[26] A few of the reasons for the inadequate involvement of foreign sources and the underdevelopment of offshore natural resources off some of the developing countries can be deduced.

First, the developed countries and the private business associations within them may have been preoccupied with the development of offshore natural resources that come under their exclusive jurisdiction. Some evidence in favor of this assumption could be found from the fact that offshore areas of Australia, the United States (Alaska, Louisiana, Gulf of Mexico), and the North Sea countries have the greatest attraction for the exploitation of oil and gas deposits therein.

The Persian Gulf is another area where private business associations have traditionally enjoyed amicable lease and political conditions, which in turn ensure a large output of oil.

See Paul M. Fye, Arthur E. Maxwell, K. O. Emery, and Bostwick Ketchum, "Ocean Science and Marine Resources," in Edmund A. Gullion (ed.), *Uses of the Seas* (Englewood Cliffs, N.J.: Prentice-Hall, 1968), pp. 17–68, at p. 44. Also see, for a mention of the World Petroleum Activity in 1968, *The New York Times,* September 11, 1969, p. 65, cols. 4, 5, 6.

Second, constraints on international politics and group alignments at the transnational level could have deterred a free flow of capital and skills to the developing countries.

For example, it was said that the Indian government in 1968 was not able to decide between a Japanese firm and an American firm in granting an offshore oil development contract because of the political and ideological overtones of the deal. For a note on this aspect, see *The Hindu Weekly Review* (Madras, India), July 8, 1968, p. 14.

Third, even where some assistance is available on a bilateral basis, supervision of the effective use of the aid is generally regarded as impossible between aid-giving and aid-receiving countries. This point has been well made in the Report of the Commission on International Development, *Partners in Development* (New York: Praeger Publishers, 1969), pp. 128–129, and 214.

Fourth, private investment in underdeveloped countries has frequently been assailed with the charge of special interest, resulting in strained and cautious relationships between the private investors and the underdeveloped countries. Some of the Latin Americans recently expropriated the leaseholdings of oil companies belonging to the United States on the assumption that the companies were unjustifiably enriching themselves at the expense of grantor countries. These expropriations have generally raised doubts among the oil companies about the reliability of their investments in those Latin American countries. For example, see the case of Peruvian expropriations reported in *International Legal Materials* (November, 1968); and Juan de Onis, "Peru's Challenge to U.S.: Oil Expropriation Poses a Difficult Problem for Nixon Administration," in *The New York Times,* February 15, 1969, p. 2, cols. 5 and 6.

[27] Many coastal states, faced with competition from highly mechanized distant water fishing fleets, are opting for extended coastal state jurisdiction to claim exclusive property rights over fish.

Even for the efficient and economic exploitation of fishing on the high seas, several commentators argue that the present "flag state" jurisdiction should be abandoned in favor of more acceptable systems of allocation. For a discussion of different systems of allocation, see Hiroshi Kashahara, "Problems of Allocation as Applied to the Exploitation of the Living Resources of the Sea" in Lewis M. Alexander, *The Law of the Sea: Needs and Interests of Developing Countries* (Proceedings of Seventh Annual Conference of Law of Sea Institute, University of Rhode Island, Kingston, R.I., 1972), pp. 94–101. See also the American Society of International Law, *Principles for Global Fisheries Management Regime: A Report of the Working Group on Living Marine Resources of the Panel on Law of the Sea* (Washington, D.C., 1974). Generally on international regulation of fishery resources, see Douglas M. Johnston, *International Law of Fisheries: A Policy-Oriented Enquiry* (New Haven: Yale University Press, 1965), and Albert Koers, *International Regulation of Marine Fisheries: A Study of Regional Fisheries Organizations* (Surrey, England: Fishing News (Books), 1973).

[28] For a discussion of several proposals on an ocean development tax, see Proceedings of the Pacem in Maribus-II: *Working Papers on the Ocean Development Tax,* Malta, June 29–July 5, 1971 (Santa Barbara, Calif.: Center for the Study of Democratic Institutions). Also see Max I. Kheden, "The Ocean Development Tax: An Instrument to Advance the Rational Development of the Marine Environment?" in Eckart Boehme and Max Ivers Kheden (eds.), *From the Law of the Sea Towards an Ocean Space Regime: Practical and Legal Implications of the Marine Revolution* (New York: International Publications Services, 1972), pp. 61–92.

Notes to Chapter 3, pp. 47–75

[1] For the text of the Convention on the Continental Shelf as adopted at the Geneva Conference of 1958, see Vol. 49, *United Nations Treaty Series,* pp. 312–320 (1964); see also Vol. 15, *United States Treaties and Other International Agreements,* pp. 473–476 (Washington, D.C.: U.S. Government Printing Office, Part I, 1964).

[2] Relying on their rights of exclusive access and invoking Article 1, many states have already issued licenses to explore and exploit the natural resources beyond the 200-meter limit. See Chapter 1.

[3] Sir Cecil J. B. Hurst, noting several occasions for claims to exclusive access to submarine areas, discussed some interesting policy implications in his article "Whose Is the Bed of the Sea?" Vol. 4, *B.Y.B.I.L.,* pp. 34–43 (1923–1924). Also, for mention of some of these occasions, see L. C. Green, "The Continental Shelf," Vol. 4, *Current Legal Problems,* pp. 54–80 (1951); P. Sreenivasa Rao, "The Law of the Continental Shelf," Vol. 6, *I.J.I.L.,* pp. 363–382 (1966); M. W. Mouton, *The Continental Shelf* (The Hague: M. Nitjhoff, 1952), at pp. 240–241; and P. C. Rao, "The Continental Shelf: The Practice and Policy of India," Vol. 3, *I.J.I.L.,* pp. 191–198 (1963).

[4] H. Lauterpacht, however, seemed to take the Treaty of the Gulf of Paria, February 26, 1942, as the starting point in evaluating the claims to exclusive access to the continental shelf. According to him,

While the various instances, prior to that date, of attempts at exploitation of the subsoil of the sea outside territorial waters and of references in official documents to the continental shelf or submarine areas generally are of some historical interest, the Paria Annexation Order may be regarded as the starting-point of development.

H. Lauterpacht, "Sovereignty over Submarine Areas," Vol. 27, *B.Y.B.I.L.*, pp. 376–433 (1950), at p. 380. The Treaty of the Gulf of Paria between the United Kingdom and Venezuela refers to submarine areas and, like the later proclamations, was not intended to affect the status of the superjacent waters as high seas. However, it differs essentially from the subsequent unilateral proclamations not only in the way in which the claims to exclusive access were advanced but also in the manner in which such rights to exclusive access were articulated. For the text of the Treaty of the Gulf of Paria of February 26, 1942, see *Laws and Regulations on Regime of the High Seas* (United Nations Legislative Series), Vol. 1 (New York: United Nations, 1951), pp. 44–46.

The principal difference was that the treaty did not regard the submarine areas as an extension of the mainland and never mentioned the term continental shelf. Also, it did not limit the submarine areas in terms of either depth or distance as was done in the later proclamations. Most important of all, it was intended to carve out two spheres of interest in the submarine areas which the contracting parties seemed to allot to each other with an understanding that each party would "recognize any rights of sovereignty or control by the other." The expectation of the parties was that, to acquire any such sovereignty "lawfully," one had to show *animus occupandi* and *corpus occupandi*, the two essential features of acquiring title to any territory under the traditional international law. On this expectation, see C. H. M. Waldock, "Legal Basis of the Claims to the Continental Shelf," Vol. 36, *Transactions of the Grotius Society,* pp. 115–148 (1951), and F. A. Vallat, "The Continental Shelf," Vol. 23, *B.Y.B.I.L.*, pp. 333–338 (1946).

As will become clear in the text, the unilateral proclamations did not seem to contemplate any future contingencies of acquisition of title on the basis of occupation. These proclamations instead seemed to adopt a new philosophy of international law, as it were, by claiming exclusive access to defined submarine areas on the basis of contiguity. It is also significant that, while some of the unilateral proclamations mentioned the Truman Proclamation as the point of reference for the novel claim, none relied on the earlier means of claiming the submarine areas. For these reasons, it is appropriate to regard the Truman Proclamation as the starting point, instead of the Treaty of the Gulf of Paria in following the trends in decision regarding the claims to the extent of the continental shelf.

[5] For the text of President Truman's Proclamation No. 2667, see "Policy of the United States with Respect to the Natural Resources of the Subsoil and Sea Bed of the Continental Shelf," (September 28, 1945), Vol. 10, *Federal Register* 12303; and Vol. 23, *Bulletin, Department of State,* No. 327 (September 30, 1945), p. 485.

[6] Ibid.

[7] For the text of the White House Press Release of September 28, 1945, see Vol. 23, *Bulletin, Department of State,* No. 327 (September 30, 1945), pp. 484–485.

[8] The twenty states, whose proclamations are collected in a United Nations Office of Legal Affairs document, are Argentina, Australia, Chile, Costa Rica, Ecuador, Guatemala, Honduras, Iceland, India, Israel, Korea (Republic of), Mexico, Nicaragua, Panama, Peru, Philippines, Portugal, Saudi Arabia, the United Kingdom [(i) on behalf of Arab states under its protection, (ii) Bahamas, (iii) British Honduras, (iv) Jamaica, (v) Trinidad and Tobago, (vi) Sarawak], and the United States of America.

For the texts of the various proclamations, see *Laws and Regulations on the Regime of the High Seas, supra* note 4, and *Supplement to the Laws and Regulations on the Regime of the High Seas* (United Nations Legislative Series; New York: United Nations, 1959).

The coastal states, in claiming exclusive competence over a portion of the submarine areas off their coasts, have used the terms "adjacent" and "contiguous" almost as if they were interchangeable. But in their exact meanings they are not synonymous. While adjacency connotes proximity, contiguity refers to continuity. Only in a loose sense can they be used to convey an identical intention. See *The Random House Dictionary of the English Language* (College Ed., 1968).

[9] For Australia, Ecuador, and Honduras, see the *Supplement,* idem, pp. 4, 9, and 10. For Portugal and the United States, *Laws and Regulations on the Regime of the High Seas,* idem, p. 19. Portugal seemed to have slightly but not substantially modified its stand later. See the *Supplement,* idem, at p. 16. For the United States, see *Laws and Regulations on the Regime of the High Seas,* idem, p. 39.

[10] For Chile, Costa Rica, Mexico, and Peru, see *Laws and Regulations on the Regime of the High Seas,* idem, pp. 6, 9, 13, and 17.

[11] For Saudi Arabia and the United Kingdom, see *Laws and Regulations on the Regime of the High Seas,* idem, pp. 22 and 23–33. For India see the *Supplement,* idem, p. 14.

[12] For Argentina and Guatemala, see the *Laws and Regulations on the Regime of the High Seas,* idem, pp. 4 and 10.

[13] For Iceland and the Republic of Korea, see the *Supplement,* idem, pp. 11, 12, and 15.

[14] For Israel, see the *Supplement,* idem, p. 14. By the time Israel passed its proclamation, on August 3, 1952, there was a growing debate in the International Law Commission on the adoption of an exploitability criterion in defining the shelf, and the government of Israel was obviously influenced by that. If this is correct, as will be noted below, the criterion of exploitability, which was accepted by the Commission, was not intended to advance a continental shelf of unlimited extent. From that point of view, Israel need not be cited as deviating unduly from the general trend of accepting a limited shelf.

[15] Nicaragua: Article 5 of the Political Constitution, November 1, 1950, describes its national territory as extending between "the Atlantic and the Pacific Oceans and the Republic of Honduras and Costa Rica. It also comprises: the adjacent islands, the subsoil, the territorial waters, the continental shelf, the submerged foundations . . . , the air space and the stratosphere." *Laws and Regulations on the Regime of the High Seas,* idem, p. 15.

Panama simply mentions "the submarine continental shelf which appertains to the national territory." Ibid.

Philippines: Article 3 of its Petroleum Act of 1949, enacted by the Republic Act No. 387, describes state ownership as follows:

All natural deposits or occurrences of petroleum or natural gas in public and/or private lands in the Philippines whether found . . . in, on, or under the surface of dry lands, creeks, rivers, lakes, or other submerged lands within the territorial waters or on the continental shelf, or its analogue Philippines which are not within the territories of other countries, belonging to the State, inalienably and imprescriptibly.

Idem, p. 19.

[16] See the subparagraph to Article 5 quoted above: "Such frontiers as may not yet be determined shall be fixed by treaties and by law." Idem, at p. 15.

[17] Nicaragua announced its Constitution on November 1, 1950, Panama on March 1, 1946, and the Philippines announced its Petroleum Act on June 18, 1949.

[18] For the differing opinions of geologists on the outer limits of continental shelf, see M. W. Mouton, *supra* note 3, pp. 6–45.

[19] According to J. L. Brierly,

Legally speaking the presence or absence of a continental shelf was of no importance. Chile, for instance, possessed no continental shelf, but if that State wished to explore, or exploit, the subsoil of the sea, and was able to do so, there was nothing against it from a legal standpoint.

Y.B.I.L.C. (1950), Vol. 1, Summary Records of the Second Session, June 5–July 29, 1950, 67th Meeting, p. 222.

The submarine areas off certain coasts are so continuously shallow that no continental shelf exists (for example, the Persian Gulf). On the other hand, off certain coasts, the depth of the waters exceeds the 200-meter limit even within the conventional territorial waters. In such cases also there is no continental shelf (for example, Peru and Chile).

[20] Idem, p. 218.

[21] Idem, p. 220. A similar recommendation was earlier made to the Copenhagen Conference of the International Law Association.

[22] Idem, p. 223.

[23] *Y.B.I.L.C.* (1951), Vol. 1, Summary Records of the Third Session, May 16–July 27, 1951, 113th meeting, p. 270.

[24] Faris El Khoury's proposals, one to adopt a maximum distance for the shelf and the other to adopt a minimum distance, were rejected 7 to 1, and 7 to 2, respectively. The proposal adopted read: "As here used, the term 'continental shelf' refers to the seabed and subsoil of the submarine areas contiguous to the coast, but outside the area of marginal seas where the depth of the superjacent water does not exceed 200 meters." Idem, p. 273.

[25] Jesús María Yepes, Roberto Cordova, and Georges Scelle were very critical of 200-meter depth limit. For their views, see idem, 117th meeting, pp., 296, 297, and 298.

[26] The Subcommittee was composed of Roberto Cordova, J. P. A. François, Jesús María Yepes, and Manley O. Hudson. For their recommendation and its approval by the Commission, see idem, 123rd meeting, p. 346. Explaining the change and the decision to drop the 200-meter limit, the report of the Commission said that, while it recognized the merits of adopting a definite limit, there were other more important considerations, such as

Technical developments in the near future might make it possible to exploit resources of the sea-bed at a depth of over 200 meters. Moreover, the continental shelf might well include submarine areas lying at a depth of over 200 meters but capable of being exploited by means of installations erected in neighboring areas where the depth does not exceed this limit. Hence the Commission decided not to specify a depth-limit of 200 meters in Article 1.

Report of the International Law Commission to the General Assembly (covering its third session), Doc. A/1858. *Y.B.I.L.C.* (1951), Vol. 2, at p. 141.

[27] For the comments of the various countries, see the Report of the International Law Commission to the General Assembly (covering work of its fifth session June 1–August 14, 1953); Doc. A/2456, *Y.B.I.L.C.* (1953), Vol. 2, Annex 1, pp. 232–269.

[28] See *Y.B.I.L.C.* (1953), Summary Records of the Fifth Session, June 1–August 14, 1953, 197th meeting, p. 83. At this time again, the Commission rejected Faris El Khouri's proposal to specify a maximum distance to the shelf by 7 votes to 4, with 2 abstentions. Also rejected was the proposal by Yepes to employ the criterion of exploitation by 7 votes to 4, with 2 abstentions.

[29] For the "Resolution of the Ciudad Trujillo," see the *Final Act of the Inter-American Specialized Conference on "Conservation of Natural Resources: The Continental Shelf*

and Marine Waters," Cuidad Trujillo, Dominican Republic, March 15–28, 1956, Organization of American States, Conference and Organizations Series, No. 50, p. 13.

For comments on the Conference and the results therein achieved see Richard Young, "Pan-American Discussions on Offshore Claims," 50 Vol. 50 *A.J.I.L.*, pp. 909–916 (1956). See also Josef L. Kunz, "Continental Shelf and International Law: Confusion and Abuse," Vol. 50, *A.J.I.L.*, pp. 828–853 (1956), at p. 848.

[30] *Y.B.I.L.C.* (1956), Vol. 1, Summary Records of the Eighth Session, April 23–July 4, 1956, 357th meeting, p. 131.

[31] Besides Rapporteur J. P. A. François, other members who opposed the amendment were Radhabinod Pal, Georges Scelle, and A. E. F. Sandström. For their views, see idem, pp. 133, 135, and 138.

[32] Idem, p. 135.

[33] Ibid. F. V. García-Amador later denied that he had ever made such a statement and that the official records of the Commission should be disregarded. For the statement of García-Amador, see Lewis M. Alexander (ed.), *The Law of the Sea: National Policy Recommendation* (Proceedings of the Fourth Annual Conference of the Law of the Sea Institute, University of Rhode Island, 1970), p. 170.

For a spirited exchange of views on this point between Henkin and Finlay, see Louis Henkin, "International Law and 'the Interests': the Law of the Seabed," Vol. 63, *A.J.I.L.*, pp. 504–510 (1969); Luke T. Finlay, "The Outer Limit of the Continental Shelf: A Rejoinder to Professor Louis Henkin," Vol. 64, *A.J.I.L.*, pp. 42–61 (1970); Louis Henkin, "A Reply to Mr. Finlay," Vol. 64, *A.J.I.L.*, pp.62–72 (1970).

We cite García-Amador's statement here not so much to show that he intended a clear outer limit when he proposed the "exploitability" clause as to point out that even he, being an advocate for a flexible definition of limits, did not think that the formula finally accepted for the limits of the shelf could be invoked to extend indefinitely coastal state jurisdiction over the "natural resources" of the sea.

[34] Idem, p. 137.

[35] Idem, p. 139.

[36] *Y.B.I.L.C.* (1956), Vol. 2, Documents of the Eighth Session, including the Report of the Commission to the General Assembly, p. 264.

From the commentary to Article 67 of the Commission's draft, one can note certain interesting points that throw light on the dilemmas faced by the Commission in arriving at the text of the article as it was finally adopted: First, referring to the adoption of exploitability criterion in 1951, it says, "It followed from this definition that areas by reason of the depth of the water, were excluded from the continental shelf." Ibid., p. 296.

Later, speaking of the adoption of 200-meter depth limit in 1953, it noted that

> The Commission considered that the limit of 200 meters would be sufficient for all practical purposes at present and probably for a long time to come. . . . The adoption of different limits by different States might cause difficulties of the same kind as differences in breadth of the territorial sea. The Commission was aware that future technical progress might make exploitation possible at a depth greater than 200 meters; in that case the limit would have to be revised, but meanwhile there is every advantage in having a stable limit.

Explaining the change in 1956 coupling the criterion of exploitability and depth, the commentary pointed out that

> Certain members thought that the Article adopted in 1953 should be modified. . . . While maintaining the limit of 200 meters in this Article as the normal limit corresponding to present needs, they wished to recognize forthwith the right to exceed that limit if exploitation of the seabed and subsoil at a greater depth than 200 meters proved technically possible.

It added,

Lastly, the Commission points out that it does not intend limiting the exploitation of the subsoil of the high seas by means of tunnels, cuttings or wells dug from *terra firma*. Such exploitation of the subsoil of the high seas by coastal States is not subject to any legal limitation by reference to the depth of the superjacent waters.

Ibid.

[37] *Summary Records of Meetings and Annexes of the Fourth Committee (Continental Shelf) of the United Nations Conference on the Law of the Sea* (Geneva, February 24– April 27, 1958), Vol. 6, p. 43.

[38] Idem, p. 2.

[39] Idem, p. 33.

[40] For the Argentinian proposal, see doc. A/CONF. 13/C.4.L. 6, idem, p. 127. For the French proposal, see A/CONF. 13/C.4/L.7, idem, p. 128; for the Lebanese proposal, which was similar to that of the French, see A/CONF. 13/C.4/L.8, idem, p. 129.

[41] Idem, p. 5. For the Panamanian proposal, see Doc. A/CONF. 13/C.4/L.4, idem, p. 127. It may be interesting to note that the proposal of Panama, while limited the outer limit of the legal shelf at the edge of the slope, was clearly intended to exclude the "great depths of the oceanic basins."

[42] Idem, p. 6. Of the other method of exploitation, the exploitation from terra firma, Mouton, like the commentary of the Commission to the Draft Article 67 adopted in 1956, felt that it need not be controlled by the provisions of the continental shelf as it interferes little with the freedom of the high seas.

[43] For the views of India, the Netherlands, Sweden, and the United Kingdom, see idem, pp. 12, 42, and 46. Ghana also favored the 550-meter depth limit; see p. 38.

[44] Idem, p. 41. See also the views of Peru on p. 10, Brazil on p. 36, Venezuela on p. 37, Uruguay on p. 34, El Salvador on p. 32, Chile on p. 31, Cuba on pp. 25–26.

[45] For the views of China, see idem, p. 4. See also the views of Republic of Korea, on p. 23.

[46] Idem, p. 21. For similar views of Pakistan, Lebanon, and the Republic of Vietnam favoring a 200-meter depth criterion, see pp. 19, 34, and 24, respectively. Guatemala also opposed Draft Article 67 because of its vagueness; see p. 31.

[47] For the proposal of Yugoslavia, see U.N. doc. A/CONF. 13/C.4/L.12, idem, p. 129.

[48] For the Canadian proposal, see U.N. doc. A/CONF. 13/C.4/L.30, idem, p. 135. At the time of voting, the Canadian representative amended the depth limit of 200 meters to 550 meters; idem, p. 46.

[49] Idem, p. 47. Apart from the proposals already mentioned, several other proposals were put to a vote and rejected. The original proposal of Canada (U.N. doc. A/CONF. 13/C.4/L.30), reintroduced by the Federal Republic of Germany, lost by 45 to 4, with 18 abstentions. The Korean proposal (A/CONF. 13/C.4/L.11, to delete the words "to a depth of 200 meters or, beyond that limit" (see p. 32), was rejected by 42 votes to 13, with 13 abstentions.

[50] The Philippine amendment was adopted by 31 votes to 10, with 25 abstentions. Countries that voted against Draft Article 67 were France, the Federal Republic of Germany, Italy, Japan, the Republic of Korea, the Netherlands, Pakistan, Argentina, and Belgium. Abstaining in the voting were Burma, Greece, Iceland, Iran, Monaco, the Philippines, Poland, Switzerland, Turkey, and the United Kingdom.

It is significant that most of the countries that wished to see a precise outer limit adopted voted in favor of Draft Article 67 for lack of a better alternative and in the interest of some agreement. Norway, one of these states, explained how its delegate voted:

The Amendments proposed by India and Canada were in general agreement with his delegation's point of view. When they were both defeated, he had voted for the Interna-

tional Law Commission's draft as amended by the Philippine proposal, because although
he considered the text lacked balance and precision, it might still form the basis of an international regime and was accordingly preferable to no agreement at all.

Ibid.

[51] *Summary Records of the Meetings and Annexes of the Plenary Meetings of the United
Nations Conference on the Law of the Sea* (Geneva, February 24–April 27, 1958), Vol.
2, Eighth Plenary Meeting, p. 13.

[52] See U.N. doc. ST/LEG/SER.D/1 (1968), pp. 332–333.

[53] For a survey of the various instruments of national legislation on the "continental
shelf," see *Survey of National Legislation Concerning the Seabed and the Ocean Floor,
and the Subsoil Thereof, Underlying the High Seas beyond the Limits of Present National Jurisdiction*, U.N. doc. A/AC. 135/11 of June 4, 1968.

[54] For the boundaries of the Australia shelf, see idem, pp. 12–25; the United Kingdom,
see pp. 50–57; Ecuador, at p. 30; and Ghana, p. 34.

[55] For the proposal of Malta of August 17, 1967, see U.N. doc. A/6695, August 18, 1967.

[56] Shigeru Oda, "Proposals for Revising the Convention on the Continental Shelf," Vol.
7, *The Columbia Journal of Transnational Law*, pp. 1–31 (1968), at p. 9. The author
himself admits that "such an interpretation was perhaps not what the delegates at the
Geneva Conference actually thought they were affirming."

John L. Mero, a marine geologist, seemed to subscribe to the same point of view. See
his *Mineral Resources of the Sea* (Amsterdam: Elsevier, 1965), at p. 289. Also see
Seymour S. Bernfeld, "Developing the Resources of the Seas—Security of Investment,"
Vol. 2, *International Lawyer*, pp. 67–76 (1967), at pp. 72–73.

[57] Ibid, p. 10. For similar views by the same author, see "The Geneva Conventions on
the Law of the Sea: Some Suggestions for Revision," Vol. 1, *Natural Resource Lawyer*
(Journal of the Section of Natural Resources Law, American Bar Association), pp. 103–
114, (1968), at pp. 105–106.

[58] M. S. McDougal and W. T. Burke, *The Public Order of the Oceans* (New Haven:
Yale University Press, 1962) pp. 688–690; Richard Young, "The Geneva Convention on
the Continental Shelf: A First Impression," Vol. 52 *A.J.I.L.*, pp. 733–738 (1958), at p.
735. Also see the views of W. T. Burke and Richard Young, Hearings before the Special
Subcommittee on the Outer Continental Shelf of the U.S. Senate Committee on Interior
and Insular Affairs, *Outer Continental Shelf*, 91st Congress, 1st and 2nd Sessions, December 17, 1969, January 22 and March 4, 1970. Washington, D.C., 1970, at pp. 172 and
181.

It is interesting to note that in the context of outer space explorations, J. C. Cooper,
as early as 1951, in discussing the extent to which a state could exercise exclusive competence over the space directly above its territory, suggested that "at any particular time
the territory of each State extends upward into space as far as the scientific progress of
any State in the international community permits such state to control space above it."
See U.S. Senate doc. No. 26, *Legal Problems of Space Exploration* (Washington, D.C.:
U. S. Government Printing Office, March 22, 1961), 87th Congress, 1st Session.

[59] L. F. E. Goldie, "The Exploitability Test: Interpretation and Possibilities," Vol. 8,
Natural Resources Journal, pp. 434–477 (1968), at p. 448.

[60] See the statement by Professor William T. Burke, in *Outer Continental Shelf, supra*
note 58, p. 162.

[61] Shigeru Oda in W. T. Burke (ed.), *Towards a Better Use of the Oceans*, a SIPRI
Monograph (New York: Humanities Press, 1969), pp. 197–206, at pp. 197–198.

[62] Mr. Richard Young in the *Outer Continental Shelf, supra* note 58, p. 176.

[63] See Northcutt Ely, "United States Seabed Minerals Policy," Vol. 4 *Natural Resources Lawyer*, pp. 597–621 (1971), at p. 609; J. A. Beesley, "Some Unresolved Issues
on the Law of the Sea" ibid., pp. 629–638, at p. 631; Ted Stevens, "The Future of Our

Outer Continental Shelf and the Seabeds," ibid., pp. 646–653, at p. 649; Luke T. Finlay, "Rights of Coastal Nations to the Continental Margins," ibid., pp. 668–675, at p. 669; and Hollis D. Hedgberg, "Limits of National Jurisdiction Over Natural Resources of the Ocean Bottom," in Lewis M. Alexander (ed.), *supra* note 33, pp. 159–170, at p. 161.

[64] R. Y. Jennings, "Note on Article 1 of the 1958 Geneva Convention on the Continental Shelf," circulated as a Memorandum (No. 12) of June 15, 1968, to the members of the Committee on Deep Sea Mineral Resources of the American Branch of International Law Association, at p. 4. See also his "General Course of International Law" in Vol. 121 *Recueil Des Cours* (1967–II), pp. 327–600, at p. 398; and his "Limits of Continental Shelf Jurisdiction, Some Possible Implications of the North Sea Case Judgement," Vol. 18, *International and Comparative Law Quarterly*, pp. 819–832 (1969).

[65] For the comment of the International Law Commission in 1953, see *Y.B.Y.L.C.* Vol. 2, pp. 213–214; R. Y. Jennings, Memorandum (No. 12), ibid., p. 4.

[66] R. Y. Jennings, ibid., p. 5.

[67] See "An Interim Report of the National Petroleum Council," *Petroleum Resources Under the Ocean Floor* (Washington, D.C., July, 1968), Appendix b.

[68] *North Sea Continental Shelf Judgment, I.C.J. Reports,* 1969. For the views of various judges of the court, which agree essentially with this interpretation, see Ian Brownlie, "Recommendations on the Limits of the Continental Shelf and Related Matters: A Commentary," in Lewis M. Alexander (ed.), *supra* note 33, pp. 133–158, at p. 138. For a more particular appraisal of the *North Sea Continental Shelf Judgment,* see W. Friedmann, "The North Sea Continental Shelf Cases: A Critique," Vol. 64, *A.J.I.L.,* pp. 229–240 (1970); R. Y. Jennings, "Limits of Continental Shelf Jurisdiction: Some Possible Implications of the North Sea Case Judgment," Vol. 18, *I.C.L.Q.,* pp. 819–832 (1969); D. H. N. Johnson, "The North Sea Continental Shelf Cases," Vol. 3, *International Relations,* pp. 522–540 (1969); Isi Foighel, "The North Sea Continental Shelf Cases," Vol. 39, *Nordisk Tidsskrift for International Ret,* pp. 109–127 (1969); L. J. Bouchez, "The North Sea Continental Shelf Cases," Vol. 1, *Journal of Maritime Law and Commerce,* pp. 113–122 (1969); and E. D. Brown, "The North Sea Continental Shelf Cases," Vol. 23, *Current Legal Problems,* pp. 187–215 (1970).

[69] See the Final Report of the National Petroleum Council, *Petroleum Resources Under the Ocean Floor* (Washington, D.C.: National Petroleum Council, March 1969), at p. 10.

[70] U.N. doc. A/AC. 135/WG. 1/SR. 8, p. 12.

[71] U.N. doc. A/AC. 135/1 p. 33.

[72] U.N. doc. A/AC. 138/SCII/SR4–23, December 2, 1971, at p. 83.

[73] See *International Law Commission Report Covering the Work of Its Eighth Session,* April 23–July 4, 1956, *Y.B.I.L.C.,* Vol. 2 (1956), pp. 253–296.

Because of the unmistakable intention of the International Law Commission, another interpretation of the limits of continental shelf jurisdiction advanced by L. F. E. Goldie should also be rejected. Referring to an earlier position of the Commission on the limits which stated that

. . . the continental shelf might well include submarine areas lying at a depth of over 200 meters, but susceptible of exploitation by means of installations erected in neighboring areas where the depth does not exceed this limit, . . .

Goldie submitted that

. . . both for policy purposes and to give effect to the most literal interpretation of Article 1 of the continental shelf convention, the exploitability test should be viewed as allowing the coastal state no more than the power of asserting its jurisdiction over exploitations *beyond* the shelf which began *on* the shelf (i.e., on the landward side of the two hundred isobath) and which subsequently developed beyond that line. [Italics in original.]

See L. F. E. Goldie, *supra* note 59, p. 447.

As a matter of policy, acceptance of Goldie's suggestion would be tantamount to reincorporating the existence of the geological shelf as a strict basis for the doctrine of the continental shelf. The disadvantages of such a proposition are noted in Chapter 2. Besides, the Commission later rightly rejected this notion as it would discriminate among states.

[74] See *supra* note 29.

[75] Roger Denrome concisely noted that if the Ciudad Trujillo conference supported anything, it was the elimination of geological inequalities from influencing the legal rights of coastal states over offshore areas. He pointed out that

> It would be ironic, indeed, to use this Latin American concern for "equality" in order to justify a geological interpretation of the "adjacency" criterion which would in effect only increase the discrimination against States which have no shelf, their coasts dropping steeply to great depths.

Roger Denrome, "The Seaward Limit of the Continental Shelf," in Lewis M. Alexander (ed.), *supra* note 33, pp. 263–274, at pp. 270–271.

[76] For a similar view, see Louis Henkin, in Lewis M. Alexander (ed.), *supra,* note 33, pp. 171–178, at p. 172. Also see his statement before the Metcalf Committee, *Outer Continental Shelf, supra* note 58, pp. 202–208, and his *Law for the Sea's Mineral Resources* (New York: Institute for the Study of Human Affairs of Columbia University, 1968); and his article cited *supra* note 33; J. Andrassy, *International Law and Resources of the Sea* (New York: Columbia University Press, 1970), at pp. 169–174; and Wolfgang Friedmann, "Selden Redivivus—Towards a Partition of the Seas?" Vol. 65, *A.J.I.L.,* pp. 757–771 (1971), at p. 762; and his *Future of the Oceans* (New York: George Braziller, 1971); and Bernard Oxman, *The Preparation of Article 1 of the Convention on the Continental Shelf* (Springfield, Va.: Clearinghouse for Federal Scientific and Technical Information, n.d.).

[77] William T. Burke, "Law and the New Technologies," Chapter XIV, in Lewis Alexander (ed.), *The Law of the Sea: Offshore Boundaries and Zones* (Columbus, Ohio: Ohio State University Press, 1967), at p. 205.

[78] Francis T. Christy, Jr., "Alternative Regime for Marine Resources Underlying the High Seas," Vol. 1, *Natural Resources Lawyer,* pp. 63–77 (1968), at pp. 63–64.

[79] See Myres S. McDougal, "Revision of the Geneva Conventions on the Law of the Sea—The Views of a Commentator," Vol. 1, *Natural Resources Lawyer,* pp. 19–28 (1968), at p. 26. Also see M. S. McDougal and W. T. Burke, *supra* note 58, pp. 685–686.

[80] *Report of the U.N. Ad Hoc Committee to Study the Peaceful Uses of the Sea-Bed and the Ocean Floor beyond the Limits of National Jurisdiction,* G.A.O.R., Twenty-Third Session, Supplement No. 21 (New York: United Nations, 1968), U.N. doc. A/7230, p. 48.

During the discussions in the United Nations either in the First Committee or the Ad Hoc Committee member-states expressed four different points of view on the issue of outer limits to the "continental shelf." One group, as noted earlier, relied on the geological appurtenance principle to assert that the outer limits fall where the slope ends and the abyssal depths begin. *Supra* note 71. A second group of states just referred to the criterion of "adjacency," without identifying any one point as the outer limit, as indicative of some limit to the legal shelf. (For example, Australia, U.N. doc. A/AC. 135/WG. 1/SR. 8 p. 2.) Yet another position was stated suggesting that the criterion of "exploitability" serves, not to stretch the exclusive access of the coastal states to unlimited depths, but only to make the definition more flexible to suit the geographical peculiarities of continental shelves around the world. (For example, Norway, U.N. doc. A/AC. 135/WG.

1/SR. 6, p. 10.) Another significant group of states was not concerned about the niceties of interpretation of the scope of Article 1. To this group the definition of "continental shelf" was vague and unrealistic in an age of rapid technological advancement. It was desirable, according to them, to clearly identify the area of exclusive access before the ambiguous formula was invoked to divide up the entire ocean floor among coastal states. (For example, Iceland, A/AC. 135/1/Add. 8, pp. 2–3; Finland, A/AC. 135/1/Add. 6, pp. 2–3; Malta, A/AC. 135/WG. 1/SR. 7, pp. 6–7.

[81] See, for example, the Report of the Thirty-Third American Assembly, May 2–5, 1968, Arden House, Harriman, New York, *Uses of the Seas*, p. 6–7 (where it proposed a narrow limit of 200-meter depth for the continental shelf); similarly, the United Nations Committee of World Peace Through Law Center, *Treaty Governing the Exploitation and Use of the Ocean Bed*, pamphlet series (No. 10, Geneva), p. 8 (200-meter depth or 50 nautical miles); *The Report of the Deep-Sea Mining Committee on the Exploration and Exploitation of Minerals on the Ocean Bed and in Its Subsoil, International Law Association*, Buenos Aires Conference (1968) (Utrecht, February 2, 1968) (500-meter depth or 20–30 nautical miles); *Summary of Discussion of the Planning Session on Law of the Seas*, February 24–26, 1968, held by the Center for the Study of Democratic Institutions, Santa Barbara, California, U.S.A. (a distance of 300 kilometers, which was, according to this group, the algebraic mean of the extension of all the continental shelves of the world); and the Nineteenth Report of the Commission to Study the Organization of Peace, *The United Nations and the Bed of the Sea* (New York, 1969), p. 24 (200-meter depth or 50 nautical miles).

According to Libya, a distance limit of 40 miles could be taken as a starting point for negotiations of the outer limit for the shelf. U.N. doc. No. A/AC.138/SCII/SR 4–23, p. 85. Iran suggested that the distance criterion should be considered only in cases where a depth limit of 200 meters would lead to inequities, p. 166.

The Soviet Union offered a 500-meter isobath or 100 nautical miles as a solution for the limits of the continental shelf. See the USSR's rough draft of basic provisions on the question of the outer limit of the continental shelf, U.N. doc. No. A/AC.138/SCII/L.26.

[82] Iceland suggested a depth limit of 3,000 meters or a distance limit of 200 nautical miles, U.N. doc. No. A/AC.138/SCII/SR.60, p. 13.

Nigeria supported a 2,500-meter depth or 200-mile distance limit for the continental shelf, A/AC.138/SCII/SR 7, p. 30.

France favored a distance limit of 200 miles, U.N. doc. A/AC.138/SCII/SR 24–32, p. 35; Norway suggested 200 miles or a 600-meter depth, U.N. doc. A/AC.138/SCII/SR 54, March 20, 1973, p. 2.

Earlier, France indicated that the limit of the shelf should be at least at the "foot of the continental slope," and where this could not be located, it should be at a depth of 200 meters; see U.N. doc. A/AC.138/WG.1/SR.7, p. 12. Also see the *Draft Report of the Committee on Deep Sea Mineral Resources of the American Branch of International Law Association* (June 1968), which suggested the "toe of the continental rise" where such a geological feature exists for the limit of the continental shelf. According to the same report, in the absence of such a feature, a depth limit of 2,500 meters, which should in no case be less than 100 nautical miles, could be substituted as a limit. E. D. Brown, *Report on the Legal Regime of Deep-Sea Mining* (for the British Branch Committee on Deep-Sea Mining, June 1, 1968), pp. 41–42, noted that a limit of 200 miles might be usefully adopted for the legal shelf. The same author later indicated that depth limit of 2,500 meters or a distance limit of 200 miles was preferable. See E. D. Brown, "Our Nation and The Sea: A Comment on the Proposed Legal-Political Framework for the Development of Submarine Mineral Resources" in Lewis M. Alexander, *supra* note 33, pp. 2–49, at p. 43.

[83] See the *Draft United Nations Convention on the International Sea-Bed Area*, submit-

ted by the United States of America to the U.N. Seabed Committee, U.N. doc. A/AC.138/25, in *Report of the Committee on the Peaceful Uses of the Sea-Bed and the Ocean Floor beyond the Limits of National Jurisdiction, G.A.O.R.*, Twenty-Fifth Session, Supp. No. 21 (New York: United Nations, 1970), U.N. doc. A/8021, pp. 130–176, at pp. 132 and 138.

The intermediate or buffer zone idea was originally suggested by Professor Louis Henkin in his *Law for the Sea's Mineral Resources* (Washington, D.C.: National Council on Marine Resources and Engineering Development, 1967), at p. 105; see also his "Changing Law for the Changing Seas," in E. A. Gullion (ed.), *Uses of the Seas* (Englewood Cliffs, N.J.: Prentice-Hall, 1968), pp. 69–97 at p. 89. The suggestion was later adopted by the United States President's Commission on Marine Science Engineering and Resources, which proposed 200 meters or 50 nautical miles for the first zone and 2,500 meters or 100 nautical miles as a limit for the second, the intermediate zone. See the Report, *Our Nation and the Sea* (Washington, D.C.: U.S. Government Printing Office, 1969). These ideas influenced the U.S. Draft Convention.

[84] See the *Preliminary Working Paper Submitted by Afghanistan, Austria, Belgium, Hungary, Nepal, Netherlands and Singapore,* U.N. doc. No. A/AC.138/55 in the *Report of the Committee on the Peaceful Uses of the Sea-Bed and the Ocean Floor beyond the Limits of National Jurisdiction, G.A.O.R.*, Twenty-Sixth Session, Suppl. No. 21 (New York: United Nations, 1971) U.N. doc. A/8421, pp. 194–197.

[85] Wolfgang Friedmann, an advocate of inclusive use and sharing of ocean resources, regarded the United States draft treaty for the creation of an international trusteeship zone as "by far the most concrete and enlightened attempt of any government to reconcile the conflicting claims of coastal states and international community and above all to put a halt to the uncertainties of Article 1." Wolfgang Friedmann, *supra* note 76, p. 759.

Professor McDougal, comparing the U.S. draft treaty's objectives with those of the claims for wide exclusive coastal state resource zones, said that "it had elements of recognition of common interest and magnanimity not shared in all the responses to it."

See his statement in the Third Seward Johnson Panel on *The Limits of National Jurisdiction and the Common Heritage Concept* (Woods Hole, Mass.: Woods Hole Oceanographic Institution, 1974), p. 27.

[86] John R. Stevenson and Bernard H. Oxman, "The Preparations for the Law of the Sea Conference," Vol. 68, *A.J.I.L.*, pp. 1–32 (1974), at p. 18.

Nigeria, for example, opposed the concept of intermediate zone, citing the following reason:

The new concept of an intermediate zone over which the coastal State would ultimately have no control and which would be controlled by an international body ran counter to the spirit [of the 1958 Convention on the Continental Shelf]. It seemed to [the Nigerian] delegation that the machinery proposed by the United States was somewhat cumbersome.

U.N. doc. A/AC.138/SCII/SR 4–23, December 2, 1971, p. 29.

Libya supported the Nigerian position in its opposition to the intermediate zone concept and added that "it would ultimately give an unfair advantage to the highly developed countries." Ibid, p. 85.

The 1971 Report of the Seabed Committee summarized the reaction of several states to the intermediate zone proposal this way: "A number of delegations could not support the concept of an intermediate-trusteeship zone." See *supra* note 85, p. 24.

For a critical review of the U.S. Draft Treaty on the intermediate zone, see "Special Report—The U.S. Position on the Seabed," in Lewis M. Alexander (ed.), *The Law of the Sea: The United Nations and Ocean Management* (Proceedings of the Fifth Annual Conference on Law of the Sea Institute, June 15–19, 1970, University of Rhode Island,

Kingston, R.I., 1971), pp. 159–186. Also see H. Gary Knight, "The Draft United Nations Convention on the International Seabed Area: Background, Description and Some Preliminary Thoughts," Vol. 8, *San Diego Law Review*, pp. 459–550 (May 1971); and M. K. Nawaz, "An Alternative Criterion for Delimiting the Continental Shelf," Vol. 13, *I.J.I.L.*, pp. 25–40 (1973).

The U.S. National Petroleum Council expressed its objections to the U.S. Draft Treaty in *Supplemental Report on Petroleum Resources Under the Ocean Floor* (Washington, D.C.: National Petroleum Council, March 4, 1971). On p. 54, it concluded that "Any treaty which fails to assure effective national jurisdiction over the entire seabed pertaining to the U.S. would be placing in jeopardy a vital national interest of this country."

[87] For a survey of the historical background bearing upon the articulation of claims for an exclusive "economic zone" or "patrimonial sea," see Douglas M. Johnston and Edgar Gold, *The Economic Zone in the Law of the Sea: Survey, Analysis and Appraisal of Current Trends* (Occasional Paper 17, Law of the Sea Institute, University of Rhode Island, June 1973).

[88] See the draft articles on the economic zone proposed by Algeria, Cameroun, Ghana, Ivory Coast, Kenya, Liberia, Madagascar, Mauritius, Senegal, Sierra Leone, Somalia, Sudan, Tunisia, and the United Arab Republic of Tanzania, in *Report of the Committee on the Peaceful Uses of the Sea-bed and the Ocean Floor beyond the Limits of National Jurisdiction*, Vol. 3, G.A.O.R., Twenty-Eighth Session, Suppl. No. 21 (New York: United Nations, 1973), U.N. doc. A/9021, pp. 87–89.

The economic zone concept was formulated earlier by Kenya, was discussed by the Asian-African legal consultative organization, the Yaoundé regional African seminar on law of the sea of 1972, and was endorsed by the Addis Ababa Declaration of the Organization of African Unity of 1973. See the statement of the Kenyan delegate, U.N. doc. A/AC.138/SC.II/SR 4–23, December 2, 1971, p. 54; the *Conclusions of the African States Regional Seminar on Law of the Sea*, Yaoundé, 1972, U.N. doc. A/AC.138/79; and the *Draft Articles on Exclusive Economic Zone Concept* submitted by Kenya, U.N. doc. A/AC.138/SCII/L.10, and the statement of the Kenyan delegate on it, U.N. doc. A/AC.138/SCII/SR 33–47, November 29, 1972, at pp. 54–55, and for the *Organization of African Unity: Declaration on the Issues of the Law of the Sea*, U.N. doc. A/AC.138/86.

[89] Fifteen countries attended the June 1972 Specialized Conference of the Caribbean Countries on Problems of the Sea. The Declaration of Santo Domingo resulting from this conference was signed by only ten countries, Colombia, Costa Rica, Guatemala, Haiti, Honduras, Mexico, Nicaragua, the Dominican Republic, Trinidad and Tobago, and Venezuela; five countries, Barbados, El Salvador, Guyana, Jamaica, and Panama, did not sign the Declaration. For the text of the Santo Domingo Declaration of 1972, see U.N. doc. A/AC.138/80.

Later, the principle of "patrimonial sea" as enunciated by the Santo Domingo Declaration was incorporated in the draft treaty articles sponsored by Colombia, Mexico, and Venezuela, 1973 Report of the U. N. Seabed Committee, Vol. 3, ibid, pp. 19–22. Also see Jorge Castañeda, "The Concept of Patrimonial Sea in International Law," Vol. 12, *I.J.I.L.*, pp. 535–543 (1972).

[90] Ibid., pp. 23, 29, 106, 111.

[91] Ibid., pp. 71–74; pp. 30 and 33.

[92] Ibid., p. 78.

[93] Ibid., pp. 79 and 80.

[94] On the interests of shelf-locked and near landlocked countries, see Lewis M. Alexander, "Indices of National Interest in the Oceans," Vol. 1, *Ocean Development and International Law Journal*, pp. 21–49 (1973), at p. 37. See also his excellent article on "Alternative Methods for Delimiting the Outer Boundary" (Office of External Research,

U.S. Department of State, February 1970); and on the interests of shelf-locked countries, see Vladimir Ibler, "The Interests of Shelf-Locked States and Proposed Development of the Law of the Sea," Vol. 11, *I.J.I.L.*, pp. 389–411 (1971). For a list of these countries, see Chapter 1, notes 3 and 4. On the interests of developing countries generally, see R. P. Anand, "Interests of the Developing Countries and the Developing Law of the Sea," in Lucius Caflisch (ed.), *Hydrospace in International Relations (Annals of International Studies*, No. 4) (Geneva: Alumni Association of Geneva Graduate Institute of International Studies, 1973), pp. 13–30.

[95] U.N. doc. A/AC.138/SCII/SR.57, April 3, 1973, p. 20. Also see the views of Czechoslovakia in favor of the rights of landlocked countries, A/AC.138/SCII/SR 56, March 27, 1973, pp. 6–7; Poland, A/AC.138/SCII/SR.60, April 6, 1973, pp. 18–20; Zaire, ibid., p. 22–24; Bolivia, A/AC.138/SCII/SR 4–23, December 2, 1971 pp. 149–153 and Nepal, ibid., p. 79.

[96] The U.N. Seabed Committee Report of 1973, Vol. 3, *supra* note 88, pp. 85–86.

[97] This restriction, however, does not, in the opinion of the sponsoring countries, "preclude the disadvantaged States from entering into arrangements with third parties for the purpose of enabling them to develop viable fishing industries of their own." Ibid., p. 86.

[98] Ibid., pp. 90, and 76. This proposal constituted a virtual abandonment by the United States of its earlier proposal for a trusteeship zone. According to the United States, this new position of agreeing to a broad coastal state economic jurisdiction and seabed areas beyond the territorial sea should be regarded as part of an overall law of the sea settlement. The components of such a settlement include international treaty standards

a. to prevent unreasonable interference with other uses of the ocean;

b. to protect oceans from pollution;

c. to protect the integrity of investments;

d. to provide for the sharing of revenues with the international community; and

e. to arrange for compulsory settlement of disputes

Ibid., p. 61. Malta, which proposed a limit of 200 miles for the "national ocean space," provided that compensation be paid to those coastal states which may have to relinquish rights already gained in seabed areas beyond a distance of 200 miles. Ibid., pp. 42, 65.

[99] Ibid., p. 88. However, in a separate draft treaty, containing articles on fisheries which were proposed as a supplement to the economic zone concept, Canada, India, Kenya, and Sri Lanka indicated (ibid., p. 83) that

This privilege will be available to the nationals of the landlocked State concerned and cannot be transferred to third parties by lease or license, by establishing joint collaboration ventures, or by any other arrangement.

This restriction may prove very onerous to the interests of a developing geographically disadvantaged state. According to it, if these countries do not already have a well-developed and growing fishing capability, they will not be allowed to improve it by seeking assistance from third parties. Adoption of such a comprehensive restriction would indeed nullify whatever advantages the coastal state purports to grant to the developing geographically disadvantaged state.

The coastal state, of course, has a legitimate concern to assure itself that the preferential treatment granted to a developing landlocked state is not abused by that state selling that right for a price to a more developed fishing industry. To guard against this abuse, preferential treatment could be granted in the form of specifying a quota for the geographically disadvantaged state, which may be fixed by taking into consideration its proved needs, the incentives necessary for the growth of its fishing industry, and such other factors as may appear reasonable in the context.

In this respect, the proposal made by a group of six geographically disadvantaged states is a reasonable one. See *supra* note 98.

[100] Ibid., p. 79. Argentina's proposal, like the four-state proposal noted above, restricts the application of a preferential regime to those enterprises of the geographically disadvantaged state which "are effectively controlled by capital and nationals of that State and [requires] that the ships which operate in the area fly the flag of that State." A similar restriction was earlier advocated by the Yaoundé African regional seminar on law of the sea; see *supra* note 88. See also ibid., pp. 29 and 73. On the Chinese position, see M. K. Nawaz, "Chinese Views on The Law of the Sea—Select Aspects," Vol. 12, *I.J.I.L.*, pp. 606–614 (1972).

[101] U.N. doc. A/AC.138/SCII/SR.58, April 4, 1973, p. 18.

[102] The Third Seward Johnson Panel, *supra* note 85, p. 30.

[103] Ibid., pp. 28–29.

[104] U.N. doc. A/AC.138/SCII/SR.57, April 3, 1973, p. 21.

[105] The Netherlands representative discussed the relevance of this consideration for the issue of limits as follows:

The allocation of a 200-mile patrimonial sea or economic zone would, in terms of area, give the greatest benefits to such states as the United States, the USSR, Canada, Australia, Japan and other developed countries, while many of the landlocked and shelf-locked countries and countries with other geographical disadvantage, which could not benefit from any extension of national jurisdiction over the seas, were developing countries. Only a system of internationalization of the seas could guarantee equitable distribution of their resources and thus contribute to bridging the gap between rich and poor countries.

See U.N. doc. A/AC.138/SCII/SR.59, April 5, 1973, pp. 12–13.

[106] This aspect will be examined in the next chapter on claims about access to deep ocean mineral resources.

[107] This point was originally made by the writer elsewhere; see P. Sreenivasa Rao, "Development and the Sea," Vol. 17, *Oceanus* (Woods Hole Oceanographic Institute Journal, Woods Hole, Mass.), pp. 6–13 (1973), at pp. 8–9.

[108] In indicating a percentage of value rather than a percentage of profits, it is suggested that sometimes a coastal state may not extract any rent or profit by leasing to other states or industries rights to exploit marine resources, and may undertake the exploitation for its own sake. Even in that case, it is possible to determine the value of the resources that the coastal state extracts. So it is much safer to leave the construction regarding revenue-sharing to a broader concept, like "value" rather than to a narrow concept of "profit."

Notes to Chapter 4, pp. 76–108

[1] For an exhaustive historical account of the emergence of the doctrine of the freedom of the seas, see Thomas Fulton, *The Sovereignty of the Seas* (Edinburgh and London: W. Blackwood and Sons, 1911). For a much briefer and handy summary of the long history through which the doctrine evolved, see H. A. Smith, *The Law and Custom of the Sea,* Third Ed. (London: Stevens and Sons, 1959), pp. 57–60; C. John Colombos, *The International Law of the Sea,* Sixth Revised Ed. (New York: D. McKay Co., 1967), pp. 47–67; L. Oppenheim and H. Lauterpacht, *International Law,* Vol. 1, Eighth Ed. (London and New York: Longmans, Green, and Co. 1955), pp. 582–593; Morton R. Kaplan and Nicholas deB. Katzenbach, *The Political Foundations of International Law* (New York: John Wiley and Sons, 1961), pp. 147–154.

[2] See Max Sørensen, *Manual of Public International Law* (New York: St. Martin's Press, 1968), p. 346.

[3] For a summary account of the conflicting theories regarding *res communis* and *res nullius* see Louis Henkin, *Law for the Sea's Mineral Resources* (Washington, D.C.: National Council on Marine Resources and Engineering Development, 1967), pp. 27–36.

[4] C. John Colombos, for example, distinguishing between the seabed and the subsoil, said,

As regards the former, the better opinion appears to be that it is incapable of occupation by any State and that its legal status is the same as that of the waters of the open sea above it. The same reasons for maintaining it unappropriated in the interests of the freedom of navigation apply, with equal force, to the bed of the sea.

Colombus, *supra* note 1, p. 67.

[5] Waldock argued, citing Fauchille, Westlake, Hurst, and Smith, that "the seabed may be occupied but subject to no unreasonable interference with the freedom of the seas." See C. H. M. Waldock, "The Legal Basis of Claims to the Continental Shelf," Vol. 36, *Transactions of the Grotius Society,* pp. 115–148 (1951), at p. 137.

[6] While almost all the writers agreed that the subsoil of the seas or the ocean floor could be occupied for purposes of claiming exclusive title, some took the view that such occupation and exclusive appropriation was permissible only by operations that were begun on the coast or in territorial waters and were carried beneath the high seas wholly underground. See C. John Colombos, *supra* note 1, p. 69; L. Oppenheim and H. Lauterpacht, *supra* note 2, p. 577. Waldock, on the other hand, believed that the limitation on the area of the ocean floor capable of "effective occupation" implied in the views of some writers was unacceptable. He said,

This view pushes the freedom of the seas too far. The most that ought to be demanded is that there should be no unreasonable interference with the use of the high seas by operations carried out on the sea-bed.

C. H. M. Waldock, *supra* note 5, p. 118.

[7] Opposing the doctrine of contiguity and geological appurtenance, which were claimed as a basis for exclusive appropriation of the mineral resources of the continental shelf by coastal states, Waldock argued that

It is my purpose to suggest that, pending the conclusion of a satisfactory convention, we should not be in a hurry to accept a totally new concept as a substitute for the existing customary law of occupation. There is probably less risk of the existing law failing to meet the legitimate requirements of States in the exploitation of the sea-bed than of a hastily advanced new doctrine undermining the international character of the high seas.

C. H. M. Waldock, ibid., at p. 147.

[8] H. Lauterpacht, "Sovereignty over Submarine Areas," Vol. 27, *The British Year Book of International Law,* pp. 376–433 (1950), at pp. 401–402.

[9] For the text of the *Abu Dhabi Award,* see Vol. 1, *International and Comparative Law Quarterly,* pp. 247–261 (1952), at p. 256–257.

[10] F. A. Vallat, "The Continental Shelf," Vol. 23, *British Year Book of International Law,* pp. 333–338 (1946), at p. 335; L. F. E. Goldie, "Australia's Continental Shelf: Legislation and Proclamations," Vol. 3, *International and Comparative Law Quarterly,* pp. 535–575 (1954), at p. 561; F. V. García-Amador, *The Exploitation and Conservation of the Resources of the Sea,* Second Ed. (Leyden: A. W. Sythoff, 1963), p. 131.

[11] M. S. McDougal and W. T. Burke, *The Public Order of the Oceans* (New Haven: Yale University Press, 1962), p. 632.

[12] See *Y.B.I.L.C.* (1950), Vol. 1, p. 227.

[13] Professor Georges Scelle of France suggested this idea. See the *Y.B.I.L.C.* (1955), Vol. 1, p. 222. The Commission in its fifth session almost endorsed the view. *Y.B.I.L.C.* (1955), Vol. 2, p. 22. But in its final draft it refused to take any position on the matter. See note 21.

[14] See *Y.B.I.L.C.* (1956), Vol. 1, p. 11.

[15] See the Report of the International Law Commission to the General Assembly of the United Nations, *Y.B.I.L.C.* (1956), Vol. 2, p. 278.

[16] For a text of the Geneva Convention on the High Seas, 1958, see United Nations, *Treaty Series,* Vol. 450, p. 82.

[17] Lt. Comdr. Bruce A. Harlow, "Legal Aspects of Claims to Jurisdiction in Coastal Waters," a paper presented at the *Conference of the U.S. Fishing Industry,* University of Washington, Seattle, Washington, March 24–27, 1968, pp. 1–25, at p. 22.

[18] Report of the National Petroleum Council, *Petroleum Resources Under the Ocean Floor* (Washington, D.C., 1969), p. 117.

[19] W. T. Burke, *Towards a Better Use of the Oceans: Contemporary Legal Problems in Ocean Development,* a SIPRI Monograph (New York: Humanities Press, 1969), at p. 52, says,

. . . there does not appear to be a serious question that any state or group can make use of the ocean floor, as for mining, so long as the activity is carried on with reasonable regard for the interests of others.

He adds, in a footnote on the same page,

This statement is based on the current general expectation that this region is open for use just as the water volume and surface above it, so long as such use is reasonable with respect to the interests of others. It may be recalled that the International Law Commission, in its commentary upon Article 27 on the "Freedom of the High Seas," noted that its list of freedoms was not restrictive and, after observing that there were other freedoms, specifically declared that it "has not made specific mention of the freedom to explore or exploit the subsoil of the high seas.

[20] U.N. doc. A/AC.135/SR.3, pp. 15–16.

[21] U.N. doc. A/AC.135/SR.5, p. 34.

[22] U.N. doc. A/AC.135/WG.1/SR.7, p. 13.

[23] U.N. doc. A/AC.135/1/Add.2.

[24] U.N. doc. A/AC.135/W.G.1/SR.7, p. 7.

[25] U.N. doc. A/C.1/PV.1597, p. 23.

[26] U.N. doc. A/C.1/PV.1600, pp. 32–35. For similar views, of China, the United Kingdom, India, Ireland, and Mexico, see U.N. doc. A/AC.135/12, pp. 19–20.

[27] U.N. doc. A/C.1/PV.1597, p. 67.

[28] U.N. doc. A/AC.135/WG.1/SR.7, p. 6.

[29] U.N. doc. A/C.1/PV.1593, p. 21.

[30] U.N. doc. A/C.1/PV.1598, p. 63. For similar views by other countries, for example: Belgium, A/C.1/PV.1596, p. 42; Chile, A/AC.138/SC.1/SR.16, p. 2; Brazil, A/C.1/PV.1591, pp. 8–10; Sudan, Sweden, India, A/AC.135/SR.7, p. 54; Mexico, A/AC.135/1, p. 3; Finland, A/AC.135/1, p. 3; and Pakistan A/AC.135/SR.8, p. 70.

[31] To the celebrated proposal of Ambassador Arvid Pardo that the seabed and ocean floor beyond the limits of national jurisdiction should be regarded as the common heritage of mankind, there were initially four different kinds of reactions from the members of the U.N. Seabed Committee.

A. The first group of states, which enthusiastically endorsed the concept of the common heritage of mankind, believed that the deep ocean mineral resources should be developed under the authority and control of international machinery with special regard for the interests of the developing nations.

See U.N. doc. A/AC.135/36, sponsored by Argentina, Brazil, Sri Lanka, Chile, Ecuador, El Salvador, India, Kenya, Liberia, Pakistan, Peru, Thailand, United Arab Republic, and United Republic of Tanzania. Several other nations had supported fifteen-nation proposals. Among them were

1. Belgium	A/C.1/PV.1596, p. 42
2. Bolivia	A/C.1/PV.1600, p. 46
3. Cyprus	A/C.1/PV.1599, p. 16
4. Finland	A/C.1/PV.1597, p. 82
5. Honduras	A/C.1/PV.1600, pp. 31–35
6. Indonesia	A/C.1/PV.1601, p. 42
7. Iraq	A/C.1/PV.1599, p. 52
8. Ireland	A/C.1/PV.1595, pp. 4–5
9. Jamaica	A/C.1/PV.1600, p. 48
10. Mexico	A/C.1/PV.1598, p. 41
11. Netherlands	A/C.1/PV.1595, pp. 21–25
12. Philippines	A/C.1/PV.1597, pp. 73–75
13. Rwanda	A/C.1/PV.1595, p. 31
14. Sierra Leone	A/C.1/PV.1600, p. 52
15. Sweden	A/C.1/PV.1596, pp. 28–30
16. Sudan	A/C.1/PV.1598, pp. 23–26
17. Turkey	A/AC.1/PV.1596, pp. 13–15
18. Yugoslavia	A/AC.1/PV.1593, p. 51

B. The second group exhibited a cautious attitude toward the idea of establishing international machinery for the deep ocean area. This group wanted further exploration and discussion of the idea before accepting it as a goal. See Cameroun, U.N. doc. A/C.1/PV.1601, p. 81; Costa Rica, U.N. doc. A/.1/PV.1602, p. 21; Colombia, U.N. doc. A/C.1/PV.1600, p. 68; and Canada, U.N. doc. A/C.1/PV.1599, p. 30.

C. The third group of states, while not openly critical of the concept of the common heritage of mankind, preferred promulgation of an agreed set of policies without the creation of international machinery for the regulation of deep ocean mineral resources. See the views of the United States, U.N. doc. A/AC.135/25; the United Kingdom, U.N. doc. A/C.1/PV.1594, pp. 61–62; France, U.N. doc. A/C.1/PV.1591, p. 41.

D. The fourth group of states was explicitly opposed both to the concept of the common heritage of mankind and to the idea of creating international machinery to govern deep ocean resource exploitation. See the views of USSR, U.N. doc. A/C.1/PV.1592, pp. 16–18; Bulgaria, U.N. doc. A/C.1/PV.1598, p. 57; Byelorussian S.S.R., U.N. doc. A/C.1/PV.1602, p. 48; Hungary, U.N. doc. A/C.1/PV.1599, p. 57; Poland, U.N. doc. A/C.1/PV.1597, p. 37; and the Ukranian S.S.R., U.N. doc. A/C.1/PV.1596, pp. 66–67.

[32] Christopher W. Pinto, "Problems of Developing States and Their Effects on Decisions on Law of the Sea," in Lewis M. Alexander (ed.), *The Law of the Sea: Needs and Interests of Developing Countries* (Proceedings of the Seventh Annual Conference of the Law of the Sea Institute, University of Rhode Island, June 26–29, 1972), pp. 3–13, at p. 8.

[33] U.N. doc. A/C.1/PV.1798, p. 32.

[34] U.N. doc. A/C.1/PV.1799, p. 6.

[35] U.N. doc. A/C.1/PV.1777, p. 27.

[36] Quoted in *Outer Continental Shelf*, Report by the Special Subcommittee on Outer Continental Shelf to the Committee on Interior and Insular Affairs of the United States Senate, 91 Congress, 2nd Session, Dec. 21, 1970, p. 21.

[37] Idem, p. 23.

[38] See Lewis M. Alexander, *supra* note 32, p. 48.

[39] E. D. Brown, "The 1973 Conference on Law of the Sea: The consequences of Failure to Agree," in Lewis M. Alexander (ed.), *The Law of the Sea: A New Geneva Conference* (Proceedings of the Sixth Annual Conference of the Law of the Sea Institute, June 21–24, 1971), pp. 1–37, at p. 23.

[40] Lewis M. Alexander (ed.), *supra* note 32, at p. 40 and p. 50.

[41] There is considerable scholarly debate about the significance of the U.N. General Assembly resolutions for creating authoritative and controlling prescriptions of law. Several scholars have alluded to the lawmaking effect of the resolutions. It is, of course, admitted that the resolutions have to be assessed in the context in which they are passed and invoked later as a basis for authoritative decision. See Rosalyn Higgins, *The Development of International Law by the Political Organs of the United Nations* (London and New York: Oxford University Press, 1963); Obed Y. Asamoah, *The Legal Significance of Declarations of the General Assembly of the United Nations* (The Hague: Martinus Nijhoff, 1966); Jorge Castañeda, *Legal Effects of United Nations Resolutions* (New York: Columbia University Press, 1970); K. V. Raman, *Customary Prescriptions of International Law* (unpublished Yale Law School dissertation, 1967).

Also see Richard A. Falk, "On the Quasi-Legislative Competence of the General Assembly," Vol. 60 *A.J.I.L.*, pp. 783–791 (1966); F. B. Sloan, "The Binding Force of a Recommendation of the General Assembly of the United Nations," Vol. 25, *B.Y.B.I.L.*, pp. 1–33 (1948); D. H. N. Johnson, "The Effect of the Resolutions of the General Assembly of the United Nations," Vol. 35, *B.Y.B.I.L.*, pp. 97–122 (1955–1956); F. A. Vallat, "The Competence of the U.N. General Assembly," Vol. 97, *Recueil Des Cours* (1959–II), pp. 207–292. Bing Cheng, "United Nations Resolutions on Outer Space: 'Instant' International Customary Law," Vol. 5, *Indian Journal of International Law*, pp. 23–45 (1965); and Samuel A. Bleicher, "The Legal Significance of Re-Citation of General Assembly Resolution," Vol. 63, *A.J.I.L.*, pp. 444–479 (1969); and Gaetano Arangio Riuz, "The Normative Role of the General Assembly of the United Nations and the Declaration of Friendly Relations," Vol. 3, *Recueil Des Cours*, pp. 431–472 (1972).

The International Court of Justice in the *Certain Expenses* case asserted that U.N. General Assembly resolutions are not merely "hortatory." *I.C.J. Reports*, 1962, p. 163.

[42] John G. Laylin, "Interim Practices and Policy for the Governing of Seabed Mining Beyond the Limits of National Jurisdiction," in *supra* note 32, pp. 25–28, p. 26, where he said that

The opinion is expressed by many scholars that while a state cannot by its activities on the ocean floor acquire sovereign rights, it can by its activities or those of its nationals acquire over a section of the Area rights, short of sovereign rights, against all other states and their nationals.

[43] See Lewis M. Alexander (ed.), *supra* note 32, p. 54.

[44] See John E. Flipse, "Impacts of Deep Ocean Mineral Development," The Charles M. Schwab Memorial Lecture, American Iron and Steel Institute, 80th General Meeting, May 24, 1972, p. 11.

[45] For the text of the proposed interim domestic legislation 52801, see Vol. 117, No. 164, U.S., *Congressional Record* (Nov. 2, 1971), pp. 2–3.

[46] John G. Laylin, *supra* note 42, pp. 27–28.

[47] Section 9 of S.2801 reads as follows:

A fund shall be established for assistance, as Congress may hereafter direct, to developing reciprocating states. The United States shall deposit in this fund each year an amount equivalent to —— percent of all license fees collected during that year by the United States pursuant to Sec. 5(a) an amount equivalent to —— percent of all income tax revenues derived by the United States which are directly attributable to recovery of hard minerals from the deep seabed pursuant to licenses issued under this Act, provided that the amount deposited by the United States per license issued and per unrelinquished square kilometer under license shall not exceed the amount contributed for assistance to developing reciprocating states by other licensing reciprocating states (except developing states) per license issued by them and per unrelinquished square kilometer licensed by them.

Supra note 45, p. 3.

[48] *Supra* note 45, p. 1.

[49] See the statements made by different delegations to the United Nations: Sweden, U.N. doc. A/C.1/PV.1527, November 14, 1967, p. 56; India, U.N. doc. A/C.1/PV.1680, November 7, 1969, pp. 23–25; Cameroun, U.N. doc. A/C.1/PV.1676, November 4, 1969, p. 76; Trinidad and Tobago, U.N. doc. A/C.1/PV.1677, November 5, 1969, p. 13; and Cyprus, U.N. doc. A/C.1/PV.1676, November 4, 1969, p. 76.

[50] See the statement by Sam Levering of Save Our Seas, an organization lobbying in Washington for an international solution to ocean problems, quoted in Lewis M. Alexander (ed.), *supra* note 32, p. 53.

[51] For a more detailed analysis of the interim legislation put before the U.S. Senate, see F. M. Auburn, "The Deep Seabed Hard Mineral Resources Bill," Vol. 9, *San Diego Law Review*, pp. 491–513 (1972). The author came to a similar conclusion (at p. 513):

> The Deep Seabed Hard Minerals Resources Bill is a carefully framed code for exploitation of ocean minerals by United States industrial enterprises, under government protection. But for the vast majority of states who do not have the technological capabilities or capital to take part in mining, it offers no benefits from the area which the General Assembly holds to be the common heritage of mankind.

[52] During the U.N. discussions, several delegations expressed the view that the concept of a "common heritage of mankind" is a new one and that it lacked precise legal content. See the views of Belgium, U.N. doc. A/AC.138/SC.1/SR.13, August 13, 1969, p. 16; Canada, idem, p. 18, and Japan, U.N. doc. A/AC.138/SC.1/SR.14, August 14, 1969, p. 24.

In one sense of the term, the oceans have always been regarded as the common heritage of mankind. As this writer pointed out elsewhere,

> . . . though occasionally claims for exclusive competence over wide stretches of the sea were put forward, they were rejected by the world community in favor of free and open access by all of its members. Oceans are a common heritage of mankind in the sense that they have been customarily open to inclusive use and enjoyment.

See P. Sreenivasa Rao, "Authority and Control Over Offshore Areas: In Defense of Common Interests," Vol. 11, *Indian Journal of International Law*, pp. 379–388 (1971), at p. 386.

Professor McDougal also rejected, as a "false and misleading idea," the contention that the concept of common heritage was novel, and he pointed out that

> If you have understood what I have said about sharability, from a factual standpoint, the whole of the oceans is a common heritage of mankind. We divide the oceans up between national jurisdiction and international jurisdiction only because of convenience in exploitation and because of different degrees in intensity of interest.

The Limits of National Jurisdiction and the Common Heritage Concept (a panel discussion, April 27, 1973, Woods Hole Oceanographic Institution, Woods Hole, Mass.), p. 6.

However, most of the delegations that supported the concept generally meant to endorse the idea of exploitation of ocean resources not for individual gain but for the good of all nations and peoples, with special regard for the needs of the developing nations. Viewed thus, the concept of the common heritage of mankind takes on a novel and technical connotation with respect to a new method of use and enjoyment of ocean resources. It is also a new concept in that it implies a more specific preference for vesting comprehensive competence over the process of ocean resource exploitation in international machinery. See the view of Sweden, U.N. doc. A/C.1/PV.1596, pp. 28–30; Cyprus, U.N. doc. A/C.1/PV.1599, p. 16; and Malta, U.N. doc. A/AC.135/WG.1/SR.3, pp. 6–14.

[53] It may be of interest that before the U.N. General Assembly had passed its Declara-

tion of Principles there were at least three proposals for the regulation of deep ocean resources through the flag-state approach. See L. F. E. Goldie, "The Contents of Davy Jones' Locker—A Proposed Regime for the Seabed and Subsoil," Vol. 22, *Rutgers Law Review*, pp. 1–66 (1967), at pp. 39–54. Goldie's intention was

. . . to propose the principles of a regime governing the assurance of titles created under the municipal law of each state, by the recognition of those titles in the courts of all the others through an international agreement, conflict of laws standards and obligations of recognition.

See L. F. E. Goldie, "The Exploitability Test—Interpretation and Potentialities," Vol. 8, *Natural Resources Journal*, pp. 434–477 (1968), at p. 458.

He also proposed at the same time the establishment of a "central index in the United Nations Secretariat" to carry out "evidentiary and recording functions" with a view to "ensure that the whole world has effective notice of the existence of recorded rights." Idem, p. 460.

A similar proposal for the "establishment of an international registry, first to serve only as a record of exploratory activity and later, after adoption of a code of conduct, to serve as a means of filing claim over minerals in a specified area" was also suggested by the U.S. National Petroleum Council. See Report of the National Petroleum Council, *supra* note 18, p. 117.

The proposal for an international registry system as suggested by Goldie and the National Petroleum Council appears to isolate the issue of peaceful and orderly exploitation of deep ocean minerals from the other equally valid issues such as accommodation of competing uses of the sea and equitable distribution of benefits arising from deep ocean mineral resources development.

The proposed international registry was intended only to keep records for self-proclaimed exclusive titles and liens to deep ocean resources. As such, it fails to comprehend all the inclusive interests involved in the process.

Compared with these two proposals, the plan of the United States President's Commission on Marine Science, Engineering and Resources, which also advocates some sort of an international registry mechanism, was more perceptive of the inclusive interests in the process of deep ocean mineral exploitation. See Report of the Commission on Marine Science, Engineering and Resources, *Our Nation and the Sea* (Washington, D.C.: U.S. Government Printing Office, 1969), p. 148.

However, even the Commission's plan was not sufficiently liberated from the crippling defects of subjecting deep ocean mineral exploitation to unorganized inclusive access. For example, its plan did not provide measures to ensure an efficient and controlled production of resources; it had no rational allocation procedures when more than one producer competes for the same resource in the same area; it also lacked policies for accommodating competing uses in the area; and finally, while the plan envisaged an international fund, the idea was not developed beyond a vague and sketchy stage.

For a discussion of these and other proposals relating to a simple secretariat for registering claims, see the Report of the U.N. Secretariat, *Study on the Question of Establishing in Due Time Appropriate International Machinery for the Promotion of the Exploration and Exploitation of the Resources of the Seabed and the Ocean Floor Beyond the Limits of National Jurisdiction and the Use of These Resources in the Interests of Mankind*, U.N. doc. A/AC.138/12 (1969). See also U.N. Secretariat, *Study on International Machinery*, U.N. doc. A/AC.138/23 (1970); B. S. Murty, "The International Regulation of the Uses of the Sea-Bed and Ocean Floor," Vol. 9, *I.J.I.L.*, pp. 72–77 (1969) and K. K. Rao, "The Legal Regime of the Sea-Bed and Ocean Floor," Vol. 9, *I.J.I.L.*, pp. 1–18 (1969).

[54] For an examination of some of these proposals, see Louis B. Sohn, "The Council of an International Sea-Bed Authority," Vol. 9, *San Diego Law Review*, pp. 404–434 (1972).

[55] See the *Y.B.I.L.C.* (1950), Vol. 1, pp. 215–216.

[56] See the Report of the International Law Commission to the General Assembly, *Y.B.I.L.C.* (1950), Vol. 2, p. 384.

[57] Georges Scelle opposed the doctrine of the continental shelf from the very beginning of its consideration by the International Law Commission. See *Y.B.I.L.C.* (1950), Vol. 1, p. 225. He regarded the concept as nothing less than a "law of grab" and, if accepted, he believed it would completely do away with the freedom of the seas. See *Y.B.I.L.C.* (1956), Vol. 1, p. 144.

[58] At one stage during the deliberations of the International Law Commission on the concept of the continental shelf, Georges Scelle declared that

It was entirely irrelevant which State laid claims to exercise rights over its continental shelf, since all States were equal before the law. All that was necessary was to establish how submarine resources could be exploited for the benefit of the world community as a whole. In [Scelle's] view, the solution lay in establishing a legal system whereby the subsoil of the high seas could not be exploited beyond the limits of territorial sea unless there was no break between the exploitation of the two zones, and unless an appropriate concession had been granted to the interested State by, say, the Economic and Social Council.

Y.B.I.L.C. (1955), Vol. 1, p. 82.

He repeated his suggestion for the international control of the offshore natural resources in his book, *Plateau Continental et Droit International* (Paris: Pedone, 1955). For a summary of his views as contained in this book, see L. F. E. Goldie, "Davy Jones' Locker," *supra* note 53, pp. 35–36.

[59] See Francis O. Wilcox and Carl M. Marcy, *Proposals for Changes in the United Nations* (Washington, D.C.: Brookings Institution, 1955), pp. 63–64.

[60] See Report of the Commission to Study the Organization of Peace, *Strengthening the United Nations* (New York: Harper and Row, 1957), at p. 213

[61] Grenville Clark and Louis B. Sohn, *World Peace Through World Law*, 3rd Rev. Ed., (Cambridge, Mass.: Harvard University Press, 1966), at p. 158.

[62] Richard N. Gardner (ed.), *Blueprint for Peace* (New York: McGraw-Hill, 1966), at p. 144.

[63] See the *Resolution 15 of the World Peace Through Law Conference*, quoted by Ambassador Pardo, see U.N. doc. A/C.1/PV.1516.

[64] The Commission to Study the Organization of Peace in its *Seventeenth Report on New Dimensions for the United Nations: The Problems of the Next Decade* (May, 1966), at p. 44, recommended that the marine resources, both living as well as mineral, "should be controlled and administered by an international agency in order to assure efficient exploitation and equitable distribution." The Commission further recommended that

There should be established a special agency of the United Nations to be called the United Nations Marine Resources Agency. It should control and administer international marine resources; hold ownership rights; and grant, lease or use these rights in accordance with the principles of economic efficiency. It should function with the independence and efficiency of the International Bank. However, it should distribute the returns from such exploitation in accordance with directives issued by the General Assembly of the United Nations. Such an agency would present a viable alternative to the anarchy that now prevails, and it would, therefore, be in the legitimate interest of most nations to encourage and support the U.N. Marine Resources Agency.

After three years, in the wake of discussions at the U.N. and elsewhere, the Commission, updating its earlier recommendations in its Nineteenth Report, *The United Nations and the Bed of the Sea* (March, 1969), at p. 27, reiterated its conviction that an International Authority for the Sea established by the United Nations is essential to create and administer a regime "for the ordered exploitation of the mineral resources of the sea-bed, with due regard to other uses of the sea" and to make "real the concept that these resources are the heritage of all mankind." See also its Draft Statute for a United Nations Sea-Bed Authority in *The United Nations and the Bed of the Sea II* (1970).

[65] The Thirty-Third American Assembly, which convened during May 2–5, 1968, observed that

Given the expanding prospects at sea, it is urgent to take measures to accommodate competing uses, to promote conservation, to refine the laws, to negotiate the appropriate international agreements, and to create international machinery to assit in the scientific investigation of the seas in orderly development of sea resources.

It also recommended that

The United States should support the creation of international machinery within the family of United Nations organizations with responsibilities in respect to the exploitation of non-living resources in the deep sea floor. Its functions might include:
—issuance of licenses for agreed activities and international registration and regulation of such activities;
—collection of an agreed share of revenues for internationally agreed purposes, including benefits for developing nations;
—referral of disputes to international arbitration or adjudication;
—encouragement of research, exploration and investment.

See the Report of the Thirty-Third American Assembly, *Uses of the Seas* (May 2–5, 1968), pp. 5–6.

[66] The New England Assembly meeting at the Woods Hole Oceanographic Institution during the May 22–25, 1969, proposed that

There will be need for a body or bodies enjoying wide international support and participation by many nations to exercise in relation to the sea-bed beyond clearly defined limits of national jurisdiction such functions as the following:
    Registration of claims
    Arbitration of disputes
    Promulgation of standards on conservation, pollution, and uses
    Inspection of operations
    Collection of fees and royalties
The United States should take the initiative to propose the form and functions of such a body or bodies and to begin the necessarily protracted negotiations involved in their creation.

See the *Final Report of the New England Assembly on the Uses of the Seas* (May 22–25, 1969).

[67] See Elizabeth Man Borgese, *The Ocean Regime, A Suggested Statute for the Peaceful Uses of the High Seas and the Sea-Bed Beyond the Limits of National Jurisdiction* (Santa Barbara, Calif.: Center for the Study of Democratic Institutions, October 1968). Article II of the Draft Statute mentions the following fundamental principles:

1. Ocean space is an indivisible ecological whole.
2. The high seas beyond the limits of territorial waters as defined in this Statute, and the sea-bed beyond the limits of the continental shelf as defined in this Statute, are the common heritage of mankind . . . .
3. The natural resources in the high seas and on or below the sea-bed as defined by this Statute are the common property of the peoples of the world. They must be developed, administered, conserved, and distributed on the basis of international cooperation and for the benefit of all mankind.

4. The use, exploration, and exploitation of the sea-bed shall be for peaceful purposes only; it shall conform to the principles of the Charter of the United Nations and to international law, and shall be conducted in a manner not causing unnecessary obstruction of the high seas or serious impairment of the marine environment.

The Draft Statute recommended an Ocean Regime to honor and safeguard these fundamental principles.

The original draft was revised several times, and a new version was presented to the Pacem In Maribus II Conference in Malta in 1971; see E. M. Borgese, *The Ocean Regime: Draft Statute* (Revised, February 1971), Pacem In Maribus II, Working Papers, *A Constitution for the Oceans* (1971). However, several of the original basic principles and hypothesis were retained even in the revised versions.

[68] U.S. Senator Claiborne Pell proposed an international licensing authority because (1) the ocean space was a common heritage of mankind; (2) there was a common interest for all mankind to explore and exploit the ocean space only for peaceful purposes; (3) there was a threat of anarchy in the exploration and exploitation of ocean space and its resources; (4) problems resulting from commercial exploitation of ocean space were imminent; and (5) such an agency would further the welfare and prosperity of mankind and their national states. See the Preamble of the *Senate Resolution 263 of March 5, 1968,* submitted by Senator Pell to the U.S. Senate, 90th Congress, 2nd Session.

[69] Rejecting the division of the ocean's natural resources among the coastal states as giving them a "disproportionately privileged position," and negating the flag-state or unorganized inclusive access approach as disproportionately biased in favor of the technologically highly developed nations, the International Committee on Deep Sea Mining of the International Law Association endorsed the establishment of international machinery. See the International Law Association, *Report of the Deep-Sea Mining Committee on the Exploration and Exploitation of Minerals on the Ocean Bed and in Its Subsoil,* Buenos Aires Conference, 1968, pp. 4–6.

See also the International Law Association's Report of the Fifty-Fourth Conference, *Deep-Sea Mining* (The Hague, 1970). (International Law Association, 3 Paper Buildings, The Temple, London, E.C.4).

[70] E. D. Brown, *Report on the Legal Regime of Deep-Sea Mining, Prepared for the British Branch Committee on Deep-Sea Mining* (June, 1968), p. 60. Brown, in *The Legal Regime of Hydrospace* (London: Stevens and Sons, 1971), at pp. 120–123, repeated his preference for the creation of international machinery to regulate deep ocean mineral resources.

[71] For the earlier recommendation of the World Peace Through Law Conference, see *supra* note 63; the United Nations Committee of the World Peace Through Law Center in a Draft Treaty proposed an Ocean Agency to "conform generally to the objectives set forth by the Committee on Conservation and Development of Natural Resources in its report to the White House Conference on International Cooperation called by President Lyndon B. Johnson." See the *Treaty Governing the Exploration and Use of the Ocean Bed,* Pamphlet Series No. 10 (Geneva: World Peace Through Law Center, 1968), at p. 24.

For a more recent version of the Draft Treaty prepared by Aaron Danzig for the World Peace Through Law Center, see *Revised Draft Treaty Governing the Exploration and Exploitation of the Ocean Bed,* Pamphlet Series No. 14, (Geneva: World Peace Through Law Center, 1971).

[72] See Alexander Rich and V. A. Engelhardt, "A Proposal from a U.S. and a Soviet Scientist: Ocean Resources and Developing Nations," Vol. 24, *Bulletin of the Atomic Scientists,* pp. 2–3 (February 1968).

[73] See the original draft statute of E. M. Borgese, *supra* note 67, p. 27.

[74] Draft working papers on international regime were presented by the following countries:

1. Canada, U.N. doc. A/AC. 138/59
2. Certain of the Latin American countries (Chile, Colombia, Ecuador, El Salvador, Guatemala, Guyana, Jamaica, Mexico, Panama, Peru, Trinidad and Tobago, Uruguay, and Venezuela), U.N. doc. A/AC. 138/49
3. Certain of the landlocked and shelf-locked countries (Afghanistan, Austria, Belgium, Hungary, Nepal, Netherlands, and Singapore), U.N. doc. A/AC. 138/55
4. France, U.N. doc. A/AC. 138/27
5. Japan, U.N. doc. A/AC. 138/63
6. Malta, U.N. doc. A/AC. 138/53
7. Poland, U.N. doc. A/AC. 138/44
8. United Kingdom, U.N. doc. A/AC. 138/26 and U.N. doc. A/AC. 138/46
9. United Republic of Tanzania, U.N. doc. A/AC. 138/33
10. United States of America, U.N. doc. A/AC. 138/25
11. Union of Soviet Socialist Republics, U.N. doc. A/AC. 138/43

For a comparative table of these draft international regimes, see the U.N. Secretariat document, *Comparative Table of Draft Treaties, Working Papers, and Draft Articles,* U.N. doc. A/AC.138/L.10 (cited hereinafter as the Comparative Table). Later in 1973, Italy also submitted separate draft articles concerning the international regime, see U.N. doc. A/AC.138/SC.I/L.26.

[75] Andres Aguilar, "How Will the Future Deep Seabed Regime Be Organized?" in John King Gamble, Jr., and Giulio Pontecorvo (eds.), *Law of the Sea: The Emerging Regime of the Oceans* (Proceedings of the Law of the Sea Institute, Eighth Annual Conference, June 18–21, 1973), (Cambridge, Mass.: Ballinger Publishing Co., 1974), pp. 43–51, at p. 47.

[76] See the Comparative Table, *supra* note 74, p. 65, col. 1, and p. 42, col. 4.

[77] See U.N. doc. A/AC.138/SC.I/SR 68, p. 9.

[78] See the *Report of the Committee on the Peaceful Uses of the Sea-Bed and the Ocean Floor beyond the Limits of National Jurisdiction,* G.A.O.R., Twenty-Sixth Session, Supplement No. 21 (New York: United Nations, 1971), U.N. doc. A/8421, p. 19.

[79] Ibid., p. 18.

[80] For information on the countries discussed, see the Comparative Table, *supra* note 74, p. 40, col. 2, and p. 70, col. 2; col. 3; col. 6; col. 5; p. 73, col. 5; col. 1; p. 65, col. 3; p. 73, col. 2; p. 110, col. 1.

[81] See the Comparative Table, *supra* note 74, for specific nations as follows: p. 75, col. 1; p. 76, col. 1; p. 74, col. 2; col. 5; p. 77, col. 2; p. 75, col. 1; p. 74, col. 4; p. 78, cols. 1 and 6, and p. 79, cols. 1 and 4.

[82] Malta divides the members of the international machinery into three categories: A, B, and C. Its draft treaty defines the categories as follows:

Article 111.1. Shall belong to category A members which are coastal States and which have a population exceeding 90 million inhabitants. 2. Shall also belong to category A members which are coastal States and which possess six of the following qualifications:
(a) Have a population greater than 45 million inhabitants;
(b) Have a length of coastline exceeding 5,000 kilometers;
(c) Possess more than 1 million gross tons of merchant shipping;
(d) Own and operate more than 20 ships and submersibles aggregating not less than 30,000 gross tons for scientific and rescue purposes;
(e) Have produced more than 1 million metric tons of fish annually over the previous three years;
(f) Have produced annually over the previous three years more than 1 million tons of hydrocarbons or other minerals from the seabed of ocean space;
(g) Own submarine pipelines or cables in International Ocean Space;
(h) Have expended more than $20 million annually from State funds, over the previous three years for scientific research in ocean space;

(i) Have contributed annually over the previous three years more than $25 million to the Institutions in respect of revenue obtained from the exploitation of natural resources in national ocean space.
3. Members belonging to category A shall review the qualifications mentioned in paragraphs 1 and 2 of this Article every six years. On such occasions the qualifications mentioned in paragraphs 1 and 2 (a), (c), (d), (e), (f), (h), and (i) may be increased by not more than 20 percent. *Article 112.* Shall belong to category B all members which are coastal States and which do not belong to category A. *Article 113.* Shall belong to category C all members which are not coastal States.

With respect to decisions in the Assembly, the Maltese draft noted that

[They] shall be made by an affirmative majority of the members present and voting, and by a majority of members present and voting belonging to category A and to one of the other two categories mentioned. . . .

Furthermore, it says that

Decisions by the Assembly relating to matters mentioned in Articles 101, 102, 103, and 104 shall be made by an affirmative majority of members present and voting and by a majority of members in each of the categories indicated. . . .

See ibid., p. 81, col. 2.
[83] For further information on the countries, in order, see ibid., the Comparative Table, p. 75, col. 4; p. 78, col. 5; p. 86, col. 1; p. 88, col. 1; p. 86, col. 2; cols. 4 and 5, and p. 87, cols. 1 and 2; p. 87, col. 6; p. 86, col. 4; p. 91, col. 2; p. 86, col. 2; p. 86, col. 5 and p. 87, cols. 1 and 6; p. 86, cols. 4 and 5; p. 87, col. 1; p. 87, col. 2; p. 85, col. 1; p. 84, col. 4; p. 84, cols. 1 and 2, and p. 85, cols. 4 and 5.

[84] According to Malta:

Article 112. 1. The Council shall consist of the following members of the Institutions: (a) all members belonging to category A; (b) an equal number of members belonging to category B; (c) five members belonging to category C. 2. Members belonging to category B and to category C shall be elected by members of their respective categories voting separately, due regard being paid in the first instance to population and to the qualifications referred to in *Article 111* and also to geographic distribution.

See ibid., p. 85, col. 2. For a definition of categories A, B, and C, see *supra* note 82.
[85] According to the Soviet draft: "The Executive Board shall consist of 30 States. The Board shall accordingly include five States from each of the following groups of countries: (a) the Socialist countries; (b) the countries of Asia; (c) the countries of Africa; (d) the countries of Latin America; (e) the Western European and other countries not coming within the categories specified in subparagraphs (a) to (d) of this paragraph; (f) one landlocked country from each of the aforementioned groups of States."
[86] Ibid., the Comparative Table, p. 84, col. 1; p. 85, col. 5; p. 85, col. 4; p. 84, col. 5; p. 85, col. 1; p. 84, col. 4; p. 84, col. 5.
[87] According to the U.S. draft, "Decisions by the Council shall require approval by a majority of all of its members, including a majority of members in each of the two categories referred to in paragraph 2 of Article 36." Ibid., p. 96, col. 1.
[88] According to Malta, ibid., p. 97, col. 2, "Decisions of the Council shall require the affirmative vote of a majority of its members and of a majority of members in category A and in one of the other categories referred to in Article 110."
[89] See ibid., the Comparative Table, p. 97, col. 6; col. 1; p. 96, col. 4 and p. 85, col. 4; p. 96, col. 5.
[90] Ibid., p. 99, col. 1. On the concept of implied powers generally, see Rahmatullah Khan, *Implied Powers of the United Nations* (New Dehli: Vikas Publication, 1970).
[91] Ibid., the Comparative Table, p. 100, col. 1; p. 102, col. 1; and p. 104, col. 1; p. 101, col. 2; p. 101, col. 4; p. 100, col. 2; p. 101, col. 5; p. 106, col. 4; p. 107, col. 1.

⁹² Ibid., p. 109, col. 2. The U.S. draft has a similar restriction according to which representatives of the International Agency are prohibited from actively associating themselves with any of the operations of any enterprise concerned with the exploitation of deep ocean resources. See also ibid., p. 72, col. 1.

⁹³ Ibid., p. 106, col. 2; p. 107, col. 5.

⁹⁴ This summary reflects in a highly simplified form several common elements among the different proposals. However, the reader is advised to refer to the individual drafts for appreciation of differences in detail and nuances.

The USSR draft did not specify any lease system and made it a part of a package deal. An explanatory note in the draft said:

> These issues are closely linked with the problems of the establishment of the 12 mile limit of the territorial sea, the securing of freedom of passage through straits used for international navigation, and fishing in waters adjacent to the territorial sea. Should a solution of the latter problems be in sight, the USSR delegation will be prepared to submit specific texts of the articles still outstanding in its draft, so that an agreement on these matters could be reached as a package deal.

See ibid., p. 34, col. 5.

⁹⁵ The Tanzanian draft allows the International Seabed Resources Authority, on an equal footing with states, to conduct or supervise offshore operations. Ibid., p. 34, col. 4. The policy to issue leases only to States, while it has the merit of ensuring that participants who engage in deep ocean mineral resource exploitation behave responsibly, is not entirely without problems. One commentator who examined a similar policy advocated by the U.S. President's Commission had this to say.

> The Commission Report, by interposing sovereigns between the entrepreneurs and the Authority, would necessarily make every dispute a dispute between sovereigns. Thus, with every dispute there would be a risk of international political controversy requiring political solution. On the other hand, there is no reason to assume, if entrepreneurs could deal directly with the Authority, that every dispute which might arise would necessarily cause a quarrel between sovereigns. It is not unthinkable that direct landlord-tenant relationships on the ocean floor would be amenable to the customary mechanisms by which men of international commerce settle their differences without direct confrontations between their governments.

George Miron, "Proposed Regimes for Exploration and Exploitation of the Deep-Seabed," in Lewis M. Alexander (ed.), *The Law of the Sea: National Policy Recommendations* (Proceedings of the Fourth Annual Conference of the Law of the Sea Institute, June 23–26, 1969), pp. 98–110, at p. 107.

⁹⁶ For U.S. and U.K. models, see ibid., cols. 1 and 2; France, p. 36, col. 3; Japan, p. 35, col. 5. According to the text, "In cases where application for a development license has been made by two or more Contracting Parties with respect to overlapping areas," Japan prefers that "The Contracting Party first submitting the application shall have priority. If two or more applications have been submitted on the same date, priority shall be determined by a lot drawn among the applying Parties."

⁹⁷ For the United States, ibid., col. 1; France, p. 36, col. 3; Japan, p. 35, col. 5. The United Kingdom model, on p. 34, col. 2, provided that

> The Convention would contain a formula for determining the total entitlement of each State party and within the quota thus made available a State would be free to apply for licenses in any part of the area irrespective of geographical location. The Convention would also provide for a phased distribution of licenses every so many years, when each State party could apply for exclusive development licenses up to a specific percentage of its quota. This would ensure the orderly development of seabed resources.

Ibid., p. 34, col. 2.

⁹⁸ See the U.S. draft, ibid., p. 36, col. 1.

[99] However, Japan prescribed that all leases, whether for exploration or for exploitation, should be exclusive. See ibid., p. 35, col. 5. France differed from other models and suggested that to issue a license offshore operations be distinguished between those that use mobile equipment and those that use fixed installations. Furthermore, it indicated that while nonexclusive licenses (preceded by simple registration with an international organization accompanied by a declaration of the areas to be explored or exploited) may be granted to the former kind of activites, exclusive licenses may be issued for the latter kinds of operations. See ibid., p. 34.

[100] See U.S. model, ibid., p. 36, col. 1, and Malta, p. 35, col. 2.

[101] U.S.A., ibid., p. 36, col. 1; U.K., p. 36, col. 2; Japan, p. 37, col. 5. The French plan on revocation of licenses is different. According to it (p. 38, col. 4):

(a) Whether or not there is any exploration activity, the area covered by the exploration licenses granted by a State to a company shall be automatically halved every five years; (b) If, in an area held by a State, the latter does not within three years allocate new licenses for the areas given back to it, the corresponding part of the area shall be regarded as once more open to the international community and may be granted to another State; (c) Withdrawal by a State of a license allocated to a company shall have the same effects for the said State as described in paragraph (b).

[102] Ibid., p. 40, col. 1; col. 2.

[103] According to the French proposal, "Should a State not fulfill this voluntarily accepted obligation, the penalty would be either the refusal of any grant of new areas, or the withdrawal of areas already held, as decided by the Conference of Plenipotentiaries." Ibid., p. 40, col. 3.

[104] Ibid., p. 40, col. 4; p. 41, col. 1; col. 2; col. 5.

[105] See, for example, Wellington Koo, Jr., *Voting Procedures in International Political Organizations* (New York: Columbia University Press, 1947), and C. Wilfred Jenks, "Unanimity, The Veto, Weighted Voting, Special and Simple Majorities and Consensus: Modes of Decision in International Organizations," in *Cambridge Essays in Honor of Lord McNair* (London: Stevens and Sons, 1965), pp. 48–63.

[106] The Polish scheme itself may be abridged, and for the transitional phase it is possible to combine the functions of the Council and the Secretariat under one autonomous organ with responsibility to report annually to the Assembly.

Compared to all the other proposals, the French plan, which proposed only two principal bodies, has the advantage of minimizing international bureaucracy. However, at times its emphasis on states, as managers of the process, leaves them too much discretion and initiative, so that a coordinated international effort at shaping and sharing the common heritage of mankind is made rather difficult.

[107] The U.N. Secretary-General's Report emphasized a similar policy in its study on "possible methods and criteria for the sharing by the international community of proceeds and other benefits derived from the exploitation of the resources of the area beyond national jurisdiction: a preliminary note." It pointed out that

It is worth noting first, however, that the volume of these funds will, for practical reasons, exert an important influence on the manner in which they might be administered, allocated and utilized. Therefore, unless the volume of seabed mineral production reaches proportions considerably higher than now anticipated, it would hardly appear practical to attempt to distribute the residual proceeds accruing to the international community directly to the countries alone, according to population size, *per capita* income, or similar criteria of need.

See U.N. doc. A/AC.138/24, reproduced in *Report of the Committee on the Peaceful Uses of the Seabed and the Ocean Floor beyond the Limits of National Jurisdiction*, G.A.O.R., Twenty-Fifth Session, Supplement No. 21 (New York: United Nations, 1970), U.N. doc. A/8021, pp. 124–129, art. 127.

250   NOTES

Notes to Chapter 5, pp. 109–165
[1] "Comment," in Vol. 2, *Fishing News International*, p. 9 (December 1972).
[2] See the *Atlas of the Living Resources of the Seas* (Rome: Food and Agricultural Organization, 1972), p. 3.
[3] C. P. Idyll, "Marine Aquaculture: Problems and Prospects," *Technical Conference on Fishery Management and Development*, Vancouver, Canada, February 13–23, 1973 (Rome: Food and Agricultural Organization, 1973), pp. 3–5.
[4] R. A. Neal, "Alternatives in Aquacultural Development: Considerations of Extensive Versus Intensive Methods," *Technical Conference on Fishery Management and Development*, Vancouver, Canada, February 13–23, 1973 (Rome: Food and Agricultural Organization, 1973), pp. 4–6. Also see C. P. Idyll, *supra* note 3, p. 7.
[5] See Thomas Kane, *Aquaculture and the Law* (Sea Grant Technical Bulletin, University of Miami, November 1970), p. 12.
[6] See Bostwick H. Ketchum (ed.), *The Water's Edge: Critical Problems of the Coastal Zone* (Cambridge, Mass.: MIT Press, 1972), p. 115. See also L. Caflisch, "Some Aspects of Oil Pollution from Merchant Shipping," in L. Caflisch (ed.), *Hydrospace in International Relations* (Annals of International Studies, No. 4) (Geneva: Alumni Association of the Graduate Institute of International Studies, 1973), pp. 213–236.
[7] John P. Albers, "Offshore Petroleum: Its Geography and Technology," in John King Gamble, Jr., and Giulio Pontecorvo (eds.), *Law of the Sea: Emerging Regime of the Oceans* (Proceedings of the Eighth Annual Conference, Law of the Sea Institute, June 18–21, 1973) (Cambridge, Mass.: Ballinger Publishing Co., 1974), pp. 293–304, at p. 13.
[8] D. G. Warner, "Oil Industry Safety and Pollution Control," Vol. 7, *Ocean Industry*, pp. 24–27 (August 1972).
[9] For a discussion on the effect of oil on the marine living organisms, see the following:
a. D. K. Button, "Petroleum-Biological Effects in the Marine Environment," in Donald W. Hood (ed.), *Impingement of Man on the Oceans* (New York: John Wiley and Sons, 1971).
b. Max Blumer and Jeremy Sass, "Oil Pollution: Persistence and Degradation of Spilled Fuel Oil," Vol. 176, *Science*, pp. 1120–1122 (June 9, 1972).
c. Max Blumer, "Scientific Aspects of the Oil Spill Problem," Vol. 1, *Environmental Affairs*, pp. 54–73 (April 1971).
d. Roger Revelle, Edward Wenk, B. H. Ketchum, and Edward Cosino, "Ocean Pollution by Petroleum Hydrocarbons," in W. Matthews, F. Smith, and E. Goldberg (eds.), *Man's Impact on Terrestrial and Oceanic Ecosystems* (Cambridge, Mass.: MIT Press, 1972), pp. 297–318.
e. J. G. Mackin, *A Review of the Significant Papers on Effects of Oil Spills and Oil Field Brine Discharges on Marine Biotic Communities* (Texas A & M Research Foundation Project 737, February 1973).
f. E. B. Cowell (ed.), *The Ecological Effects of Oil Pollution on Littoral Communities* (Proceedings of a symposium organized by the Institute of Petroleum and held at the Zoological Society of London, November 30–December 1, 1970) (London: Institute of Petroleum, 1971).
g. Report of Study No. VI, by the United Kingdom, *The Environmental and Financial Consequences of Oil Pollution from Ships: Main Report,* submitted to IMCO as part of the preparations for the International Marine Pollution Conference, 1973 (Programs Analysis Unit, Chilton, Dedcot, Berks, 1973).
h. Food and Agricultural Organization, *Pollution: An International Problem for Fisheries* (Rome, 1971).
i. M. Waldichuk, "Coastal Marine Pollution and Fish," Vol. 2, *Ocean Management*, pp. 1–61 (1974).

[10] Bostwick H. Ketchum (ed.), *supra* note 6, pp. 117–118. On the Santa Barbara oil spill, see also Carol E. Steinhart and John S. Steinhart, *Blowout* (North Scituate, Mass.: Duxbury Press, 1972), and A. E. Keir Nash, Dean E. Mann, and Phil G. Olsen, *Oil Pollution and the Public Interest* (Berkeley: University of California, 1972).

[11] Max Blumer, Howard L. Sanders, J. Fred Grassle, and George R. Hampson, "A Small Oil Spill," Vol. 13, *Environment*, pp. 2–12 (March 1971), at p. 11.

[12] Idem, p. 6.

[13] John P. Albers, *supra* note 7, pp. 13–14; see also Milner B. Schaeffer, "Conservation of Biological Resources of the Coastal Zone," in J. F. Peel Brahtz (ed.), *Coastal Zone Management: Multiple Use with Conservation* (New York: John Wiley and Sons, 1972), pp. 35–77, at pp. 72 and 75.

[14] See John W. Paden, "Marine Mining and the Environment," in Donald W. Hood, *supra* note 9, pp. 553–561, at p. 559; see also the U.N. Secretary-General's Report, *Marine Pollution and Other Hazardous and Harmful Effects Which Might Arise from the Exploration and Exploitation of the Sea-bed and the Ocean Floor, and the Subsoil Thereof beyond the Limits of National Jurisdiction*, A/7924; and U.S. Department of Interior, "Draft Environmental Statement Prepared for the United States Involvement in the Law of the Sea Negotiations Governing the Mining of Deep Seabed Hard Mineral Resources Seaward of the Limits of National Jurisdiction" (Washington, D.C., 1974).

[15] See A. L. Rice, "H.M.S. *Challenger:* Midwife to Oceanography," Vol. 18, *Sea Frontiers*, pp. 291–305 (September–October 1972).

[16] See Susan Schlee, *The Edge of an Unfamiliar World* (New York: E. P. Dutton and Co., 1973), pp. 11–12.

[17] See *United Nations, Ecosoc, Marine Science and Technology Survey and Proposals, Report to the Secretary-General* (New York, April 24, 1968), p. 35 and 36, for a list of number of research and survey vessels owned by different countries and their expenditures for oceanographic research as of 1968. See also several reports on national activities in ocean science research issued in 1968 by the *U.S. National Council on Marine Resources and Engineering Development.*

[18] See Brenda Horsfield and Peter Bennet Stone, *The Great Ocean Business* (Coward, McCann and Geoghegan, New York, 1972)

[19] See Paul M. Fye, *Ocean Policy and Scientific Freedom* (Columbus O'Donnell Iselin Memorial Lecture, Marine Technology Society, Washington, D.C., September 11, 1972), pp. 14–17.

[20] See Roger Revelle, "Scientific Research on the Seabed: International Cooperation in Scientific Research and Exploration of the Seabed," in Jerzy Sztucki (ed.), *Symposium on the International Regime of the Seabed* (Rome: Instituto Affari Internazionale, 1970), pp. 649–663, at p. 654.

[21] See Charles C. Bates and Paul Yost, "Where Trends the Flow of Merchant Ships?" in John Gamble and Giulio Pontecorvo (eds.), *supra* note 7, pp. 249–276.

[22] National Petroleum Council, *Law of the Sea: Particular Aspects Affecting the Petroleum Industry* (Washington, D.C., May 1973), p. 10.

[23] Ibid., Appendix F, pp. 61–67 and p. 13.

[24] See V. E. McKelvey, "Environmental Protection in Offshore Petroleum Operations," Vol. 1, *Ocean Management*, pp. 119–128 (1973), at p. 124.

[25] Personal communication received by the author from Captain S. A. Wallace of the U.S. Coast Guard, Chief Marine Environmental Protection Division, letter dated October 5, 1973.

For a mention of the conflict situations that arose and might again arise between commercial vessels and offshore installations, see Commission on Marine Science, Engineering and Resources, *Report of the Panel on Management and Development of the Coastal Zone,* Part III (1969), at p. 25; see also Baker, "Navigation Hazards in the Gulf," paper presented to the Institute of Navigation, November 6, 1969, cited in H. Gary Knight, "Shipping Safety Fairways: Conflict Amelioration in the Gulf of Mexico," Vol. 1, *Journal of Maritime Law and Commerce*, pp. 1–20 (1969), at p. 2; and William L. Griffin, "Accommodation of Conflicting Uses of Ocean Space with Special Reference to Navigation Safety Lanes," in Lewis M. Alexander (ed.), *The Law of the Sea: The Future of Sea's Resources* (Proceedings of the Second Annual Conference on the Law of the Sea Institute, June 26–29, 1967, University of Rhode Island, Kingston), pp. 73–83, at p. 73. On the legal regulation of merchant shipping generally, see Nagendra Singh, *The Legal Regime of Merchant Shipping* (Bombay: University of Bombay, 1969), and also Nagendra Singh, "International Law Problems of Merchant Shipping," Vol. 107, *Hague Recueil des Cours*, pp. 8–186 (1962–II).

[26] Bostwick H. Ketchum (ed.), *supra* note 6, pp. 129–130.

[27] For a comprehensive survey of present or proposed deep water port developments, see Institute for Water Resources, *Foreign Deep Water Port Development: A Selective Overview of Economics, Engineering and Environmental Factors*, Vols. 1, 2, and 3 (U.S. Department of the Army Corps of Engineers, December 1971). Also Bostwick H. Ketchum (ed.), *supra* note 6, p. 226.

On the possible conflict between the deep-draft harbor facilities and other uses of ocean space, see H. Gary Knight, "International Legal Problems in the Construction and Operation of Offshore Deep Draft Port Facilities," in T. Clingan, and L. M. Alexander (eds.), *Hazards of Maritime Transit* (Cambridge, Mass.: Ballinger Publishing Co., 1973), pp. 91–127, at pp. 115–117.

[28] The Chase Manhattan Bank, Energy Division, *Outlook for Energy in the United States* (New York, October 1968), p. 47, cited in Dennis W. Ducsik, Paul Mertens, and George Neill, "Offshore Siting of Electric Power Plants" in Dennis W. Ducsik (ed.), *Power, Pollution and Public Policy* (Cambridge, Mass.: MIT Press, 1971), pp. 29–89, at p. 34. Also see the statement of Sherman R. Knapp, Chairman of Northeast Utilities, quoted in Dennis W. Ducsik and others, ibid.

[29] See the United Nations estimate, cited in Roger H. Charlier, "Harnessing the Energies of the Oceans: A Review–Part II," Vol. 3, *Marine Technology Society Journal*, pp. 59–81 (1969), at p. 75.

[30] See Dennis W. Ducsik and others, *supra* note 28.

[31] Peter Gwyne, "Nuclear Power Goes to Sea," Vol. 55, *New Scientist*, pp. 474–476 (September 21, 1972).

[32] Roger H. Charlier, *supra* note 29.

[33] For a comprehensive analysis of the Rance River project, see Roger H. Charlier, "Harnessing the Energies of the Oceans: A Review–Part I," Vol. 3, *Marine Technology Society Journal*, pp. 13–23 (May 1969), at pp. 19–22 and p. 13.

[34] See Bos Kalis Westminister Dredging Group, "Study on Sea Island Project," *The Building of Islands in the Open Sea Offers Possibilities for Industrial Development* (June 1972); also see another study by the same group on *Sea Island Project: A Solution for Waste Disposal Problems* (June, 1972).

[35] See the Preface to the study of waste disposal problems, ibid.

[36] See the study on industrial development, *supra* note 34, p. 10.

[37] Ibid.; see also Bostwick H. Ketchum (ed.), *supra* note 6, p. 226; J. Lear, "Cities on the Sea," Vol. 54, *Saturday Review*, pp. 80–90 (1971).

[38] Bostwick H. Ketchum (ed.), ibid., pp. 84. Also see Dennis W. Ducsik and Rolyn Seitz, "The Crisis in Shoreline Use," in Dennis W. Ducsik (ed.), *supra* note 28, pp. 90–186.

[39] E. Winslow and A. B. Bigler, "A New Perspective on Recreational Use of the Ocean," Vol. 10, *Undersea Technology*, pp. 51–55 (1969).

[40] Bostwick H. Ketchum (ed.), *supra* note 6, p. 88.

[41] A. Nelson-Smith, *Oil Pollution and Marine Ecology* (London: Paul Elek Science Publishers, 1972), pp. 168–169.

[42] For very interesting details on underwater archaeology, see Kennth A. Kovaly, "Underwater Archaeology," Vol. 3, *Oceanology International*, pp. 27–30 (January–February 1968). See also Crane Miller, *International Law and Marine Archaeology* (Belmont, Mass.: Academy of Applied Science, 1973); and F. M. Auburn, "Deep Sea Archaeology and the Law," Vol. 2, *International Journal of Nautical Archaeology and Underwater Exploration*, pp. 159–162 (1973).

[43] Lionel A. Walford and John R. Clark, "Artificial Reefs," Vol. 2 *Oceanology International*, pp. 27–30 (1967).

[44] See Edward M. MacCutcheon, "Traffic and Transport Needs at the Land-Sea Interface," in J. F. Peel Brahtz (ed.), *supra* note 13, pp. 105–148, at p. 118.

[45] For a similar view, see Richard Young, "Offshore Claims and Problems in the North Sea," Vol. 59, *American Journal of International Law*, pp. 505–522 (1965) at p. 521. However, Jan Jacobson and Thomas Hanlon in a recent article prefer, in rather absolute terms, aesthetic consideration and renewable resource use over petroleum and hard mineral exploitation. See Jon Jacobson and Thomas A. Hanlon, "Regulation of Hard-Mineral Mining on the Continental Shelf," Vol. 50, *Oregon Law Review*, pp. 425–461 (1971), at p. 432. The authors were articulating their preferences at a time when in the United States environmental considerations were becoming very appealing to the general public. But it is doubtful that they would express the same preferences in such absolute terms at a time when the "energy crisis" is being accepted as a serious concern of the United States, and indeed of most of the world. See also Lewis A. Dexter, "Priorities for Ecology," *New York Times*, February 8, 1974, p. 31, warning against absolute priorities in favor of ecology.

[46] These factors are taken from the suggestions of M. S. McDougal and W. T. Burke, *The Public Order of the Oceans* (New Haven: Yale University Press, 1962), pp. 579–582. See also J. F. Paul Brahtz, Introduction to J. F. Paul Brahtz, *supra* note 13, p. 14.

[47] Jon Jacobson and Thomas A. Hanlon detail several procedures aimed at minimizing conflicts among multiple uses in the continental shelf area. These steps include (a) requiring governmental permission before exploitation or exploration activity can begin; (b) consulting different branches of the government before permission can be granted; (c) holding a public hearing on the request for exploration or exploitation of offshore resources; (d) prescribing permit terms that detail off-limits locations, methods and equipment that can be used, monitoring by environmental protection agencies, pollution-presentation devices needed, liability in case of damage, and conditions under which the permit can be revoked or amended. See Jon Jacobson and Thomas A. Hanlon, *supra* note 45, pp. 442–451.

[48] Quoted in Herbert W. Briggs, *The Law of Nations: Cases, Documents, and Notes*, Second Ed. (New York: Appleton-Century-Crofts, 1952), p. 329.

[49] Wolfgang Friedmann, Oliver J. Lessitzyn, and Richard C. Pugh, *International Law: Cases and Materials* (St. Paul, Minn.: West Publishing Co., 1969), p. 554.

[50] *The Laws and Regulations on the Regime of the High Seas* (United Nations, Legislative Series), Vol. 1 (New York: United Nations, 1951), p. 39.

[51] See P. Sreenivasa Rao, "The Law of the Continental Shelf," Vol. 6, *The Indian Journal of International Law*, pp. 363–382 (1966), at p. 365.

[52] See L. F. E. Goldie, "Australia's Continental Shelf: Legislation and Proclamations," Vol. 3, *International and Comparative Law Quarterly*, pp. 535–575 (1954), at pp. 553–555; and Joseph L. Kunz, "Continental Shelf and International Law: Confusion and Abuse," Vol. 50, *American Journal of International Law*, pp. 828–853 (1956).

[53] George Schwargenberger, "The Fundamental Principles of International Law," Vol. 87, *Recueil Des Cours*, pp. 191–385 (1955), at p. 364. Shigeru Oda, a well-known

Japanese scholar, expressed a similar view in his book on *International Control of Sea Resources* (Leyden: A. W. Sythoff, 1963), at p. 157.

[54] Sir Hersch Lauterpacht, "Sovereignty over Submarine Areas," Vol. 27, *British Year-book of International Law*, pp. 376–433 (1950), at p. 403.

[55] Idem., p. 409.

[56] M. W. Mouton, *The Continental Shelf* (The Hague: M. Nijhoff, 1952), pp. 190, 220, and 229.

[57] *The Report of the International Law Commission to the General Assembly*, 1953, *Y.B.I.L.C.*, Vol. 2 (1953), pp. 200–271, para. 75, at p. 215. See also *The Report of the International Law Commission to the General Assembly*, 1956, *Y.B.I.L.C.*, Vol. 2 (1956), pp. 251–303, article 68, commentary para. 2, at p. 297.

[58] See the 1953 I.L.C. Report to the General Assembly, idem, para. 80, at p. 216.

[59] F. V. García-Amador, *The Exploitation and Conservation of the Resources of the Sea*, Second Ed. (Leyden: A. W. Sythoff, 1963), p. 114.

[60] *The 1953 I.L.C. Report to the General Assembly, supra* note 57, draft article 6(3), at p. 213, and commentary para. 79, at p. 216. See also *The 1956 I.L.C. Report to the General Assembly*, ibid., article 71(3), and commentary para. 6; article 61, p. 293, and commentary, pp. 293–294; article 70 and commentary, p. 298; article 68 and commentary para. 10, p. 298.

[61] M. S. McDougal and W. T. Burke, *supra* note 46, p. 713.

[62] *The 1956 I.L.C. Report to the General Assembly, supra* note 57, article 71, commentary para. 2, p. 299.

[63] Shigeru Oda, *supra* note 53, pp. 170–171.

[64] For a similar conclusion, see M. S. McDougal and W. T. Burke, *supra* note 46, p. 715; and D. W. Bowett, *The Law of the Sea* (Dobbs Ferry, N.Y.: Oceana Publications, Inc., 1967), pp. 37–38.

[65] For texts of the various national legislation on the continental shelf regulations, see United Nations, Legislative Series, *National Legislation and Treaties Relating to the Law of the Sea*, Vols. I and II (New York: United Nations, 1972); United Nations, Legislative Series, *National Legislation and Treaties Relating to Law of the Sea: Addendum* (New York: United Nations, 1973); United Nations, Legislative Series, *National Legislation and Treaties Relating to the Territorial Sea, the Contiguous Zone, the Continental Shelf, the High Seas and Fishing and Conservation of the Living Resources of the Sea* (New York: United Nations, 1970). For the Norwegian legislation, see pp. 396–403, 405, 421. Also see *Law of the Sea*, Vol. 2, pp. 151, 152, for regulations on the conduct of scientific research.

There is also a good deal of literature on the United States' management of continental shelf operations, specifically with respect to its Outer Continental Shelf Lands Act, 1953. The Act was in later years amended and elaborated to take into consideration changing uses and technology of the sea. See the following articles on U.S. legislation: Warren Christopher, "The Outer Continental Shelf Lands Act: Key to a New Frontier," Vol. 6, *Stanford Law Review*, pp. 23–68 (1953); Russel G. Wayland, "Federal Regulations of the U.S. Offshore Oil Industry," in *Pollution Control in the Marine Industries* (proceedings of the conference sponsored by the International Association for Pollution Control, May 11–12, 1972, Washington, D.C.), pp. 219–229; W. A. Radlinski, "Safety and Pollution Control in OCS Petroleum Operations" (paper presented at the *Second Annual Meeting, Division of Production, American Petroleum Institute*, Houston, Texas, March 7, 1972, manuscript, pp. 3–4; W. F. McIlhenny, "Pollutional Aspects of Marine Mineral Exploitation," *First Offshore Technology Conference* (held in Houston, Texas, May 18–21, 1969), paper no. 1032, pp. I-229–304; V. E. McKelvey, "Environmental Protection in Offshore Petroleum Operations," Vol. I, *Ocean Management and Development*, pp. 119–128 (1973); and National Academy of Engineering, *Outer Continental Shelf Resource*

Development Safety: A Review of Technology and Regulation for Systematic Minimization of Environmental Intrusion from Petroleum Products (Panel on Operational Safety in Offshore Resource Development), (Washington, D.C.: Government Printing Office, December, 1972).

For a review of national legislation, see Francisco Durante, "The Present Regime of the Exploration and Exploitation of the Seabed Resources in International Law and in National Legislation" in Jerzy Sztucky (ed.), *supra* note 20, pp. 279–294.

[66] For the Brazilian Decree of August 26, 1968, see *Law of the Sea, Addendum,* pp. 67–70; for the People's Democratic Republic of Yemen Law, see *Law of the Sea,* Vol. 1, p. 32; and for the USSR legislation, see *Law of the Sea,* Vol. 2, p. 159, and *National Legislation,* p. 443.

[67] The warning of V. E. McKelvey of the U.S. Geological Survey in this regard is to the point. He said that

Even though the accident rate has been low, we must recognize that we are still dealing with high-risk operations and that we must strive to improve our ability to conduct offshore operations safely. We can do this by further development of comprehensive safety systems that incorporate risk assessment, hazard analysis, early warning and weakness detection, standards and quality control, fail-safe and back-up, personnel training, and regulations enforced by inspection procedures.

V. E. McKelvey, *supra* note 65, p. 127.

[68] See statement of Richard S. Whitehead, Santa Barbara County Director of Planning, Hearings on S.7 and S.544, Before the Sub-Committee on Air and Water Pollution of the U.S. Senate Committee on Public Works, 91st Congress, 1st Session, Series 2, at p. 271 (1969).

[69] David J. Walmsley, "Oil Pollution Problems Arising out of Exploitation of the Continental Shelf: The Santa Barabara Disaster," Vol. 9, *San Diego Law Review,* pp. 514–568 (1972), at p. 518. See also Robert Easton, *Black Tide: The Santa Barbara Oil Spill and Its Consequences* (New York: Delacorte Press, 1972).

[70] Idem, p. 521. It seems that the decision to lease out the Santa Barbara Channel area for oil exploitation was made for four possible reasons: (1) that the West Coast was a crude oil deficit area; (2) that the U.S. Bureau of the Budget at that time was suffering from a deficit of its own and was "hungry for revenues"; (3) that the oil companies, which spent considerable money for exploratory work, were pressing for return on their investments, and (4) that there was no apprehension or reluctance on the part of the Interior Department personnel with respect to the proposed leasing. See F. de G. Harlow, "The Oil Men and the Sea," Vol. 2, *Arizona Law Review,* pp. 677–730 (1969), at pp. 694–695.

[71] David J. Walmsley, idem, p. 516.

[72] For a detailed account of the claims and counterclaims involved in the Santa Barbara case, see idem, pp. 538–560.

[73] See *Fletcher v. Rylands* (1866) *Law Reports* 1 Ex. 265, 279. For a general discussion of various theories of liability, see L. F. E. Goldie, "Liability for Damage and the Progressive Development of International Law," Vol. 14, *International and Comparative Law Quarterly,* pp. 1189–1264 (1965).

[74] Quoted in David J. Walmsley, *supra* note 69, pp. 549–550.

[75] See Vol. 34, *Federal Regulations,* Section 250.43.

[76] According to William L. Prosser, a leading American authority on torts, some twenty states in the United States accepted the strict liability principle; and nearly eleven explicitly rejected the same. See his *Law of Torts,* Third Ed. (St. Paul, Minn.: West Publishing Co., 1964), pp. 524–525. Also see, for a leading article on the subject, Samuel Bergman, "No Fault Liability for Oil Pollution Damage," Vol. 5, *The Journal of*

Maritime Law and Commerce, pp. 1–50 (1973). The writer cited Arkansas, Illinois, Indiana, Kansas, Missouri, and Ohio as being among the states that adopted absolute liability. Idem, p. 27.

[77] Milton Katz, "The Function of Tort Liability in Technology Assessment," Vol. 38, *University of Cincinnati Law Review,* pp. 587–662 (1969), at p. 607.

[78] See Joseph F. Singleton, "Pollution of the Marine Environment from Outer Continental Shelf Oil Operations," Vol. 22, *South Carolina Law Review,* pp. 228–241 (1970), at p. 237. Also see Michael Hardy, "Offshore Development and Marine Pollution," Vol. 1, *Ocean Development and International Law Journal,* pp. 239–273 (1973); and 230 U.S. 46 (1913) cited in idem, p. 238.

[79] Clyde Eagleton, *The Responsibility of States in International Law* (New York: New York University Press, 1928), pp. 207, 214.

[80] Jon Jacobson and Thomas A. Hanlon argued for imposition of absolute liability on offshore hard mineral exploitation because the operation is in its infancy and all the risks attendant upon it cannot be reasonably foreseen; they supported the choice as a way of internalizing the costs of doing business that is potentially harmful to the environment. See Jon L. Jacobson and Thomas A. Hanlon, *supra* note 45; see also *supra* note 67.

[81] C. Wilfred Jenks, "Liability for Ultra-Hazardous Activities in International Law," Vol. 117, *Hague Recueil Des Cours,* pp. 105–193 (1966), at p. 107. See also Anthony D'Amato and John L. Hargrove, *Environment and the Law of the Sea* (Report of the American Society of International Law, Washington, D.C., May 1974), for articulation of standards of liability for causing massive pollution; and John M. Kelson, "State Responsibility and the Abnormally Dangerous Activity," Vol. 13, *Harvard International Law Journal,* pp. 197–244 (1972).

[82] L. F. E. Goldie, *supra* note 73, p. 1260.

[83] Milton Katz, *supra* note 77, pp. 654–655. Several forms of insurance are already available to the petroleum industry. For a description of the industry's efforts in this regard, see George A. Birrell, "TOVALOP and CRISTAL: A Case Study in Policy-Making for the Control of Ocean Pollution" (paper presented to the Annual Meeting of American Association for the Advancement of Science, held in Washington, D.C., December 27, 1972).

[84] L. F. E. Goldie, *supra* note 73, p. 1261.

[85] For a very interesting account of the development of the concept of shipping fairways, see H. Gary Knight, *supra* note 25, pp. 3–12; see also idem, pp. 7, 10.

[86] Charles C. Bates and Paul Yost, *supra* note 21.

[87] For a system of traffic separation schemes in the Dover Strait and adjacent areas, see *IMCO Resolution A.227 (VII),* adopted on October 12, 1971, A VII/Resolution 227; November 2, 1971. Also for traffic separation schemes for Chesapeake Bay (U.S.A.), Cani Island (Tunisia), German Bight (West Germany), Chedabucto Bay (Canada), Hook of Holland (Netherlands), River Elbe (West Germany), Kiel (West Germany), and others, see *IMCO Resolution A.226 (VII),* adopted on October 12, 1971, A/VII/Resolution 226, November 2, 1971. For the work of IMCO in this regard, see Repkin, "Routing of Ships at Sea" (paper presented to *Technical Symposium of Ships' Gear International,* July 29, 1968). Also see W. Griffin, *supra* note 25, p. 78. See also the *Annual Report of the IMCO,* 1972/73, p. 7.

[88] This point can be illustrated by referring to the following exchange of views, which took place at the Second Annual Conference on the Law of the Sea Institute; referring to the Gulf Coast situation, the dialogue went thus:

Christy: . . . as the oil rigs move out along the Gulf Coast and the fairways are built, shipping incurs extra costs in moving into and going through one of the fairways. It is particularly true with coastwise shipping, where it has to move out, say, of Galveston

and then through a fairway and then around the oil rigs and, say, back in to New Orleans or some other port. The interesting aspect here is to determine the relative values of the different uses of the area and to find out whether the economy benefits more from oil that we produced or more from having greater freedom of navigation.
Question: Chris, I could drive to Washington in a straight line over farmer's country if I wanted to but I have to stick to highways, which is a longer route than going straight would be, and I believe that the shipping is going to have to suffer some inconvenience, too. Shipping has had free access to the seas for a long time; if we are going to exploit the oceans for other purposes, shipping must expect some regulations.
Christy: Well, I don't necessarily agree with you. I think there may be advantages in proving fairways parallel to the coast at slight additional costs to the oil operations.
Question: But the oil is where you find it.
Christy: Yes. But there are techniques, for example, for slant-well drilling.
Question: That is too much cost for the oil producers.
Christy: All right. Maybe it would be beneficial for the economy of the United States to have the cost borne by the oil producer rather than by the navigator, or perhaps it may be the other way around. The point is we don't know yet.
Griffin: May I say on this point that the location of these fairways was agreed upon by the oil industry's offshore operators committee and by the American Merchant Marine Institute and then they went jointly to the Corps of Engineers and said here are the places where we want fairways and we agree that they can be moved if we don't find oil alongside a fairway and slant drilling is not feasible in a given situation. So this is a cooperative industry type of arrangement.

See Lewis M. Alexander (ed.), *supra* note 25, p. 89.

[89] For a lucid account of the law in this regard, see Ed Bluestein, Jr., "Admirality Law and Its Effect on Offshore Development" (paper no. OTC 1212 presented to Second Annual Offshore Technology Conference held in Houston, Texas, April 22–24, 1970), pp. I 651–662. See also Jack L. Allbritton, "Division of Damages in Admiralty: A Rising Tide of Confusion," Vol. 2, *Journal of Maritime Law and Commerce*, pp. 323–348 (1971).

[90] Ed Bluestein, idem, pp. I 658 and I 659.

[91] See Herman T. Franssen, "Research vs. Regulation," Vol. 17, *Oceanus*, pp. 18–22 (1973), at pp. 18–19.

[92] See M. R. Schaefer, "The Changing Law of the Sea—Effects on Freedom of Scientific Investigation," in Lewis M. Alexander, *supra* note 25, pp. 113–117, at p. 115. See also Michael Redfied, "The Legal Framework for Oceanic Research," in Warren S. Wooster (ed.), *Freedom of Oceanic Research* (New York: Crane, Russak and Co., 1973), pp. 41–95, at pp. 54–57.

[93] The regional African seminar on law of the sea held at Yaoundé, Cameroun, June 20–30, 1972, significantly omits freedom of scientific research from the list of freedoms protected by the concept of economic zone advocated by Kenya and other members of the OAU. The Yaoundé seminar concluded that "The establishment of such a zone shall be without prejudice to the following freedoms: freedom of navigation, freedom of overflight, freedom to lay submarine cables and pipelines." See conclusions in the General Report of the African States Regional Seminar on Law of the Sea, held in Yaoundé from June 20 to 30, 1972, in the *Report of the Committee on the Peaceful Uses of the Sea-Bed and the Ocean Floor beyond the Limits of National Jurisdiction*, G.A.O.R., 27th Session, Supplement No. 21 (A/8721) (New York: United Nations, 1972), pp. 73–75, at p. 74 (hereinafter cited as the 1972 Report). The Addis Ababa Conference of the OAU states more positively claimed that scientific research in the exclusive resource zones should be subject to the prior consent of the coastal state; see *Report of the Committee on Peaceful Uses of the Sea-Bed and the Ocean Floor beyond the Limits of National Jurisdiction*, G.A.O.R., 28th Session, Supplement No. 21 (A/9021) (New York: United Nations, 1973), Vol. 2, p. 6 (hereinafter cited as 1973 Report).
   The Santo Domingo Declaration said:

The coastal state has the duty to promote and the right to regulate the conduct of scientific research within the patrimonial sea, as well as the right to adopt the necessary measures to prevent marine pollution and to ensure its sovereignty over the resources of the area.

See the text of the Declaration of Santo Domingo, approved by the meeting of ministers of the Specialized Conference of the Caribbean Countries on Problems of the Sea, held on June 7, 1972, in 1972 Report idem, pp. 70–73, at p. 71.

For the Chinese position, see the *Working Paper on Marine Scientific Research,* submitted by the Chinese delegation to the U.N. Committee on Law of the Sea Problems, A/AC.138/SCIII/L.42, July 19, 1973, where it said that

To conduct marine scientific research in the sea area within the national jurisdiction of a coastal state, prior consent of the coastal state concerned must be sought, and the relevant laws and regulations of the coastal state must be observed.

For the Pakistani position, see U.N. doc. A/AC.138/SCIII/SR.55, pp. 2–3; for Yugoslavia's position, see U.N. doc. A/AC.138/SCII/SR.60, pp. 9–11; for the Iranian position, see U.N. doc. A/AC.138/SCIII/SR.38, p. 5.

See the document sponsored by Algeria, Brazil, China, Ethiopia, Egypt, Iran, Kenya, Pakistan, Peru, Philippines, Romania, Somalia, Trinidad and Tobago, Tunisia, and Yugoslavia, entitled "Draft Article on Consent to Conduct Marine Scientific Research." U.N. doc. A/AC.138/SCIII/L.55, August 17, 1973.

For the Italian position see U.N. doc. A/AC.138/SCIII/L.50, August 14, 1973.

[94] For a summary of the views of the developing nations on the conduct of scientific research at sea, see Edwardo Ferrero, "The Latin American Position on Legal Aspects of Maritime Jurisdiction and Oceanic Research;" Herman T. Franssen, "Developing Country Views of Sea Law and Marine Science;" Maureen N. Franssen, "Oceanic Research and the Developing Nation Perspective," in Warren S. Wooster, *supra* note 92, at pp. 97–136, 137–177, and 179–200.

[95] See the summary of the views expressed to this effect by several delegations during the 1973 meetings of the U.N. Committee on Law of the Sea Problems. See 1973 Report *supra* note 93, Vol. 1, pp. 78–79.

[96] The case for the scientists was presented in the following articles by leading oceanographers of the United States: (a) Warren S. Wooster and Michael D. Bradley, "Access Requirements of Oceanic Research: The Scientists' Perspective," in Warren S. Wooster (ed.), *supra* note 92, pp. 29–39; (b) Dr. John Knauss's views, presented before the U.N. Committee on Law of the Sea problems, U.N. doc. A/AC.138/SCIII/SR.26; (c) Paul M. Fye, *supra* note 19; (d) Roger Revelle, *supra* note 20.

[97] See the Draft Articles for a Chapter on Marine Scientific Research, submitted by the United States to the U.N. Committee on Law of the Sea Problems, U.N. doc. A/AC.138/SCIII/L.44.

[98] See W. Burger, "Treaty Provisions Concerning Marine Science Research," Vol. 1, *Ocean Development and International Law Journal,* pp. 159–184 (1973), at p. 166. For a critical review of the problems associated with the transfer of marine technology from developed to developing countries, see G. Pontecorvo, "Ocean Science and Mutual Assistance: An Uneasy Alliance," Vol. 1, *Ocean Development and International Law Journal,* pp. 51–64 (1973); John A. Knauss, "Development of the Freedom of Scientific Research Issue of the Third Law of the Sea Conference," Vol. 1, *Ocean Development and International Law Journal,* pp. 93–120 (1973); and George Cadwalader, "Freedom for Science in the Oceans," Vol. 182, *Science,* pp. 15–20 (October 1973).

[99] Some of these views were expressed by the author in an article " 'Law of the Sea' Threatens Research," published in *The Christian Science Monitor,* December 11, 1973,

p. 16. Also see Conrad H. Check, "Law of the Sea: Effects of Varying Coastal State Controls on Marine Research," Vol. 1, *Ocean Development and International Law Journal*, pp. 209–220 (1973).

[100] For a discussion of the case *United States* v. *Ray*, see David P. Stang, "Individuals' Right to Question United States Administrative Jurisdiction over Continental Shelf Areas," in L. M. Alexander, *supra* note 25, pp. 86–87; also see H. Gary Knight, "Non-Extractive Uses of the Seabed," Vol. 6, *Marine Technology Society*, pp. 18–22 (1972), at pp. 19–20.

[101] For a discussion of the "Abalonia incident," see David P. Stang, idem, pp. 87–88.

[102] For the Dutch case and others involving pirate broadcasting, see N. March Hunnings, "Pirate Broadcasting in European Waters," Vol. 14, *International and Comparative Law Quarterly*, pp. 410–436 (1965), at p. 423.

[103] UNESCO, Intergovernmental Oceanographic Commission and Intergovernmental Maritime Consultative Organization, *Legal Problems Associated with Ocean Data Acquisition Systems*, Vol. 8 (IOC/INF.108, 1969), at p. 9.

[104] See M. S. McDougal and W. T. Burke, *supra* note 46. For an application of some of these factors to determine whether occupation of Cobb Seamount in offshore areas adjacent to the northwest coast of the United States for the conduct of scientific research was justified, see Stewart Riley, "The Legal Implications of the Sea Use Program," Vol. 4, *Marine Technology Society Journal*, pp. 31–46 (1970).

[105] See the Letter dated April 23, 1971, from the Belgian representative addressed to the U.N. Secretary-General, in the *Report of the Committee on the Peaceful Uses of the Sea-Bed and the Ocean Floor beyond the Limits of National Jurisdiction*, G.A.O.R., 26th Session, Supplement No. 21 (A/8421) (New York: United Nations, 1971), pp. 65–66, at p. 66 (hereinafter cited as 1971 Report).

[106] See *supra* note 102.

[107] See U.N. doc. A/AC.138/SCII/SR.4–23, pp. 83 84.

[108] See idem, pp. 173–174. See also U.N. doc. A/AC.138/SCII/SR.51, p. 5; U.N. doc. A/AC.138/SCII/SR.57, p. 17; U.N. doc. A/AC.138/SCII/L.21.

[109] See Pardo's draft ocean space treaty, Articles 62, 63, and 64 in 1971 Report *supra* note 105, p. 143. Belgium itself proposed that the artificial structures in the exclusive resource zones be subject to the authority of the coastal state. See 1973 Report *supra* note 93, Vol. 2, pp. 9–10. For the U.S. proposal on the subject, see U.N. doc. A/AC.138/SCII/L.35, article I(3).

[110] M. S. McDougal and W. T. Burke, *supra* note 46, p. 705.

[111] See U.N. doc. A/AC.138/SCII/SR.33–47, p. 55; the 1972 Report, *supra* note 93, p. 70; idem, p. 74; U.N. doc. A/AC.138/SCII/L.21; U.N. doc. A/AC.138/SCII/SR.33–47, at p. 55.

[112] See *supra* note 109, p. 127.

[113] M. S. McDougal and W. T. Burke, *supra* note 46, pp. 761–762.

[114] The author noted the implications of open and inclusive access to the high seas elsewhere thus:

Oceans are a common heritage of mankind in the sense that they have been customarily open for inclusive use and enjoyment. That is, a community of participants can use them for different purposes and should do so with a minimum of mutual interference. The concept also means that whenever certain exclusive rights are granted to a participant or a category of participants, to own and enjoy a particular resource, or to authorize and control access to certain areas of the sea to the exclusion of others, such exclusive rights are granted as an exception and they carry with them, or should do so, a responsibility for rational use and management. Such an exception has been and should be recognized only when there is an understanding among the members of the world community that it is in the interest not only of a single participant who will enjoy the exclusive competence, but in the common interest of all of them. What is more, the concept of common heritage of mankind also demands that it is those participants, who claim exclusive authority and control over specific processes of use and enjoyment of oceans, who will have to prove that the grant of such exclusive competence to them would in fact benefit the entire international community.

See Pemmaraju Sreenivasa Rao, "Authority and Control over Offshore Areas: In Defense of Common Interests," Vol. 11, *Indian Journal of International Law*, pp. 379–388 (1971), at p. 386.

The purport of the comment is that even if the future regime of the sea is fundamentally replaced by the doctrine of the common heritage of mankind, many of the expectations generated in terms of the doctrines of freedom of the seas remain unchanged. The new doctrine of the common heritage of mankind would only strengthen those expectations by attempting to provide more centrally organized procedures to regulate human interaction on the high seas than were necessary under the doctrine of the freedom of the seas. For a comparison of the expectations under the two doctrines, see George Cadwalader, *supra* note 98, p. 17. Essentially in agreement with this thesis is Fritz Münch, "Lex Lata of Deep-Sea Mining," in *Legal Foundations of the Ocean Regime* (Pacem in Maribus: Proceedings of the Preparatory Conference on the Continental Shelf and Legal Framework, January–February 1970), Vol. 2 (Royal University of Malta Press, 1971), pp. 142–147, at pp. 144–145.

[115] In view of the comments in note 114, the problems of incompatibility between the doctrine of freedom of the seas and the common heritage of mankind may not indeed be great.

[116] The full text of the "Principles" resolution is reproduced in S. H. Lay, R. Churchill, and M. Nordquist (eds.), *New Directions in Law of the Sea: Documents,* Vol. 2 (Dobbs Ferry, N.Y.: Oceana Publications, 1973), pp. 740–741.

[117] There are several scholars who subscribe to this view. Shigeru Oda, for example, noted that

. . . When exploration and exploitation of the deep ocean floor are concerned, the time-honoured and well-established principles of international law relating to the high seas should be applied. In this respect, exploration and exploitation of the continental shelf, on the one hand, and of the areas beyond, namely the deep ocean floor, on the other, are identical in respect of application of the principles of the freedom of the high seas to the activities carried on in the superjacent waters of the respective seabed areas.

Shigeru Oda, "Future Regime of the Deep Ocean Floor," in Jerzy Sztucky (ed.), *supra* note 20, pp. 343–361, at p. 358.

For a similar treatment of the problems in the international areas of the seabed, see E. D. Brown, "The Present Regime of the Exploration and Exploitation of Sea-Bed Resources in International Law and in National Legislation: An Evaluation," in idem, pp. 241–278, especially at pp. 272–275.

Also refer to the opinion of L. F. E. Goldie, who suggested that the practice of requiring agencies planning on proposing environmentally hazardous activities to compile environmental impact statements, a practice now almost mandatory within the United States domestic legislation, could be usefully extended to the conduct of resource exploration activity in the international area. See L. F. E. Goldie, "International Impact Reports and the Conservation of the Ocean Environment," Vol. 13, *Natural Resources Journal,* pp. 256–281 (1973).

[118] For a comparative table of different drafts on international regime submitted to the U.N. Seabed Committee, see the U.N. document prepared by the Secretariat, *Comparative Table of Draft Treaties, Working Papers and Draft Articles,* U.N. doc. A/C.138/L.10, January 28, 1972. Draft articles of the United States, United Republic of Tanzania, Malta, and the Latin American countries characterized the international seabed

areas as the common heritage of mankind. See pp. 16–17. See also ibid, p. 17; idem, pp. 22–23. Japan and Poland also agreed with the recommendation of the United Kingdom. See idem, pp. 23 and 64.

[119] Idem, p. 23. Poland did not think that the international organization should deal with the laying of submarine cables and pipelines, idem, pp. 64 and 33.

[120] See the draft treaties of the United States, United Kingdom, United Republic of Tanzania, USSR, Malta, and Japan, idem, pp. 54–55.

[121] Ibid. Japan, Poland, and the Latin American draft treaties agreed with this provision; see idem, pp. 64–65, 55, and 74.

[122] Idem, pp. 77.

[123] Idem, pp. 86–88, 93, and 111–113.

[124] Idem, pp. 56–57. Canada, the United States, United Kingdom, and the USSR believed that offshore exploitation activities should be undertaken exclusively by states and did not favor assumption of such activities by international organizations.

[125] The views of the working group summarized hereunder were not officially recorded; however, they were presented to the first committee in a statement by the chairman of the working group, Christopher Pinto of Ceylon. See U.N. doc. A/AC.138/SC.I/SR.73, August 3, 1973. These views reflect the latest trend in thinking available as of the end of 1973.

[126] The term "creeping jurisdiction" was coined by John P. Craven, who is currently associated with the University of Hawaii. According to this view, certain features of the limited exclusive competence granted to coastal states over the seabed and the ocean floor will cause it to evolve naturally into comprehensive coastal state authority not only over the seabed and ocean floor of the shelf but also over its superjacent waters.

It may be noted that a similar concern was expressed by G. Schwargenberger and S. Oda. See *supra* note 53.

However, Burke agrees with our view that the fear has no basis in practice; see William T. Burke, *Law, Science and the Ocean* (Law of the Sea Institute, University of Rhode Island, Occasional Paper No. 3), pp. 14–15.

Notes to Chapter 6, pp. 166–200

[1] For an account of the significance of the traditional maritime military strategy, see Captain A. T. Mahan, *Influence of Sea Power upon History, 1660–1783* (Boston: Little, Brown and Co., 1894); and for an essay on naval strategy in the nuclear age, see Rear Admiral Edward Wegener, "Theory of Naval Strategy in the Nuclear Age," in *Proceedings of the United States Naval Institute* (May, 1972), pp. 190–208.

[2] See William A. Nierenberg, "Militarized Oceans," in Nigel Calder (ed.), *Unless Peace Comes* (New York: Viking Press, 1968), pp. 115–128, at p. 120. For a detailed breakdown of the U.S. Naval strength as of 1972, see *Proceedings*, idem, p. 338.

[3] See the Center for Strategic and International Studies, *Soviet Sea Power* (Georgetown University, Washington, D.C., June 1969), at p. 4.

[4] See the following literature and Table 6.1 for an indication of a select group of states' maritime capabilities.

a. *SIPRI Yearbook of World Armaments and Disarmament*, 1969/70 (Stockholm: Stockholm International Peace Research Institute, 1970), p. 138, where the undersea capabilities of vehicles belonging to the USSR, France, Japan, the United Kingdom, and Switzerland are described.

b. Captain A. P. S. Bindra, "The Indian Ocean as Seen by an Indian," in the *Proceedings of the United States Naval Institute* (May, 1970), pp. 178–203, where the relevance of Indian Ocean to various Indian Ocean states was analyzed. According to a note on p. 193, the Indian Navy now possesses a small aircraft carrier, the *Vikrant*, two old light cruisers, four submarines, sixteen destroyers and frigates, six minesweepers, and an assortment of lesser ships. The note also mentions that submarines, some frigates, and some fast patrol craft came from the Soviet Union and most of the other ships came from England.

c. Commander Hideo Sekino, "Japan and Her Maritime Defense," in the *Proceedings of the United States Naval War Institute* (May 1971), pp. 98–121, at p. 110, where statistics regarding navies of the Pacific East are presented. (See Table 6.1 below.)

d. Arthur Davidson Baker III, "Small Combatants—1972," in the *Proceedings, supra* note 1, pp. 240–265, at pp. 257–262, where major small combatants either being operated or acquired by different countries by 1972 were noted.

e. Harold E. Nash, "Challenges in National Defense—Particularly Antisubmarine Warfare" in *Proceedings of the Marine Frontiers Conference at the University of Rhode Island,* July 27–28, 1967 (University of Rhode Island, July 1968), pp. 15–26. On p. 16 the author noted that, according to *Jane's Fighting Ships,*

. . . 31 countries own and operate some 849 submarines; 736 of these are conventionally powered and 113 are nuclear-powered.

Of these 849, 380, or nearly 45%, belong to Russia, 203 to the United States, 45 to the United Kingdom, 30 to the People's Republic of China, 22 to Sweden, 21 to France, 14 to Rumania, 12 to Indonesia, 11 to West Germany, 10 to Turkey and 9 to the United Arab Republic. The balance of 81 are distributed among 19 other nations.

Of the 113 nuclear-powered submarines included in the above total of 849, 70 belong to the United States, 40 to Russia, and 3 to the United Kingdom.

[5] The following description of the military uses of the sea is substantially summarized from "The Militarization of the Deep Ocean," *SIPRI Yearbook* idem, note 5(a), pp. 92–153; see also Gordon I. F. McDonald, "An American Strategy for the Oceans," in E. A. Guillien (ed.), *Uses of the Seas* (Englewood Cliffs, N.J.: Prentice-Hall, 1968), pp. 163–194.

[6] See A. T. Mahan, *supra* note 1, for illustrations. Participating in the Washington Naval Conference of 1921, the United Kingdom argued that lack of appropriate military strength in land and aerial warfare made it essential for her to rely on seapower for security and

Table 6.1 Navies of the Pacific East [See note 4, item c.]

Country	Sub-marines	Cruisers	De-stroyers and Escorts	Mine Counter-measures Aircraft	Patrol	Am-phibious Aircraft	Aux-iliary	Air-craft Carrier	Other
Soviet Pacific Fleet	100	7	50	70	200	100	200	—	—
North Korea	4	—	—	30	130	10	—	—	40
Communist China	30	—	27	50	535	305	130	—	300
Japan	10	—	38	44	43	52	0	—	16
Republic of Korea	—	—	23	12	10	20	20	—	6
Nationalist China	—	—	12	12	73	95	20	—	25
Philippines	—	—	10	2	37	6	3	—	8
U.S. Seventh Fleet	10	1	30	—	—	—	—	4	70

Note: a dash represents 0.

survival. And she was not ready to consider proposals for naval disarmament unless proposals for reduction of land and aerial power were also discussed. Other participants—France, Italy, the United States, and Japan—were equally concerned about maintaining a relative balance of maritime power among them. See United States Naval War College, *International Law Documents: Conference on the Limitation of Armaments, 1921* (Washington, D.C., 1923).

[7] Wilbert M. Chapman, a U.S. expert on maritime affairs, said this:

Whatever the contemporary attitude of the government and citizenry, the one incontestable fact that stands out in this history, and in our present posture, is that the ocean and its uses control the power position of the United States in the world whether we see this or ignore it at the moment. The control and use of the ocean is the difference between life and death of our society, our economy, and our way of life.

Wilbert M. Chapman, "Statement before the Subcommittee on Oceanography of the Committee on Merchant Marine and Fisheries," House of Representatives, Eighty-Ninth Congress, First Session, *National Oceanographic Program Legislation* (Washington, D.C.: U.S. Government Printing Office, 1965), p. 409. See also pp. 428 and 433.

An Indian Naval officer, in a similar vein, believes that

History teaches us that he who controls the Indian Ocean controls the commerce and governs the destiny of indigenous people. This is an essential lesson of history and the countries of Southern Asia can afford to neglect their elements of maritime power only if they are prepared to surrender their freedom.

Captain A. P. S. Bindra, "My India: Diversity and Harmony," Vol. 94, *U.S. Naval Institute Proceedings*, pp. 43–55 (July 1968).

[8] In the continuing competition between submarine forces and the antisubmarine warfare forces, despite advancements in the latter sphere, the former still holds upper hand. See *SIPRI Yearbook, supra* note 4(a), pp. 118–119, where it is noted that

The discussion of ASW may have created the impression that the submarine is losing ground to the ASW side. This impression would certainly be wrong. Most advantages are still on the side of the modern nuclear-powered submarine, which is undergoing continuous improvements. It has enormous possibilities for hiding just by moving submerged in the vast ocean, undetectable by sonar in certain thermal layers. Since it is also becoming quieter and faster and soon will go deeper, it will have every chance of escape. It can also use active countermeasures: put out false targets to distract the ASW forces; employ mine countermeasures such as towing noise-making devices or magnetic generating equipment; or in a war, hide behind a nuclear explosion.

[9] United States Secretary of Defense, Melvin R. Laird, evaluated the Soviet-U.S. mutual deterrence forces thus:

Even if the Soviet Union levels off at roughly the present number of ICBM's operational and under construction, it could still have more than 1,900 reentry vehicles in its ICBM force by the mid-1970's. This force, alone, would be more than enough to destroy all U.S. cities of any substantial size. Practically all of the U.S. population also lies within the range to take into account the Soviet bomber force, which is expected to decline only gradually in the near term.
We continue to believe that an effective defense of our population against a major Soviet attack is not now feasible. Thus, we must continue to rely on our strategic offensive forces to deter a Soviet nuclear attack on our cities.
. . . We do have reliable and survivable strategic retaliatory forces, and their capabilities for retaliation today cannot be denied by nuclear attack.

Laird further noted that by the end of fiscal year 1972 the strategic offensive forces of the United States would "consist of 1,000 MINUTEMAN missiles, 54 TITAN missiles, 450 B-52 aircraft (26 squadrons), and 656 POLARIS and POSEIDON missiles carried on 41 nuclear submarines." See the statement of Secretary of Defense, Melvin R. Laird, before the House Armed Services Committee on the *FY 1972–1976 Defense Program and 1972 Budget,* March 9, 1971 (Washington, D.C.: U.S. Government Printing Office, 1972), at pp. 63–64.

[10] See Donella H. Meadows, Dennis L. Meadows, Jørgen Randers, and William W. Behrens III, *The Limits to Growth* (New York: Universe Books, 1972), for a warning that the earth's interlocking resources probably cannot support present rates of economic and population growth much beyond the year 2100, if that long, even with advanced technology.

[11] A few years ago, William A. Nierenberg expressed a similar opinion.

We are now, in the 1960's, just beginning to explore this vast unknown marine province for mineral deposits. This decade of exploration will be followed by a period of development of the tools for the extraction of the wealth and finally by actual installations for deep-sea mining. This great technological development will ultimately merge with the military technology. At that stage, many nations will have very large investments in the deep ocean, both on the bottom and throughout the ocean levels immediately above these installations. There will be teams of men working in these installations at all depths. We cannot foresee all the legal problems at this time, but we can tell that these massive investments will have a value that will make them attractive military targets, a source of international blackmail and friction, and in general, a central concern of naval planners.

See William A. Nierenberg, *supra* note 2, p. 119.

[12] For the British position, see U.S. Naval War College, *supra* note 6.

[13] The Marine Resources and Engineering Development Act of 1966, which was intended to coordinate and contribute to the marine activities of the United States, listed as one of its objectives "the preservation of the role of the United States as a leader in maritime science and development." See *Marine Science Affairs—A Year of Transition,* The First Report of the President to the Congress on Marine Resources and Engineering Development (Washington, D.C.: U.S. Government Printing Office, 1967), p. 14.

[14] Ambassador Amerasinghe of Sri Lanka endorses the view:

At the time the Ad Hoc Committee on the Seabed and the Ocean Floor began its study there was abundant evidence that the threat of extension of the arms race, and particularly the nuclear arms race, beyond the limits of territorial waters into the area of the seabed and the ocean floor was no longer a matter of speculation but was assuming gravely disquieting proportions. It was evident that scientific research and development in regard to the seabed and the ocean floor have received its principal stimulus from the military possibilities of that area and from considerations of military strategy.

See Hamilton S. Amerasinghe, "The Third World and the Seabed," in Pacem in Maribus–1, Vol. 2, *Legal Foundations of the Ocean Regime,* pp. 234–242 (Royal University of Malta Press, 1971), at p. 237.

[15] For an elaboration of the basic goals, see Chapter 2; also see M. S. McDougal, H. D. Lasswell, and I. A. Vlasic, *Law and Public Order in Outer Space* (New Haven: Yale University Press, 1963), Chapter II, and P. Sreenivasa Rao, "Authority and Control over Offshore Areas: In Defense of Common Interests," *Indian Journal of International Law,* pp. 379–388 (1971).

[16] We refer here mainly to the preamble of the Charter, which commits the members of the United Nations "to save succeeding generations from the scourge of war" and "to promote social progress and better standards of life in larger freedom," and to the "purposes of the United Nations" enumerated under Article I.

[17] As part of the contemporary realities of the global situation, we refer here to the divided world arena with more than 130 independent territorial entities, representing di-

verse political, ideological, economic, and military positions; to the existence of nuclear weapons, whose power to destroy seems to multiply with time; to the constant occurrence of actual armed conflict in one corner or the other of the world; and to the accelerating pace of application of science and technology to human needs and the resultant dangers to environmental preservation.

For exposition of one or more of these trends in the world social process and for articulation of appropriate basic policies of the world community, see M. S. McDougal and H. D. Lasswell, "The Identification and Appraisal of Diverse Systems of Public Order," Vol. 53, *A.J.I.L.*, pp. 1–30 (1959); Oscar Schachter, "Scientific Advances and International Law Making," Vol. 55, *California Law Review*, pp. 423–430 (1967); Richard A. Falk, *This Endangered Planet* (New York: Random House, 1971); Gunnar Myrdal, *The Challenge of World Poverty: A World Anti-Poverty Program in Outline* (New York: Pantheon Books, 1970); Robert S. McNamara, *The Essence of Security: Reflections in Office* (New York: Harper and Row, 1968); and Nigel Calder (ed.), *supra* note 2.

[18] The definition of value used here is taken from Harold D. Lasswell and Abraham Kaplan, *Power and Society: A Framework for Political Inquiry* (New Haven: Yale University Press, 1950), p. 16.

[19] M. S. McDougal, H. D. Lasswell, and I. A. Vlasic, *supra* note 15, pp. 779–780, where the authors defined a spatial-extension resource as follows:

. . . those resources whose most distinctive characteristic is their utility as media of transportation and communication. Among the most striking examples of this reference are the land and ocean surfaces, airspaces, and the void of outer space. The land masses obviously contain various stock and flow resources, as do the oceans and air space and outer space. The particular reference we make is, however, to the spatial or extension of quality of the resource which makes it a highly advantageous medium of transportation and communication; for present purposes, the material aspects are relevant, not for their characteristics as flow or stock resources, but because they form a surface or extension which can be made use of for movement.

[20] See M. S. McDougal and W. T. Burke, *The Public Order of the Oceans* (New Haven: Yale University Press, 1962), Chapter 7, where claims to shared use and competence upon the high seas are discussed. Especially see pp. 769–773.

[21] For a survey of the status of United States strategic capabilities, see the statement by the Secretary of Defense, Melvin R. Laird, *Toward a National Security Strategy of Realistic Deterrence* (Washington, D.C.: U.S. Government Printing Office, March 10, 1971), before the United States House Armed Services Committee. Also see the statement by Admiral Thomas H. Moorer, USN, Chairman, Joint Chiefs of Staff, before the same committee on the same day.

Admiral Rickover gave his assessment of the scope and magnitude of Soviet maritime capabilities in comparison with those of the United States. See his statement of March 10, 1971, before the House Joint Committee on Atomic Energy, 92nd Congress, First Session, *Naval Nuclear Propulsion Program—1971* (1971), pp. 109–128.

[22] See Lane C. Kendall, "Capable of Serving as a Naval and Military Auxiliary . . . ," *Proceedings of the Naval Review Issue* (U.S. Naval Institute, May 1971), pp. 212–227.

[23] This aspect was discussed by John A. Knauss, "The Military Role in the Ocean and Its Relation to the Law of the Sea," in Lewis M. Alexander (ed.), *The Law of the Sea: A New Geneva Conference* (Proceedings of the Sixth Annual Law of the Sea Institute Conference, University of Rhode Island), pp. 77–87 (1972). Also see, by the same author, *Factors Influencing a U.S. Position in a Future Law of the Sea Conference* (Law of the Sea Institute, University of Rhode Island, Occasional Paper no. 10, April 1971).

[24] The research by military personnel is, however, to be distinguished from the military intelligence activity, which is not supported by these policies.

[25] See A. T. Mahan, *supra* note 1. See also Bernard Brodie, *Sea Power in the Machine Age* (New York: Greenwood Press, 1969); Anthony Eugene Sokol, *Seapower in the Nuclear Age* (Washington, D.C.: Public Affairs Press, 1961); K. M. Panikkar, *India and the Indian Ocean: An Essay on the Influence of Sea Power on Indian History* (London: G. Allen and Unwin, 1951); The Center for Strategic and International Studies, *supra* note 3; and David D. Lewis, *The Fight for the Sea* (New York: The World Publishing Co., 1961).

[26] See, for example, the Agreement on Prevention of Incidents at Sea between the Soviet Union and the U.S.A., Vol. 11, *International Legal Materials*, p.778 (1972). The Agreement, which went into force on signature, aims at reducing the dangers inherent in the practice of "shadowing," "buzzing," and otherwise harassing each other's vessels in the course of surveillance of naval exercises or maneuvers.

[27] For a discussion of these attempts, see M. S. McDougal and W. T. Burke, *supra* note 20, p. 717.

[28] See U.N. doc. A/C.1/PV.1763, pp. 16–17. See also CCD/PV.477, at p. 19.

[29] For the Indian view, see U.N. doc. A/C.1/PV.1758, p. 23; for the Canadian view, see ENDC/PV.410, pp. 6–7; in addition, Brazil, ENDC/PV.423, pp. 24–28; Argentina, ENDC/PV.432, p. 12; Ethiopia, ENDC/PV.430, p. 32, Italy, ENDC/PV.432, p. 14; and Nigeria, ENDC/PV.430, pp. 19–20, all expressed sympathy with the Canadian, Indian, and Mexican positions.

[30] M. S. McDougal and W. T. Burke, *supra* note 20, p. 719. For a similar opinion, see E. D. Brown, *Arms Control in Hydrospace: Legal Aspects* (Washington, D.C.: Woodrow Wilson International Center for Scholars, Ocean Series 301, 1971), p. 32.

[31] The concept of the contiguous zone has emerged through a long history. States are known to have claimed limited exclusive authority and control, on occasion, for specified purposes over adjacent maritime areas of varying distances. The limits of the claimed zones of special jurisdiction have extended beyond twelve miles and covered more interests than the ones noted in the Geneva Convention. These interests included such values as power and security (zones of military interest), wealth (fisheries, nonliving resources and customs), well-being (health and sanitation), skills and affection (immigration), and rectitude (prohibition of liquor and antismuggling laws).

Indeed, well-known authorities, like Philip Jessup, M. S. McDougal, and W. T. Burke, believe that limits of the contiguous zone and the interests that the coastal state may seek to protect in the area are best left open, as they may vary with the context. However, there are other experts, such as George Schwargenberger, and Gerald Fitzmaurice, who argue that the authority over the contiguous zone should be allowed for only very specific limited purposes and, where such authority is claimed, that it should be interpreted as restrictively as possible. For a fuller discussion of the concept of the contiguous zone, see M. S. McDougal and W. T. Burke, *supra* note 20, pp. 582–607.

The concept of the contiguous zone is fast changing in its relevance to modern international law of the sea, as claims for a twelve-mile territorial sea are accepted and as claims for exclusive coastal state competence over living and nonliving resources and over their conservation are increasingly favored by the international community. Nevertheless, the basic idea that states, to protect their legitimate interests, on occasion can claim special jurisdiction over specified areas, for limited time intervals, remains valid. The legitimacy of such claims, however, depends on the context.

[32] *I.C.J. Reports,* 1949, pp. 4–26. The Court noted that

> It is, in the opinion of the Court, generally recognized and in accordance with international custom that States in time of peace have a right to send their warships through straits used for international navigation between two parts of the high seas without the previous authorization of a coastal State, provided that the passage is innocent. Unless otherwise prescribed in an international convention, there is no right for a coastal State to prohibit such a passage through straits in time of peace.

Quoted in Herbert W. Briggs, *The Law of Nations,* Second Ed. (New York: Appleton-Century-Crofts, 1952), at p. 292.

[33] See *Status of Multilateral Conventions, Law of the Sea* XXI–8 (U.N. doc. ST/LEG/e/Rev.1, December 31, 1959). For a comment on the practice of these states, see A. Kobadkin, "Territorial Waters and International Law," No. 8, *International Affairs* (Moscow, 1969), p. 78.

[34] Quoted in M. S. McDougal and W. T. Burke, *supra* note 20, p. 239.

[35] See H. W. Briggs, *supra* note 32, pp. 294–295.

[36] M. S. McDougal and W. T. Burke, *supra* note 20, p. 238.

[37] See the records of the International Law Commission, Seventh Session, Vol. 1, *Y.B.I.L.C.* (1955).

[38] Idem, p. 254.

[39] M. S. McDougal and W. T. Burke, *supra* note 20, p. 249.

[40] Max Sørensen, "The Law of the Sea," No. 520, *International Conciliation,* p. 234 (November 1958).

[41] J. H. W. Verzijl, "The United Nations Conference on the Law of the Sea, Geneva, 1958:I," Vol. 6, *Nederlands Tijdschrift voor International Recht 1,* pp. 1–9 (1959).

[42] See Friedhelm Kruger-Sprengel, *The Role of NATO in the Use of the Sea and the Seabed* (Washington, D.C.: Woodrow Wilson International Center for Scholars, Ocean Series 304, October 1972), p. 22.

[43] See the map issued by the Office of Geographer in the U.S. Department of State, "World Straits Affected by a 12-Mile Territorial Sea."

[44] The views of the United States and the Soviet Union are reflected in Article 2 of their 1968 Joint Draft Convention on the Breadth of Territorial Sea, cited in Friedhelm Kruger-Sprengel, *supra* note 42, p. 23. More recently the Soviet Union presented similar views to the United Nations Seabed Committee, in the form of draft articles on straits used for international navigation; see U.N. doc. A/AC.138/SCII/L.7. Also see the Soviet delegate's statement on the issue

. . . [the Soviet] delegation considered that there should be a distinct category of international straits including straits which linked up the high seas and the oceans or linked two parts of the same high sea, and which had over a considerable period of history served as waterways for international shipping and consequently were open for unhindered passage by all vessels in accordance with the principle of equality of all flags.
  It was therefore difficult to agree with the arguments of delegations which were opposed to freedom of navigation through international straits—as on the high seas—on the ground that it would enable warships and other vessels to pass unhindered through the straits and thus pose a threat to the coastal states. Hitherto such straits had not constituted territorial waters; yet no threat had arisen for the coastal states when warships as well as merchant vessels had sailed through them or when on occasion aircraft had flown over them. It was not easy to understand why some delegations felt that such vessels, particularly warships, now suddenly constituted a threat when they had been passing through the straits for so long, in some cases for centuries.

U.N. doc. A/AC.138/SCII/SR.4–23, December 2, 1971, at pp. 22–23.
  The U.S. delegate defended these views on the basis of inherent right of self-defense and collective security; see idem, pp. 45–47.
  Supporting the U.S. and USSR views were Turkey, idem, p. 7, Bulgaria, idem, p. 34, Czechoslovakia, idem, p. 52, Poland, idem, p. 115, the Ukrainian S.S.R., idem, p. 133. To a certain extent, Ethiopia supported the international corridor concept, and on account of its geographical position, it favored a liberalization of the rule of innocent passage rather than advocate absolute freedom, idem, p. 90.

[45] Alleging that the freedoms of the sea have helped the interests of the developed rather than developing countries, the Indonesian delegate argued that

  The freedom of navigation, for instance, had been used by the maritime Powers [not only] for trade purposes but also for purposes of war and conquest. History had evolved but today it was necessary that, while recognizing this freedom, the coastal states should have the right to take action to protect themselves against the dangers caused by the passage of foreign ships and particularly against the danger of pollution.

Further, in his opinion,

. . . the right of innocent passage in relation to warships should be considered from the standpoint of the peaceful uses of the sea and the security interests of the coastal states.

Idem, pp. 111 and 113.

Malaysia cited the threat of oil pollution in the Malacca Strait from the huge cargo carriers and possibly irreparable damage to its fish, tourism, and wildlife and pointed out that "there were no guarantees against those risks and there could never be adequate compensation for them." In addition, it argued that

The super-Powers were clamouring for freedom of transit for their warships through territorial straits. Malaysia could not be expected to invite potential calamity by encouraging their war of nerves. In the present age, it was essential to ensure that the seas, the sea-bed, and the ocean floor were used for peaceful purposes. Malaysia therefore insisted upon prior authorization for the passage of warships, including submarines, through its territorial strait. It would guarantee the right of innocent passage, but must be absolutely certain that the passage was innocent.

Idem, p. 88. See also, V. S. Mani, and S. Balupuri, "Malacca Straits and International Law," Vol. 12, *I.J.I.L.*, pp. 455–467 (1973).

[46] States belonging to the third group are Australia, idem, pp. 153–156; Denmark, idem, pp. 35–36; Gabon, idem, p. 84; Greece, idem, pp. 115–116; Italy, idem, p. 157–160; Kenya, idem, p. 55; Madagascar, idem, p. 72; Singapore, idem, p. 180; Mexico, idem, p. 95.

[47] F. Krueger-Sprengel, a West German specialist in international law and security problems, in a recent persuasive study indicated that the security interests of the United States and those of its West European allies were well served by maintaining the traditional concept of innocent passage. In rejecting the international corridor concept, he even saw certain advantages for the United States and NATO. See *supra* note 42.

The author in this connection made these interesting points:

1. Noting the claims of the U.S. and USSR that the concept of innocent passage was inadequate to serve their strategic needs, he pointed out that such claims were "mainly based on military needs." From a political point of view, he continued, "more emphasis should be placed on the fact that the United States naval forces can, contrary to the Navy of the Soviet Union, afford to rely on friendly or even allied coastal states" (p. 3, footnote 4).

2. Referring to different proposals dealing with the extension of coastal state jurisdiction over the maritime areas, he observed that "as part of the analysis of the geographical facts, NATO holds a generally favorable position under any partition of the North Atlantic Seabed area" (p. 9).

3. After thoroughly examining the strategic significance of different straits, F. Krueger-Sprengel came to the conclusion that "From the point of view of the NATO states in Europe, there is no necessity to strengthen the right of passage in the seas around Europe, for such a measure would only favor the navies of the Soviet Union and other Warsaw Pact states" (p. 30).

4. Finally, the same author noted that

From a military point of view only a few straits among the 16 above mentioned major straits affected by a 12-mile territorial sea can be classified as being of vital importance to the United States and indirectly to NATO. These are: the Malacca Strait, the Sunda Strait, the Bering Strait (West), the Dover Strait, the Bab el Mandeb (Red Sea) and the Hormuz Strait (Persian Gulf).

Passage through these straits could be negotiated with relatively few countries, namely Great Britain, France, Spain, Indonesia, Iran and the Soviet Union. In regional and bilateral arrangements, the concept of "innocent passage" which is the basic rule of existing international law, could form the basis for defining the necessary rights of transit. Such a regional or bilateral approach, which might include arrangements with the Soviet Union concerning the passage through the Bering Strait, could serve the interests of the United States as well as NATO's military and political aims. It could even help the United States reject charges that U.S. cooperation with the Soviet Union on the future law of the sea has been aimed at strengthening the hegemonic position of these two major naval powers over all parts of the seas and oceans. [p. 40]

[48] On the subject of the Washington and London Naval Conference, consult the following literature:

1. United States Naval War College, *supra* note 6.
2. Proceedings of the *London Naval Conference of 1930* (Washington, D.C.: Publication of the U.S. Department of State, Conference Series 6, 1931).
3. Hugh Latimer, *Naval Disarmament* (London: The Royal Institute of World Affairs, 1930).
4. Raymond Gish O'Connor, *Perilous Equilibrium* (Watson, Lawrence, Kans.: University of Kansas Press, 1962).
5. Arnold Toynbee, *Survey of International Affairs, 1930* (London: Oxford University Press, 1931).

[49] For the text of the Antarctica Treaty, which was signed on December 1, 1959, and has been in force since June 23, 1961, see Vol. 42, *United Nations Treaty Series,* p. 72 (1961). The Treaty on Outer Space was signed on January 27, 1967, and has been in force since October 10, 1967. For its text, see U.N. doc. A/RES.2222 (XXI) of December 19, 1967.

However, the term "peaceful purposes" as used in those two treaties is subject to differing interpretations. For a discussion of the differences in this connection, see M. S. McDougal, H. D. Lasswell, and I. A. Vlasic, *supra* note 15. Also see Leon Lipson and Nicholas de B. Katzenbach, *The Law of Outer Space: Report to the National Aeronautics and Space Administration* (Chicago: American Bar Foundation, July 1961). Also see the comments of Stephen Grove in Lewis M. Alexander (ed.), *supra* note 23, pp. 98–99; Robert K. Woetzel, "Comments on U.S. and Soviet Viewpoints Regarding the Legal Aspects of Military Uses in Space," *Proceedings of the Fifty-Seventh Annual Meeting of the American Society of International Law* (1963), pp. 195–205.

[50] For the statement of Ambassador Pardo, see U.N. doc. A/C.1/PV.1515 of November 1, 1967. Alva Myrdal of Sweden expressed a similar opinion in an address delivered before the Hague Academy of International Law on August 9, 1971:

The majority of states would like to see a comprehensive banning of all weapons of the seabed . . . one can hardly imagine that the international machinery could fulfill its tasks if states were permitted secretly to use the area for military purposes. The development of peaceful international activities on the seabed cannot coexist with national military wants . . . military installations in the areas concerned are not most defensible because they are defensive in character. In my view, shared by many, they should be banned from the international area as offensive to the aims and purposes of declaration of principles.

Quoted in Friedhelm Krueger-Sprengel, *supra* note 42, footnote 27, p. 21.

[51] For the views of the United States, see U.N. doc. A/C.1/PV.1590, p. 13; and for the United Kingdom, U.N. doc. A/C.1/PV.1594, pp. 63–65.

[52] See U.N. doc. A/C.1/PV.1592, pp. 6–7.

⁵³ See, for example, the views of the Trinidad and Tobago, U.N. doc. A/C.1/PV.1601, pp. 71–72; Sweden, U.N. doc. A/C.1/PV.1596, pp. 32–36; Yugoslavia, U.N. doc. A/C.C1/PV.1593.

⁵⁴ U.N. General Assembly Resolution 2340 (XXII) December 18, 1967, and U.N. General Assembly Resolution 2467 (XXIII) of December 21, 1968.

⁵⁵ U.N. doc. A/7134, July 8, 1968; ENDC/240, March 19, 1969.

⁵⁶ ENDC/PV.440, pp. 8–9.

⁵⁷ ENDC/PV.424, p. 11.

⁵⁸ ENDC/PV.397, pp. 11–12.

⁵⁹ ENDC/PV.424, pp. 9–10.

⁶⁰ ENDC/PV.423, p. 17.

⁶¹ ENDC/PV.411, p. 10; ENDC/249, May 22, 1969; and ENDC/PV.414, p. 5.

⁶² For example, see the views of Mexico, ENDC/PV.426, p. 15; Nigeria, ENDC/PV.430, p. 19; the USSR, ENDC/PV.400, p. 7; and Canada, ENDC/PV.424, p. 11.

⁶³ ENDC/PV.411, p. 10. The Soviet Union, however, disputed this assertion. Its representative said that

As to the possibilities of the development of a conventional arms race on the sea-bed they may prove in practice no less realistic than the use of this sphere for the emplacement of nuclear weapons. As far back as the Second World War wide use was made of ground mines, surfacing mines (without contact) and later also of torpedo mines which, when a ship passed over them, would surface and overtake the ship. With present rates of development of science and technology one cannot rule out the possibility of the emergence of new types of conventional weapons which could be used to strike from the sea-bed both at ships and at the territories of States. . . . Thus it is impossible to agree with the argument that "realistic possibilities" do not now and will not soon exist for conventional military uses of the sea-bed.

ENDC/PV.423, p. 18.

⁶⁴ ENDC/PV.414, p. 5. For the Polish suggestion, see ENDC/PV.406, para. 11–31.

⁶⁵ CCD/PV.440, p. 9.

⁶⁶ CCD/PV.444, pp. 22 and 44.

⁶⁷ Sweden championed this suggestion and submitted a draft on the operative paragraph. See CCD/PV.443, and CCD/271.

⁶⁸ See the views of the United Kingdom, CCD/44, p. 22; and Malta, U.N. doc. A/C.1/PV.1706, pp. 53–55.

⁶⁹ This suggestion was made by Canada, CCD/PV.441, p. 9; Netherlands, CCD/PV.442, p. 11; India, CCD/PV.444, p. 19; the United Kingdom, idem, p. 26; and Yugoslavia, CCD/PV.445, p. 32.

⁷⁰ The joint draft treaty originally stipulated that the amendments were subject to the veto of the nuclear powers. However, this stipulation was dropped at the insistence of several delegations; see, for example, the views of Italy, CCD/441, p. 14; Japan, CCD/PV.442, p. 8; Netherlands, idem, p. 12; India, CCD/PV.444, p. 18; the United Kingdom, idem, p. 39; and Yugoslavia, CCD/PV.445, p. 32.

⁷¹ ENDC/PV.400, p. 12.

⁷² ENDC/PV.409, p. 12; and ENDC/PV.410, pp. 6–7.

⁷³ The representative of the United States estimated that, as compared with the 12-mile width, it would add roughly 2 million square miles of the seabed to the area of prohibition.

⁷⁴ ENDC/PV.414, p. 6. See, for example, the views of India, ENDC/PV.428, p. 9; Poland, ENDC/PV.429, p. 43; Nigeria, ENDC/PV.430, p. 19, and Romania, ENDC/PV.434, p. 7.

It can be stated roughly that less than one-third of the total number of coastal states claim a length of three miles of territorial sea.

[75] The Mexican representative, a well-known international lawyer, Jorge Castañeda, said that

It is a sound principle of legal drafting that treaties should possess the greatest possible degree of autonomy. Every agreement should contain clear and precise judicial elements likely to make it self-explanatory and self-sufficient on perusal, thus obviating the need to refer to international instruments separate from the treaty. The draft treaty we are considering is far from fulfilling that requirement.

He then went on to elaborate on several confusions engendered by the joint draft treaty in defining the maritime area. See CCD/PV.477, pp. 10–14.

[76] For the views of Brazil, see U.N. doc. A/C.1/PV.1092, p. 12; for Nigeria, U.N. doc. A/C.1/PV.1693, p. 13; for Nepal, U.N. doc. A/C.1/PV.1694, p. 12; and for the United Kingdom, idem, p. 28.

[77] Ecuador, U.N. doc. A/C.1/PV.1696, p. 31; Philippines, U.N. doc. A/C.1/PV.1702, p. 31.

[78] Argentina, CCD/PV.445, p. 18 and El Salvador, U.N. doc. A/C.1/PV.1698, pp. 33–35.

[79] For example, see the views of Japan, CCD/PV.460, p. 6.

[80] Japan, CCD/PV.442, pp. 6–7, and Poland, CCD/PV.444, p. 12; United Kingdom, CCD/PV.444, p. 23.

[81] U.N. doc. A/C.1/997, December 11, 1969.

[82] See CCD/209/Rev. 2, April 23, 1970, especially Articles I and II.

[83] CCD/PV.477, p. 14.

[84] For the text and comment on the Tlatelolco Treaty provisions, see *SIPRI Year Book of World Armaments and Disarmament,* 1969–1970 (Stockholm: International Peace Research Institute, 1970), pp. 218–256; for Argentina and Chile, see idem, pp. 459 and 460.

[85] U.N. doc. A/C.1, 995, December 1, 1969.

[86] CCD/PV.480, pp. 13–14.

[87] For the United States, see U.N. doc. A/C.1/PV.1762, p. 36; for the statement of the Soviet representative, see idem, p. 47.

[88] Elaborating the concept of defensive maritime zone, the Canadian representative said,

No State, not even the coastal State, would be allowed to emplace in this zone weapons prohibited by the treaty. Within this security zone, however, the coastal State, or any other State acting with the explicit consent of the coastal State, would be able to perform those defensive activities not prohibited under the treaty, while other States will have no such rights. We believe that a provision along these lines should be considered for the purpose of satisfying the legitimate defense requirements of coastal States under the Charter. This concept clearly recognizes that the security interests of a coastal State would be jeopardized if other States, without its permission, were to install military devices on the seabed in the waters adjacent to the coastal State.

ENDC/PV.424, p. 12.

[89] Ibid, and see also ENDC/PV.410, pp. 6–7.

[90] See the views of Brazil, ENDC/PV.423, pp. 24, 28; Argentina, ENDC/PV.432, p. 12 (but the zone it suggested would have to include the entirety of the continental shelf area); Burma, U.N. doc. A/C.1/PV.1697, p. 42; Ethiopia, ENDC/PV.430, p. 32; Italy, ENDC/PV.423, p. 14; and Nigeria, ENDC/PV.430, pp. 19–20 (but in relation to a 50-mile zone).

[91] ENDC/PV.400, pp. 10–11.

[92] See the views of the United Arab Republic, ENDC/PV.403, p. 11; Brazil, ENDC/PV.405, p. 10; Sweden, idem, p. 25; and Canada, ENDC/PV.410, p. 8.

[93] Nigeria, ENDC/PV.411, p. 9.

[94] India, ENDC/PV.404, p. 24 and Italy, ENDC/PV.410, p. 20.

[95] See ENDC/PV.411, p. 11; and ENDC/PV.414, p. 9.

[96] For example, see the views of Mexico, ENDC/PV.426, p. 22, and India, ENDC/PV.428, p. 12.

[97] Brazil, for example, made this point, ENDC/PV.430, pp. 35–36. See also the views of Romania, ENDC/PV.434, pp. 6–9.

[98] For the Canadian Working Paper, see CCD/270, October 8, 1969; for the Brazilian Working Paper, see U.N. doc. A/C.1/993, November 28, 1969, and A/C.1/993/Rev/1, December 10, 1969.

[99] See *supra* note 98. Contrast this Brazilian view with the Romanian view, which suggests that the consent of the coastal state for verification of installations under its exclusive jurisdiction should be required. Ibid.

[100] ENDC/PV.421, pp. 16 and 17.

[101] ENDC/PV.428, p. 12. See also the explanation of Nigeria, ENDC/PV.430, p. 21.

[102] ENDC/PV.424, p. 14.

[103] For a rather dissatisfied outlook on the Treaty, note, for example, that France, though it welcomed the Treaty as a "praiseworthy measure" in itself, pointed out that it "does not satisfy us" because in its opinion, the Treaty applied the policy of reserving the oceans exclusively for peaceful purposes only in part. France declared that complete demilitarization, not denuclearization, should be the goal. U.N. doc. A/C.1/PV.1754, p. 13.

Arvid Pardo, who introduced the agenda item reserving the oceans exclusively for peaceful purposes in the United Nations, regarded the Treaty as of marginal value for arms control. U.N. doc. A/C.1/PV.1758, p. 37.

The People's Republic of China, another nuclear power, condemned the United States–Soviet Joint Draft Treaty, which was finally approved to become the SACT, as a "new swindle to legalize their intensive efforts in carrying out the nuclear armament race on the seabed" in order to perpetuate their "nuclear monopoly." See *Documents on Disarmaments,* 1969 (United States Arms Control and Disarmament Agency, August 1970), at p. 498.

See also Lord Kennet, "Arms Race Without End?" in Vol. 104, *The Manchester Guardian Weekly,* p. 7 (No. 21, May 22, 1971). Referring to the activities of the Conference of the Committee on Disarmament, he said, "It is producing a series of 'collateral measures' which get less and less useful, though the last of this series to be completed, the Seabed Treaty was the first to be entirely useless."

[104] For an account of the agreement reached between the United States and the USSR through the first phase of SALT, see E. D. Brown, "The Demilitarization and Denuclearization of Hydrospace," in Lucius Caflisch (ed.), *Annals of International Studies,* No. 4 (Geneva: Alumni Association of the Graduate Institute of International Studies, 1973), pp. 71–92, at pp. 87–90; also see "Towards SALT II: Interpretation and Policy Implications of the SALT Agreements," *Proceedings of the 67th Annual American Society of International Law* (November 1973), pp. 28–47.

[105] This was also the feeling expressed by a number of delegations to the United Nations at the time when they were approving the Treaty.

The Yugoslavian delegation called it a "building block" in the arms control structure. U.N. doc. A/C.1/PV.1748, p. 32.

Ireland noted that it signified the "beginning of arms control measures in relation to the sea-bed and the ocean floor." U.N. doc. A/C.1/PV.1751, p. 13.

Italy thought the Treaty offered a valuable and realistic solution to the problems concerning the limitation of armaments in the seabed. U.N. doc. A/C.1/PV.1752, p. 23.

Nigeria and Belgium characterized it as a "first step" toward preventing an arms race in the seabed. Idem, pp. 28 and 43. See also Argentina, U.N. doc. No. A/C.1/PV.1754, p. 36; Finland, U.N. doc. A/C.1/PV.1758, p. 52. See also Louis Henkin, "The Sea-Bed

Arms Treaty—One Small Step More," Vol. 10, *Columbia Journal of Transnational Law*, pp. 60–65 (Spring 1971).

The Treaty went into force on May 18, 1972, and about 35 countries have ratified it. See Pemmaraju Sreenivasa Rao, "The Seabed Arms Control Treaty: A Study in the Contemporary Law of the Military Uses of the Seas," Vol. 4, *Journal of Maritime Law and Commerce*, pp. 67–92 (1972).

[106] See *supra* note 85.

[107] Preambular Paragraph 2 of the U.N. Resolution 2832 (XXVI).

[108] Report of the Secretary-General, Declaration of the Indian Ocean as a Zone of Peace, U.N. doc. A/8809, September 14, 1972.

[109] See U.N. doc. A/C.1/PV.1911, December 5, 1972, pp. 7–10; p. 6; pp. 18–19; p. 12.

[110] Idem, pp. 21–22. See also M. Sornarajah, "Indian Ocean as a Peace Zone—Possible Legal Framework," Vol. 12, *I.J.I.L.*, pp. 543–563 (1972); and S. Balupuri, "Indian Ocean as a Peace Zone—Possible Legal Framework (Comment)," Vol. 12, *I.J.I.L.*, pp. 621–625 (1972).

Bibliography

(Books, articles, and reports cited in this volume)

Books
Albers, John P., Devereux M. Carter, Allen L. Clark, Anny B. Coury, and Stanley P. Schweinfurth. *Summary of Petroleum and Selected Mineral Statistics for 120 Countries, Including Offshore Areas,* Geological Survey Professional Paper 817. Washington, D.C.: U.S. Government Printing Office, 1973.

Alexander, Lewis M. (ed.). *The Law of the Sea: Needs and Interests of Developing Countries.* Proceedings of the Seventh Annual Conference of the Law of the Sea Institute, University of Rhode Island, Kingston, R.I., 1973.

Alexander, Lewis M. (ed.) *The Law of the Sea: A New Geneva Conference.* Proceedings of the Sixth Annual Conference of the Law of the Sea Institute, University of Rhode Island, Kingston, R.I., 1972.

Alexander, Lewis M. (ed.). *The Law of the Sea: The United Nations and Ocean Management.* Proceedings of the Fifth Annual Conference of the Law of the Sea Institute, University of Rhode Island, Kingston, R.I., 1971.

Alexander, Lewis M. (ed.). *The Law of the Sea: National Policy Recommendations.* Proceedings of the Fourth Annual Conference of the Law of the Sea Institute, University of Rhode Island, Kingston, R.I., 1970.

Alexander, Lewis M. (ed.). *The Law of the Sea: The Future of the Sea's Resources.* Proceedings of the Second Annual Conference of the Law of the Sea Institute, University of Rhode Island, Kingston, R.I., 1968.

Alexander, Lewis M. (ed.). *The Law of the Seas: Offshore Boundaries and Zones.* Columbus, Ohio: Ohio State University Press, 1967.

American Branch of the International Law Association. *Draft Report of the Committee on Deep Sea Mineral Resources* (June 1968), a report of the Thirty-Third American Assembly, *Uses of the Seas* (May 2–5, 1968).

American Society of International Law. *Principles for Global Fisheries Management Regime: A Report of the Working Group on Living Marine Resources of the Panel on Law of the Sea.* Washington, D.C., 1974.

Andrassy, J. *International Law and Resources of the Sea.* New York: Columbia University Press, 1970.

Arms Control and Disarmament Agency (U.S.). *Documents on Disarmament, 1969.* Washington, D.C.: U.S. Government Printing Office, August 1970.

Asamoah, Obed Y. *Legal Significance of Declarations of the General Assembly of the United Nations.* The Hague: Martinus Nijhoff, 1966.

Böhme, Eckart, and Max Ivers Kheden. *From the Law of the Sea towards an Ocean Space Regime: Practical and Legal Implications of the Marine Revolution.* New York: International Publications Services, 1972.

Borgese, Elizabeth Mann. *The Ocean Regime.* Santa Barbara, Calif.: Center for the Study of Democratic Institutions, October 1968.

Bos Kalis Westminister Dredging Group. *Study on Sea Island Project: The Building of Islands in the Open Sea Offers Possibilities for Industrial Development.* June 1972.

Bos Kalis Westminister Dredging Group. *Study on Sea Island Project: A Solution for Waste Disposal Problem.* June 1972.

Bowett, D. W. *The Law of the Sea.* Dobbs Ferry, N.Y.: Oceana Publications, 1967.

Brahtz, J. F. Peel (ed.). *Coastal Zone Management: Use with Conservation.* New York: John Wiley and Sons, 1972.

Briggs, Herbert W. *The Law of Nations: Cases, Documents and Notes.* Second Ed. New York: Appleton-Century-Crofts, 1952.

Brodie, Bernard. *Sea Power in the Machine Age.* New York: Greenwood Press, 1969.

Brooks, David B. *Low-Grade and Nonconventional Sources of Manganese.* Baltimore: Johns Hopkins University Press, 1966.

Brown, E. D. *The Legal Regime of Hydrospace.* London: Stevens and Sons, 1971.

Brown, E. D. *Arms Control in Hydrospace: Legal Aspects.* Washington, D.C.: Woodrow Wilson International Center for Scholars, Ocean Series 301, 1971.

Brown, E. D. *Report on the Legal Regime of Deep-Sea Mining.* For the British Branch of the International Law Association, Committee on Deep-Sea Mining, June 1, 1968.

Burke, William T. *Law, Science and the Ocean.* Law of the Sea Institute, University of Rhode Island, Occasional Paper No. 3.

Burke, William T. *Towards a Better Use of the Oceans: A Study and Prognosis.* A SIPRI Monograph. New York: Humanities Press, 1969.

Burke, William T. *Ocean Science, Technology and the Future of International Law of the Sea.* Columbus, Ohio: Ohio State University Press, 1968.

Caflisch, Lucius C. (ed.). "Hydrospace in International Relations." No. 4, *Annals of International Studies.* Geneva: Alumni Association of the Graduate Institute of International Studies, 1973.

Calder, Nigel. *Technopolis.* New York: Simon and Schuster, 1970.

Calder, Nigel (ed.). *Unless Peace Comes.* New York: Viking Press, 1968.

Cambridge Essays in Honor of Lord McNair. London: Stevens and Sons, 1965.

Center for Strategic and International Studies, *Soviet Sea Power*. Washington, D.C.: Georgetown University, June 1969.

Castañeda, Jorge. *Legal Effects of United Nations Resolutions*. New York: Columbia University Press, 1970.

Chase Manhattan Bank, Energy Division. *Outlook for Energy in the United States*. New York, November 1968.

Chayes, Abram, and Jerome B. Wiesner. *ABM: An Evaluation of the Decision to Deploy on an Antiballistic Missile System*. New York: Harper and Row, Publishers, 1969.

Ciriacy-Wantrup, S. *Resources Conservation Economics and Policies*. Berkeley, Calif.: University of California Press, 1952.

Clark, G., and L. Sohn. *World Peace through World Law*. Third Revised Ed. Cambridge, Mass.: Harvard University Press, 1967.

Clingan, T., and L. M. Alexander (eds.). *Hazards of Maritime Transit*. Cambridge, Mass.: Ballinger Publishing Co., 1973.

Colombos, C. John. *The International Law of the Sea*. Sixth Ed. New York: D. McKay Co., 1967.

Commission on International Development. *Partners in Development*. New York: Praeger Publishers, 1969.

Commission on Marine Science. *Our Nation and the Sea: A Plan for National Action*. Washington, D.C.: U.S. Government Printing Office, 1969.

Commission on Marine Science, Engineering and Resources. *Report of the Panel on Management and Development of the Coastal Zone—Part III*. Washington, D.C.: U.S. Government Printing Office, 1969.

Commission to Study the Organization of Peace. *The United Nations and the Bed of the Sea II*. New York, 1970.

Commission to Study the Organization of Peace. Nineteenth Report. *The United Nations and the Bed of the Sea*. New York, 1969.

Commission to Study the Organization of Peace. Seventeenth Report. *New Dimensions for the United Nations: The Problems of Next Decade*. New York, May 1966.

Commission to Study the Organization of Peace. *Strengthening the United Nations*. New York: Harper and Row, Publishers, 1957.

Cowell, E. B. (ed.). *The Ecological Effects of Oil Pollution on Littoral Communities*. Proceedings of the symposium organized by the Institute of Petroleum and held at the Zoological Society of London. London: Institute of Petroleum, 1971.

D'Amato, Anthony, and John L. Hargrove. *Environment and the Law of the Sea*. A Report of the Working Group on Ocean Environment, American Society of International Law, Washington, D.C., May 1974.

Degens, Egon T., and David A. Ross. *Hot Brines and Recent Heavy Metal Deposits in the Red Sea: A Geochemical and Geophysical Account.* New York: Springer-Verlag, 1969.

Documents on Disarmament, 1969. U.S. Arms Control and Disarmament Agency. Washington, D.C.: U.S. Government Printing Office, August 1970.

Drucker, Peter F. *The Age of Discontinuity: Guidelines for Our Changing Society.* New York: Harper and Row, Publishers, 1969.

Ducsik, Dennis W., ed. *Power, Pollution and Public Policy.* Cambridge, Mass.: MIT Press, 1971.

Eagleton, Clyde. *The Responsibility of States in International Law.* New York: New York University Press, 1928.

Easton, Robert. *Black Tide: The Santa Barbara Oil Spill and Its Consequences.* New York: Delacorte Press, 1972.

Emery, K. O. *Eastern Atlantic Continental Margin Program of the International Decade of Ocean Exploration (Gx28193). Some Results of 1972 Cruise of R/V Atlantis II.* Washington, D.C.: National Academy of Science, 1972.

Engler, Robert. *The Politics of Oil: Private Power and Democratic Directions.* Chicago: University of Chicago Press, 1967.

Falk, Richard A. *This Endangered Planet.* New York: Random House, 1971.

Falk, Richard A., and Saul M. Mendlovitz. *The Strategy of World Public Order: Disarmament and Economic Development,* Vol. 4. New York: World Law Fund, 1966.

Final Report of the New England Assembly on Uses of the Seas. May 22–25, 1969.

First Scientific Meeting of the Undersea Medical Society in Conjunction with the Aerospace Medical Association. Miami, Fla., 1968.

First Report of the U.S. President to the Congress on Marine Resources and Engineering Development. *Marine Science Affairs: A Year of Transition.* Washington, D.C.: U.S. Government Printing Office, 1967.

Flipse, John E. "Impacts of Deep Ocean Mineral Development." The Charles M. Schwab Memorial Lecture, American Iron and Steel Institute, 80th General Meeting, May 24, 1972.

Food and Agricultural Organization. *Atlas of the Living Resources of the Seas.* Rome, 1972.

Food and Agricultural Organization. *Pollution: An International Problem for Fisheries.* Rome, 1971.

Friedmann, Wolfgang. *The Future of the Oceans.* New York: George Braziller, 1971.

Friedmann, Wolfgang, Oliver J. Lissitzyn, and Richard C. Pugh. *International Law: Cases and Materials*. St. Paul, Minn.: West Publishing Co., 1969.

Fulton, Thomas. *The Sovereignty of the Seas*. Edinburgh and London: W. Blackwood and Sons, 1911.

Fye, Paul M. *Ocean Policy and Scientific Freedom*. Columbus O'Donnell Memorial Lecture, Marine Technology Society, September 11, 1972.

Gamble, John King, Jr., and Giulio Pontecorvo (eds.). *Law of the Sea: The Emerging Regime of the Oceans*. Proceedings of the Eighth Annual Conference of the Law of the Sea Institute, June 18–21, 1973. Cambridge, Mass.: Ballinger Publishing Co., 1974.

García-Amador, F. V. *The Exploitation and Conservation of the Resources of the Sea*. Second Ed., Leyden: A. W. Sythoff, 1963.

Gardner, Richard N. (ed.). *Blueprint for Peace*. New York: McGraw-Hill, 1966.

Goodrich, Leland M. *The United Nations*. London: Stevens and Sons, 1959.

Grieves, Forest L. *Supranationalism and International Adjudication*. Urbana, Ill.: University of Illinois Press, 1969.

Gullion, Edmund A. (ed.). *Uses of the Sea*. Englewood cliffs, N.J.: Prentice-Hall, 1968.

Haas, Ernst B. *Tangle of Hopes: American Commitments and World Order*. Englewood Cliffs, N.J.: Prentice-Hall, 1969.

Henkin, Louis. *Law for the Sea's Mineral Resources*. New York: Institute for the Study of Human Affairs of Columbia University, 1968.

Higgins, Rosalyn. *The Development of International Law by the Political Organs of the United Nations*. London and New York: Oxford University Press, 1963.

Hood, Donald (ed.). *Impingement on Man on the Oceans*. New York: John Wiley and Sons, 1971.

Horn, D. R., B. M. Horn, and M. N. Delach. *Ocean Manganese Nodules, Metal Values and Mining Sites*. Technical Report No. 4. International Decade of Ocean Exploration. Washington, D.C.: National Science Foundation 1973.

Horsfield, Brenda, and Peter Bennet Stone. *The Great Ocean Business*. New York: Coward, McCann and Geoghegan, 1972.

Institute of Water Resources. *Foreign Deep Water Port Development: A Selective Overview of Economics, Engineering and Environmental Factors*, Vols. I, II, and III. U.S. Department of the Army, Corps of Engineers, December 1971.

International Law Association. Report of the Fifty-Fourth Conference. *Deep-Sea Mining*, The Hague, 1970. International Law Association, 3 Paper Buildings, The Temple, London, E.C. 4.

International Law Association. *The Report of the Deep-Sea Mining Committee on the Exploration and Exploitation of Minerals on the Ocean Bed and in Its Subsoil.* Buenos Aires Conference, 1968. International Law Association, 3 Paper Buildings, The Temple, London, E.C. 4.

Jenks, C. Wilfred. *The World Beyond the Charter.* London: George Allen and Unwin, 1969.

Johnston, Douglas M. *International Law of Fisheries: A Policy-Oriented Enquiry.* New Haven: Yale University Press, 1965.

Johnston, Douglas M., and Edgar Gold. *The Economic Zone in the Law of the Sea: Survey, Analysis, and Appraisal of Current Trends.* Occasional Paper 17, Law of the Sea Institute, University of Rhode Island, June 1973.

Kane, Thomas. *Aquaculture and the Law.* Sea Grant Technical Bulletin, University of Miami, November 1970.

Kaplan, Norman (ed.). *Science and Society.* Chicago: Rand McNally Co., 1965.

Kaplan, Morton, and Nicholas de B. Katzenbach. *The Political Foundation of International Law.* New York: John Wiley and Sons, 1961.

Ketchum, Bostwick H. (ed.). *The Water's Edge: Critical Problems of the Coastal Zone.* Cambridge, Mass.: MIT Press, 1972.

Khan, Rahmatullah. *Implied Powers of the United Nations.* New Delhi, Nikas Publications, 1970.

King, C. A. M. *An Introduction to Oceanography.* New York: McGraw-Hill, 1963.

Knauss, John A. *Factors Influencing a U.S. Position in a Future Law of the Sea Conference.* Occasional Paper No. 10, Law of the Sea Institute, University of Rhode Island, April 1971.

Koers, Albert. *International Regulation of Marine Fisheries: A Study of Regional Fisheries Organizations.* Surrey, England: Fishing News (Books), 1973.

Koo, Wellington, Jr. *Voting Procedures in International Political Organizations.* New York: Columbia University Press, 1947.

Kruger-Sprengel, Friedhelm. *The Role of NATO in the Use of the Sea and Seabed.* Washington, D.C.: Woodrow Wilson International Center for Scholars, Ocean Series 304, October 1972.

Kuenen, P. H. *Marine Geology.* New York: John Wiley and Sons, 1950.

Laird, Melvin R. *Statement before the House Armed Services Committee on the FY 1972–1976 Defense Program and 1972 Budget, March 9, 1971.* Washington, D.C.: U.S. Government Printing Office, 1972.

Laird, Melvin R. *Toward a National Security Strategy of Realistic Deterrence.* Washington, D.C.: U.S. Government Printing Office, 1971.

Lasswell, Harold D., and Abraham Kaplan. *Power and Society: A Framework for Political Inquiry*. New Haven: Yale University Press, 1950.

Latimer, Hugh. *Naval Disarmament*. London: Royal Institute of World Affairs, 1930.

Lay, S. Houston, Robin Churchill, and Myron Nordquist (eds.). *New Directions in Law of the Sea: Documents*, Vols. I and II. Dobbs Ferry, N.Y.: Oceana Publications, 1973.

Lewis, David D. *The Fight for the Sea*. New York: World Publishing Co., 1961.

Legal Foundations of the Ocean Regime. Pacem in Maribus: Proceedings of the Preparatory Conference, 1970. The Royal University of Malta Press, 1971.

Lipson, Leon, and Nicholas de B. Katzenbach. *The Law of Outer Space: Report to NASA*. Chicago: American Bar Association, 1961.

McDougal, Myres S., and William T. Burke. *The Public Order of the Oceans*. New Haven: Yale University Press, 1962.

McDougal, Myres S., and David Haber. *Property, Wealth and Land: Allocation, Planning and Development*. Charlottesville, Va.: Michie Case Book Corporation, 1948.

McDougal, Myres S., Harold D. Lasswell, and Ivan A. Vlasic. *Law and Public Order in Outer Space*. New Haven: Yale University Press, 1963.

Mackin, J. G. *A Review of Significant Papers on Effects on Oil Spills and Oil Fields Brine Discharges on Marine Biotic Communities*. Texas A & M Research Foundation, Project 737, February 1973.

McNamara, Robert S. *The Essence of Security: Reflections in Office*. New York: Harper and Row, Publishers, 1968.

Mahan, Captain A. T. *Influence of Sea Power upon History, 1660–1783*. Boston: Little, Brown and Co., 1894.

Marine Technology Society. *Exploiting the Ocean*. Washington, D.C., 1968.

Matthews, W., F. Smith, and E. Goldberg (eds.). *Man's Impact on Terrestrial and Oceanic Ecosystems*. Cambridge, Mass.: MIT Press, 1972.

Meadows, Donella H. and Dennis L., Jørgen Randers, and William W. Beherens III. *The Limits to Growth*. New York: Universe Books, 1972.

Mero, John L. *The Mineral Resources of the Sea*. Amsterdam: Elsevier, 1965.

Mero, John L. *The Mining and Processing of Deep-Sea Manganese Nodules*. Berkeley, Calif.: Institute of Marine Resources, 1959.

Miller, Crane. *International Law and Marine Archaeology*. Belmont, Mass.: Academy of Applied Science, 1973.

Mouton, M. W. *The Continental Shelf*. The Hague: M. Nijhoff, 1952.

Murty, B. S. *Propaganda and World Public Order: The Legal Regulation of the Ideological Instrument of Coercion.* New Haven: Yale University Press, 1968.

Myrdal, Gunnar. *The Challenge of World Poverty: A World Anti-Poverty Program in Outline.* New York: Pantheon Books, 1970.

Nash, A. E. Keir, Dean E. Mann, and Phil G. Olsen. *Oil Pollution and the Public Interest.* Berkeley, Calif.: University of California, 1972.

National Academy of Engineering. *Outer Continental Shelf Resource Development Safety: A Review of Technology and Regulation for the Systematic Minimization of Environmental Intrusion from Petroleum Products.* Panel on Operational Safety in Offshore Resource Development. Washington, D.C.: U.S. Government Printing Office, December 1972.

National Council on Marine Resources and Engineering Development (U.S.). *International Decade of Ocean Exploration.* Washington, D.C.: U.S. Government Printing Office, 1968.

National Petroleum Council. *Law of the Sea: Particular Aspects Affecting Petroleum Industry.* Washington, D.C., 1973.

National Petroleum Council. *Supplemental Report on Petroleum Resources under the Ocean Floor.* Washington, D.C., March 4, 1971.

National Petroleum Council. Final Report. *Petroleum Resources under the Ocean Floor.* Washington, D.C., March, 1969.

National Petroleum Council. Interim Report. *Petroleum Resources under the Ocean Floor.* Washington, D.C., 1968.

Naval Oceanographic Office (U.S.). *Science and the Sea.* Washington, D.C.: U.S. Government Printing Office, 1967.

Nelson-Smith, A. *Oil Pollution and Marine Technology.* London: Paul Elek Science Publishers, 1972.

O'Connor, Raymond Gish. *Perilous Equilibrium.* Lawrence, Kans.: University of Kansas Press, 1962.

Oda, Shigeru. *International Control of Sea Resources.* Leyden: A. W. Sythoff, 1963.

Oppenheim, L., and H. Lauterpacht. *International Law,* Vol. I. Eighth Ed., London and New York: Longmans, Green and Co., 1955.

Oxman, Bernard. *The Preparation of Article 1 of the Convention on the Continental Shelf.* Springfield, Va.: Clearinghouse for Federal Scientific and Technical Information, n.d.

Pacem in Maribus II. *Working Papers on the Ocean Development Tax.* Malta, June 29–July 5, 1971. Santa Barbara, Calif.: Center for the Study of Democratic Institutions.

Panikkar, K. M. *India and the Indian Ocean: An Essay on the Influence of Seapower on Indian History*. London: George Allen and Unwin, 1951.

President's Science Advisory Committee Report of the Panel on Oceanography (U.S.). *Effective Use of the Sea*. Washington, D.C.: U.S. Government Printing Office, 1968.

Proceedings of the Marine Frontiers Conference at the University of Rhode Island. Kingston, R.I., July 1968.

Prosser, William L. *Law of Torts*. Third Ed. St. Paul, Minn.: West Publishing Co., 1964.

Reisman, Michael. *Nullity and Revision: The Review and Enforcement of International Judgments and Awards*. New Haven: Yale University Press, 1971.

Report of Study No. VI by the United Kingdom. *The Environmental and Financial Consequences of Oil Pollution from Ships: Main Report*. Submitted to IMCO as part of the preparations for the International Marine Pollution Conference, 1973. Programs Analysis, University of Chilson, Dedcot, Berks, England, 1973.

Ross, David A. *Introduction to Oceanography*. New York: Appleton-Century-Crofts, 1970.

Schlee, Susan. *The Edge of an Unfamiliar World*. New York: E. P. Dutton and Co., 1973.

Sears, Mary (ed.). *Oceanography*. Washington, D.C.: Publication No. 67, American Association for the Advancement of Science, 1961.

Second Report of the President to the Congress on Marine Resources and Engineering Development (U.S.). *Marine Science Affairs: A Year of Plans and Progress*. Washington, D.C.: U.S. Government Printing Office, 1968.

Shepard, F. P. *Submarine Geology*. Third Ed. New York: Harper and Row, Publishers, 1973.

Shepard, F. P. *Submarine Geology*. First Ed. New York: Harper and Brothers, Publishers, 1948.

Singh, Nagendra. *The Legal Regime of Merchant Shipping*. Bombay: University of Bombay, 1969.

SIPRI Year Book of World Armaments and Disarmament. Stockholm: Stockholm International Peace Research Institute, 1969/70.

Smith, H. A. *The Law and Custom of the Sea*. Third Ed., London: Stevens and Sons, 1959.

Sokol, Anthony Eugene. *Seapower in the Nuclear Age*. Washington, D.C.: Public Affairs Press, 1961.

Sørensen, Max (ed.). *Manual of Public International Law*. New York: St. Martin's Press, 1968.

Sørensen, Max. *The Law of the Sea.* International Conciliation, No. 520. Carnegie Endowment for International Peace, New York: November, 1958.

Steinhart, Carol E. and John S. *Blowout.* N. Scituate, Mass.: Duxbury Press, 1972.

Subcommittee on Oceanography of the Committee on Merchant Marine and Fisheries, U.S. House of Representatives. *National Oceanographic Program Legislation,* 89th Congress, First Session, 1965.

Sverdrup, H., M. W. Johnson, and R. H. Fleming. *The Oceans.* Englewood Cliffs, N.J.: Prentice-Hall, 1942.

Sztucki, Jerzy (ed.). *Symposium of the International Regime of the Seabed.* Rome: Instituto Affari Internazionale, 1970.

Thompson, Murray. *Militarism 1969: A Survey of World Trends,* Vol. II. Peace Research Reviews, No. 5. Clarkson, Ontario, Canada: Canadian Peace Research Institute, October 1968.

Toynbee, Arnold. *Survey of International Affairs, 1930.* London: Oxford University Press, 1931.

United Kingdom. Report of Study No. VI. *The Environmental and Financial Consequences of Oil Pollution from Ships: Main Report.* Submitted to IMCO as part of the preparations for the International Marine Pollution Conference, 1973. Program Analysis, University of Chilson, Dedcot, Berks, England, 1973.

United Nations Committee, World Peace through Law Center. *Treaty Governing the Exploitation and Use of the Ocean Bed.* Pamphlet series No. 10, Geneva.

U.S. Department of State. *Proceedings of the London Naval Conference of 1930.* Conference Session 6, Washington, D.C. 1931.

U.S. Naval Oceanographic Office. *Science and the Sea.* Washington, D.C.: U.S. Government Printing Office, 1967.

U.S. Naval War College. *International Law Documents: Conference on the Limitation of Armaments,* 1921. Washington, D.C. 1923.

U.S. President. President's Science Advisory Committee Report of the Panel on Oceanography. *Effective Use of the Sea.* Washington, D.C.: U.S. Government Printing Office, 1968.

U.S. President. Second Report of the President to the Congress on Marine Resources and Engineering Development. *Marine Science Affairs: A Year of Plans and Progress.* Washington, D.C.: U.S. Government Printing Office, 1968.

U.S. President. First Report to the Congress on Marine Resources and Engineering Development. *Marine Science Affairs: A Year of Transition.* Washington, D.C.: U.S. Government Printing Office, 1967.

U.S. Senate. *Hearings before the Special Sub-Committee on Outer Continental Shelf of the United States Senate Committee on Interior and Insular Affairs.* 91st Congress, First and Second Sessions, 1970.

U.S. Senate. *Hearings before the Special Sub-Committee on Outer Continental Shelf of the U.S. Senate Committee on Interior and Insular Affairs, Outer Continental Shelf,* 91st Congress, First and Second Sessions. December 17, 1969, January 22, and March 4, 1970.

U.S. Senate. *Hearings on S. 7 and S. 544 before the Sub-Committee on Air and Water Pollution of the U.S. Senate Committee on Public Works.* 91st Congress, First Session, Section 2, 1969.

U.S. Senate. Doc. No. 26. *Legal Problems of Space Exploration,* March 22, 1961. 81st Congress, First Session. Washington, D.C.: U.S. Government Printing Office, 1961.

University of Chicago and World Brotherhood. *Conference on World Tensions.* May 11–13, 1960.

Ward, Barbara. *Spaceship Earth.* New York: Columbia University Press, 1966.

Wilcox, Francis O., and Carl M. Marcy. *Proposals for Changes in the United Nations.* Washington, D.C.: Brookings Institution, 1955.

Woodrow Wilson International Center for Scholars. *Ocean Affairs Bibliography, 1971.* Ocean Series 302. Washington, D.C. 1971.

Wooster, Warren (ed.). *Freedom of Oceanic Research.* New York: Crane, Russak and Co., 1973.

Articles
Aguilar, Andres. "How Will the Future Deep Seabed Regime Be Organized?" In J. K. Gamble and G. Pontecorvo (eds.), *Law of the Sea: The Emerging Regime of the Oceans,* pp. 43–51 (1974).

Albers, John P. "Offshore Petroleum: Its Geography and Technology" In J. K. Gamble and G. Pontecorvo (eds.), *Law of the Sea: The Emerging Regime of the Oceans,* pp. 293–304 (1974).

Albers, John P., and Richard F. Mayer. "New Information on World-Wide Seabed Resources," Vol. 2, *Ocean Management,* pp. 61–74 (1974).

Alexander, Lewis M. "Indices of National Interest in the Oceans." Vol. 1, *Ocean Development and International Law Journal,* pp. 21–49 (1973).

Allbritton, Jack L. "Division of Damages in Admiralty—A Rising Tide of Confusion." Vol. 2, *Journal of Maritime Law and Commerce,* pp. 323–348 (1971).

Amerasinghe, Hamilton S. "The Third World and the Seabed." In Pacem in Maribus-I, Vol. 2, *Legal Foundations of the Ocean Regime,* pp. 234–242 (The Royal University of Malta Press, 1971).

Anand, R. P. "Interests of the Developing Countries and the Developing Law of the Sea." In Lucius Caflisch (ed.), *Hydrospace in International Relations,* pp. 13–30 (1973).

Anderson, Harry. "Oil Crisis Has Made Global Trade Wars Real Threat." *The Boston Globe*, p. 29 (February 2, 1974).

Arangio-Ruiz, Gaetano. "The Normative Role of the General Assembly of the United Nations and the Declaration of Friendly Relations." Vol. 3, *Recueil des Cours*, pp. 431–472 (1972).

Auburn, F. M. "Deep Sea Archaeology and the Law." Vol. 2, *International Journal of Nautical Archaeology and Underwater Exploration*, pp. 159–162 (1973).

Auburn, F. M. "The Deep Seabed Hard Mineral Resources Bill." Vol. 9, *San Diego Law Review*, pp. 491–513 (1972).

Baker, Arthur Davidson III. "Small Combatants—1972." *Proceedings of the U.S. Naval Institute* (May 1972), pp. 240–265.

Balpuri, S. "Indian Ocean as a Peace Zone—Possible Legal Framework (Comment)." Vol. 12, *I.J.I.L.,* pp. 621–625 (1972).

Barkenlens, Jack N. "The International Implications of Manganese Nodules." Vol. 136, *World Affairs* (April 1974).

Bates, Charles C., and Paul Yost. "Where Trends the Flow of Merchant Ships." In J. K. Gamble and G. Pontecorvo (eds.), *Law of the Sea: Emerging Regime of the Oceans,* pp. 249–276 (1974).

Becher, William. "The New Submarine-Hunter Plane Is Shown on the Coast." *The New York Times* (October 13, 1968).

Beesley, Alan J. "Some Unresolved Issues on the Law of the Sea." Vol. 4, *Natural Resources Lawyer,* pp. 629–638 (1971).

Bergman, Samuel. "No Fault Liability for Oil Pollution Damage." Vol. 5, *Journal of Maritime Law and Commerce,* pp. 1–50 (1973).

Bergsten, C. Fred. "The Threat is Real." No. 14, *Foreign Policy,* pp. 84–90 (Spring 1974).

Bergsten, C. Fred. "The Threat from the Third World," No. 11, *Foreign Policy,* pp. 102–124 (Summer 1973).

Bernfeld, Seymour S. "Developing the Resources of the Seas—Security of Investment." Vol. 2, *International Lawyer,* pp. 67–76 (1967).

Bindra, Captain A. P. S. "The Indian Ocean as Seen by an Indian." *Proceedings of the U.S. Naval Institute* (May 1970), pp. 178–203.

Bindra, Captain A. P. S. "My India: Diversity and Harmony." *U.S. Naval Institute Proceedings* (July 1968).

Birrell, George A. "TOVALPO and CRISTAL: A Case Study in Policy-Making for the Control of Ocean Pollution." Paper presented at the Annual Meeting of the American Association for the Advancement of Science (Washington, D.C., December 27, 1972).

Bleicher, Samuel A. "The Legal Significance of Re-Citation of General Assembly Resolution." Vol. 63, *American Journal of International Law*, pp. 444–479 (1969).

Bluestein, Ed, Jr. "Admirality Law and Its Effects on Offshore Development." Paper No. OTC 1212, presented to *Second Annual Offshore Technology Conference* (Houston, Texas, April 22–24, 1970), pp. I-651–662.

Blumer, Max, and Jeremy Saas. "Oil Pollution: Persistence and Degradation of Spilled Fuel Oil." Vol. 176, *Science*, pp. 1120–1122 (June 9, 1972).

Blumer, Max. "Scientific Aspects of the Oil Spill Problem." Vol. 1, *Environmental Affairs*, pp. 54–73 (1971).

Blumer, Max, Howard L. Sanders, J. Fred Grassle and George R. Hampson, "A Small Oil Spill." Vol. 13, *Environment*, pp. 2–12 (March 1971).

Bouchez, L. J. "The North Sea Continental Shelf Case." Vol. 1, *Journal of Maritime Law and Commerce*, pp. 113–122 (1969).

Boulding, Kenneth E. "The Concept of World Interest." In Richard A. Falk and Saul H. Mendlovitz, *The Strategy of World Public Order: Disarmament and Economic Development* (1966).

Brooks, David B. "Deep Sea Manganese Nodules: From Scientific Phenomenon to World Resource." In L. M. Alexander (ed.), *The Law of the Sea: The Future of the Sea's Resources*, pp. 32–42 (1968).

Brown, E. D. "The Demilitarization and Denuclearization of Hydrospace." In Lucius Caflisch (ed.), "Hydrospace in International Relations." Vol. 4, *Annals of International Studies*, pp. 71–92 (1973).

Brown, E. D. "The 1973 Conference on Law of the Sea: The Consequences of Failure to Agree." In Alexander, L. M. (ed.), *The Law of the Sea: A New Geneva Conference*, pp. 1–37, (1972).

Brown, E. D. "Our Nation and the Sea: A Comment on the Proposed Legal-Political Framework for the Development of Submarine Mineral Resources." In L. M. Alexander, *The Law of the Sea: National Policy Recommendations*, pp. 2–49 (1970).

Brown, E. D. "The Present Regime of the Exploration and Exploitation of Sea Bed Resources in International Law and in National Legislation: An Evaluation." In Jerzy Sztucki (ed.), *Symposium on the International Regime of the Seabed*, pp. 241–278 (1970).

Brown, E. D. "The North Sea Continental Shelf Cases." Vol. 23, *Current Legal Problems*, pp. 187–215 (1970).

Brownlie, Ian. "Recommendations on the Limits of the Continental Shelf and Related Matters: A Commentary." In L. M. Alexander (ed.), *The Law of the Sea: National Policy Recommendation*, pp. 133–158 (1970).

Burger, W. "Treaty Provisions Concerning Marine Science Research." Vol 1, *Ocean Development and International Law Journal*, pp. 159–184 (1973).

Burke, William T. "A Negative View of the Proposal for the United Nations Ownership of Ocean Mineral Resources." Vol. 1, *Natural Resources Lawyer*, pp. 42–62 (1968).

Burke, William T. "Law and the New Technologies." In L. M. Alexander (ed.), *The Law of the Sea: Offshore Boundaries and Zones*, pp. 204–227 (1967).

Button, D. K. "Petroleum—Biological Effects in the Marine Environment." In Donald Hood (ed.), *Impingement of Man on the Oceans*, pp. 421–430 (1971).

Cadwalader, George. "Freedom for Science in the Oceans." Vol. 182, *Science*, pp. 15–20 (October 1973).

Caflisch, Lucius. "Some Aspects of Oil Pollution from Merchant Shipping." In L. Caflisch (ed.), *Hydrospace in International Relation*, pp. 213–236 (1973).

Castañeda, Jorge. "The Concept of Patrimonial Sea in International Law." Vol. 12, *I.J.I.L.*, pp. 535–543 (1972).

Chanslor, J. W. "Treasures from the Sea." In U.S. Naval Oceanographic Office, *Science and the Sea*, pp. 9–16 (1967).

Charlier, Roger H. "Harnessing the Energies of the Oceans: A Review, Parts I and II." Vol. 3, *Marine Technology Society Journal*, pp. 13–32 and 59–81 (1969).

Cheek, Conrad H. "Law of the Sea: Effects of Varying Coastal State Controls on Marine Research." Vol. 1, *Ocean Development and International Law Journal*, pp. 209–220 (1973).

Cheng, Bing. "United Nations Resolutions on Outer Space: 'Instant' International Customary Law." Vol. 5, *Indian Journal of International Law*, pp. 23–45 (1965).

Christy, Francis T., Jr. "Alternative Regimes for Marine Resources Underlying the High Seas." Vol. 1, *Natural Resources Lawyer*, pp. 63–77 (1968).

Craven, John P. "The Challenge of Ocean Technology to the Law of the Sea." Vol. 22, *Judge Advocate General Journal*, pp. 31–38 (1967).

Craven, John P. "Sea Power and the Sea Bed." Vol. 92, *U.S. Naval Institute Proceedings*, pp. 36–51 (April 1966).

Crawford, John E., and John W. Padan. "The Bureau of Mine's Expanding Role in Undersea Mining." Vol. 17, *Mining Engineering*, pp. 67–70 (March 1965).

Denrome, Roger. "The Seaward Limit of the Continental Shelf." In L. M. Alexander (ed.), *The Law of the Sea: National Policy Recommendations*, pp. 263–274 (1970).

Dexter, Lewis A. " Priorities for Ecology," *The New York Times* (Friday, February 8, 1974).

Ducsik, Dennis W., Paul Mertens, and George Neill. "Offshore Siting of Electric Power Plants." In Dennis W. Ducsik (ed.), *Power, Pollution and Public Policy*, pp. 29–89 (1971).

Ducsik, Dennis W., and Robyn Seitz. "The Crisis in Shoreline Recreation." In Dennis W. Ducsik (ed.), *Power, Pollution and Public Policy*, pp. 90–186 (1971).

Durante, Francesco. "The Present Regime of the Exploration and Exploitation of the Seabed Resources in International Law and in National Legislation." In Jerzy Sztucky (ed.), *Symposium on the International Regime of the Seabed*, pp. 279–294 (1970).

Ely, Northcutt. "United States Seabed Minerals Policy." Vol. 4, *Natural Resources Lawyer*, pp. 597–621 (1971).

Ely, Northcutt. "The Laws Governing Exploitation of the Minerals beneath the Sea." In Marine Technology Society, *Exploiting the Oceans*, pp. 373–378 (1968).

Emery, K. O. "Oil of the Shelf." Vol. 27, *Oceanus*, pp. 11–17 (Spring 1973).

Emery, K. O., and Zir Ben-Avraham, "Structure and Stratigraphy of the China Basin." Vol. 6, *United Nations ECAFE, CCOP Technical Bulletin* (July 1972).

Emery, K. O., Paul M. Fye, and George Cadwalader. "The Seabed." In *Public Policy towards Environment 1973: A Review and Appraisal*, Vol. 216, *Annals of the New York Academy of Sciences*, pp. 51–55 (May 18, 1973).

Emery, K. O., and Hiroshi Niino. "Stratigraphy and Petroleum Prospects of Korea Strait and the East China Sea." Vol. 1, *Report of Geophysical Exploration*, pp. 1–19 (1967).

Emery, K. O., Elazar Uchupi, John Sunderland, H. L. Oktolseja, and E. M. Young. "Geological Structure and Some Water Characteristics of the Java Sea and Its Adjacent Continental Shelf." Vol. 6, *United Nations ECAFE, CCOP Technical Bulletin* (July 1972).

Ewing, Maurice, and Mark Landisman. "Shape and Structure of Ocean Basins." In Mary Sears (ed.), *Oceanography*, pp. 3–38 (1961).

Falk, Richard A. "On the Quasi-Legislative Competence of the General Assembly." Vol. 60, *American Journal of International Law*, pp. 783–791 (1966).

Ferrero, Eduardo. "The Latin Position on Legal Aspects of Maritime Jurisdiction and Oceanic Research." In Warren S. Wooster (ed.), *Freedom of Oceanic Research*, pp. 97–136 (1973).

Finlay, Luke T. "Rights of Coastal Nations to the Continental Margins." Vol. 4, *Natural Resources Lawyer*, pp. 668–675 (1971).

Finlay, Luke T. "The Outer Limit of the Continental Shelf: A Rejoinder to Professor Louis Henkin." Vol. 64, *A.J.I.L.*, pp. 42–61 (1970).

Finney, John W. "Why Inspection Can No Longer Be Critical for Arms Control." *The New York Times* (April 13, 1969).

Fisher, Joseph L. "Limits on Exploitation of Natural Resources." Vol. 70, *Technology Review* (MIT), pp. 49–54 (May 1968).

Foighel, Isi. "The North Sea Continental Shelf Case." Vol. 39, *Nordisk Tidsskrift for International Ret,* pp. 109–127 (1969).

Franssen, Herman T. "Oil and Gas in the Oceans." Vol. 26, *Naval War College Review,* pp. 50–64 (May–June, 1974).

Franssen, Herman T. "Developing Country Views of Sea Law and Marine Science." In Warren S. Wooster (ed.), *Freedom of Oceanic Research,* pp. 137–177 (1973).

Franssen, Herman T. "Research v. Regulation." Vol. 17, *Oceanus,* pp. 18–22 (1973).

Franssen, Maureen N. "Oceanic Research and the Developing Nation Perspective." In Warren S. Wooster (ed.), *Freedom of Oceanic Research,* pp. 179–200 (1973).

Friedmann, Wolfgang. "Selden Redivirus—Towards a Partition of the Seas?" Vol. 65, *A.J.I.L.,* pp. 757–771 (1971).

Friedmann, Wolfgang. "The North Sea Continental Shelf Cases: A Critique." Vol. 64, *A.J.I.L.,* pp. 229–240 (1970).

Fye, Paul M., Arthur E. Maxwell, K. O. Emery, and Bostwick Ketchum. "Ocean Sciences and Marine Resources." In Edmund Gullion (ed.), *Uses of the Sea,* pp. 10–68 (1968).

Girad, Claude. "Military Uses of the Continental Shelf and the Sea Bed Beyond." In William T. Burke, *Towards a Better Use of the Oceans,* pp. 175–182 (1968).

Goldie, L. F. E. "International Impact Reports and the Conservation of the Ocean Environment." Vol. 13, *Natural Resources Journal,* pp. 256–281 (1973).

Goldie, L. F. E. "The Exploitability Test: Interpretation and Possibilities." Vol. 8, *Natural Resources Journal,* pp. 434–477 (1968).

Goldie, L. F. E. "The Contents of Davy Jones' Locker—A Professed Regime for the Seabed and Subsoil." Vol. 22, *Rutgers Law Review,* pp. 39–54 (1967).

Goldie, L. F. E. "Liability for Damage and the Progressive Development of International Law." Vol. 14, *International and Comparative Law Quarterly,* pp. 1189–1264 (1964).

Goldie, L. F. E. "Australia's Continental Shelf: Legislation and Proclamation." Vol. 3, *International and Comparative Law Quarterly,* pp. 535–575 (1954).

Green, L. C. "The Continental Shelf." Vol. 4, *Current Legal Problems,* pp. 54–80 (1951).

Griffin, William L. "Accommodation of Conflicting Uses of Ocean Space with Special Reference to Navigation Safety Lanes." In L. M. Alexander (ed.), *The Law of the Sea: Future of Sea's Resources,* pp. 73–83 (1968).

Gurr, Ted. "A Causal Model of Civil Strife: A Comparative Analysis Using New Indices." Vol. 62, *American Political Science Review,* pp. 1104–1124 (1968).

Gwyne, Peter. "Nuclear Power Goes to Sea." Vol. 55, *New Scientist*, pp. 474–476 (September 21, 1972).

Hardy, Michael. "Offshore Development and Marine Pollution." Vol. 1, *Ocean Development and International Law Journal*, pp. 239–273 (1973).

Harlow, Lt. Comdr. Bruce A. "Legal Aspects of Claims to Jurisdiction in Coastal Waters." *Conference of the U.S. Fishing Industry*, Seattle, Washington, March 24–27, 1968.

Harlow, F. de G. "The Oil Men and the Sea." Vol. 11, *Arizona Law Review*, pp. 677–730 (1969).

Hearn, Rear Admiral Wilfred A., U.S.N. "The Role of the United States Navy in the Formulation of Federal Policy Regarding the Sea." Vol. 1, *Natural Resources Lawyer*, pp. 23–31 (June 1968).

Hedberg, Hollis D. "Limits of National Jurisdiction over Natural Resources of the Ocean Bottom." In L. M. Alexander (ed.), *The Law of the Sea: National Policy Recommendations*, pp. 159–170 (1970).

Henkin, Louis. "The Sea-Bed Arms Treaty—One Small Step More." Vol. 10, *Columbia Journal of Transnational Law*, pp. 60–65 (Spring 1971).

Henkin, Louis. "A Reply to Mr. Finlay." Vol. 64, *A.J.I.L.*, pp. 62–72 (1970).

Henkin, Louis. "International Law and the 'Interests': The Law of the Seabed." Vol. 63, *A.J.I.L.*, pp. 504–510 (1969).

Henkin, Louis. "Changing Law for the Changing Seas." In Edmund A. Gullion (ed.), *Uses of the Seas*, pp. 69–97 (1968).

Hess, H. D. "The Ocean: Mining's Newest Frontier." Vol. 166, *Engineering and Mining Journal*, pp. 79–96 (August 1965).

Horigan, James E. "Unitization of Petroleum Reservoirs Extending across Subsea Boundary Lines of Bordering Seas in the North Sea." Vol. 7, *Natural Resources Lawyer*, pp. 67–76 (Winter 1974).

Hunnings, N. March. "Pirate Broadcasting in European Waters." Vol. 14, *I.C.L.Q.*, pp. 410–436 (1965).

Hurst, Cecil J. B. "Whose Is the Bed of the Sea?" Vol. 4, *B.Y.B.I.L.*, pp. 34–43 (1923–1924).

Ibler, Vladimir. "The Interests of Shelf-Locked States and Proposed Development of the Law of the Sea." Vol. 11, *I.J.I.L.*, pp. 389–411 (1971).

Idyll, C. P. "Marine Aquaculture: Problems and Prospects." *Technical Conference on Fishery Management and Development* (Vancouver, Canada, February 13–23, 1973).

Jacobson, Jon, and Thomas A. Hanlon. "Regulation of Hard-Mineral Mining and the Continental Shelf." Vol. 50, *Oregon Law Review*, pp. 425–461 (1971).

Jenks, C. Wilfred. "Liability for Ultra-Hazardous Activities in International Law." Vol. 117, *Hague Recueil des Cours,* pp. 105–193 (1966).

Jenks, C. Wilfred. "Unanimity, the Veto, Weighted Voting, Special and Simple Majorities and Consensus: Modes of Decisions in International Organizations." In *Cambridge Essays in Honor of Lord McNair,* pp. 48–63 (London 1965).

Jennings, R. Y. "Limits of Continental Shelf Jurisdiction, Some Possible Implications of the North Sea Case Judgement." Vol. 18, *International and Comparative Law Quarterly,* pp. 819–832 (1969).

Jennings, R. Y. "Note on Article 1 of the 1958 Geneva Convention of the Continental Shelf." Memorandum, June 15, 1968, No. 12, circulated to the members of the Committee on Deep Sea Mineral Resources of the American Branch of International Law Association.

Jennings, R. Y. "General Course of International Law." Vol. 121, *Recueil des Cours,* 327–600 (1967-II).

Johnson, D. H. N. "The North Sea Continental Shelf Cases." Vol. 3, *International Relations,* pp. 522–540 (1969).

Johnson, D. H. N. "The Effect of the Resolutions of the General Assembly of the United Nations." Vol. 35, *British Year Book of International Law,* pp. 97–122 (1955–1956).

Johnston, Douglas M. "Law, Technology and the Sea." Vol. 55, *California Law Review,* pp. 449–472 (May 1967).

Kashahara, Hiroshi. "Problems of Allocation as Applied to the Exploitation of the Living Resources of the Sea." In Lewis M. Alexander (ed.), *The Law of the Sea: Needs and Interests of Developing Countries,* pp. 94–101 (1972).

Katz, Milton. "The Function of Tort Liability in Technology Assessment." Vol. 38, *University of Cincinnati Law Review,* pp. 587–662 (1969).

Kelson, John M. "State Responsibility and the Abnormally Dangerous Activity." Vol. 13, *Harvard International Law Journal,* pp. 197–244 (1972).

Kendall, Lane C. "Capable of Serving as a Naval and Military Auxiliary . . ." *Proceedings of the Naval Review Issue,* U.S. Naval Institute, May 1971, pp. 212–227.

Kennet, Lord, "Arms Race without End?" Vol. 104, *The Manchester Guardian Weekly,* p. 7 (May 22, 1971).

Kolodkin, A. "Territorial Waters and International Law." No. 8, *International Affairs,* pp. 78–81 (Moscow, 1969).

Kovaly, Kenneth A. "Underwater Archeology." Vol. 3, *Oceanology International,* pp. 27–30 (January–February, 1968).

Knauss, John A. "Development of the Freedom of Scientific Research Issue of the Third Law of the Sea Conference." Vol. 1, *Ocean Development and International Law Journal,* pp. 93–120 (1973).

Knauss, John A. "The Military Role in the Ocean and Its Relation to the Law of the Sea." In Lewis M. Alexander (ed.), *The Law of the Sea: A New Geneva Conference,* pp. 77–87 (1972).

Knight, H. Gary. "International Legal Problems in the Construction and Operation of Offshore Deep Draft Port Facilities." In T. Clingan and L. M. Alexander (eds.), *Hazards of Maritime Transit,* pp. 91–127 (1973).

Knight, H. Gary. "Non-Extractive Uses of the Seabed." Vol. 6, *Marine Technology Society,* pp. 18–22 (1972).

Knight, H. Gary. "The Draft United Nations Convention on the International Seabed Area: Background, Description and Some Preliminary Thoughts." Vol. 8, *San Diego Law Review,* pp. 459–550 (May 1971).

Knight, H. Gary. "Shipping Safety Fairways: Conflict Amelioration in the Gulf of Mexico." Vol. 1, *Journal of Maritime Law and Commerce,* pp. 1–20 (1969).

Krasner, Stephen D. "Oil Is the Exception." No. 14, *Foreign Policy,* pp. 68–74 (Spring 1974).

Kunz, Joseph L. "Continental Shelf and International Law: Confusion and Abuse." Vol. 50, *American Journal of International Law,* pp. 828–853 (1956).

Kuzminov, I. "Superiorities of Socialism." Vol. 12, *International Affairs,* pp. 32–36 (Moscow, December 1967).

Lasswell, Harold D. "The Relevance of International Law to the Development Process." *Proceedings of the American Society of International Law* (April 28–30, 1966), pp. 1–8.

Lauterpacht, H. "Sovereignty over Submarine Areas." Vol. 27, *B.Y.B.I.L.,* pp. 376–433 (1950).

Laylin, John G. "Interim Practices and Policy for the Governing of Seabed Mining beyond the Limits of National Jurisdiction." In Lewis M. Alexander (ed.), *The Law of the Sea: Needs and Interests of the Developing Countries,* pp. 25–28 (1973).

Lear, J. "Cities on the Sea." Vol. 54, *Saturday Review,* pp. 80–90 (1971).

Lurie, Meyer G. "Ocean Miners Prepare for the Big Plunge." Vol. 96, *Chemical Week,* pp. 131–144 (April 17, 1965).

MacCutcheon, Edward M. "Traffic and Transport Needs at the Land-Sea Interface." In J. F. Peel Brahtz (ed.), *Coastal Zone Management: Multiple Use with Conservation,* pp. 105–148 (1972).

MacDonald, Gordon J. F. "An American Strategy for the Oceans" in Edmund A. Gullion (ed.), *Uses of the Sea,* pp. 163–194 (1968).

McDougal, M. S. "Revision of the Geneva Conventions on the Law of the Sea. The Views of a Commentator." Vol. 1, *Natural Resources Lawyer,* pp. 19–28 (July 1968).

McDougal, M. S., and H. D. Lasswell. "The Identification and Appraisal of Diverse Systems of Public Order." Vol. 53, *American Journal of International Law,* pp. 1–30 (1959).

McDougal, M. S., H. D. Lasswell, and M. Reisman. "The World Constitutive Process of Authoritative Decision-Making." Vol. 19, *Journal of Legal Education*, pp. 253–300 and 403–437 (1967).

McIlhenny, W. F. "Pollutional Aspects of Marine Mineral Exploitation." *First Offshore Technology Conference* (Houston, Texas, May 18–21, 1969), Paper No. 1032, pp. I-299–304.

McKelvey, V. E. "Environmental Protection in Offshore Petroleum Operations." Vol. 1, *Ocean Management*, pp. 119–128 (1973).

Mani, V. S., and S. Balapuri. "Malacca Straits and International Law." Vol. 13, *I.J.I.L.*, pp. 455–467 (1973).

Mero, John L. "Review of Mineral Values on and under the Ocean Floor." In Marine Technology Society, *Exploiting the Oceans* (Washington, D.C., 1966), pp. 61–78.

Mero, John L. "Minerals on the Ocean Floor." Vol. 203, *Scientific American*, pp. 64–72 (December 1960).

Mikdashi, Zuhyr. "Collision Could Work." No. 14, *Foreign Policy*, pp. 57–68 (Spring 1974).

Miron, George. "Proposed Regimes for Exploration and Exploitation of the Deep-Seabed." In L. M. Alexander (ed.), *The Law of the Sea: National Policy Recommendation* (1969).

Münch, Fritz. "Lex Lata of Deep-Sea Mining." In *Legal Foundations of the Ocean Regime*, pp. 142–147 (1971).

Murty, B. S. "The International Regulation of the Uses of the Sea-Bed and the Ocean Floor." Vol. 9, *I.J.I.L.*, pp. 72–77 (1969).

Nash, Harold E. "Challenges in National Defense—Particularly Antisubmarine Warfare." In *Proceedings of the Marine Frontiers Conference* (University of Rhode Island, July 1968), pp. 15–26.

Nawaz, M. K. "An Alternative Criterion for Delimiting the Continental Shelf." Vol. 13, *Indian Journal of International Law*, pp. 25–40 (January–March 1973).

Nawaz, M. K. "Chinese Views on Law of the Sea—Select Views." Vol. 12, *I.J.I.L.*, pp. 606–614 (1972).

Neal, R. A. "Alternatives in Aquacultural Development: Considerations of Extensive versus Intensive Methods." *Technical Conference in Fishery Management and Development* (Vancouver, Canada, February 13–23, 1973), FMD/73/S-37 (January 1973).

Nierenberg, William A. "Militarized Oceans." In Nigel Calder (ed.), *Unless Peace Comes*, pp. 115–127 (1968).

Oda, Shigeru. "Future Regime of the Deep Ocean Floor." In Jerzy Sztucky (ed.), *Symposium on the International Regime of the Seabed*, pp. 343–362 (1970).

Oda, Shigeru. "Proposals for Revising the Convention on the Continental Shelf." Vol. 7, *The Columbia Journal of Transnational Law*, pp. 1–31 (1968).

Oda, Shigeru. "The Geneva Conventions on the Law of the Sea: Some Suggestions for the Revision." Vol. 1, *Natural Resources Lawyer*, pp. 103–114 (1968).

Onis, Juan de. "Peru's Challenge to U.S.: Oil Expropriation Poses a Difficult Problem for Nixon Administration." *The New York Times* (February 15, 1969).

Paden, John W. "Marine Mining and the Environment." In Donald Hood (ed.), *Impingement of Man on the Oceans*, pp. 553–561 (1971).

Pardo, Arvid. "A Statement on the Future Law of the Sea in Light of Current Trends in Negotiation." Vol. 1, *Ocean Development and International Law*, pp. 315–335 (1974).

Parry, Clive. "The Function of Law in the International Community." In Max Sørensen, *Manual of Public International Law*, pp. 1–54 (1968).

Paust, Jordan, and Albert Blaustein. "The Arab Oil Weapon—A Threat to International Peace." Vol. 68, *A.J.I.L.*, pp. 410–439 (1974).

Pinto, Christopher W. "Problems of Developing States and the Effects on Decisions on Law of the Sea." In L. M. Alexander (ed.), *The Law of the Sea: Needs and Interests of Developing Countries*, pp. 3–13 (1973).

Pontecorvo, G. "Ocean Science and Mutual Assistance: An Uneasy Alliance." Vol. 1, *Ocean Development and International Law Journal*, pp. 51–64 (1973).

Radlinski, W. A. "Safety and Pollution Control in OCS Petroleum Operations." Paper presented at the Second Annual Meeting, Division of Production, American Petroleum Institute, Houston, Texas, March 7, 1972 (manuscript)

Rao, K. K. "The Legal Regime of the Sea-Bed and Ocean Floor." Vol. 9, *I.J.I.L.*, pp. 1–18 (1969).

Rao, P. C. "The Continental Shelf: The Practice and Policy of India." Vol. 3, *I.J.I.L.*, pp. 191–198 (1963).

Redfield, Michael. "The Legal Framework for Oceanic Research." In Warren Wooster (ed.), *Freedom of Oceanic Research*, pp. 41–96 (1973).

Repkin, "Routing of Ships at Sea." Paper presented to the Technical Symposium of Ships' Gear International.

Revelle, Roger. "Scientific Research on the Seabed: International Cooperation in Scientific Research and Exploration of the Seabed." In Jerzy Sztucki (ed.), *Symposium of the International Regime of the Seabed*, pp. 649–663 (1970).

Revelle, Roger, Edward Wenk, B. H. Ketchum, and Edward R. Cosino. "Ocean Pollution by Petroleum Hydrocarbons." In W. Matthews, F. Smith, and E. Goldberg (eds.), *Man's Impact on Terrestrial and Oceanic Ecosystems*, pp. 297–318 (1972).

Rice, A. L. "H.M.S. Challenger: Midwife to Oceanography." Vol. 18, *Sea Frontiers*, pp. 291–305 (September–October 1972).

Rich, Alexander, and V. A. Engelhardt. "A Proposal from a U.S. and a Soviet Scientist: Ocean Resources and Developing Nations." Vol. 24, *Bulletin of the Atomic Scientist*, pp. 2–3 (February 1968).

Rickover, Admiral Hyman G. "Naval Nuclear Propulsion Program—1971." In *Hearings before U.S. House Joint Committee on Atomic Energy*, 92nd Congress, First Session (1971).

Riley, Stewart. "The Legal Implications of the Sea Use Program." Vol. 4, *Marine Technology Society Journal*, pp. 31–46 (1970).

Rothstein, A. J., and R. Kaufman. "The Approaching Maturity of Deep Ocean Mining—The Pace Quickens." Vol. 1, *Offshore Technology Conference Preprints*, pp. 323–344 (1973).

Saikowski, Charlotte. "The U.S. Way of Oil-Crisis Impact on 'Third World'." *The Christian Science Monitor* (Thursday, January 24, 1974).

Schacter, Oscar. "Scientific Advances and International Law Making." Vol. 55, *California Law Review*, pp. 423–430 (1967).

Schaeffer, M. B. "Conservation of Biological Resources of the Coastal Zone." In J. F. Peel Brahtz (ed.), *Coastal Zone Management: Multiple Use with Conservation*, pp. 35–77 (1972).

Schaeffer, M. B. "The Changing Law of the Sea—Effects on Freedom of Scientific Investigation." In Lewis M. Alexander (ed.), *The Law of the Sea: The Future of Sea's Resources*, pp. 113–117 (1968).

Schwargenberger, George. "The Fundamental Principles of International Law." Vol. 87, *Recueil des Cours*, p. 196 (1955).

Sekino, Commander Hideo. "Japan and Her Maritime Defense." *Proceedings of the U.S. Naval Institute* (May 1971), pp. 98–121.

Singh, Nagendra. "International Law Problems of Merchant Shipping." Vol. 107, *Hague Recueil des Cours*, pp. 8–166 (1962-II).

Singleton, Joseph F. "Pollution of the Marine Environment from Outer Continental Shelf Operations." Vol. 22, *South Carolina Law Review*, pp. 228–241 (1970).

Sloan, F. B. "The Binding Force of a Recommendation of the General Assembly of the United Nations." Vol. 25, *British Year Book of International Law*, pp. 1–33 (1948).

Sohn, Louis B. "The Council of an International Sea-Bed Authority." Vol. 9, *San Diego Law Review*, pp. 404–434 (1972).

Smith, Wayne J. "International Control of Deep Sea Mineral Resources." Vol. 24, *Naval War College Review*, pp. 82–90 (June 1972).

Snow, Lord C. P. Comments, *The New York Times* (Wednesday, November 13, 1968).

Sørensen, Max. "Institutionalized Cooperation in Economic, Social and Cultural Fields." In Max Sørensen, *Manual of Public International Law*, pp. 605–672 (1968).

Sornarajah, M. "Indian Ocean as a Peace Zone—Possible Legal Framework." Vol. 12, *I.J.I.L.*, pp. 543–563 (1972).

Sreenivasa Rao, Pemmaraju. "Development and the Sea." Vol. 17, *Oceanus* (Woods Hole Oceanographic Institution Journal, Woods Hole, Mass.), pp. 6–13 (1973).

Sreenivasa Rao, Pemmaraju. "Law of the Sea Threatens Research." *The Christian Science Monitor* (December 11, 1973).

Sreenivasa Rao, Pemmaraju. "The Seabed Arms Control Treaty: A Study on the Contemporary Law of the Military Uses of the Seas." Vol. 4, *Journal of Maritime Law and Commerce*, pp. 67–92 (1972).

Sreenivasa Rao, Pemmaraju. "Authority and Control over Offshore Areas: In Defense of Common Interests." Vol. 2, *Indian Journal of International Law*, pp. 379–388 (1971).

Sreenivasa Rao, Pemmaraju. "The Law of the Continental Shelf." Vol. 6, *I.J.I.L.*, pp. 363–382 (1966).

Stang, David P. "Individuals' Right to Question United States Administrative Jurisdiction over Continental Shelf Areas." In Lewis M. Alexander (ed.), *The Law of the Sea: The Future of the Sea's Resources*, pp. 86–88 (1968).

Stevens, Ted. "The Future of our Outer Continental Shelf and the Seabeds." Vol. 4, *Natural Resources Lawyer*, pp. 646–653 (1971).

Stevenson, John R., and Bernard H. Oxman. "The Preparations for the Law of the Sea Conference." Vol. 68, *American Journal of International Law*, pp. 1–32 (1974).

Stone, Jeremy J. "Can the Communists Deceive US?" In Abram Chayes and Jerome B. Wiesner, *ABM: An Evaluation of the Decision to Deploy an Antiballistic Missile System*, pp. 193–198 (1969).

Third Seward Johnson Panel on *The Limits of National Jurisdiction and the Common Heritage Concept* (Woods Hole Oceanographic Institution, Woods Hole, Mass. 1974).

Utton, Albert E. "Institutional Arrangements for Developing North Sea Oil and Gas." Vol. 9, *Virginia Journal of International Law*, pp. 66–81 (1968).

Vallat, F. A. "The Competence of the U.N. General Assembly." Vol. 97, *Recueil des Cours*, pp. 207–292 (1959-II).

Vallat, F. A. "The Continental Shelf." Vol. 23, *B.Y.B.I.L.*, pp. 333–338 (1946).

Verzijl, J. H. W. "The United Nations Conference on Law of the Sea, Geneva 1958: I." Vol. 6, *Nederlands Tijdschrift Voor International Recht*, p. 1 (1959).

Wageman, John M., Thomas W. C. Hilde, and K. O. Emery. "Structural Framework of East China Sea and Yellow Sea." Vol. 54, *The American Association of Petroleum Geologists Bulletin*, pp. 1611–1643 (September 1970).

Wegener, Edward. "Theory of Naval Strategy in the Nuclear Age." *Proceedings of the U.S. Naval Institute* (May 1972), pp. 190–208.

Waldichuk, M. "Coastal Marine Pollution and Fish." Vol. 12, *Ocean Management*, pp. 1–61 (1974).

Waldock, C. H. M. "Legal Basis of the Claims to the Continental Shelf." Vol. 36, *Transactions of the Grotius Society*, pp. 115–148 (1951).

Walford, Lionel A., and John R. Clark. "Artificial Reefs." Vol. 2, *Oceanology International*, pp. 27–30 (1967).

Walmsley, David J. "Oil Pollution Problems Arising out of Exploitation of the Continental Shelf: The Santa Barbara Disaster." Vol. 9, *San Diego Law Review*, pp. 514–568 (1972).

Warner, D. G. "Oil Industry Safety and Pollution Control." Vol. 7, *Ocean Industry*, pp. 24–27 (August 1972).

Waters, Odale D., Jr. "The Navy's Role in Oceanography." *Proceedings of the Marine Frontiers Conference* (1967).

Wayland, Russell G. "Federal Regulations of the U.S. Offshore Oil Industry." In *Pollution Control in the Marine Industries—Proceedings of the Conference Sponsored by the International Association for Pollution Control* (May 11–12, 1972), pp. 219–229.

Wilson, Thomas A. "Undersea Mining: Where Do We Stand Today?" Vol. 166, *Engineering and Mining Journal*, pp. 81–88 (May 1965).

Winslow, E., and A. B. Bigler. "A New Perspective on Recreational Use of the Ocean." Vol. 10, *Undersea Technology*, pp. 51–55 (1969).

Woetzel, Robert K. "Comments on U.S. and Soviet Viewpoints Regarding the Legal Aspects of Military Uses in Space." *Proceedings of the Fifty-Seventh Annual Opening of American Society of International Law*, pp. 195–205 (1963).

Wooster, Warren S., and Michael D. Bradley. "Access Requirements and Oceanic Research: The Scientists' Perspective." In Warren S. Wooster (ed.), *Freedom of Oceanic Research*, pp. 29–39 (1973).

Yost, Charles W. "World Order and American Responsibility." Vol. 47, *Foreign Affairs*, pp. 1–14 (1968).

Young, Richard. "Offshore Claims and Problems in the North Sea." Vol. 59, *A.J.I.L.*, pp. 505–522 (1965).

Young, Richard. "The Geneva Convention of the Continental Shelf: A First Impression." Vol. 52, *American Journal of International Law*, pp. 733–738 (1958).

Young, Richard. "Pan American Discussions on Offshore Claims." Vol. 50, *A.J.I.L.*, pp. 909–916 (1956).

U.N. Documents
Conclusions of the African States Regional Seminar on Law of the Sea (Yaoundé, Cameroun, 1972), U.N. doc. A/AC.138/79.

ECOSOC. Report to the Secretary-General. *Marine Science and Technology: Survey and Proposals* (United Nations, New York, April 24, 1968).

Final Act of the Inter-American Socialized Conference on "Conservation of Natural Resources: The Continental Shelf and Marine Waters" (Cuidad Trujillo, Dominican Republic, March 15–28, 1956). OAS, *Conference and Organization Lines,* No. 50.

IMCO Resolution A 227 (VII), October 12, 1971. Resolution A226 (VII) October 12, 1971.

Legislative Series. *National Legislation and Treaties Relating to Law of the Sea: Addendum* (United Nations, New York, 1973).

Legislative Series. *National Legislation and Treaties Relating to the Law of the Sea,* Vol. I and Vol. II (United Nations, New York, 1972).

Legislative Series. *National Legislation and Treaties Relating to the Territorial Sea, the Contiguous Zone, the Continental Shelf, the High Seas and to Fishing and Conservation of the Living Resources of the Sea* (United Nations, New York, 1970).

Legislative Series. *Supplement to the Laws and Regulations on the Regime of the High Seas* (United Nations, New York, 1959).

Legislative Series. *Laws and Regulations on Regime of the High Seas,* Vol. 1 (United Nations, New York, 1951).

Mineral Resources of the Sea Including Annexes (1970), U.N. doc. ST/ECA/125.

Organization of African Unity. *Declaration on the Issues of the Law of the Sea* (Addis Ababa, 1973), UN doc. A/AC. 138/86.

Report of the Ad Hoc Committee to Study the Peaceful Uses of the Sea-Bed and Ocean Floor beyond the Limits of National Jurisdiction, A/7230 (1968).

Report of the U.N. Committee on the Peaceful Uses of the Sea-Bed and the Ocean Floor beyond the Limits of National Jurisdiction, Vols. I–VI, G.A.O.R. 28th Session, A/9021 (1973).

Report of the U.N. Committee on the Peaceful Uses of the Sea-Bed and the Ocean Floor beyond the Limits of National Jurisdiction, G.A.O.R., 26th Session, A/8421 (1971).

Report of the U.N. Committee on the Peaceful Uses of the Sea-Bed and the Ocean Floor beyond the Limits of National Jurisdiction, G.A.O.R., 25th Session, A/8021 (1970).

Report of the U.N. Secretariat. *Study on International Machinery,* U.N. doc. A/AC. 138/23 (1970).

(Report of the) U.N. Secretariat. *Study on the Question of Establishing in Due Time Appropriate International Machinery for the Promotion of the Exploration and Exploitation of the Resources of the Seabed and the Ocean Floor beyond the Limits of National Jurisdiction and the Use of These Resources in the Interests of Mankind,* U.N. doc., A/AC. 138/12 (1969).

(Report of the) U.N. Secretariat. *Comparative Table of Draft Treaties, Working Papers, and Draft Articles,* U.N. doc. A/AC. 138/L. 10 (January 28, 1972).

(Report by) the U.N. Secretary-General. *Sea-Bed Mineral Resources: Recent Developments,* U.N. doc. A/AC. 138/90 (July 1973).

Report of the U.N. Secretary-General. *Economic Significance in Terms of Sea-Bed Mineral Resources of the Various Limits Proposed for National Jurisdiction,* U.N. doc. A/AC. 137/87 (June 4, 1973).

Report of the U.N. Secretary-General. *Marine Pollution and Other Hazardous and Harmful Effects Which Might Arise from the Exploration and Exploitation of the Seabed and the Ocean Floor and the Subsoil Thereof beyond the Limits of National Jurisdiction,* A/7924 (June 11, 1970).

Report of the U.N. Secretary-General. *Marine Science and Technology: Survey and Proposals,* U.N. doc. E/4487 (April 24, 1968).

Report of the U.N. Secretary-General. *Resources of the Sea,* U.N. doc. E/4449/Add. 1 (February 21, 1968).

Specialized Conference of the Caribbean Countries on Problems of the Sea (Santo Domingo, 1972), U.N. doc. A/AC.128/80.

Status of Multilateral Conventions, Law of the Sea, XXI-8, U.N. doc. ST/Leg/e/Rev. 1 (December 31, 1959).

Summary Records of Proposals and Documents before the U.N. Committee on the Peaceful Uses of the Sea-Bed and the Ocean Floor beyond the Limits of National Jurisdiction (1969–1973).

Summary Records of Proposals and Documents before the U.N. Ad Hoc Committee to Study the Peaceful Uses of the Sea-Bed and the Ocean Floor beyond the Limits of National Jurisdiction (1968).

Summary Records of Meetings and Annexes of the Fourth Committee (Continental Shelf) of the United Nations Conference on Law of the Sea (Geneva, February 26–April 2, 1958), Vol. VI.

Summary Records of the Meetings and Annexes of the Plenary Meetings of the United Nations Conference on Law of the Sea (Geneva, February 26–April 2, 1958), Vol. II, Eighth Plenary Meetings.

Summary Records of the Year Book of International Law Commission, Vol. 1 (1950),

Vol. 1 (1951), Vol. 2 (1951), Vol. 1 (1953), Vol. 2 (1953), Vol. 1 (1956), Vol. 2 (1956). *Survey of National Legislation Concerning the Seabed and the Ocean Floor, and the Subsoil Thereof, Underlying the High Seas beyond the Limits of Present National Jurisdiction,* U.N. doc. A/AC.135/11 (June 4, 1968).

UNESCO, IOC, and IMCO. *Legal Problems Associated with Ocean Data Acquisition Systems,* 8 (10C/INF.108), (1969).

U.S. *Draft of United Nations Convention of the International Seabed Area,* U.N. doc., A/AC.138/25.

Verbatim Records and Proposals before the Conference of the Committee on Disarmament (1969–1970).

Verbatim Records and Proposals before the Eighteen Nation Disarmament Conference (1968–1969).

Miscellaneous
Abu Dhabi Award. Vol. 1, *International and Comparative Law Quarterly,* pp. 247–261 (1952).

"Agreement on Prevention of Incidents at Sea between the Soviet Union and the USA." Vol. XI, *International Legal Materials,* p. 778 (1972).

Alexander, Lewis M. "Alternative Methods for Delimiting the Outer Boundary of the Continental Shelf." Unpublished manuscript, Office of External Research, U.S. Department of State (February 1970).

The Antarctic Treaty, Vol. 42, United Nations Treaty Series, p. 72 (1961).

Certain Expenses Case. ICJ Reports (1962).

"Comment," Vol. 2, *Fishing News International,* p. 9 (December 1972).

The Corfu Channel Case. ICJ Reports (1949).

Emery, K. O. "Pagoda Structures in Marine Sediments." In press.

Fletcher vs. *Rylands* (1866). *Law Reports,* 1 Ex. 265, 279.

"Inflation Goes around the World." *The New York Times* (July 1974).

The New York Times, Editorial (February 2, 1969 and February 4, 1969).

The New York Times, Editorial (February 10, 1974).

North Sea Continental Shelf Judgment. ICJ Reports (1969).

"Ocean Raw Materials." Vol. 14, *Kirk-Othmer Encyclopedia of Chemical Technology* (Second Ed. 1967).

"The Oil Industry Caught in a Tug-of-War." *The New York Times* (July 7, 1974).

"Perspectives for the Oceanography," *The New York Times*, Editorial (January 18, 1969).

President Truman's Proclamation No. 2667. "Policy of the United States with Respect to the Natural Resources of the Subsoil and Sea Bed of the Continental Shelf." Vol. 10, *Federal Register*, p.12303 (September 28, 1948).

Raman, K. V. *Customary Prescriptions of International Law*. Unpublished Yale Law School dissertation (1967).

Shell International Petroleum. *Licenses and Leases Awarded in Water Deeper Than 200 Meters* (March 1973). Map obtainable through the U.N. Secretariat.

Smith, Wayne J. "An Assessment of the Deep Ocean Manganese Nodule Exploration Technology." An unpublished draft, Woods Hole Oceanographic Institution, Woods Hole, Mass., (1972).

The Tlatelolco Treaty. In *SIPRI Yearbook of World Armaments and Disarmament, 1969–1970*, pp. 218–256 (1970).

"Towards Salt II: Interpretation and Policy Implications of the SALT Agreements." *Proceedings of the 67th Annual Conference of the American Society of International Law* (November 1973), pp. 28–47.

The Treaty on Outer Space, June 27, 1967, U.N. doc. A/Res222(XXI), (December 19, 1967).

"U.S. Asks NATO to Help Save Man's Environment." *The New York Times* (October 22, 1969).

U.S. Department of the Interior. "Draft Environmental Statement Prepared for United States Involvement in Law of the Sea Negotiations Governing the Mining of Deep Seabed Hard Mineral Resources Seaward of the Limits of National Jurisdiction" (March 1974).

U.S. Department of State. "World Straits Affected by a 12 Mile Territorial Sea." Map.

U.S. Interim Domestic Legislation 52901. Vol. 117, No. 164, *U.S. Congressional Record* (November 2, 1971).

U.S. Senate Resolution 263 of March 5, 1968, 90th Congress, 2nd Session.

Index